P9-AGF-317

Studies in Social, Political, and Legal Philosophy

General Editor: James P. Sterba, University of Notre Dame

This series analyzes and evaluates critically the major political, social, and legal ideals, institutions, and practices of our time. The analysis may be historical or problem-centered; the evaluation may focus on theoretical underpinnings or practical implications. Among the recent titles in the series are:

Moral Rights and Political Freedom
by Tara Smith, University of Texas at Austin

Morality and Social Justice: Point/Counterpoint
by James P. Sterba, University of Notre Dame; Tibor Machan, Auburn University; Alison Jaggar, University of Colorado at Boulder; William Galston, White House Domestic Policy Council; Carol C. Gould, Stevens Institute of Technology; Milton Fisk, Indiana University; and Robert C. Solomon, University of Texas at Austin

Faces of Environmental Racism: Confronting Issues of Global Justice
edited by Laura Westra, University of Windsor, and Peter S. Wenz, Sangamon State University

Plato Rediscovered: Human Value and Social Order
by T. K. Seung, University of Texas at Austin

Liberty for the Twenty-First Century: Contemporary Libertarian Thought
edited by Tibor R. Machan, Auburn University, and Douglas B. Rasmussen, St. John's University

In the Company of Others: Perspectives on Community, Family, and Culture
edited by Nancy E. Snow, Marquette University

Perfect Equality: John Stuart Mill on Well-Constituted Communities
by Maria H. Morales, Florida State University

Citizenship in a Fragile World
by Bernard P. Dauenhauer, University of Georgia

Critical Moral Liberalism: Theory and Practice
by Jeffrey Reiman, American University

Nature as Subject: Human Obligation and Natural Community
by Eric Katz, New Jersey Institute of Technology

Can Ethics Provide Answers? And Other Essays in Moral Philosophy
by James Rachels, University of Alabama at Birmingham

Character and Culture
by Lester H. Hunt, University of Wisconsin at Madison

Racist Symbols and Reparations: Philosophical Reflections on Vestiges of the American Civil War
by George Schedler, Southern Illinois University at Carbondale

Same Sex: Debating the Ethics, Science, and Culture of Homosexuality
edited by John Corvino, University of Texas at Austin

SAME SEX

Same Sex

Debating the Ethics, Science, and Culture of Homosexuality

Edited by

John Corvino

ROWMAN & LITTLEFIELD PUBLISHERS, INC.
Lanham • Boulder • New York • Oxford

ROWMAN & LITTLEFIELD PUBLISHERS, INC.

Published in the United States of America
by Rowman & Littlefield Publishers, Inc.
4720 Boston Way, Lanham, Maryland 20706

12 Hid's Copse Road
Cummor Hill, Oxford OX2 9JJ, England

First paperback edition printed by Rowman & Littlefield in 1999.

British Library Cataloguing in Publication Information Available

The hardback edition of this book was previously catalogued by the Library of Congress as follows:

Library of Congress Cataloging-in-Publication Data

Same sex : debating the ethics, science, and culture of homosexuality / edited by John Corvino
p. cm.—(Studies in social, political, and legal philosophy)
Includes bibliographical references and index.
I. Homosexuality. 2. Homosexuality—Moral and ethical aspects. 3. Gays.
4. Gay Rights I. Corvino, John, 1969– . II. Series.
HQ76.25.S24 1997 97-22315
CIP

ISBN 0-8476-8483-0 (paper : alk. paper)

The cover art is taken from *The Death of Hyacinth*, by the eighteenth-century French painter Jean Broc. According to Cecile Beurdeley in *L'Amour Bleu* (Evergreen [a label of Benedikt Taschen Verlag GmbH], 1994),

> Hyacinth was so beautiful that even Apollo could not resist him. One day, as they were throwing the discus together, Hyacinth, with the impetuousness of youth, ran to pick up the god's discus—which rebounded, striking him in the face. Another story says that Zephyr, who was also madly in love with Hyacinth, deflected the discus in flight out of jealousy. Despite Apollo's attempts to revive him, the boy died. Filled with despair, the god lamented: "What is my crime? Is it a crime to play? Is it a crime to love . . . ?"

Printed in the United States of America

⊗™ The paper used in this publication meets the minimum requirements of American National Standard for Information Sciences—Permanence of Paper for Printed Library Materials, ANSI Z39.48-1984.

For My Parents

sine quibus non.

Contents

Acknowledgments

. . . . .

I am indebted to countless others for their assistance in producing this volume. First and foremost, I wish to thank the contributors, many of whom acted above and beyond the call of duty in tailoring their work for the volume or in helping me obtain permission to reprint previously published work.

The following chapters have been revised and reprinted from other sources:

Chapters 3 and 22 are reprinted with revisions from *Notre Dame Journal of Law, Ethics & Public Policy* Vol. IX Issue 1 (1995) pp. 11–40, 185–213.

Chapter 5 is reprinted from *First Things* No. 41 (March 1994) pp. 15–20.

Portions of chapter 10 are reprinted with substantial revisions from *Psychological Review* 103 (1996) pp. 320–335.

Portions of chapters 11 and 13 are reprinted with substantial revisions from *Journal of Homosexuality* Vol. 27 No. 3/4 (1994) pp. 269–308, 223–268.

Chapter 12 is reprinted with revisions from *Lesbian Psychologies: Explorations and Challenges* (Urbana: University of Illinois Press, 1987) pp. 18–34.

Chapter 15 is reprinted with revisions from *Salmagundi* No. 58–59 (Fall 1982/Winter 1983) pp. 89–113, and from *Hidden from History: Exploring the Gay and Lesbian Past* (New York: Penguin, 1990) pp. 34–36.

Chapter 16 is reprinted with revisions from *Hidden from History: Exploring the Gay and Lesbian Past* (New York: Penguin, 1990) pp. 37–53.

Chapter 17 is reprinted with revisions from *Passion and Power: Sexuality in History* (Philadelphia: Temple University Press, 1989) pp. 241–256.

Chapter 18 is reprinted with revisions from *Journal of Social History* 19 (1985) pp. 189–212.

Chapter 19 is reprinted with revisions from *Out/Look* No. 16 (Spring 1992) pp. 23, 29–33.

Chapter 20 is reprinted with revisions from *Policy Review* (Spring 1993) pp. 68–71.

Chapter 24 is reprinted with revisions from *Insight*, a bulletin of the Family Research Council.

Chapter 25 is reprinted with revisions from *Beyond Queer: Challenging Gay Left Orthodoxy* (New York: Free Press, 1996) pp. 296–313.

Chapter 26 is reprinted with revisions from *Hypatia* Vol. 11 No. 3 (Summer 1996).

This project began with a phone call in 1995 from my old roommate and friend Melissa Barry, who put me in touch with James Sterba, who put me in touch with Jennifer Ruark, who was then philosophy editor at Rowman & Littlefield. I wish to thank Melissa for her serendipitous phone call, Jennifer for her expertise and enthusiasm in the early stages of the project, and Jim for his assistance and support throughout.

Jennifer left Rowman & Littlefield just as the collection was beginning to take shape. Since then, I have had the good fortune to work with Jonathan Sisk (editor in chief), Robin Adler (assistant editor), Christa Acampora (then acquisitions editor), and Lynn Weber (production editor). I thank all four of them for their confidence, insight, and patience.

Thanks to Patrick D. Hopkins for suggesting the title and to Laura Schwartz, Susan Macicak, and Mary Beth Mader for helping me track down the cover art. Thanks to Kim Hewitt and Robert Schuessler for helping me prepare the final manuscript.

Among those who offered especially helpful suggestions and assistance along the way are William Byne, Claudia Card, Carlos Casillas, David Cleaves, Thomas Denton, Yve Golan, Jacob Hale, David M. Halperin, Kevin Keim, Kevin Lamb, Mary Beth Mader, A. P. Martinich, Kevin Milstead, Timothy F. Murphy, Jason Nichols, Jonathan Rauch, Robert Schuessler, Alan Soble, Robert C. Solomon, Edward Stein, Frederick Suppe, and Nicholas Will. I am especially grateful to Richard D. Mohr, who not only provided invaluable guidance throughout the project, but also has been a generous mentor more broadly.

Throughout this project (and indeed, all of my projects), Thomas Williams has been a tireless colleague and quintessential friend. I cannot thank him enough for his wisdom, patience, and encouragement.

Finally, I am deeply indebted to my sister, Jennifer Corvino; and to my parents, John and Annette Corvino, for their abiding love and support.

Introduction

. . . . .

Just a century ago Lord Alfred Douglas, lover (and later enemy) of Oscar Wilde, referred to homosexuality as "the love that dare not speak its name." Since then, the love that dare not speak its name has become the love that won't shut up—or so several observers have quipped. Yet discussions of homosexuality, though increasingly common, are typically strident and polemical. This book responds to this cacophony by providing a forum for reasoned dialogue. It brings together respected philosophers, scientists, theologians, and historians who present a variety of perspectives on this complex and controversial topic. Although the authors clash on many issues, they share a commitment to careful rational discussion.

The book is divided into four parts. In part I, philosophers and theologians debate the moral status of homosexuality. Part II looks at some of the scientific research on sexual orientation and considers possible ethical implications of that research. Part III investigates some historical manifestations of homosexuality in an attempt to answer the question, "What does it mean to be gay, lesbian, or bisexual?" Finally, part IV explores various public policy debates on homosexuality: Are gay rights "equal rights" or "special rights"? Should gay marriages be legally recognized? Should gays and lesbians be permitted to serve openly in the military? Is "outing"—the revealing of a closeted person's homosexuality—ever justified? The contributors respond to such questions from various philosophical and political perspectives.

A word about the "balance" of the book. On each of the controversial moral debates—gay marriage, homosexuality in the Bible, gays in the military, and so on—I have sought out the best available articles by both defenders and opponents of homosexuality. But there is more to understanding homosexuality than debating its moral and social status. Some of the debates in this book occur between gay rights advocates and gay rights opponents, others reflect differing views within the gay community. For example, Richard D. Mohr and James S. Stramel differ on when outing is justified, John Boswell and David M. Halperin differ on whether homosexual people existed in ancient times, and Jonathan Rauch and Claudia Card differ on whether gays and lesbians should seek the legal right to marry. Other articles do not appear in "debate" format at all, but simply present the authors' views for critical assessment by the reader. I encourage readers to approach each selection in the volume with a critical eye and an open mind.

One problem with the point/counterpoint format, which dominates portions of the book (especially the first and last parts), is that it may promote a simplistic "either/or" mentality. Readers should keep in mind that the collection, though broad and diverse, by no means exhausts the range of possible views.

What Is Homosexuality?

Since this book is about "homosexuality," we ought briefly to consider what that term means. People often make a distinction between homosexual orientation (being sexually or romantically attracted predominantly to members of one's own sex) and homosexual activity or conduct (engaging in sexual or romantic physical contact with members of one's own sex). The distinction can be useful because it recognizes that not all or only those who have a homosexual orientation engage in homosexual sex; the orientation merely suggests an inclination toward the activity.

Nevertheless, the distinction raises various questions. One might ask, for instance, what "counts" as homosexual activity. Does kissing count? What about holding hands? Gazing into a same-sex partner's eyes during a romantic dinner? Homosexual experience, like heterosexual experience, comprises many more activities than simply sexual ones. Interestingly, some common objections to homosexual activity (e.g., that it involves misuse of genital organs) don't cover such activities, at least not in any obvious ways. Moreover, as several contributors point out, genital homosexual acts appear to be neither necessary nor sufficient for causing antigay discrimination.

Even focusing on genital homosexual acts leaves questions open. Are motives and intentions a part of the acts? For the purposes of ethical evaluation, motives and intentions usually matter: cutting someone's throat is a fundamentally different act when done as part of an emergency tracheotomy than when done as part of a mugging. Similarly, male-male intercourse may be a fundamentally different act when done as part of a loving relationship in contemporary America than when done as part of a Canaanite ritual in ancient Palestine. Thus, insofar as the orientation/activity distinction separates physical acts from their larger social contexts, it oversimplifies the matter. For the purposes of this introduction, I will use the catch-all term "homosexuality" to cover various kinds of homosexual experience and will distinguish between orientation and activity only when my meaning would be ambiguous otherwise.

The concept of sexual orientation is itself problematic. Many researchers believe that sexuality is better characterized as a continuum than as a set of two (or possibly three) discrete categories—homosexual, heterosexual, and bisexual. Moreover, even if we rely on such categories for the sake of convenience, it is not clear what criteria to use to assign people to them. Should a woman who has primarily homosexual fantasies but who generally prefers intercourse with men count as a heterosexual, a bisexual, or a lesbian? Does the answer depend on how she labels herself? What if her self-understanding changes over time? The answers aren't as simple as they might initially seem.

Enriching the taxonomy are the related issues of bisexuality and transgender. Bisexual people are attracted to both males and females (which does not mean that they're attracted to everyone or that they're incapable of monogamy). Since bisexual people may experience homosexual desires or engage in homosexual activity (or both), much of what is said about homosexual people should apply to them as well—(which is not to say, of course, that discussions of homosexuality will cover all that needs to be said about bisexuality). This collection includes one article devoted specifically to bisexuality.

The issue of transgender is more complex; here, I can offer only a very rough sketch. Transgendered people are those whose biological sex (whether they were born with male or female bodies) differs from their gender identity (whether they experience themselves as male or female). Transgender is different from homosexuality: most lesbians do not desire to be men, and most gay men do not desire to be women. Yet we might still group transgendered people with both homosexual and bisexual people under the broad rubric of "sexual minorities," insofar as all three groups deviate from certain widespread social expectations about sex and gender.

Given the complex terrain of human sexuality, we might be tempted to define homosexuality by borrowing the old quip about pornography: "I know it when I see it." These days, like it or not, we're seeing it more frequently. The articles in this book should help us see it more clearly as well—in all its various forms.

Synopsis of the Book

Part I. Morality and Religion

Intelligent, well-educated people disagree sharply on homosexuality's moral status. In that respect, homosexuality is not unique: intelligent people also disagree sharply on the moral status of capital punishment, euthanasia, and a host of other issues. What distinguishes homosexuality is that it is not immediately clear what's at stake in the debate. Euthanasia and capital punishment end lives; abortion ends a potential or budding life—but what does homosexuality do?

Debates about the moral status of homosexuality usually focus on one of three points: nature, harm, and religion. Many people contend that homosexual sex is unnatural. But what does that mean? And is unnaturalness necessarily a bad thing? After all, many things that humans value—like housing, eyeglasses, and government, to take a random list—are unnatural in some sense. And many things that humans detest—like disease—are *natural* in some sense. Thus, those who argue that homosexual sex is wrong because it is unnatural must do two things: they must find a sense of "unnatural" that applies to homosexual sex, and they must show that things that are unnatural in that sense are therefore immoral.

Others claim that homosexuality is wrong because it is harmful either to homosexual people or to society at large. This claim raises several questions. First, how is homosexuality harmful (if at all)? Conversely, how might it be beneficial? Second, if it is harmful, are the harms inherent to homosexuality, or are they a result of society's response to it (or both)? Finally, what is the relevance of harm to our moral judgments?

Still others claim that homosexuality violates God's will as revealed in the Judeo-Christian Bible. (Articles in this collection focus on the Judeo-Christian tradition mainly because it is the most influential one in the United States.) Biblical scholars interested in homosexuality commonly engage both in exegetical debates on how to translate specific words or phrases that seem to condemn homosexuality and in hermeneutical debates on whether and how the biblical perspective is relevant to our own.

In chapter 1, I consider all three issues—nature, harm, and religion—though the bulk of the discussion focuses on harm. I argue that, far from being harmful, homosexual relationships can be beneficial both for those who engage in them and for the community at large. I also consider various senses of the term "natural" and conclude that homosexuality is not unnatural in any morally relevant sense. In chapter 2, David Bradshaw disagrees with this assessment and argues that many of our moral intuitions—for example, our abhorrence of bestiality—cannot be captured by considerations of benefit and harm. He reaffirms the traditional prohibition of homosexual acts by situating it in a larger moral framework that focuses on the given form of the human body.

Chapters 3 and 4, by John Finnis and Andrew Koppelman, respectively, contain a sophisticated debate on the naturalness of homosexuality. As one of the "new natural lawyers," Finnis holds that there are certain "basic goods" that are intrinisically worthy of human pursuit. Heterosexual marriage, with its twofold values of procreation and friendship, is one such basic good. Finnis argues that homosexual conduct is unreasonable, wrong, and therefore unnatural, because instead of bringing about either of these values (or some other basic good), it achieves only the illusion of doing so, and moreover involves treating sexual organs as mere instruments of pleasure rather than as integrated parts of the whole human person. Koppelman responds that Finnis's argument, if it were sound, would prove that intercourse by sterile heterosexual couples is immoral, a conclusion that neither he nor Finnis accepts. He argues further that arguments like Finnis's rest on several misunderstandings about the goods achievable by sexual partners in general and homosexual partners in particular.

Chapter 5 is by the Ramsey Colloquium, a group of Jewish and Christian scholars who meet periodically to discuss public policy questions from a biblical perspective. In their selection, they criticize "the homosexual movement" as part of a larger trend of moral degeneration. In chapter 6, Thomas Williams replies that the Ramsey Colloquium's argument focuses on features of the homosexual movement that homosexuals need not, and often do not, accept; furthermore, he argues that their position depends on several false dichotomies and a mistaken view of chastity.

Chapter 7 by Daniel A. Helminiak and chapter 8 by Thomas E. Schmidt examine the Bible directly. Focusing on St. Paul's letter to the Romans, Helminiak and Schmidt agree that the text must be understood in its historical context but disagree about its message regarding homosexuality. Helminiak argues that Paul's remarks involve ritual purity concerns, whereas Schmidt argues that they involve Paul's Creation-based view of marriage. Accordingly, Helminiak concludes that the Bible regards homosexual acts as ethically neutral, whereas Schmidt concludes that it regards them as ethically sinful. These issues are also touched upon in chapters 1 and 2.

Part II. Science and Identity

Ethical questions are also raised occasionally in part II, this time in the context of scientific discussion. Recent scientific discussions of homosexuality usually focus on the etiology (cause or origin) of same-sex desire. The current wave of interest in etiology began in 1991 when Simon LeVay, then a neurobiologist at the Salk Institute, published his study suggesting a correlation between sexual orientation and hypothalamic structure. That same year, J. Michael Bailey and Richard Pillard announced the results of their research on gay men and their brothers, which indicated a possible genetic influence on sexual orientation. Their genetic hypothesis was bolstered two years later when Dean Hamer at the National Cancer Institute published his study of Xq28, which was quickly (and inaccurately) dubbed "the gay gene." What Hamer in fact discovered was not a gene, but rather a tendency among gay brothers to share a certain group of genetic "markers" inherited from the same X chromosome.

Reactions to these studies were swift and strident. Gay rights advocates touted the studies as proving that homosexuality is "natural" and that discrimination against gays is unjust, since homosexuality is "not a choice." Opponents pointed to flaws in the research and argued further that it failed to prove that homosexuality is any more natural than alcoholism, which also appears to have a genetic basis. Unfortunately, both sides' reactions manifested a good deal of scientific and ethical confusion, a problem that part II attempts to alleviate.

One common problem is the conflation of two distinct issues: the debate over the etiology of sexual orientation (sometimes called "the nature/nurture debate") and the debate over the mutabililty of sexual orientation (sometimes called "the determinist/voluntarist debate"). Proving that sexual orientation is "biological" is not the same as proving that it is permanent, and proving that it is learned is not the same as proving that it can be unlearned. Some genetically influenced characteristics, like myopia, can be changed, and some acquired characteristics, like tinnitus (a hearing problem), cannot. Moreover, even if sexual orientation is more or less permanent, sexual activity still involves an element of choice. Thus it is not clear that etiological studies, even if they are sound, have the ethical relevance that gay rights advocates sometimes claim for them.

Part II begins in chapter 9 with William Byne and Mitchell Lasco's overview of the etiological research. Byne and Lasco first note that, because we are physical beings, *all* of our desires have some biological basis. Thus, the question is not "Is homosexuality biological?" but rather "How do biological and environmental factors interact to influence sexual orientation?" Byne and Lasco explore three different models for conceptualizing biology's role in the formation of sexual orientation. They then examine the aforementioned etiological studies in light of these models. In chapter 10, Daryl J. Bem explores how environmental factors—in particular, the experience of feeling "different" from opposite- or same-sex peers—might factor into the explanation of sexual orientation. He also analyzes the concept of sexual orientation and discusses some of the political implications of his theory.

In chapter 11, Edward Stein addresses the political issue directly by asking what relevance sexual orientation research has to lesbian and gay rights. Stein argues that even if science were to establish that homosexuality is biologically "fixed," that finding would prove nothing about the moral or political status of homosexuality. Moral and political arguments, not scientific arguments, are needed to support gay rights claims.

The final two contributions in part II move beyond the question of cause or origin to discuss sexual orientation more broadly, as well as to pose challenges to those who do research on sexual orientation. In chapter 12, Carla Golden discusses lesbian identity from the perspective of a psychologist who has extensively interviewed college-aged women (among others); she argues that many women experience their sexuality as fluid rather than fixed. In her postscript, she criticizes the androcentrism of some of the recent etiological research and discusses how attitudes toward female homosexuality have changed on college campuses since the mid-1980s. Finally, in chapter 13, Frederick Suppe criticizes sexual orientation research more generally—first, because it treats sexual orientation as if it were monolithic rather than multifaceted, and second, because the research does not have the marks of a legitimate scientific project. Suppe's chapter includes a useful discussion of the various components of sexual orientation.

An important thing to remember throughout part II is that scientific questions about sexual orientation must be resolved by scientific inquiry, not by political debates or by isolated personal testimony (even while one recognizes the subtle influences of politics and culture on science). Although scientific inquiry can tell us more about who we are as sexual beings, it can also pose certain ethical challenges as well—challenges that scientific data alone cannot answer.

Part III. Identity and History

Science is one way for us to understand ourselves as sexual beings; history is another. One debate that arises in historical studies of homosexuality, and that is sometimes conflated with the nature/nurture debate, is the essentialist/constructionist debate. Although scholars widely disagree about the ongoing significance of this debate, no one denies its prominence in gay and lesbian studies. Thus, a brief explanation—including an explanation of its difference from the scientific debates discussed above—is in order.

Essentialists believe that sexual orientation is an objective, culturally independent property that one can attribute to people irrespective of their particular historical situations. Thus, for example, an essentialist would claim that there were homosexuals and heterosexuals in ancient Greece, even though the ancient Greeks might not have understood themselves in precisely those terms. Constructionists, on the other hand, believe that sexual orientation is a product of culture and that, prior to the modern era, there was no such thing as a "homosexual" or "heterosexual." The constructionists do not claim, of course, that there were no same-sex desires or same-sex acts before the modern era, but rather that the people who experienced these should not be labeled "homosexuals"—that mode of self-understanding simply did not exist until fairly recently. According to constructionists, the world is no more naturally divided into homosexuals and heterosexuals than the globe is naturally divided into various countries. Rather, culture imposes sexual categories, and different cultures have drawn the lines in different ways.

Many people take the essentialist/constructionist debate to correspond with either the debate on the origins of homosexuality, or the debate on the mutability of homosexuality, or both. Specifically, they take it that all essentialists believe that homosexuality is genetically determined and immutable and that all constructionists believe that homosexuality is learned and mutable. But the essentialist is not committed to either the innateness or the immutability of homosexuality, and the constructionist is at least not committed to its mutability. (In what follows, I am indebted to Edward Stein's careful discussion of these matters in his book *Forms of Desire*.)

Take first the essentialist. The essentialist merely holds that there is some culturally independent characteristic or set of characteristics that qualifies someone as homosexual, apart from cultural surroundings. He or she may simultaneously (and consistently) hold that the characteristic is acquired rather than innate and, furthermore, that it is mutable rather than immutable. What makes this person an essentialist is simply the claim that the characteristic is culturally independent.

On the other hand, the social constructionist need not claim that sexual orientation is mutable. On the contrary, the vast cultural framework that gives shape and identity to a person's desires, not to mention the desires themselves, may be largely beyond an individual's control. So a constructionist may hold that a person's sexual orientation is more or less fixed, even though that orientation is a cultural construct.

Can a constructionist also believe that homosexuality is innate? At first it would seem not. After all, a genetic marker for homosexuality would be precisely the kind of transcultural objective property that constructionists reject and essentialists support. But the idea that there is a genetic marker *for homosexuality* is overly simplistic. Rather, there are genes that affect various physical structures and psychological states, which may or may not add up to homosexuality, depending on various environmental influences. Indeed, even if biological factors guaranteed same-sex desires regardless of environmental influences, a constructionist could still deny that a person with such desires "counts" as a homosexual without the proper cultural framework and consequent self-understanding. Thus, although constructionists (and probably everyone else) should reject talk of "gay genes"—that is, genes that make people gay and lesbian regardless of environmental influences or cultural circumstances—they can certainly accept that genes influence sexual desire.

The essentialist/constructionist debate is especially relevant to the first few readings in part III, which begins in chapter 14 with Aristophanes' speech from Plato's *Symposium* (with notes and a new translation by Leah Himmelhoch). Aristophanes shares a myth of three ancient "genders" to explain the origin of love. Many modern readers believe that the myth's three genders correspond to contemporary lesbians, gay men, and heterosexuals. In chapter 15, John Boswell takes what many would label an essentialist position, arguing that classical texts like Aristophanes' speech demonstrate that the categories of sexual orientation existed throughout history, even if only implicitly. (Boswell actually rejects the essentialist label and suggests that it is often misapplied.) Boswell situates his argument in a larger philosophical debate between "realists," who hold that universal categories exist whether or not humans acknowledge them, and "nominalists," who hold that universal categories are convenient social devices that humans impose upon the world. The realists correspond to the essentialists in the current debate, the nominalists to the social constructionists.

In chapter 16, David M. Halperin discusses similar questions from a constructionist perspective. Building on the work of the late French philosopher Michel Foucault, Halperin argues that "sexuality"—as a positive, distinct, and constitutive feature of human personalities—is a relatively modern invention. In contrast to Boswell, he argues that ancient texts like Aristophanes' speech illustrate the radical difference between the ancient Greek experience of sex and our own. More broadly, he argues that sexuality is historical or cultural rather than biological or "natural."

Chapters 17 and 18 explore the construction of sexuality in twentieth-century America. Their focus is rather specific—and necessarily so, since the authors argue that cultural circumstance deeply affects sexual self-understanding. In chapter 17, Elizabeth Lapovsky Kennedy and Madeline Davis provide a constructionist perspective on butch-fem roles in Buffalo, New York, from 1930 to 1965. They argue that although such roles might seem fixed and objective, they in fact changed in response to social conditions and had different meanings for different people. In chapter 18, George Chauncey analyzes sexual relations between men at a naval training station in Newport, Rhode Island around 1920. Chauncey reveals that many sailors did not consider themselves "queer," even though they had sex with other men whom they labeled as such; he also recounts a fascinating court case involving the U.S. Navy and the Episcopal Church. Although these accounts are specialized, they shed light on our primary question in this section: What is homosexuality?

In chapter 19, the final selection in part III, Carol Queen discusses the challenges of being bisexual in the contemporary lesbian and gay rights movement. Queen argues that although bisexuals are often misunderstood by their homosexual counterparts, their membership in the "queer" community is both inescapable and instructive.

Part IV. Public Policy

The final section of the book deals with the question of how society should treat lesbians, gays, and bisexuals. It is tempting here to divide the debate into "conservatives," who oppose gay rights, and "liberals," who support them. But this division is misleading. For one thing, "gay rights" encompasses a number of disparate aims, including, for example, freedom from antisodomy laws, the right to legal marriage, the right to serve openly in the military, and the right to be included in antidiscrimination statutes. Many people support one or two such aims while opposing others. Moreover, one can be morally conservative while being politically liberal—one might hold, for example, that homosexual conduct is immoral yet insist that the state has no right to regulate it. That said, there does seem to be some connection between morality and politics in the gay rights debate. Those who oppose gay rights often do so because they believe that homosexuality is immoral; those who support gay rights typically do not believe that homosexuality is immoral. Thus, there is an important connection between parts I and IV.

Some commentators have likened the political debate about homosexuality to the conflict between communitarians, who emphasize community values, and classical liberals (or "libertarians"), who emphasize individual freedom. Communitarians supposedly correspond to the conservatives in the current debate, and classical liberals to the current liberals. But this division is misleading as well. It is true that classical liberals reject government interference in people's lives beyond what is necessary to prevent harm to nonconsenting parties; thus, classical liberals typically oppose antisodomy laws. Yet classical liberals also typically oppose antidiscrimination laws, since such laws infringe upon the liberty of individual citizens to hire or rent to whomever they please. Moreover, although classical liberals believe in maximizing individual freedom, they need not believe that homosexual relations are a good way of exercising that freedom, and they may support noncoercive measures to discourage such relations. Thus, classical liberals are not politically equivalent to contemporary liberals.

Likening contemporary conservatives to communitarians is even more misleading. It is possible to believe (as communitarians do) that part of the function of government is to enforce morals, without also believing that homosexuality is immoral or otherwise to be discouraged. Moreover, there are even people within the lesbian and gay community who take "conservative" stances on certain gay rights issues. So while it is tempting to divide the gay rights debate into conservatives and liberals, that division is overly simple at best.

Part IV begins with the debate over gays in the military, which climaxed during the 1992 presidential campaign when Bill Clinton announced his intention to end the ban against homosexual servicemembers. After considerable controversy, Clinton eventually settled for the current "Don't Ask, Don't Tell, Don't Pursue" policy. The policy forbids military personnel from asking recruits about their sexual orientation and from initiating investigations solely for the purpose of determining sexual orientation. Yet it also continues to forbid homosexual conduct by servicemembers, and it maintains that a servicemember's statement that he or she is homosexual creates the presumption that the servicemember is engaging in homosexual conduct; thus, such statements may be grounds for dismissal. Supporters of this policy feel that it is a useful compromise, while critics argue either that it is too permissive or that it actually makes conditions worse for homosexual servicemembers.

In his defense of the military ban, John Luddy argues in chapter 20 that the key issue is not gay rights, but rather saving lives: whatever the moral status of homosexuality may be, the ban on gays and lesbians is essential to unit cohesion and combat effectiveness. Paul Siegel responds in chapter 21 that those who oppose gays in the military, like those who once opposed blacks in the military, typically display a kind of "secondhand prejudice": they claim not to be prejudiced themselves, but they argue that since most young recruits are prejudiced, the integration of the disfavored group would undermine cohesion and is thus wrong. Siegel also rejects the "privacy rationale" for the military ban.

Following the military section is a brief discussion of "outing," the revealing of a closeted person's sexual orientation. Although this is not a public policy issue in the usual sense, it does raise important questions regarding how individuals and institutions should treat gays and lesbians who might prefer to keep their sexual orientation private. In chapter 22, Richard D. Mohr argues that treating homosexuality as "secret" reinforces the notion that gays and lesbians are somehow inferior; he thus supports outing not as a means to embarrass or punish people (a practice he labels "vindictive outing"), but rather as a way of living honestly and rejecting conventions that degrade gays and lesbians. James S. Stramel responds in chapter 23 that the concrete harmful effects of outing outweigh the abstract hypothetical benefits suggested by Mohr.

A more visible public controversy over homosexuality is the gay marriage debate, which came to the fore in 1996 when a Hawaii circuit court ruled that Hawaii's ban on gay marriage violated the state constitution, which prohibits sex-based discrimination. At the time of this writing, the Hawaii Supreme Court is preparing to issue a final judgment on the matter; most parties expect that it will uphold the circuit court ruling. Meanwhile, the Hawaii legislature has proposed a constitutional amendment banning same-sex marriage; a statewide referendum on the amendment is scheduled for November 1998. On the national level, Congress has passed the Defense of Marriage Act (DOMA), which allows individual states to refuse to recognize same-sex marriages performed in other states. President Clinton signed DOMA into law in September 1996.

Part IV contains three distinct perspectives on the issue of same-sex marriage. In chapter 24, Robert H. Knight argues that same-sex marriages are not really marriages at all, since "marriage" by definition requires one man and one woman. Knight sees the push for same-sex marriage and domestic partnership legislation as part of a larger trend of moral decay. By contrast, Jonathan Rauch argues in chapter 25 that homosexual marriage achieves some of the same key social goods as heterosexual marriage: namely, domesticating males and providing people with dedicated partners in times of need. If these are good justifications for recognizing heterosexual marriages, Rauch argues, then they are good justifications for recognizing homosexual marriages as well. Then, Claudia Card argues in chapter 26 against same-sex marriage from a lesbian feminist perspective. Card opposes legal marriage (both heterosexual and homosexual) not because she believes that committed partnerships are a bad thing, but because she believes that state involvement in such partnerships has serious moral costs.

In the book's final chapter (27), Richard D. Mohr examines the changing cultural climate regarding homosexuality. His essay represents the views of one prominent philosopher on many of the themes covered in part IV and the rest of the book: equal rights versus special rights, gay and lesbian identity, privacy versus community, and others. Mohr's vision of "A Gay and Straight Agenda" forms a fitting closing to the volume, since it not only surveys the current landscape, but also offers challenges to the various participants in the ongoing discussion. As editor, I hope that this volume will render that discussion more rational, more civil, and more productive.

· PART ONE ·

Morality and Religion

· CHAPTER ONE ·

Why Shouldn't Tommy and Jim Have Sex?

A Defense of Homosexuality

JOHN CORVINO

John Corvino, the editor of this volume and a frequent lecturer on homosexuality, defends homosexual relationships against three main objections: that they are unnatural, that they are harmful, and that they violate biblical teaching. Corvino examines several common arguments behind each objection and argues that none overcome the main point in favor of homosexual relationships: namely, that they promote the happiness and well-being of those who engage in them (and thus, the community at large).

.....

Tommy and Jim are a homosexual couple I know. Tommy is an accountant; Jim is a botany professor. They are in their forties and have been together fourteen years, the last five of which they've lived in a Victorian house that they've lovingly restored. Although their relationship has had its challenges, each has made sacrifices for the sake of the other's happiness and the relationship's long-term success.

I assume that Tommy and Jim have sex with each other (although I've

This paper grew out of a lecture, "What's (Morally) Wrong with Homosexuality?" which I first delivered at the University of Texas in 1992 and have since delivered at numerous other universities around the country. I am grateful to countless audience members, students, colleagues, and friends for helpful dialogue over the years. I would especially like to thank the following individuals for detailed comments on recent drafts of the paper: Edwin B. Allaire, Jonathan M. Bell, Daniel Bonevac, David Bradshaw, David Cleaves, Mary Beth Mader, Richard D. Mohr, Jonathan Rauch, Robert Schuessler, James Sterba, Alan Soble, and Thomas Williams. I dedicate this article to Carlos Casillas.

never bothered to ask). Furthermore, I contend that they probably *should* have sex with each other. For one thing, sex is pleasurable. But it is also much more than that: a sexual relationship can unite two people in a way that virtually nothing else can. It can be an avenue of growth, of communication, and of lasting interpersonal fulfillment. These are reasons why most heterosexual couples have sex even if they don't want children, don't want children yet, or don't want additional children. And if these reasons are good enough for most heterosexual couples, then they should be good enough for Tommy and Jim.

Of course, having a reason to do something does not preclude there being an even better reason for not doing it. Tommy might have a good reason for drinking orange juice (it's tasty and nutritious) but an even better reason for not doing so (he's allergic). The point is that one would need a pretty good reason for denying a sexual relationship to Tommy and Jim, given the intense benefits widely associated with such relationships. The question I shall consider in this paper is thus quite simple: Why shouldn't Tommy and Jim have sex?[1]

Homosexual Sex Is "Unnatural"

Many contend that homosexual sex is "unnatural." But what does that mean? Many things that people value—clothing, houses, medicine, and government, for example—are unnatural in some sense. On the other hand, many things that people detest—disease, suffering, and death, for example—are "natural" in the sense that they occur "in nature." If the unnaturalness charge is to be more than empty rhetorical flourish, those who levy it must specify what they mean. Borrowing from Burton Leiser, I will examine several possible meanings of "unnatural."[2]

What Is Unusual or Abnormal Is Unnatural

One meaning of "unnatural" refers to that which deviates from the norm, that is, from what most people do. Obviously, most people engage in heterosexual relationships. But does it follow that it is wrong to engage in homosexual relationships? Relatively few people read Sanskrit, pilot ships, play the mandolin, breed goats, or write with both hands, yet none of these activities is immoral simply because it is unusual. As the Ramsey Colloquium, a group of Jewish and Christian scholars who oppose homosexuality, writes, "The statistical frequency of an act does not determine its moral status."[3] So while homosexuality might be unnatural in the sense of being unusual, that fact is morally irrelevant.

What Is Not Practiced by Other Animals Is Unnatural

Some people argue, "Even animals know better than to behave homosexually; homosexuality must be wrong." This argument is doubly flawed. First, it rests on a false premise. Numerous studies—including Anne Perkins's study of "gay" sheep and George and Molly Hunt's study of "lesbian" seagulls—have shown that some animals do form homosexual pair-bonds.[4] Second, even if animals did not behave homosexually, that fact would not prove that homosexuality is immoral. After all, animals don't cook their food, brush their teeth, participate in religious worship, or attend college; human beings do all of these without moral censure. Indeed, the idea that animals could provide us with our standards—especially our sexual standards—is simply amusing.

What Does Not Proceed from Innate Desires Is Unnatural

Recent studies suggesting a biological basis for homosexuality have resulted in two popular positions. One side proposes that homosexual people are "born that way" and that it is therefore natural (and thus good) for them to form homosexual relationships. The other side maintains that homosexuality is a lifestyle choice, which is therefore unnatural (and thus wrong). Both sides assume a connection between the origin of homosexual orientation, on the one hand, and the moral value of homosexual activity, on the other. And insofar as they share that assumption, both sides are wrong.

Consider first the pro-homosexual side: "They are born that way; therefore it's natural and good." This inference assumes that all innate desires are good ones (i.e., that they should be acted upon). But that assumption is clearly false. Research suggests that some people are born with a predisposition toward violence, but such people have no more right to strangle their neighbors than anyone else. So while people like Tommy and Jim may be born with homosexual tendencies, it doesn't follow that they ought to act on them. Nor does it follow that they ought *not* to act on them, even if the tendencies are not innate. I probably do not have any innate tendency to write with my left hand (since I, like everyone else in my family, have always been right-handed), but it doesn't follow that it would be immoral for me to do so. So simply asserting that homosexuality is a lifestyle choice will not show that it is an immoral lifestyle choice.

Do people "choose" to be homosexual? People certainly don't seem to choose their sexual *feelings*, at least not in any direct or obvious way. (Do you? Think about it.) Rather, they find certain people attractive and certain activities arousing, whether they "decide" to or not. Indeed, most people at some point in their lives wish that they could control their feelings more—for example, in situations of unrequited love—and find it frustrating that they cannot. What they *can* control to a considerable degree is how and when they act upon those feelings. In that sense, both homosexuality and heterosexuality involve lifestyle choices. But in either case, determining the origin of the feelings will not determine whether it is moral to act on them.

What Violates an Organ's Principal Purpose Is Unnatural

Perhaps when people claim that homosexual sex is unnatural they mean that it cannot result in procreation. The idea behind the argument is that human organs have various natural purposes: eyes are for seeing, ears are for hearing, genitals are for procreating. According to this argument, it is immoral to use an organ in a way that violates its particular purpose.

Many of our organs, however, have multiple purposes. Tommy can use his mouth for talking, eating, breathing, licking stamps, chewing gum, kissing women, or kissing Jim; and it seems rather arbitrary to claim that all but the last use are "natural."[5] (And if we say that some of the other uses are "unnatural, but not immoral," we have failed to specify a morally relevant sense of the term "natural.")

Just because people can and do use their sexual organs to procreate, it does not follow that they should not use them for other purposes. Sexual organs seem very well suited for expressing love, for giving and receiving pleasure, and for celebrating, replenishing, and enhancing a relationship—even when procreation is not a factor. Unless opponents of homosexuality are prepared to condemn heterosexual couples who use contraception or individuals who masturbate, they must abandon this version of the unnaturalness argument. Indeed, even the Roman Catholic Church, which forbids contraception and masturbation, approves of sex for sterile couples and of sex during pregnancy, neither of which can lead to procreation. The Church concedes here that intimacy and pleasure are morally legitimate purposes for sex, even in cases where procreation is impossible. But since homosexual sex can achieve these purposes as well, it is inconsistent for the Church to condemn it on the grounds that it is not procreative.

One might object that sterile heterosexual couples do not *intentionally* turn away from procreation, whereas homosexual couples do. But this distinction doesn't hold. It is no more possible for Tommy to procreate with a woman whose uterus has been removed than it is for him to procreate with Jim.[6] By having sex with either one, he is intentionally engaging in a nonprocreative sexual act.

Yet one might press the objection further and insist that Tommy and the woman *could* produce children if the woman were fertile: whereas homosexual relationships are essentially infertile, heterosexual relationships are only incidentally so. But what does that prove? Granted, it might require less of a miracle for a woman without a uterus to become pregnant than for Jim to become pregnant, but it would require a miracle nonetheless. Thus it seems that the real difference here is not that one couple is fertile and the other not, nor that one couple "could" be fertile (with the help of a miracle) and the other not, but rather that one couple is male-female and the other male-male. In other words, sex between Tommy and Jim is wrong because it's male-male—i.e., because it's homosexual. But that, of course, is no argument at all.[7]

What Is Disgusting or Offensive Is Unnatural

It often seems that when people call homosexuality "unnatural" they really just mean that it's disgusting. But plenty of morally neutral activities—handling snakes, eating snails, performing autopsies, cleaning toilets, and so on—disgust people. Indeed, for centuries, most people found interracial relationships disgusting, yet that feeling—which has by no means disappeared—hardly proves that such relationships are wrong. In sum, the charge that homosexuality is unnatural, at least in its most common forms, is longer on rhetorical flourish than on philosophical cogency. At best it expresses an aesthetic judgment, not a moral judgment.

Homosexual Sex Is Harmful

One might instead argue that homosexuality is harmful. The Ramsey Colloquium, for instance, argues that homosexuality leads to the breakdown of the family and, ultimately, of human society, and it points to the "alarming rates of sexual promiscuity, depression, and suicide and the ominous presence of AIDS within the homosexual subculture."[8] Thomas Schmidt marshals copious statistics to show that homosexual activity undermines physical and psychological health.[9] Such charges, if correct, would seem to provide strong evidence against homosexuality. But are the charges correct? And do they prove what they purport to prove?

One obvious (and obviously problematic) way to answer the first question is to ask people like Tommy and Jim. It would appear that no one is in a better position to judge the homosexual lifestyle than those who know it firsthand. Yet it is unlikely that critics would trust their testimony. Indeed, the more homosexual people try to explain their lives, the more critics accuse them of deceitfully promoting an agenda. (It's like trying to prove that you're not crazy. The more you object, the more people think, "That's exactly what a crazy person would say.")

One might instead turn to statistics. An obvious problem with this tack is that both sides of the debate bring forth extensive statistics and "expert" testimony, leaving the average observer confused. There is a more subtle problem as well. Because of widespread antigay sentiment, many homosexual people won't acknowledge their romantic feelings to themselves, much less to researchers.[10] I have known a number of gay men who did not "come out" until their forties and fifties, and no amount of professional competence on the part of interviewers would have been likely to open their closets sooner. Such problems compound the usual difficulties of finding representative population samples for statistical study.

Yet even if the statistical claims of gay rights opponents were true, they would not prove what they purport to prove, for several reasons. First, as any good statistician realizes, correlation does not equal cause. Even if homosexual people were more likely to commit suicide, be promiscuous, or contract AIDS than the general population, it would not follow that their homosexuality causes them to do these things. An alternative—and very plausible—explanation is that these phenomena, like the disproportionately high crime rates among African Americans, are at least partly a function of society's treatment of the group in question. Suppose you were told from a very early age that the romantic feelings that you experienced were sick, unnatural, and disgusting. Suppose further that expressing these feelings put you at risk of social ostracism or, worse yet, physical violence. Is it not plausible that you would, for instance, be more inclined to depression than you would be without such obstacles? And that such depression could, in its extreme forms, lead to suicide or other self-destructive behaviors? (It is indeed remarkable that couples like Tommy and Jim continue to flourish in the face of such obstacles.)

A similar explanation can be given for the alleged promiscuity of homosexuals.[11] The denial of legal marriage, the pressure to remain in the closet, and the overt hostility toward homosexual relationships are all more conducive to transient, clandestine encounters than they are to long-term unions. As a result, that which is challenging enough for heterosexual couples—settling down and building a life together—becomes far more challenging for homosexual couples.

Indeed, there is an interesting tension in the critics' position here. Opponents of homosexuality commonly claim that "marriage and the family . . . are fragile institutions in need of careful and continuing support."[12] And they point to the increasing prevalence of divorce and premarital sex among heterosexuals as evidence that such support is declining. Yet they refuse to concede that the complete absence of similar support for homosexual relationships might explain many of the alleged problems of homosexuals. The critics can't have it both ways: if heterosexual marriages are in trouble despite the various social, economic, and legal incentives for keeping them together, society should be little surprised that homosexual relationships—which not only lack such supports, but face overt hostility—are difficult to maintain.

One might object that if social ostracism were the main cause of homosexual people's problems, then homosexual people in more "tolerant" cities like New York and San Francisco should exhibit fewer such problems than their small-town counterparts; yet statistics do not seem to bear this out. This objection underestimates the extent of antigay sentiment in our society. By the time many gay and lesbian people move to urban centers, they have already been exposed to (and may have internalized) considerable hostility toward homosexuality. Moreover, the visibility of homosexuality in urban centers makes gay and lesbian people there more vulnerable to attack (and thus more likely to exhibit certain difficulties). Finally, note that urbanites *in general* (not just homosexual urbanites) tend to exhibit higher rates of promiscuity, depression, and sexually transmitted disease than the rest of the population.

But what about AIDS? Opponents of homosexuality sometimes claim that even if homosexual sex is not, strictly speaking, immoral, it is still a bad idea, since it puts people at risk for AIDS and other sexually transmitted diseases. But that claim is misleading: it is infinitely more risky for Tommy to have sex with a woman who is HIV-positive than with Jim, who is HIV-negative. Obviously, it's not homosexuality that's harmful, it's the virus; and the virus may be carried by both heterosexual and homosexual people.

Now it may be true (in the United States, at least) that homosexual males are statistically more likely to carry the virus than heterosexual females and thus that homosexual sex is *statistically* more risky than heterosexual sex (in cases where the partner's HIV status is unknown). But opponents of homosexuality need something stronger than this statistical claim. For if it is wrong for men to have sex with men because their doing so puts them at a higher AIDS risk than heterosexual sex, then it is also wrong for women to have sex with men because their doing so puts them at a higher AIDS risk than homosexual sex (lesbians as a group have the lowest incidence of AIDS). Purely from the standpoint of AIDS risk, women ought to prefer lesbian sex.

If this response seems silly, it is because there is obviously more to choosing a romantic or sexual partner than determining AIDS risk. And a major part of the decision, one that opponents of homosexuality consistently overlook, is considering whether one can have a mutually fulfilling relationship with the partner. For many people like Tommy and Jim, such fulfillment—which most heterosexuals recognize to be an important component of human flourishing—is only possible with members of the same sex.

Of course, the foregoing argument hinges on the claim that homosexual sex can only cause harm indirectly. Some would object that there are certain activities—anal sex, for instance—that for anatomical reasons are intrinsically harmful. But an argument against anal intercourse is by no means tantamount to an argument against homosexuality: neither all nor only homosexuals engage in anal sex. There are plenty of other things for both gay men and lesbians to do in bed. Indeed, for women, it appears that the most common forms of homosexual activity may be *less* risky than penile-vaginal intercourse, since the latter has been linked to cervical cancer.[13]

In sum, there is nothing *inherently* risky about sex between persons of the same gender. It is only risky under certain conditions: for instance, if they exchange diseased bodily fluids or if they engage in certain "rough" forms of sex that could cause tearing of delicate tissue. Heterosexual sex is equally risky under such conditions. Thus, even if statistical claims like those of Schmidt and the Ramsey Colloquium were true, they would not prove that homosexuality is immoral. At best, they would prove that homosexual people—like everyone else—ought to take great care when deciding to become sexually active.

Of course, there's more to a flourishing life than avoiding harm. One might argue that even if Tommy and Jim are not harming each other by their relationship, they are still failing to achieve the higher level of fulfillment possible in a heterosexual relationship, which is rooted in the complementarity of male and female. But this argument just ignores the facts: Tommy and Jim are homosexual *precisely because* they find relationships with men (and, in particular, with each other) more fulfilling than relationships with women. Even evangelicals (who have long advocated "faith healing" for homosexuals) are beginning to acknowledge that the choice for most homosexual people is not between homosexual relationships and heterosexual relationships, but rather between homosexual relationships and celibacy.[14] What the critics need to show, therefore, is that no matter how loving, committed, mutual, generous, and fulfilling the relationship may be, Tommy and Jim would flourish more if they were celibate. Given the evidence of their lives (and of others like them), this is a formidable task indeed.

Thus far I have focused on the allegation that homosexuality harms those who engage in it. But what about the allegation that homosexuality harms other, nonconsenting parties? Here I will briefly consider two claims: that homosexuality threatens children and that it threatens society.

Those who argue that homosexuality threatens children may mean one of two things. First, they may mean that homosexual people are child molesters. Statistically, the vast majority of reported cases of child sexual abuse involve young girls and their fathers, stepfathers, or other familiar (and presumably heterosexual) adult males.[15] But opponents of homosexuality argue that when one adjusts for relative percentage in the population, homosexual males appear more likely than heterosexual males to be child molesters. As I argued above, the problems with obtaining reliable statistics on homosexuality render such calculations difficult. Fortunately, they are also unnecessary.

Child abuse is a terrible thing. But when a heterosexual male molests a child (or rapes a woman or commits assault), the act does not reflect upon all heterosexuals. Similarly, when a homosexual male molests a child, there is no reason why that act should reflect upon all homosexuals. Sex with adults of the same sex is one thing; sex with *children* of the same sex is quite another. Conflating the two not only slanders innocent people, it also misdirects resources intended to protect children. Furthermore, many men convicted of molesting young boys are sexually attracted to adult women and report no attraction to adult men.[16] To call such men "homosexual," or even "bisexual," is probably to stretch such terms too far.[17]

Alternatively, those who charge that homosexuality threatens children might mean that the increasing visibility of homosexual relationships makes children more likely to become homosexual. The argument for this view is patently circular. One cannot prove that doing *X* is bad by arguing that it causes other people to do *X*, which is bad. One must first establish independently that *X* is bad. That said, there is not a shred of evidence to demonstrate that exposure to homosexuality leads children to become homosexual.

But doesn't homosexuality threaten society? A Roman Catholic priest once put the argument to me as follows: "Of course homosexuality is bad for society. If everyone were homosexual, there would be no society." Perhaps it is true that if everyone were homosexual, there would be no society. But if everyone were a celibate priest, society would collapse just as surely, and my friend the priest didn't seem to think that he was doing anything wrong simply by failing to procreate. Jeremy Bentham made the point somewhat more acerbically roughly 200 years ago: "If then merely out of regard to population it were right that [homosexuals] should be burnt alive, monks ought to be roasted alive by a slow fire."[18]

From the fact that the continuation of society requires procreation, it does not follow that *everyone* must procreate. Moreover, even if such an obligation existed, it would not preclude homosexuality. At best, it would preclude *exclusive* homosexuality: homosexual people who occasionally have heterosexual sex can procreate just fine. And given artificial insemination, even those who are exclusively homosexual can procreate. In short, the priest's claim—if everyone were homosexual, there would be no society—is false; and even if it were true, it would not establish that homosexuality is immoral.

The Ramsey Colloquium commits a similar fallacy.[19] Noting (correctly) that heterosexual marriage promotes the continuation of human life, it then infers that homosexuality is immoral because it fails to accomplish the same.[20] But from the fact that procreation is good, it does not follow that childlessness is bad—a point that the members of the colloquium, several of whom are Roman Catholic priests, should readily concede.

I have argued that Tommy and Jim's sexual relationship harms neither them nor society. On the contrary, it benefits both. It benefits them because it makes them happier—not merely in a short-term, hedonistic sense, but in a long-term, "big picture" sort of way. And, in turn, it benefits society, since it makes Tommy and Jim more stable, more productive, and more generous than they would otherwise be. In short, their relationship—including its sexual component—provides the same kinds of benefits that infertile heterosexual relationships provide (and perhaps other benefits as well). Nor should we fear that accepting their relationship and others like it will cause people to flee in droves from the institution of heterosexual marriage. After all, as Thomas Williams points out, the usual response to a gay person is not "How come *he* gets to be gay and I don't?"[21]

Homosexuality Violates Biblical Teaching

At this point in the discussion, many people turn to religion. "If the secular arguments fail to prove that homosexuality is wrong," they say, "so much the worse for secular ethics. This failure only proves that we need God for morality." Since people often justify their moral beliefs by appeal to religion, I will briefly consider the biblical position.

At first glance, the Bible's condemnation of homosexual activity seems unequivocal. Consider, for example, the following two passages, one from the "Old" Testament and one from the "New":[22]

> You shall not lie with a male as with a woman; it is an abomination. (Lev. 18:22)

> For this reason God gave them up to degrading passions. Their women exchanged natural intercourse for unnatural, and in the same way also the men, giving up natural intercourse with women, were consumed with passion for one another. Men committed shameless acts with men and received in their own persons the due penalty for their error. (Rom. 1:26–27)

Note, however, that these passages are surrounded by other passages that relatively few people consider binding. For example, Leviticus also declares,

> The pig . . . is unclean for you. Of their flesh you shall not eat, and their carcasses you shall not touch; they are unclean for you. (11:7–8)

Taken literally, this passage not only prohibits eating pork, but also playing football, since footballs are made of pigskin. (Can you believe that the University of Notre Dame so flagrantly violates Levitical teaching?)

Similarly, St. Paul, author of the Romans passage, also writes, "Slaves, obey your earthly masters with fear and trembling, in singleness of heart, as you obey Christ" (Eph. 6:5)—morally problematic advice if there ever were any. Should we interpret this passage (as Southern plantation owners once did) as implying that it is immoral for slaves to escape? After all, God himself says in Leviticus,

> [Y]ou may acquire male and female slaves . . . from among the aliens residing with you, and from their families that are with you, who have been born in your land; and they may be your property. You may keep them as a possession for your children after you, for them to inherit as property. (25:44–46)

How can people maintain the inerrancy of the Bible in light of such passages? The answer, I think, is that they learn to interpret the passages *in their historical context.*

Consider the Bible's position on usury, the lending of money for interest (for *any* interest, not just excessive interest). The Bible condemns this practice in no uncertain terms. In Exodus God says that "if you lend money to my people, to the poor among you, you shall not exact interest from them"

(22:25). Psalm 15 says that those who lend at interest may not abide in the Lord's tent or dwell on his holy hill (1–5). Ezekiel calls usury "abominable"; compares it to adultery, robbery, idolatry, and bribery; and states that anyone who "takes advanced or accrued interest . . . shall surely die; his blood shall be upon himself" (18:13).[23]

Should believers therefore close their savings accounts? Not necessarily. According to orthodox Christian teaching, the biblical prohibition against usury no longer applies. The reason is that economic conditions have changed substantially since biblical times, such that usury no longer has the same negative consequences it had when the prohibitions were issued. Thus, the practice that was condemned by the Bible differs from contemporary interest banking in morally relevant ways.[24]

Yet are we not in a similar position regarding homosexuality? Virtually all scholars agree that homosexual relations during biblical times were vastly different from relationships like Tommy and Jim's. Often such relations were integral to pagan practices. In Greek society, they typically involved older men and younger boys. If those are the kinds of features that the biblical authors had in mind when they issued their condemnations, and such features are no longer typical, then the biblical condemnations no longer apply. As with usury, substantial changes in cultural context have altered the meaning and consequences—and thus the moral value—of the practice in question. Put another way, using the Bible's condemnations of homosexuality against contemporary homosexuality is like using its condemnations of usury against contemporary banking.

Let me be clear about what I am *not* claiming here. First, I am not claiming that the Bible has been wrong before and therefore may be wrong this time. The Bible may indeed be wrong on some matters, but for the purpose of this argument I am assuming its infallibility. Nor am I claiming that the Bible's age renders it entirely inapplicable to today's issues. Rather, I am claiming that when we do apply it, *we must pay attention to morally relevant cultural differences between biblical times and today.* Such attention will help us distinguish between specific time-bound prohibitions (for example, laws against usury or homosexual relations) and the enduring moral values they represent (for example, generosity or respect for persons). And as the above argument shows, my claim is not very controversial. Indeed, to deny it is to commit oneself to some rather strange views on slavery, usury, women's roles, astronomy, evolution, and the like.

Here, one might also make an appeal to religious pluralism. Given the wide variety of religious beliefs (e.g., the Muslim belief that women should cover their faces, the Orthodox Jewish belief against working on Saturday, the Hindu belief that cows are sacred and should not be eaten), each of us inevitably violates the religious beliefs of others. But we normally don't view such violations as occasions for moral censure, since we distinguish between beliefs that depend on particular revelations and beliefs that can be justified independently (e.g., that stealing is wrong). Without an independent justification for condemning homosexuality, the best one can say is, "My religion says so." But in a society that cherishes religious freedom, that reason alone does not normally provide grounds for moral or legal sanctions. That people still fall back on that reason in discussions of homosexuality suggests that they may not have much of a case otherwise.

Conclusion

As a last resort, opponents of homosexuality typically change the subject: "But what about incest, polygamy, and bestiality? If we accept Tommy and Jim's sexual relationship, why shouldn't we accept those as well?" Opponents of interracial marriage used a similar slippery-slope argument in the 1960s when the Supreme Court struck down antimiscegenation laws.[25] It was a bad argument then, and it is a bad argument now.

Just because there are no good reasons to oppose interracial or homosexual relationships, it does not follow that there are no good reasons to oppose incestuous, polygamous, or bestial relationships. One might argue, for instance, that incestuous relationships threaten delicate familial bonds, or that polygamous relationships result in unhealthy jealousies (and sexism), or that bestial relationships—do I need to say it?—aren't really "relationships" at all, at least not in the sense we've been discussing.[26] Perhaps even better arguments could be offered (given much more space than I have here). The point is that there is no logical connection between homosexuality, on the one hand, and incest, polygamy, and bestiality, on the other.

Why, then, do critics continue to push this objection? Perhaps it's because accepting homosexuality requires them to give up one of their favorite arguments: "It's wrong because we've always been taught that it's wrong." This argument—call it the argument from tradition—has an obvious appeal: people reasonably favor tried-and-true ideas over unfamiliar ones, and they recognize the foolishness of trying to invent morality from scratch. But the argument from tradition is also a dangerous argument, as any honest look at history will reveal.

I conclude that Tommy and Jim's relationship, far from being a moral abomination, is exactly what it appears to be to those who know them: a morally positive influence on their lives and on others. Accepting this conclusion takes courage, since it entails that our moral traditions are fallible. But when these traditions interfere with people's happiness for no sound reason, they defeat what is arguably the very point of morality: promoting individual and communal well-being. To put the argument simply, Tommy and Jim's relationship makes them better people. And that's not just good for Tommy and Jim: that's good for everyone.

· CHAPTER TWO ·

A Reply to Corvino

DAVID BRADSHAW

David Bradshaw, assistant professor of philosophy at the University of Kentucky, responds to the previous essay by John Corvino. Bradshaw distinguishes between various types of arguments against homosexuality and then proceeds to defend the one he believes to be most important. Specifically, he argues that homosexuality is immoral because it fails to respect the given form of the human body as male or female. In the process, he explains how the conservative position on homosexuality is a natural extension of a larger moral framework.

· · · · ·

After reading John Corvino's essay "Why Shouldn't Tommy and Jim Have Sex? A Defense of Homosexuality," one is left with the impression that the conservative position on homosexuality is nothing but a tissue of confusions. Surely it is a marvel that so many otherwise reasonable people have for so long persisted in such an erroneous view. Perhaps, as Corvino suggests, the explanation is mere prejudice. Or perhaps it is not. I believe that much of the confusion that Corvino finds is of his own making, caused by his insistence on treating arguments that really have quite distinct purposes as if they were all trying to show the same thing: that homosexual intercourse is always wrong. Now this is certainly a position that many conservatives (myself included) do hold, but it does not follow that every conservative argument is aimed at defending it. Many have more modest aims, and to treat them all as if they were intended to show that homosexuality *in every case* is immoral can only lead to confusion. (I will use the term "homosexuality" throughout to indicate the practice of same-sex intercourse and not merely homosexual orientation.)

In what follows, I will first attempt to clarify how the various elements of the conservative position fit together. I will distinguish three levels of opposition to homosexuality, only the third of which is concerned to maintain that homosexual intercourse is always wrong. Although I will not attempt to defend every conservative argument in detail, placing the arguments within their proper context will make it apparent that most of Corvino's objections are misguided. Following this preliminary survey, the bulk of the essay will be devoted to elaborating the single argument which I think best illuminates the deeper issues involved.

A Taxonomy of Conservatism

Most public debate over homosexuality tends to focus, not on the morality of homosexual intercourse as such, but on the various changes to public policy advocated by the gay rights movement. It is important to recognize that one need not hold a moral belief against homosexuality in order to oppose the gay rights movement. Consider the analogy of smoking. Many Americans would deny that it is immoral to smoke, but would also resist any concerted effort to increase public acceptance of smoking. (Imagine, for example, an attempt by the tobacco companies to infiltrate pro-smoking material into the public schools.) Such a position is perfectly consistent, for not every decision about public policy need be based on strictly moral considerations. Other factors that rightly carry weight include public health and safety, demands on the public treasury, the well-being of institutions that are essential to society, and respect for established custom and the wishes of the majority, even when one personally believes those wishes to be ill-founded.

Much of the opposition to the gay rights movement is grounded on considerations such as these. We must therefore distinguish the first level of opposition from one that goes further. The second level lodges a specifically moral objection to homosexuality. It is limited, however, in that it objects to what may be called the "homosexual lifestyle"—that is, to the persistent practice of homosexuality as that practice *typically* exists in our society. As Corvino rightly observes, many of the points most frequently made in this connection really apply only to the practices of male homosexuals: they include that sex among male homosexuals is wildly promiscuous, that it spreads disease, and that it is highly correlated with other evils both sexual (sadism, masochism, child molestation) and non-sexual (suicide, alcoholism, drug abuse). What makes all of this a bit confusing is that an argument based on such premises may belong to either of the two levels. The distinction is one of purpose. If the aim is to show that, as a matter of public policy, homosexuality ought not to be conceded the same legitimacy as heterosexuality, then the argument belongs to the first level; if the aim is to show that it is wrong for an individual to follow a homosexual lifestyle, then the argument belongs to the second.

There is another type of objection to the homosexual lifestyle, one that applies equally to males and females. This one deserves special mention because only a garbled version of it appears in Corvino's essay. Properly stated, the argument is that the mutual attraction of male and female is so important to the foundations of society that to adopt a way of life that publicly and persistently repudiates it is a moral evil. Note that religious celibates do not repudiate the heterosexual norm in the relevant way; they confirm it, for their celibacy is recognized by both themselves and others as a sacrifice made in pursuit of a higher good. Nor is there any repudiation in the attitude of those who, for whatever reason, simply do not feel or act upon an attraction to the opposite sex. The source of offense is the proffering of homosexuality as an *alternative* to heterosexuality—an "alternative lifestyle," one capable of providing the same sort of companionship and sexual pleasure as heterosexual marriage. This is felt by opponents to be a sort of counterfeiting of a basic human good. Like any counterfeit, it is bogus, but it is also sufficiently plausible to have the potential for doing serious harm.

Just as with the arguments directed against male homosexuality, an argument against the public acceptance of homosexuality as an equal alternative to heterosexual marriage can work at two levels. The first level argues that to give homosexuality the same sort of legitimacy as heterosexuality tends to destroy the delicate web of sanctions and incentives through which society channels the sexual impulse in a constructive direction. The second level argues that anyone who lives publicly as a homosexual by that very action endorses and helps propagate a sort of counterfeit good, a false alternative to the heterosexual norm.

All of these arguments are interesting and important. In the interests of space, however, I will not pursue them further here.[1] There is yet a third level of opposition to homosexuality, and it is the one that goes deepest. In describing the second level, I emphasized the word "typically," for of course there are many varieties of homosexual practice. Let us imagine a homosexual act performed in such a way that it does not damage bodily tissues (as does anal sex, for example), does not spread disease, is not part of a promiscuous lifestyle, has no harmful public repercussions, and, in general, shares none of the characteristics that have so far been mentioned as objectionable. Is such an act wrong? Is it wrong *simply in virtue of being a sexual act between two persons of the same sex,* without regard to its further characteristics? That is the question that is at the heart of the moral issues surrounding homosexuality, and it is the one on which I wish to focus.

At least two sorts of arguments can be brought to bear at this point.[2] One is based on religious authority. Although in this essay my main interest does not lie in that direction, I must say a word about such arguments because of what seems to me the misleading treatment of them by Corvino. Like Corvino, I will take the biblical injunctions as representative. It should be noted, however, that opposition to homosexuality is the dominant tradition in most of the world's major religions, including not only Judaism and Christianity, but also Hinduism and Islam.[3]

Corvino writes that "[v]irtually all scholars agree that homosexual relations during biblical times were vastly different from relationships like Tommy and Jim's." This is true as far as it goes; monogamous and committed homosexuality did not exist in antiquity, particularly among males. But why should that affect the meaning of the biblical commandments? They are not stated in a way that would restrict them to acts occurring in a particular context. The passages in Leviticus refer simply to a man lying with a man as with a woman (18:22, 20:13). Even more to the point, St. Paul explicitly bases his position on the deviation of same-sex intercourse from "natural" intercourse—that between man and woman (Rom. 1:26–27). This makes it clear that his objection is to same-sex intercourse as such, and not solely to its associations in the culture of his time.[4]

Corvino also appeals to religious pluralism. He claims that, whatever one thinks of the biblical teachings, they do not "provide grounds for moral or legal sanctions." The question of what are the appropriate grounds for *legal* sanctions is a large one that raises tricky issues of constitutional interpretation. Since Corvino does not address those issues, he can scarcely be said to have argued for his view, and I shall simply register my disagreement without pursuing the issue further. The main point at issue between us is that of the appropriate grounds for *moral* judgment. Here, Corvino's examples blur an important distinction. Many biblical commandments, such as the dietary laws and the prohibition of working on Saturday, are clearly intended as binding only on Jews; others, like the commandment against murder given to Noah (Gen. 9:6), are clearly meant to be universally applicable. The reason they are conceived as universally applicable is that they purport to make explicit a standard that, in some sense, is already given in the nature of things; thus Cain, for example, was at fault for his murder of Abel, although there was at that time no explicit commandment against murder.

To which of these two classes do the commandments against homosexuality belong? One important clue is the fact that the people of Sodom and Gomorrah were held accountable for their homosexual acts, despite the fact that they were non-Jews and lived long before the time of Leviticus.[5]

More generally, a strong case can be made—although I will not attempt to make it here—that the commandments against homosexuality are simply one aspect of a broader sexual ethic rooted in the creation account in Genesis.[6] As such, they are binding upon the entire human race.

What all this means is that, *if* one takes the Bible as authoritative, one is bound to regard homosexuality as wrong. That may seem an elementary point, but it is so widely denied (or ignored) today that it bears emphasizing. Of course, we can hardly stop with this conclusion. Many people do not accept the authority of the Bible, and even those who accept it recognize that there is a need to do more than simply repeat the traditional teaching. In the remainder of this essay, I will provide an argument against same-sex intercourse that does not rely on religious authority. The argument will proceed in two stages. In the first, I will attempt to make plausible the idea that the very form of the body carries with it certain moral restrictions. In the second, I will apply this general insight to the particular case of homosexuality.

The Body and Its Moral Space

One of the more decadent Roman emperors, Domitian, is said to have enjoyed pulling the wings off flies and watching them suffer.[7] I will assume that the reader agrees with me that such a practice is not only disgusting, but also has about it at least a faint whiff of evil. How are we to understand its moral dimension? One way would be to say that what Domitian does is wrong because it contributes to the total amount of suffering in the world. The problem with this approach is that the act also contributes to the total amount of happiness—namely, by giving pleasure to Domitian. To arrive at a proper assessment of it, therefore, we presumably would have to weigh these two factors against one another. In the first place, of course, there is no plausible way of doing so; even more to the point, part of what seems wrong about the act is precisely that Domitian *does* take pleasure in it. There is something about the pleasure itself that seems debased and degrading. The suffering of flies, on the other hand, is something that we generally do not feel obligated to take account of at all. Surely a better way to understand the moral dimension of Domitian's act would be to say that what is wrong is Domitian's taking pleasure in the sufferings of his fellow creatures. This attitude and the pleasure deriving from it are wrong, even if the sufferings themselves happen to be morally inconsequential.

I would now like to examine a case where the cruelty of Domitian is writ large. It is an episode from C. S. Lewis's novel *Perelandra.*[8] In the novel, an adventurer named Ransom is transported to Venus (called "Perelandra" by its inhabitants). He discovers there a world of stunning natural beauty that has not experienced—not yet—its own equivalent of the Fall. But soon Ransom sees a sign that something is wrong. Ransom finds on the ground a frog-like creature, still living, but with its back ripped open in a V-shaped gash. The discovery leaves him stunned.

> On earth it would have been merely a nasty sight, but up to this moment Ransom had seen nothing dead or spoiled in Perelandra, and it was like a blow in the face. . . . The milk-warm wind blowing over the golden sea, the blues and silvers and greens of the floating garden, the sky itself—all these had become, in one instant, merely the illuminated margin of a book whose text was the struggling little horror at his feet, and he himself, in that same instant, had passed into a state of emotion which he could neither control nor understand. He told himself that a creature of that kind probably had very little sensation. But it did not much mend matters. It was not merely pity that had suddenly changed the rhythm of his heart-beats. The thing was an intolerable obscenity which afflicted him with shame.[9]

Ransom soon discovers that there is a whole string of mutilated frogs, twenty-one in all, leading downward to the water's edge. He forces himself to follow the trail. At its end he finds Weston, another man who has made the journey from Earth to Perelandra. Weston has devoted his life to interplanetary exploration in service to what he calls "the great, inscrutable Force" driving all cosmic progress. In a previous scene, Ransom had warned him that this so-called Force might very well be the devil. Ransom now observes Weston quietly and methodically ripping open the twenty-second frog. As Weston tosses it to the ground their eyes meet.

> If Ransom said nothing, it was because he could not speak. . . . He saw a man who was certainly Weston, to judge from his height and build and colouring and features. In that sense he was quite recognisable. But the terror was that he was also unrecognisable. He did not look like a sick man: but he looked very like a dead one. The face which he raised from torturing the frog had that terrible power which the face of a corpse sometimes has of simply rebuffing every conceivable human attitude one can adopt towards it. The expressionless mouth, the unwinking stare of the eyes, something heavy and inorganic in the very folds of the cheek, said clearly: "I have features as you have, but there is nothing in common between you and me." . . .

> And now, forcing its way into consciousness, thrusting aside every mental habit and every longing not to believe, came the conviction that this, in fact, was not a man: that Weston's body was kept, walking and undecaying, in Perelandra by some wholly different kind of life, and that Weston himself was gone.[10]

It soon becomes all too clear that Ransom's earlier hunch was correct. What Weston had called the "Force" is in reality the devil. The man who was Weston is gone; in his place is a demonically possessed corpse whom Ransom comes to call "the Un-man."

This tale nicely illustrates what I was getting at in my remarks about Domitian and the flies. Clearly, what makes the mutilation wrought by the Un-man evil is not just the harm done to the frogs; nor is it the harm done to Ransom and other observers, for the act would be just as evil even if it were observed by no one. What makes it evil is its gratuitous cruelty.

Yet there is something else going on here as well. Notice that Ransom reacts to what he has seen as an obscenity *before* he is aware that it is due to a (partly) human agent. There is something about the thing itself—the way the body of the frog has been warped and defiled—that stands out as an offense against nature, even apart from the malicious intent that has produced it. True, the incident strikes Ransom in this way only because of the idyllic conditions of Perelandra. But that does not negate the point, for it is at least possible (and Lewis certainly means to suggest) that these idyllic conditions have merely heightened Ransom's sensitivity to a kind of moral reality that in some degree is always present.

Another point to notice is the way that Weston's act of mutilation effectively places him beyond the bounds of the human race. "I have features as you have, but there is nothing in common between you and me." In the novel, of course, this dehumanization is entirely literal; the Un-man is no longer a human being, but a corpse moved by the devil. Even apart from demonic possession, however, there is a clear sense in which to take pleasure in the sufferings of others renders one inhuman. We frequently refer to torturers and those who run death camps in precisely that way. Cruelty of this kind is more than the violation of a moral rule, for it affects the very being of the agent, extinguishing whatever there is in the agent that is distinctively human. It is thus, to repeat a phrase I have already used, an offense against nature—this time, specifically against human nature, a violation of what it is to be human.

Admittedly, this is something of a paradox. Surely, to take pleasure in the sufferings of others *is* distinctively human, for it is done by no animal other than man. Why, then, do we call it inhuman? The reason is that man alone, unlike the other animals, has a certain control over his own nature. Any human being has the capacity to give up his humanity; that is part of the glory and curse of what it is to be human.

I now wish to focus on the connection between the evil that we find so repellent in the Un-man and the elementary fact that we possess bodies. First, I must bring forward another example. A few years ago, it was widely reported that the flesh of fetuses aborted in China was being sold there as a health food. It turns out that such flesh contains nutrients that inhibit the formation of wrinkles and other aspects of the aging process. Those in America who in any degree oppose abortion were swift and unanimous in denouncing this practice. More surprisingly, even those who find nothing wrong with abortion for the most part shied away from defending it and in some cases even joined in its denunciation. The parallel to cannibalism was apparently too close for comfort, despite their official position that the fetus is not a human being.

In light of this history, I feel reasonably safe in assuming that the reader will share my own reaction to this practice: that it is obscene and inhuman. I choose these words advisedly, for they are of course the same words that appeared in our discussion of the Un-man. But notice that in this case there is no gratuitous cruelty. If cruelty figures at all, it is much earlier, at the point of the abortion; by the time that the flesh is sold and consumed, the fetus is already dead. Indeed, one could argue that the entire process involves a net gain to humanity, for it puts a substance that would otherwise be wasted to good use. From a utilitarian standpoint, it is actually laudable.

Why, then, do we feel toward it a kind of visceral abhorrence? Are we simply being irrational? I think not. What is at work here is the same deeply rooted form of understanding that determines our reaction to Domitian and the Un-man. Our existence as bodily creatures carries with it what I shall call a moral "space," a sort of overlay that assigns to the field of possible actions and attitudes varying kinds of moral significance. I conceive this space as much like the space surrounding an airplane in flight. Movement in certain directions is permitted but carries no special significance; movement in other directions is not only permitted, but is positively enjoined, in that it is necessary if the airplane is to reach its destination; and movement in yet other directions is strictly forbidden and can lead to disaster.

Similarly, in some cases, the significance that the body attaches to a given type of action is purely negative. That is true in the case of cannibalism: to eat human flesh, such as that of the fetuses, is wrong because it is an offense against the dignity of the human body. It treats human flesh like any other flesh, whereas what is important is precisely that this is *human* flesh and demands to be respected as such. To deny this truth is implicitly to degrade one's own flesh as well; it is, in some degree, to relinquish one's humanity.

A similar explanation applies in the case of the Un-man. Here, the circle widens to include not only human life, but animal life as well. We share with animals certain fundamental capacities, such as those for movement and perception. That is why the wanton infliction of pain on small animals is not only wrong, but degrading and somehow an insult to one's own nature. It betrays human nature by betraying the bond that ties us to the animal world.

Although my main focus here must be on the negative aspect of the body's moral space, I wish to emphasize that there is a positive aspect as well. An example is the virtue of compassion. It is an interesting fact that what we call "compassion" plays scarcely any role in ancient Greek philosophical ethics. Aristotle recognizes the virtue of giving pleasure in social intercourse, and he has a great deal to say about friendship, but there is nothing in his system corresponding specifically to compassion. The Stoics went so far as to deny outright that the wise man feels pity or indulges in forgiveness.[11] The reason for this is that ancient Greek ethics saw moral obligation as arising primarily from two sources, the needs of the soul and the needs of society. The body remained for the most part an afterthought.

Few today would question that compassion is a virtue; nonetheless, there is much to be learned by considering how one might argue that it is. The argument I would offer runs as follows. Because one's own body is subject to the same ailments and passions as the body of one's neighbor, it is right that one should ache with him and feel with him. The point is not merely that what happens to him might happen to you as well; it is that your embodiment binds you to him in a kind of fellowship of suffering, one that cannot be broken by any divergence in character or belief.[12] This is simultaneously a bond that the body imposes and an opportunity that it offers. In accepting the bond *as* an opportunity, accepting it freely and willingly, one moves appropriately within the moral space created by the body. One turns away from the brutish and toward the full richness of humanity.

Homosexuality

Now we must ask whether the moral framework that I have described provides any help in thinking about homosexuality. Homosexuality is one of a number of sexual practices that traditionally have been regarded as perversions. Others include bestiality, necrophilia, coprophilia, fetishism, and pederasty. To classify all of these as perversions does not mean that they are all wrong to the same degree or for the same reasons, but it does suggest that they share a certain inner kinship. I wish to explore that traditional view by examining bestiality and homosexuality in parallel with each other. I will argue that, despite their manifest differences, both practices involve a similar violation of the body's moral space.

Although there is an enormous variety of sexual mores and customs, virtually all societies regard at least one kind of sex as morally unproblematic: that of a married man and woman who engage in intercourse with the willingness (and often the positive hope) that their union will be blessed with children. Since a union of this sort directly contributes to the perpetuation of society, it is not surprising that it should escape moral censure. The first point I wish to argue is that there is also a deeper reason at work—namely, that this sort of intercourse "fits" the body's moral space uniquely well. I do not wish to argue (here, at any rate) that only such intercourse is morally acceptable. My claim is, rather, that it provides a paradigmatic case through which we can begin to understand the relationship between sexual intercourse and the body's moral space.

What is it about intercourse of this particular type that makes it morally appealing? Part of the answer is surely that in such a case the sexual act is the consummation of a joint commitment of the persons involved to share their lives together and to enter together the great enterprise of bearing and rearing children. The word "consummation" is worth pausing to weigh carefully. It comes from *consummare*, "to sum up, complete, finish." Implicit in the word is the assumption that the commitment is incomplete and unfinished without the corresponding physical act. The act expresses and realizes the commitment, making it tangibly present and giving it a place in the bodily order. When it does so, the act attains special significance, for it manifests in the body the decision made by the two persons to entrust to each other their past achievements and future hopes. They grant to their union a certain causal autonomy; they pledge with their bodies, as it were, that they are willing to accept whatever consequences their union produces, up to and including the possibility of new life.

This is not yet the whole answer. It is also important that in such cases the sexual act typically evinces (and is partly motivated by) a delight in the *kind* of being that the other is. "O brave new world that has such people in't!"—that is what Miranda in *The Tempest* exclaims upon encountering men.[13] Much though we may smile at her naiveté, she speaks for the whole human race. Every lover knows that love is more than simply a delight in the other qua individual; man also delights in the femininity of woman, and woman delights in the masculinity of man. Part of what makes erotic love such a powerful experience is the surprise and gratitude one feels in finding that what one has admired from afar even in strangers is now available as a kind of gift in the beloved. What had seemed foreign and unapproachable becomes as close as one's own flesh.

Now it is precisely the masculinity or femininity of the beloved, in its physical dimension, that is engaged in the sexual act. This means that there is possible in the type of intercourse that I have described a certain integration between the physical act, the attitude of commitment it consummates, and the larger dimensions of human society. The act is a reenactment at a personal level of the drama of the mutual need, attraction, and union of man and woman that has been repeated in countless times and countless ways throughout human history. As such, it is a way of personally participating in one of the deepest roots of human society. I do not mean to suggest that an explicit awareness of this dimension is always present. What is present is the participation itself, the fact that this private and particular act recapitulates in a small way the universal bonding of man and woman.

Here, then, are at least two important reasons why intercourse in a committed, monogamous, heterosexual relationship, with an openness to the possibility of children, is a paradigmatic case of a "fit" between the sexual act and the body's moral space. First, such an act consummates the mutual commitment of the two persons involved. It unites body and spirit in a single harmonious endeavor; it raises the body to the level of the spirit and focuses the spirit within the body. Second, the act engages the body in a profoundly human way. It integrates the body within a drama that is and always has been the primary means by which the two halves of the human race come to value one another.

Let us now see whether this discussion can shed any light on bestiality. I shall simply assume that the reader shares with me the intuition that bestiality is wrong. Discussing sexual morality with one who does not share such a basic intuition would be a bit like discussing music with one who is tone-deaf. Perhaps something could be said to get through in the end, but the discussion would have to begin much further back than is possible here.

The question I would ask is not whether bestiality is wrong, but *why* it is wrong. Corvino remarks that a bestial relationship is not a "relationship" at all. That is true as far as it goes, but it scarcely scratches the surface of the problem. Why, after all, should we require that sex must take place within a "relationship"? What is so special about that? Furthermore, merely to remark that a man and an animal cannot share a "relationship" seems far too weak. Bestiality is not only wrong, but abhorrent and perverse—more like, say, cannibalism or wanton cruelty to small animals than like fraud or drunken driving. Nothing in the requirement that sex take place within a "relationship" seems to answer to the deep-seated feeling of disgust that bestiality arouses within us.

I submit that the reason why bestiality is wrong is that it is an abuse of the body. It is a paradigmatic case of a sexual violation of the body's moral space. And, if we ask why that is so, we have only to compare it to the opposite paradigm, that of intercourse within a heterosexual, monogamous relationship. Intercourse with an animal allows the possibility neither of commitment nor of procreation. It consummates nothing. It also fails to engage the body in a uniquely human way, a way that would resonate with the larger dimensions of human existence. For these reasons, there is an important sense in which it disengages the body both from the individual psyche and from society at large. The net result is a sort of fragmentation of the person. The body is left isolated from the other dimensions of personhood, having no other role than that of providing a coarse kind of pleasure.

Consider now a somewhat different case. Suppose that the act were with a talking animal, one as fully rational as a human being and fully engaged in human society. In such a case, an attitude of commitment could be present. But how much else could not! First, because of the biological mismatch of the two bodies, there could be no procreation. This means that the attitude of commitment would remain permanently unfulfilled; there could be no consummation, no "drawing down" of the commitment to the level of physical and tangible reality. Second, the sexual act would not resonate with the larger dimensions of human existence; it would remain isolated from the mutual fascination of man and woman, together with all the structures of society to which that fascination has given shape. Indeed, it would actually be a repudiation of that fascination, for it would be an attempt to find the solaces that men and women traditionally have found in one another in an entirely different source.

For these reasons, regardless of how tenderly or affectionately such an act might be performed, it would fail to achieve anything like the integration among body, soul, and society that is present in the paradigmatic case. Like "normal" bestiality, though to a lesser degree, it would contribute to the fragmentation, rather than the integration, of the person. And for that reason, like "normal" bestiality, though to a lesser degree, it would be a violation of the body's moral space.[14]

This case seems to me identical in its morally relevant characteristics to same-sex intercourse among human beings. In saying this, I do not wish to invoke whatever feelings of disgust may attach to the thought of intercourse with even an intelligent animal. Readers who have such feelings are asked to lay them aside for the moment. The morally relevant characteristics I have in mind are the two that I have emphasized: the inability of the sexual act, due to the permanent structure of the bodies involved, to serve as a *consummation* in the sense that I have described; and its inability, for the same reason, to connect in any significant way with the larger dimensions of human existence.

I conclude that same-sex intercourse is a violation of the body's moral space, in the same way and for the same reasons as would be intercourse with an intelligent animal. Again, in saying this, I do not wish to transfer to homosexuality precisely the same feelings of disgust that (rightly) attach to bestiality. I readily concede that intercourse with an animal is worse than that with a human being of the same sex. The only likeness I wish to assert between same-sex intercourse and bestiality is that both are perversions, in that both involve a very fundamental abuse of the body.

Before closing, I should attempt to head off an important objection. There are various reasons that may result in even a heterosexual couple being permanently unable to bear children. Does my argument imply that sex would be illegitimate in their case as well? Not at all. One important difference is that, even in such a case, the second of the characteristics I have mentioned—the participation of the act within the larger human drama—is fully present. In addition, there is a fundamental difference between the bar that prevents such a couple from bearing children and that which similarly prevents two persons of the same sex from doing so. In the heterosexual case, the inability is due to some special circumstance, such as sterility or dismemberment, whereas in the homosexual case, it is due to the given form of the body. If our aim is to respect the moral space created by the body, then it is entirely reasonable that the latter sort of bar should have important moral consequences, whereas the former does not.

Conclusion

The argument that I have presented regarding the body's moral space does not rely on those discussed in the first section of this chapter. However, once this argument is grasped the others gain considerably in force and coherence. We can now understand why homosexuality is so widely viewed as a kind of counterfeit of married, heterosexual love. We can also understand why so many religions forbid same-sex intercourse and why the Jewish and Christian Scriptures, in particular, treat it as a serious offense before God. Finally—though I think too much can be made of this point—it becomes a bit more intelligible why homosexuality is regularly correlated with promiscuity and a variety of other unseemly and reckless kinds of behavior. Lacking the capacity of heterosexuality to integrate body, spirit, and society, it leaves those who partake in it isolated both from society at large and from their own bodily existence. This is not the fault of prejudice against homosexuals; it is an intrinsic limitation of the act itself.

There is a cliché—a wholly true cliché—that one must hate the sin and love the sinner. I would add that part of loving the sinner *is* to hate the sin. Only when the sin is seen as what it is, as wrong and destructive, can the truly important work of repentance and healing begin.

· CHAPTER THREE ·

Law, Morality, and "Sexual Orientation"

JOHN FINNIS

John Finnis, professor of law and legal philosophy at Oxford University and the University of Notre Dame, offers an intellectually sophisticated natural law argument against homosexuality. As one of the "new natural lawyers," Finnis holds that there are certain "basic goods" that are intrinisically worthy of human pursuit. Heterosexual marriage, with its twofold values of procreation and friendship, is one such basic good. Finnis argues that homosexual conduct is unreasonable, wrong, and therefore unnatural, because instead of bringing about either of these values (or some other basic good), it pursues an illusion of doing so, and moreover involves treating sexual organs as mere instruments of pleasure rather than as integrated parts of the whole human person. In his last section, Finnis responds to some criticisms of his argument, including that offered by Andrew Koppelman in the next essay.

I

Since the mid-1960s there has emerged a standard form of legal regulation of sexual conduct. This "standard modern position" has two limbs. On the one hand, the state is not authorized to, and does not, make it a punishable offense for adult consenting persons to engage, in private, in immoral sexual acts (for example, homosexual acts). On the other hand, states do have the authority to discourage, say, homosexual conduct and "orientation" (i.e., overtly manifested active willingness to engage in homosexual conduct).

This chapter is a revised version of "Law, Morality, and 'Sexual Orientation,'" *Notre Dame Journal of Law, Ethics, and Public Policy* 9 (1995). Section IV was written especially for this volume.

Throughout this essay I shall use the terms "homosexual activity," "homosexual acts," and "homosexual conduct" synonymously, to refer to bodily acts on a person of the same sex, which are engaged in with a view to securing orgasmic sexual satisfaction for one or more of the parties. The standard modern position recognizes the objectionable ambiguity of the phrase "sexual orientation." Particularly as used by promoters of "gay rights," that phrase equivocally assimilates and confuses (I) a psychological or psychosomatic disposition inwardly orienting one *towards* homosexual activity, with (II) the deliberate *decision* so to orient one's public *behavior* as to express or *manifest* one's active interest in and endorsement of homosexual *conduct* and/or forms of life which presumptively involve such conduct.

The concern of the standard modern position itself is with the latter, not the former. It draws a distinction not drawn in earlier legal arrangements, between (a) supervising the truly private conduct of adults and (b) supervising the *public realm or environment.* Supervision of the public environment is important for a number of reasons: this is the environment or public realm in which young people (of whatever sexual inclination) are educated; it is the context in which and by which everyone with responsibility for the well-being of young people is helped or hindered in assisting them to avoid bad forms of life; it is the milieu in which and by which all citizens are encouraged and helped, or discouraged and undermined, in their own resistance to being lured by temptation into falling away from their own aspirations to be people of integrated good character, and to be autonomous, self-controlled persons rather than slaves to impulse and sensual gratification.

Supervision of truly private adult consensual conduct is now (and rightly) considered to be outside the state's normally proper role (with exceptions such as sado-masochistic bodily damage, and with apparent but not real exceptions such as assisting in suicide). But supervision of the moral-cultural-educational environment is maintained as a very important part of the state's justification for claiming legitimately the loyalty of its decent citizens.

Laws outlawing "discrimination based on sexual orientation" are always interpreted by "gay rights" movements as going far beyond discrimination based merely on A's belief that B is sexually attracted to persons of the same sex—discrimination which the standard modern position rightly treats as unjust. "Gay rights" movements interpret laws against "discrimination based on sexual orientation" as extending full legal protection to *public* activities intended specifically to promote, procure and facilitate homosexual *conduct.* So the standard position wisely rejects the idea that discrimination of the kind it recognizes as unjust would be appropriately remedied by such laws. It wisely holds that such a "remedy" would work significant discrimination and injustice against (and would indeed damage) families, associations and institutions which have organized themselves to live out and transmit ideals of family life that include a high conception of the worth of truly conjugal sexual intercourse.

II

The standard modern position includes a judgment that homosexual conduct is morally wrong. This judgment need not be a manifestation of mere hostility to a hated minority, of purely religious, theological, and sectarian belief, or of prejudice. It can be supported by reflective, critical, publicly intelligible and rational considerations.

All three of the greatest Greek philosophers, Socrates, Plato, and Aristotle, regarded homosexual *conduct* as intrinsically immoral.[1] All three rejected the linchpin of modern "gay" ideology and lifestyle.

At the heart of the Platonic-Aristotelian and later ancient philosophical rejections of all homosexual conduct, and thus of the modern "gay" ideology, are three fundamental theses: (1) The commitment of a man and woman to each other in the sexual union of marriage is intrinsically good and reasonable, and is incompatible with sexual relations outside marriage. (2) Homosexual acts are radically and peculiarly non-marital, and for that reason intrinsically unreasonable and unnatural. (3) Furthermore, according to Plato, if not Aristotle, homosexual acts have a special similarity to solitary masturbation,[2] and both types of radically non-marital act are manifestly unworthy of the human being and immoral.

Plato's mature concern, in the *Laws*, for familiarity, affection and love between spouses in a chastely exclusive and fertile marriage, like Aristotle's representation of marriage as an intrinsically desirable friendship between quasi-equals, and as a state of life even more natural to human beings than political life,[3] is developed in first-century A.D. Rome by the "third founder of Stoicism," Musonius Rufus, in a conception of marriage as having an inseparable double good: procreation and education of children but also, equally and essentially, complete community of life and mutual care and affection between husband and wife. All these concerns and conceptions find expression in Plutarch's second-century (but still entirely non-Christian) celebration of marriage—as a union not of mere instinct but of reasonable love, and not merely for procreation but for mutual help, goodwill, and cooperation for their own sake.[4] Plutarch's severe critiques of homosexual conduct (and of the disparagement of women implicit in homosexual ideology)[5] develop Plato's critique of homosexual and all other extra-marital sexual conduct. Like Musonius Rufus, Plutarch does so by bringing much closer to explicit articulation the following thought. Genital intercourse between spouses enables them to actualize and experience (and in that sense express) *their marriage itself*, as a single reality with two blessings (children and mutual affection). Non-marital intercourse, especially *but not only* homosexual, has no such point and therefore is unacceptable.

Why cannot non-marital friendship be promoted and expressed by sexual acts? Why is the attempt to express affection by orgasmic non-marital sex the pursuit of an illusion? Why did Plato and Socrates, Xenophon, Aristotle, Musonius Rufus, and Plutarch, right at the heart of their reflections on the homoerotic culture around them, make the very deliberate and careful judgment that homosexual *conduct* (and indeed all extra-marital sexual gratification) is radically incapable of participating in, actualizing, the common good of friendship?

Implicit in the philosophical and commonsense rejection of extra-marital sex is the answer to these questions. The union of the reproductive organs of husband and wife really unites them biologically (and their biological reality is part of, not merely an instrument of, their *personal* reality); reproduction is *one* function and so, in respect of that function, the spouses are indeed one reality. So their union in a sexual act of the reproductive kind (whether or not actually reproductive or even capable of resulting in generation in this instance) can *actualize* and allow them to *experience* their real *common good*. That common good is precisely *their marriage* with the two goods, parenthood and friendship, which are the parts of its wholeness as an intelligible common good even if, independently of what the spouses will, their capacity for biological parenthood will not be fulfilled by that act of genital union. But the common good of friends who are not and cannot be married (for example, man and man, man and boy, woman and woman) has nothing to do with their having children by each other, and their reproductive organs cannot make them a biological (and therefore personal) unit.[6] So their sexual acts together cannot do what they may hope and imagine. Because their activation of one or even each of their reproductive organs cannot be an actualizing and experiencing of the *marital* good—as marital intercourse (intercourse between spouses in a marital way) can, even between spouses who *happen* to be sterile—it can *do* no more than provide each partner with an individual gratification. For want of a *common good* that could be actualized and experienced *by and in this bodily union*, that conduct involves the partners in treating their bodies as instruments to be used in the service of their consciously experiencing selves;

their choice to engage in such conduct thus dis-integrates each of them precisely as acting persons.[7]

Reality is known in judgment, not in emotion. In reality, whatever the generous hopes and dreams and thoughts of *giving* with which some same-sex partners may surround their "sexual" acts, those acts cannot express or do more than is expressed or done if two strangers engage in such activity to give each other pleasure, or a prostitute pleasures a client to give him pleasure in return for money, or (say) a man masturbates to give himself pleasure and a fantasy of more human relationships after a gruelling day on the assembly line. This is, I believe, the substance of Plato's judgment—at that moment in the *Gorgias* 494–495 which is also decisive for the moral and political philosophical critique of hedonism[8]—that there is no important distinction in essential moral worthlessness between solitary masturbation, being sodomized as a prostitute, and being sodomized for the pleasure of it. Sexual acts cannot *in reality* be self-giving unless they are acts by which a man and a woman actualize and experience sexually the real giving of themselves to each other—in biological, affective, and volitional union in mutual commitment, both open-ended and exclusive—which like Plato and Aristotle and most peoples we call *marriage*.

In short, sexual acts are not unitive in their significance unless they are marital (actualizing the all-level unity of marriage) and (since the common good of marriage has two aspects) they are not marital unless they have not only the generosity of acts of friendship but also the procreative significance, not necessarily of being intended to generate or capable in the circumstances of generating but at least of being, as human conduct, acts of the reproductive kind—actualizations, so far as the spouses then and there can, of the reproductive function in which they are biologically and thus personally one.

The ancient philosophers do not much discuss the case of sterile marriages, or the fact (well known to them) that for long periods of time (e.g. throughout pregnancy) the sexual acts of a married couple are naturally incapable of resulting in reproduction. They appear to take for granted what the subsequent Christian tradition certainly did, that such sterility does not render the conjugal sexual acts of the spouses non-marital. (Plutarch indicates that intercourse with a sterile spouse is a desirable mark of marital esteem and affection.)[9] For: a husband and wife who unite their reproductive organs in an act of sexual intercourse which, so far as they then can make it, is of a kind suitable for generation, do function as a biological (and thus personal) unit and thus can be actualizing and experiencing the two-in-one-flesh common good and reality of marriage, even when some biological condition happens to prevent that unity resulting in generation of a child. Their conduct thus differs radically from the acts of a husband and wife whose intercourse is masturbatory, for example sodomitic or by fellatio or coitus interruptus.[10] In law such acts do not consummate a marriage, because in reality (whatever the couple's illusions of intimacy and self-giving in such acts) they do not actualize the one-flesh, two-part marital good.

Does this account seek to "make moral judgments based on natural facts"?[11] Yes and no. No, in the sense that it does not seek to infer normative conclusions or theses from only non-normative (natural-fact) premises. Nor does it appeal to any norm of the form "Respect natural facts or natural functions." But yes, it is to the realities of our constitution, intentions and circumstances that the argument applies the relevant practical reasons (especially that marriage and inner integrity are basic human goods) and moral principles (especially that one may never *intend* to destroy, damage, impede, or violate any basic human good, or prefer an illusory instantiation of a basic human good to a real instantiation of that or some other human good).

III

Societies such as classical Athens and contemporary England (and virtually every other) draw a distinction between behaviour found merely (perhaps extremely) offensive (such as eating excrement) and behaviour to be repudiated as destructive of human character and relationships. Copulation of humans with animals is repudiated because it treats human sexual activity and satisfaction as something appropriately sought in a manner as divorced from the expressing of an intelligible common good as is the instinctive coupling of beasts—and so treats human bodily life, in one of its most intense activities, as appropriately lived *as* merely animal. The deliberate genital coupling of persons of the same sex is repudiated for a very similar reason. It is not simply that it is sterile and disposes the participants to an abdication of responsibility for the future of humankind. Nor is it simply that it cannot *really* actualize the mutual devotion which some homosexual persons hope to manifest and experience by it, and that it harms the personalities of its participants by its dis-integrative manipulation of different parts of their one personal reality. It is also that it treats human sexual capacities in a way which is deeply hostile to the self-understanding of those members of the community who are willing to commit themselves to real marriage in the understanding that its sexual joys are not mere instruments or accompaniments to, or mere compensations for, the accomplishment of marriage's responsibilities, but rather enable the spouses to *actualize and experience* their intelligent commitment to share in those responsibilities, in that genuine self-giving.

Now, as I noted at the outset, "homosexual orientation," in one of the two main senses of that highly equivocal term, is precisely the deliberate willingness to promote and engage in homosexual acts—the state of mind, will, and character whose self-interpretation came to be expressed in the deplorable but helpfully revealing name "gay." So this willingness, and the whole "gay" ideology, treats human sexual capacities in a way which is deeply hostile to the self-understanding of those members of the community who are willing to commit themselves to real marriage.

Homosexual orientation in this sense is, in fact, a standing denial of the intrinsic aptness of sexual intercourse to actualize and in that sense give expression to the exclusiveness and open-ended commitment of marriage as something good in itself. All who accept that homosexual acts can be a humanly appropriate use of sexual capacities must, if consistent, regard sexual capacities, organs and acts as instruments for gratifying the individual "self" who has them. Such an acceptance is commonly (and in my opinion rightly) judged to be an active threat to the stability of existing and future marriages; it makes nonsense, for example, of the view that adultery is inconsistent with conjugal love, in an important way and *intrinsically*—not merely because it may involve deception. A political community which judges that the stability and protective and educative generosity of family life are of fundamental importance to the whole community's present and future can rightly judge that it has compelling reasons for judging that homosexual conduct—a "gay lifestyle"—is never a valid, humanly acceptable choice and form of life, for denying that same-sex partners are capable of marrying, and for doing whatever it *properly*[12] can, as a community with uniquely wide but still subsidiary functions (see section I above), to discourage such conduct.

IV

The preceding sections of this essay—an essay which bears the marks of its origin in 1993 as an affidavit of evidence in the "Colorado Amendment 2 case," *Evans v. Romer*—were published (in a considerably fuller version) in 1994[13] and have attracted various responses including the essay by Andrew Koppelman in the present collection (whose editor has kindly allowed me to add the following remarks). Koppelman takes it for granted that the kind of argument developed in my essay, the argument of "the new natural lawyers," is radically different from (and, he claims, less coherent than) Aquinas' insistence on natural teleology. He is right in thinking that, like Germain Grisez, Robert George, and Gerard Bradley, I reject as fallacious (and never argue on the basis of) any proposition like "natural functions or tendencies are moral standards and ought to guide deliberation and choice." But, though this fallacy is certainly to be found from time to time in the tradition, Koppelman is mistaken in thinking that Aquinas' sex ethics depends upon it.

The question of sex ethics which Aquinas took up more often than any other is as follows: When must sex acts *between spouses*, even acts of intercourse of the generative kind, be regarded as seriously wrongful? His answer is, in effect: When such acts are de-personalized, and de-maritalized. That is to say, if I choose this act of intercourse with my spouse, not for the sake of pleasurably actualizing and expressing our marital commitment, but "*solely* for pleasure," or *solely* for the sake of my health, or *solely* as a relief from temptations to masturbation or extra-marital sex, and *if I would be just as (or more!) willing* to be having intercourse with someone else—so that I am seeing in my spouse, in this act of intercourse, no more than I would see in a goodtime girl or a gigolo or another acquaintance or someone else's spouse—then my sex act with my spouse is *non-marital* and is in principle seriously wrong.[14] It is contrary to reason, and therefore[15] contrary to nature. It is contrary to reason because it is dis-integrated from—indeed, contrary to—an intrinsic good to which we are directed by one of the first principles of practical reason (and therefore of natural law), a good which may therefore be called primary, fundamental, or basic: the good of marriage itself.[16]

Why are sex acts (seeking the orgasm of one or more of the parties) unreasonable unless marital? Implicit in Aquinas' often misunderstood work[17] is a rarely recognized train of thought, substantially as follows.

Marriage, in which a man and a woman would find their friendship and devotion to each other fulfilled in their procreation, nurture, protection, education and moral formation of their children,[18] is an intrinsic, basic human good. Sexual intercourse between the spouses, provided it is authentically marital, actualizes and promotes the spouses' mutual commitment in marriage (their marital *fides*). But one's sex act with one's spouse will not be truly marital—and will not authentically actualize, and allow one in a non-illusory way to experience, one's marriage—if one engages in it while one *would be willing* in some circumstance(s) to engage in a sex act of a non-marital kind—e.g. adultery, fornication, intentionally sterilized intercourse, solitary masturbation or mutual masturbation (e.g. sodomy), and so forth. Such willingness takes various forms, whose incompatibility with the marital character of one's sex acts is of varying degree. But even to regard one or more of the non-marital types of sex act as morally acceptable is to regard it or them as something one might under some circumstances engage in, and this state of mind undermines the marital character of one's sex acts with one's spouse. In short, the complete *exclusion* of non-marital sex acts from the range of acceptable human options is a pre-condition for the truly marital character of any spouses' intercourse. Blindness or indifference to the inherent wrongness of non-marital sex acts is among the states of mind which render non-marital the choosing and carrying out of even those actual sex acts which in all other respects are marital in kind.

Moreover, without the possibility of truly marital intercourse, the good of marriage is seriously impaired. Any willingness to (counterfactually or actually) engage in non-marital sex radically undermines my marriage itself. For it dis-integrates the intelligibility of my marriage; our sex acts no longer truly actualize and enable us authentically to experience our *marriage*; they are unhinged from the other aspects of our mutual commitment and project. And this unhinging or dis-integration threatens—runs contrary to—both of the goods inherent in the complex basic good of marriage:[19] not only the good of friendship and *fides,* but also the good of procreation and of the children whose education etc. so depends on the context of a *good* marriage. *So* any kind of assent—even if conditional—to non-marital sex is unreasonable. (Indeed, all sexual immorality, including all willingness to treat it as a potentially acceptable option, is contrary to love-of-neighbour, i.e. of children.)[20] *And so* it is immoral, *and* out of line with human nature.[21]

This line of thought may seem complex when spelled out on the page. But it is no more than the articulation of married people's commonsense appreciation of the offensiveness of adultery and of being treated by one's spouse as a mere object of sexual relief, sexual servicing, de-personalized sex—"he/she doesn't love me, he/she only wants me for my body [or: as a baby-maker]." The traditional sex ethic which, despite all backsliding, was fairly perspicuous to almost everyone until the acceptance by many people of divorce-for-remarriage and contraception began to obscure its coherence a few decades ago, is no more and no less than a drawing out of the implications of this same reasonable thought: the intending, giving, and receiving of pleasure in sex acts is reasonably respectful of and coherent with intelligible human goods *only* when those acts are fully expressive of and (so far as my willing goes) instantiations of the complex good of marriage. Behaviour of the kind that same-sex partners engage in (intended to culminate in orgasmic satisfaction by finger in vagina, penis in mouth, etc., etc.) remains non-marital, and so unreasonable and wrong, when chosen with like intention by a married couple.[22]

Every married couple is sterile most of the time. Outside one or two remote tribes, that has always been well known, even when the limited periods of fertility in the female cycle were mislocated. Koppelman and Stephen Macedo absurdly think that *most of the time*, therefore, (1) the couple's genitals are not reproductive organs at all,[23] and (2) the couple's intercourse cannot be of a reproductive kind. The same line of thought also drives these writers towards the equally arbitrary conclusion that a man and a woman can never be biologically united—only sperm and egg can be biologically united! While in this reductivist, word-legislating mood, one might declare that sperm and egg unite only physically and only their pronuclei are *biologically* united. But it would be more realistic to acknowledge that the whole process of copulation, involving as it does the brains of the man and woman, their nerves, blood, vaginal and other secretions, and coordinated activity (such that conception is much less likely to result from rape), is biological through and through. The dualism embraced by Koppelman and Macedo[24] neatly shows how far humanness itself—the radical *unity* of body ("biology"), sense, emotion, reason, and will—becomes unintelligible once one loses one's grip on the way in which a marital sexual act, uniting *us*[25] in a *particular bodily* (and therefore biological) *way* can really *actualize*, express, and enable us truly to experience something as *intelligent and voluntary* as a freely chosen commitment to serving each other as friends in a form of life adapted to serving also (if fortune so provides) our children as the living embodiments and fruit peculiarly appropriate to our kind of (comm)union.[26]

Sexual acts which are marital are "of the reproductive kind" because in willing such an act one wills sexual behavior which is (1) the very same as causes generation (intended or unintended) in every case of human *sexual* reproduction, and (2) the very same as one would will if one were intending precisely sexual reproduction as a goal of a particular marital sexual act. This kind of act is a "natural kind," in the morally relevant sense of "natural," not (as Koppelman supposes) if and only if one is intending or attempting to produce an *outcome*, viz. reproduction or procreation. Rather it is a distinct rational kind—and therefore in the morally relevant sense a natural kind—because (1) in engaging in it one is intending a *marital* act, (2) its being of the reproductive kind is a necessary though not sufficient condition of it being marital, and (3) marriage is a rational and natural kind of institution. One's reason for action—one's rational motive—is precisely the complex good of *marriage*.

For marriage is rational and natural primarily because it is the institution which physically, biologically, emotionally, and in every other practical way is peculiarly apt to promote suitably the reproduction of the couple by the generation, nurture, and education of ultimately mature offspring. And here we touch on another point of importance in understanding and evaluating the version of "gay" ideology defended by Koppelman and Macedo. These writers claim that sex acts between persons of the same sex can be truly marital, and that to perform such acts two such persons can indeed marry each other. They want us to evaluate homosexual sex acts by focusing upon this sort of activity of this sort of couple. Koppelman adopts Sidney Callahan's claim that, *when engaged in "with a faithful partner,"* such same-sex sex acts "produce . . . intense intimacy, bodily confirmation, mutual sanctification, and fulfilling happiness." It seems rather careless of Koppelman to accept that "mutual sanctification" is "produced" by sex acts in a universe he proclaims to be "disenchanted." But more interesting is his failure to explain why this and the other effects allegedly "produced" by sex acts depend upon the faithfulness of one's partner, or partners,[27] and, I assume, upon one's own faithfulness.

The "gay" ideology, even in the sanitized Koppelman/Macedo version, has no serious account whatever of why it makes sense to regard faithfulness—reservation of one's sex acts exclusively for one's spouse—as an intelligible, intelligent, and reasonable requirement. Only a small proportion of homosexual men who live as "gays" seriously attempt anything even resembling marriage as a permanent commitment. Only a tiny proportion seriously attempt marital fidelity, the commitment to exclusiveness; the proportion who find that the attempt makes sense, in view of the other aspects of their "gay identity," is even tinier.[28] Thus, even at the level of behaviour—i.e. even leaving aside its inherent sterility—gay "marriage," precisely because it excludes or makes no sense of a *commitment* utterly central to *marriage*, is a sham.

And this is no mere happenstance. The reason why marriage involves the commitment to permanence and exclusiveness in the spouses' sexual union is that, as an institution or form of life, it is fundamentally shaped by its dynamism towards, appropriateness for, and fulfilment in, the generation, nurture, and education of children who each can only have two parents and who are fittingly the primary responsibility (and object of devotion) of *those two parents*. Apart from this orientation towards children, the institution of marriage, characterized by marital *fides* (faithfulness), would make little or no sense. Given this orientation, the marital form of life does make good sense, and the marital sexual acts which actualize, express, and enable the spouses to experience that form of life make good sense, too.

Moreover, a man and a woman *who can engage in precisely the same marital acts with precisely the same behaviour and intentions*, but who have reason to believe that in their case those very same acts will never result in children, can still opt for this *form of life* as one that makes good sense. Given the bodily, emotional, intellectual, and volitional complementarities with which that combination of factors we call human evolution[29] has equipped us as men and women, such a commitment can be reasonable as a participation in the good of marriage in which these infertile spouses, if well-intentioned, would wish to have participated more fully than they can. [30] By their model of fidelity within a relationship involving acts of the reproductive kind, these infertile marriages are, moreover, strongly supportive of marriage as a valuable social institution.

But same-sex partners cannot engage in acts of the reproductive kind, i.e. in marital sexual intercourse. For them the permanent, exclusive commitment of marriage—in which bodily union in such acts is the biological actuation of the multi-level (bodily, emotional, intellectual, and volitional) marital relationship—is inexplicable. Of course, two, three, four, five or any number of persons of the same sex can band together to raise a child or children. That may, in some circumstances, be a praiseworthy commitment. It has nothing to do with marriage. Koppelman and Macedo remain discreetly silent on the question of why the same-sex "marriage" they offer to defend is to be between two persons rather than three, four, five, or more, all engaging in sex acts "faithfully" with each other. They are equally silent on the question of why this group sex-partnership should remain constant in membership, rather than revolving like other partnerships.

The plain fact is that those who propound a homosexual ideology have no principled moral case to offer against (prudent and moderate) promiscuity, indeed the getting of orgasmic sexual pleasure in whatever friendly touch or welcoming orifice (human or otherwise) one may opportunely find it. In debate with opponents of their ideology, these proponents are fond of postulating an idealized (two-person, lifelong . . .) category of relationship—"gay marriage"—and of challenging their opponents to say how relationships of such a (not too carefully delimited) kind differ from *marriage* at least where husband and wife know themselves to be infertile. As I have argued, the principal difference is simple and fundamental: the artificially delimited category named "gay marriage" or "same-sex marriage" corresponds to no intrinsic reason or set of reasons at all. When we realize that—and why—the core of marriage is *fides*, the stringently exclusive commitment whose rationale and implications for sexual activity's integrity, purity, and reasonableness were well understood by Aquinas, we realize that—and why—the world of same-sex partnerships (in the real world outside the artifice of debate) offers no genuine instantiations, equivalents, or counterparts to marriage, and so very few whole-hearted imitations. *Marriage* is the category of relationships, activities, satisfactions, and responsibilities which can be intelligently and reasonably chosen by a man together with a woman, and adopted as their demanding mutual commitment and common good, because its components respond and correspond coherently to that complex of interlocking, complementary good *reasons.*

Following the great philosophers and the mass of ordinary participants in the tradition of civilized life, I have been describing that complex as the good of marriage. And I have been arguing that true and valid sexual morality does no more, and no less, than unfold what is involved in understanding, promoting, and respecting that basic human good. It sets forth the conditions for instantiating that common good of two friends in a real, non-illusory way, integrating all the levels of their human reality, in all the phases of the marital act.

· CHAPTER FOUR ·

Homosexual Conduct

A Reply to the New Natural Lawyers

ANDREW KOPPELMAN

Andrew Koppelman, assistant professor of law at Northwestern University, responds to the arguments of John Finnis in chapter 3 and other "new natural lawyers." Specifically, he addresses the charge that homosexual relationships cannot be "marital," that is, that they cannot achieve the goods typically associated with marriage. According to Koppelman, if sterile heterosexual relationships can be marital, then homosexual relationships can be marital as well. Koppelman also addresses the claim that homosexual relationships necessarily involve using the body as a mere instrument of pleasure.

· · · · ·

Many people believe that marriage is necessarily a relation between persons of different sexes. These people think that, whatever goods a same-sex couple is capable of achieving together, marriage is simply impossible for them, because of the kind of thing that marriage is. The writings of the new natural lawyers—such as John Finnis, Germain Grisez, Robert P. George, and Gerard V. Bradley—are valuable because they are the most rigorous philosophical attempt that has been made to defend this intuition. In this essay, I will argue that the defense fails and that there is no reason to think that the goods associated with marriage cannot be realized by same-sex couples.

A foundational concept of the new natural law theory is that certain goods are intrinsically and not just instrumentally worthy of being pursued. These "basic goods" are intelligible ends, capable of motivating us to act as a matter of free choice by appealing to our practical understanding.

Such goods are worth pursuing even at the price of discomfort or even pain. The good that spouses can bring about by engaging in marital sexual acts is their genuine bodily union. Such acts achieve this good because, and only because, of that union's aptness for procreation. Reproduction differs from other biological functions in that, with respect to it,

> each animal is incomplete, for a male or a female individual is only a potential part of the mated pair, which is the complete organism that is capable of reproducing sexually. This is true also of men and women: as mates who engage in sexual intercourse suited to initiate new life, they complete each other and become an organic unit. In doing so, it is literally true that "they become one flesh."[1]

Put simply, the marital union is a sexual union, and the one-flesh unity that sexuality has the potential to achieve can only be achieved by the coming together of a male and a female body in a way that is suitable for reproduction. Only then do they genuinely become a single organism.

Homosexuals obviously cannot become one flesh in this sense, because "the coupling of two bodies of the same sex cannot form one complete organism and so cannot contribute to a bodily communion of persons."[2] Two persons of the same sex therefore cannot achieve the good that is marriage. The intimacy they achieve in sexual activity is a mere appearance; "each one's experience of intimacy is private and incommunicable, and is no more a common good than is the mere experience of sexual arousal and orgasm."[3]

The above argument provokes an obvious objection. Even if one agrees that there is a self-evident good, over and above mere pleasure, that is achievable by sex, why should one think that that good has precisely the dimensions that the new natural lawyers offer for it? Why is communion of the reproductive type the only bodily communion between persons that is possible?

Robert George observes that "intrinsic values, as *ultimate* reasons for action, cannot be deduced or inferred. We do not, for example, infer the intrinsic goodness of health from the fact, if it is a fact, that people everywhere seem to desire it. . . . We see the point of acting for the sake of health, in ourselves or in others, just for its own sake, without the benefit of any such inference."[4] The intrinsic nature of these goods can only be defended dialectically. Thus, in order to show that the basic good of marriage has the dimensions they claim, the new natural law theorists would have to offer a dialectical defense of their view.

Any such defense must address a widely held contrary view. For at least some same-sex couples, sexual intercourse is valued not merely as a pleasurable experience unintegrated with the rest of one's life, but as an activity that is an important constituent of one of the primary relationships in one's life, exactly as is the case with many heterosexual couples. In a sexual relationship, homosexual or heterosexual, the activity of pleasuring each other sexually may have the real and intended effect of constituting a relationship that is different and better—more intense, more committed, closer, and more enduring—than it would be if the partners substituted, say, conversation. "For most persons, gay or straight," Sidney Callahan observes, "chaste friendships and general charity cannot produce the same intense intimacy, bodily confirmation, mutual sanctification, and fulfilling happiness that come from making love with a faithful partner."[5] One may reasonably wonder whether the new natural lawyers simply do not understand the good that is being pursued by these couples.

The Response to the Sterility Objection

The new natural lawyers' argument appears, on first blush, to confer an uncertain status on infertile heterosexual couples. Several recent writings from this perspective attempt to account for the disparity between their treatment of the homosexual couple and of the sterile heterosexual couple. These clarify their understanding of the good of marriage. Indeed, to the extent that the promised dialectical defense of their understanding has occurred, it has occurred in the course of their responses to the sterility objection.

Sterile heterosexual couples, too, one might argue, are incapable of becoming one procreative organism, because it is impossible that in them sperm and egg could be united. If "the organic complementarity of man and woman in respect to reproduction is the necessary condition for the very possibility of marriage,"[6] then the infertile heterosexual couple would seem to lack that complementarity in the same way as the homosexual couple. They may differ from the homosexual couple in that they *seem* to the untrained observer to be capable of becoming a "complete organism that is capable of reproducing sexually,"[7] but medical science can show that this is an illusion and that they are *in fact* like the homosexual couple in lacking that capacity. If "two persons can become one flesh in marriage only because they are a male and a female *who can join together as a single principle of reproduction*,"[8] then one might infer that persons who cannot so join together cannot marry. What John Finnis says of homosexual couples might equally be said of sterile heterosexual couples: "In reality, whatever the generous hopes and dreams and thoughts of *giving* with which some same-sex partners may surround their "sexual" acts, those acts cannot express or do more than is expressed or done if two strangers engage in such activity to give each other pleasure, or a prostitute pleasures a client to give him pleasure in return for money, or (say) a man masturbates to give himself pleasure and a fantasy of more human relationships after a gruelling day on the assembly line."[9]

Moreover, this argument would imply, a fertile person ought not to choose a sterile spouse, particularly when a fertile partner is also available. The illusion of marital communion would have been chosen instead of the reality. Finnis does not draw these conclusions, of course, but other natural law theorists have been less diffident. Philo, a Judeo-Platonist philosopher of the early Christian period, condemned as "unnatural" not only homosexuality and masturbation, but also celibacy and failure to divorce a barren wife.[10] "Those who woo women who have been shown to be barren with other husbands are simply mounting them in the manner of pigs or goats and should be listed among the impious as enemies of God."[11]

The new natural lawyers, of course, take an altogether different line. "If a couple know or come to learn that they will never be able to have children, their marital communion is no less real and no less fulfilling as a communion of complementary persons, even though it always will lack the fulfillment of parenthood."[12] But this line is equally applicable to the homosexual couple. Although the good of procreation is unavailable to them, they may find marriage "fulfilling for them in itself, apart from the fruitfulness of their cooperation."[13] Their sexual acts would not be merely instrumental, or the choice of appearance over reality; rather, they would be integrated with their commitments. "The willing of a good leads to the integration of acts with it, and the full integration of sexual acts in marriage with the good of marriage makes those acts reasonable and worthy."[14] But then, it appears that the unitary good of marriage is realizable even when the one-flesh communion of a single reproductive organism cannot be achieved. Moreover, the possibility of adoption or artificial insemination means that they, like sterile heterosexual couples, can become parents. "For parenthood is far more a moral than a biological relationship: its essence is not so much in begetting and giving birth as in readiness to accept the gift of life, commitment to nurture it, and faithful fulfillment of that commitment through many years."[15] All the evidence we now have indicates that children raised by gay couples turn out as well as those raised by heterosexual couples.[16] In short, if the basic good of marriage is available to, and thereby can make intelligible and appropriate the sexual activity of, the sterile heterosexual couple, the same seems true of the gay couple. No distinction between the two kinds of couple seems capable of bearing the weight that the new natural lawyers want to place upon it.

Finnis has attempted to defend the distinction in the following way. Even when a heterosexual couple cannot reproduce, he writes, "[t]he union of the reproductive organs of husband and wife really unites them biologically (and their biological reality is part of, not merely an instrument of, their *personal* reality)."[17] The homosexual couple differs from the heterosexual couple, Finnis explains, precisely in that "their reproductive organs cannot make them a biological (and therefore personal) unit."[18] Thus, Finnis rejects Stephen Macedo's critique of his position. Macedo observes that "[a]ll we can say is that conditions would have to be more radically different in the case of gay and lesbian couples than sterile married couples for new life to result from sex . . . but what is the moral force of that? The new natural law theory does not make moral judgments based on natural facts."[19] Finnis replies that, although values cannot be directly derived from facts, the moral character of acts may depend on natural facts—most prominently here, "that the human mouth is not a reproductive organ."[20] The relevance of that fact is, however, disputable. One might reply that the vagina of a woman whose "diseased uterus has been removed" is similarly "not a reproductive organ."

Finnis is certainly correct that the moral character of acts may crucially depend on natural facts. If someone points a gun at me and pulls the trigger, he exhibits the behavior that, as behavior, is suitable for shooting, but it still matters a lot whether the gun is loaded and whether he knows it. Intent matters: the act is a homicidal kind of act even if the actor mistakenly thinks the gun is loaded, when in fact it is not. Material reality matters, too: if, knowing the gun is unloaded, he points it and pulls the trigger, intending homicide, then fantasy has taken leave of reality. But the only aspect of material reality that matters is whether the gun, as it now is, is in fact capable of killing. Contingencies of deception and fright aside, all objects that are *not* loaded guns are morally equivalent in this context: it is not more wrong, and certainly not closer to homicide, to point a gun known to be unloaded at someone and pull the trigger than it is to point one's finger and say, "Bang!" And if the two acts have the same moral character in this context, why is the same not equally true of, on the one hand, vaginal intercourse between a heterosexual couple who know they cannot reproduce and, on the other, anal or oral sex between any couple? Just as, in the case of the gun, neither act is more homicidal than the other, so in the sexual cases, neither act is more reproductive than the other. As Macedo has observed, "penises and vaginas do not unite biologically, sperm and eggs do."[21]

Nonetheless, Germain Grisez insists that an act can be of a reproductive kind even when reproduction is neither intended nor possible. He appears to place considerable weight on the fact that no sex act is ever certain to achieve conception. "In most instances, of course, physiological conditions preclude conception. However, those conditions are not part of the human act of intercourse, for they are neither included in the couple's behavior nor subject to their choice."[22] But this equivocates on what it means to intend something. I can intend to produce an outcome, even if I know it is unlikely. If I fire a gun at someone, hoping to hit him, I have attempted homicide even if I know that I'm a lousy shot and that I'm very likely to miss. The matter is altogether different if the outcome is not merely unlikely, but actually impossible. "One cannot choose unless one thinks of something, sees it as interesting, *and considers it possible.*"[23] If I know the gun is unloaded, then it simply is not possible for me to pull its trigger while intending homicide.

In order to maintain a distinction between sterile heterosexual unions and homosexual unions, the new natural lawyers seem to assume a kind of Aristotelian hylomorphism, in which the infertile heterosexual couple participates imperfectly in the idea of one-flesh unity, but the homosexual couple does not participate at all. The infertile heterosexual couple does become one organism, albeit an organism of a handicapped sort that cannot do what a perfectly functioning organism of that kind can do. The heterosexual couple is only accidentally infertile, while the homosexual couple is essentially so. But unless one posits a divine artificer whose intentions are knowable, it is not clear how the essence/accident distinction can do any moral work. In what sense *are* they one flesh? Procreative unity isn't realized *in them.* Their unity, if it exists outside of the ideational community in which they participate (and in which the homosexual couple obviously can also participate), consists in their membership in a class, a natural kind that ideally *can* procreate.

Why should we think that such a natural kind is a real thing, rather than an ex post facto mental construct? We could do it with the unloaded gun, because the gun was constructed by an intelligent designer for a purpose. An unloaded gun remains a *gun,* a device designed for shooting. In contrast, it's far from clear in what sense, that has any moral weight, the genital organ of a sterile man can properly and precisely be called a *reproductive* organ. It is not fit for reproduction. Moreover, if the Darwinian model is correct, it cannot be said to be *designed* for reproduction, except in a metaphorical sense that can only mislead in this context. The structure is what it is because it just happened, in the past, to increase the gene's likelihood of reproducing itself. The gene wasn't *trying* to reproduce itself. A gene has neither mind nor intention. Grisez and Finnis have not fully come to grips with what Leo Strauss argued is the central dilemma for moderns, including modern followers of Aquinas: "a fundamental, typically modern, dualism of a nonteleological natural science and a teleological science of man."[24]

What Is Bad about Bad Sexual Acts?

A question that I have thus far not explored is why acts that are not marital in the sense meant by new natural law writers are thought to be positively wrong. Even if the lawyers' argument as set forth thus far can answer the objections I have raised, without more it implies nothing about the status of homosexual unions, which might be good in their own way even if they do not realize the distinctive marital good. Perhaps we can say that homosexual couples cannot achieve "marriage," but only some deviant variation, which we might call "schmarriage."[25] Why should we think that schmarriages are sufficiently different from marriages that the law ought to distinguish between them in allocating rights?[26]

One might answer by pointing to some of the alleged harms of homosexuality. But that approach will likely fail. The claim that homosexuality is wrong because it is unnatural cannot be salvaged by pointing to homosexuals' painful and solitary lives, because many homosexuals do not lead such lives, and there is little reason to think that homosexuality per se, rather than societal intolerance, brings about such lives. Now that the closet has to some extent been opened and openly gay people have become commonplace, it has become increasingly clear that many of them are well adjusted and have formed enduring, loving relationships.

That fact might be taken to end the discussion, but it does not. Grisez and Finnis emphasize, and I think correctly, that human well-being cannot adequately be assessed solely on the basis of utilitarian considerations of pleasure, pain, and social adjustment. The new natural law theory has as one of its central tenets the rejection of the view that human well-being consists in subjective satisfaction. Finnis writes that "for anyone who has accurately understood the relations between desire and understanding, the correlate and object of desire is *perfection*, i.e., what makes the one who desires *better off*, what is for him a *good thing*. Satisfaction is a good aspect of the attainment of that good, but it is not that good, and 'satisfying for me' is in very many cases not part of the description under which he pursues that object of desire."[27] Thus, the new natural lawyers can coherently claim that homosexuality is wrong and harmful even if homosexuals themselves are satisfied and feel contented with their lives.

Finnis offers a powerful argument for his claim that the good is not simply identical with pleasure or pleasant experiences. Borrowing from Robert Nozick, he offers the thought experiment of the "experience machine": suppose that you could spend your life plugged into a machine that, by stimulating your brain while you lay floating in a tank, would afford you a lifetime of nothing but pleasurable experiences, which would include the illusion of activities, achievements, and fulfillments?[28] If pleasure or good experiences were what was really good, one would not hesitate to plug into the machine, which would almost certainly provide one with more such experiences than one could otherwise have. But, of course, the reverse is true. Such a lifetime is obviously not to be chosen. This, Finnis thinks, teaches three important lessons. First, human flourishing consists in action, not experience; the point of human activity is the activity itself. Second, one's character and identity are good things; it is unreasonable to plug into the machine because it dissolves these things, so plugging in is, as Nozick says, "a kind of suicide."[29] Third, appearances are not a good substitute for reality. One wants a real life that consists of real activities.[30]

Grisez and Finnis both think that the lessons of the experience machine have implications for sexual ethics that are relevant to the moral assessment of homosexual conduct. First, because appearances are not a good substitute for reality, if a genuine good is achievable through sexuality, one ought to pursue that good itself rather than its mere appearance. Second, because the good is not reducible to good experiences, pleasure alone is not a good reason to pursue anything. As Grisez puts it, "[o]ne should not choose to satisfy an emotional desire except as part of one's pursuit and/or attainment of an intelligible good other than the satisfaction of the desire itself."[31] Third, and most important, because one's character and identity are good things, the use of one's sexual faculties solely for the pursuit of pleasure is wrong. Such use tends to destroy one's character and identity: empty pleasures have an addictive quality that are likely to overwhelm one's ability to discern and to pursue what is truly good. The pursuit of pleasure for its own sake is tantamount to plugging oneself into the machine.[32]

The new natural lawyers' basis for condemning sexual activities that aim solely at pleasure is set out most clearly in their argument against masturbation. "[I]n choosing to masturbate, one does not choose to act for a goal which fulfills oneself as a unified, bodily person. The only immediate goal is satisfaction for the conscious self; and so the body, not being part of the whole for whose sake the act is done, serves only as an extrinsic instrument."[33] Finnis argues that masturbation involves "a threefold lack of personal integrity": it is not part of any chosen project; the stimulation and fantasizing activity is unintegrated with real goods; it is unintegrated with any other real person.[34] The self-alienation that occurs when one uses one's body as an instrument for the gratification of one's consciousness, Grisez writes, "is an existential dualism between the body and the conscious self, that is, a division between the two insofar as they are coprinciples of oneself considered as an integrated, acting, sexual person. Therefore, to choose to masturbate is to choose a specific kind of self-disintegrity."[35]

Disintegrity is bad because self-integration, "harmony among all the parts of a person which can be engaged in freely chosen action,"[36] is a basic good—a good that is intrinsically worthy of pursuit. It is self-evidently good to be a single, coherent self rather than a mess of conflicting desires and impulses. To the extent that one makes one's reason the slave of one's passions, one sacrifices this good. As a consequence, one loses sight of all of the real goods that are not available on the experience machine; "one tends to regard only two realities as important: the conscious experience in which that satisfaction is obtained and the instruments—the alienated body and desacralized world—used to bring about the satisfaction."[37] The argument obviously can be extended beyond masturbation to other sexual activities, such as many acts of casual fornication of either the homosexual or heterosexual variety, the sole end of which is pleasure.

The new natural lawyers do not think that there is anything uniquely monstrous about homosexual acts. These same considerations equally condemn other nonmarital sexual acts. Fornicators achieve only the experience, not the reality, of marital communion, which requires marital commitment. Married couples who contracept, or who engage in oral or anal sex, cannot achieve the reality of one-flesh communion. In both of these heterosexual cases, what the couples are doing, according to the new natural lawyers, is essentially mutual masturbation rather than marital intercourse. Sodomites differ from these in that, if their orientation is exclusively homosexual, they are not choosing an illusory good *instead* of a real one, but "they do choose to use their own and each other's bodies to provide subjective satisfactions, and thus they choose self-disintegrity as masturbators do."[38]

This argument depends crucially on the premise that the procreative, marital communion of a man and a woman not only is good, but is the only good thing that is achievable through sex. Is this credible? Are the only gratifications achieved by the homosexual couple the same kind of gratifications that are provided by the experience machine?

First of all, it should be noted that the argument against actions taken solely for the sake of pleasure is a non sequitur. It depends on an illegitimate inference from the case of the experience machine. The experience machine argument, it will be recalled, demonstrated that pleasurable experience was not the *only* criterion of well-being. Here, however, it is being argued that pleasure alone is never a good reason to do anything. The lessons of the experience machine, however, are equally consistent with the view that pleasure is a good of an inferior kind, which is worthy of pursuit in itself, but the value of which can easily be trumped by other and higher goods. On this view, pleasure is not a sufficient reason to forgo or damage a higher good, such as friendship or knowledge, but its pursuit is at worst morally neutral unless there is some good reason *not* to pursue it.[39]

There is reason to suspect that Grisez does not believe all the implications of what he is saying. He observes that the old scholastic natural law theory, which holds that faculties should only be used in ways that realize their natural powers, produces the absurd result that it is immoral to chew sugarless gum just for the pleasure of chewing, apart from nutrition.[40] This example, however, creates a similar problem for his own theory. When one chews gum, is not one choosing to have a sentient experience, merely for its own sake? Grisez's suspicion of bodily pleasures is curiously selective, holding sexual pleasure to a burden of justification that he does not place upon other kinds of pleasure.

Grisez recognizes that one uses one's body as an instrument all the time and that ordinarily this is not morally problematic. "This is done when one works and plays, and also when one communicates, using the tongue to speak, the finger to point, the genitals to engage in marital intercourse."[41] In such cases, however, "the body functions as part of oneself, serving the whole and sharing in the resulting benefits."[42] It is hardly clear, however, that this is never the case with masturbation or casual fornication. Often the pursuit of sexual gratification is thought of as responding to a bodily need, rather than inducing one: the arousal typically precedes the act. I feel an itch before I scratch it. In scratching an itch, I am not abusing my body or regarding it as "a lower form of life with its own dynamism,"[43] but tending respectfully to its needs, which are my needs. The pleasure that is involved may indeed be unintegrated with one's other projects, but this is true of pleasures that Grisez finds unproblematic. "The mother who writes poetry in her free moments, the pope who occasionally skis, are engaging in humanly fulfilling activities which they need not direct to any of the purposes set by their commitments and which they can undertake without making any additional commitment."[44] Why cannot sex at least sometimes be one more kind of harmless play?

Moreover, the pursuit of sexual gratification may serve some end beyond itself. Grisez acknowledges the example of one who masturbates in order to relieve sexual tension in order to get to sleep. Even if masturbation is undertaken for the sake of an ulterior end, however, Grisez concludes that the choice to masturbate "remains the adoption of a proposal to have the sentient and emotional experience of masturbating" and thus "is to choose a bad means to a good end."[45] The pursuit of sexual pleasure is no longer bad because, like the experience machine, it is unintegrated with and diverts one from the achievement of real ends. Rather, it is bad even if it facilitates the achievement of those ends.

Grisez's argument does point to an important truth. Sex does have the potential to be exploitative or instrumental or both. That potential is far more likely to be realized when persons regard their sexual faculties primarily as means for producing good experiences. Since many of us are at least sometimes tempted to engage in sex on those terms, and since such sex is an inferior kind that has the potential to distract from or disrupt more valuable and enduring relationships, it makes moral and prudential sense to distinguish more valuable from less valuable expressions of sexuality and to discourage the latter. The question is whether Grisez and Finnis have drawn this line in a sensible way.

The answer depends upon whether the deliberate inducement of pleasurable states of consciousness can sometimes facilitate the achievement of goods beyond pleasure. Grisez acknowledges that this sometimes can be the case. Consider his discussion of psychoactive drugs. In some places, he takes a very hard line against them. Thus he writes that when one uses such substances solely for the experience they provide (as opposed to, e.g., relief of disabling pain, promotion of alertness in one's work, or some other intelligible good), one alienates one's consciousness from one's own body, making the latter a tool of the former. The pattern of reasoning is quite similar to that he applies to the case of masturbation:

> But a person's capacity to embody himself or herself completely in his or her acts is necessary for the self-giving involved in the communication which establishes and nurtures interpersonal communion. Hence, to choose to use a psychoactive substance precisely for the experience is to accept damage to the capacity of one's bodily self for interpersonal communion. But to damage an intrinsic and necessary condition for attaining a good is to damage the good itself. Thus, in choosing to use a psychoactive substance, not for the sake of some intelligible good, but precisely for the experience, a person accepts damage to the basic human good of friendship or association.[46]

It's obviously true that a person in a drugged stupor is incapable of friendship or association. But in this passage, Grisez seems to want to go beyond this extreme case and condemn *any* use of psychoactive substances not absolutely necessary to the attainment of some good beyond good experience. In the same discussion, however, Grisez concedes the possibility of "drinking that serves sociability": "if several people, having set out to celebrate an occasion or engage in conversation, drink only to facilitate their common activity, their incommunicable states of consciousness must remain subordinate to their interpersonal communion; and, if one party's drinking begins to interfere with communication, the others will consider that an unfortunate excess."[47] In this passage, it appears that the good of friendship or association may be promoted by the inducement of altered states of consciousness among the participants, so long as this alteration is not carried to excess.

Evidently, Grisez understands that the activity of inducing pleasure can be a fundamentally different *kind* of activity when a group undertakes it together than when someone undertakes it alone. If this is true, then the same may be true of sexual acts that are not "marital" in his sense of the word: it is true that each of the participants is trying to induce, in herself and in the other, an experience of pleasure that is (like all experiences) essentially solitary and incommunicable, but the activity of bringing about this experience is a collective one. Why is it not the case that here, too, "their incommunicable states of consciousness must remain subordinate to their interpersonal communion"?

We have returned to the question of whether the new natural lawyers have understood the good of marriage. Bradley and George say that pleasure is innocent when it is the by-product of a certain kind of activity, one in which "the body is not typically commandeered into the service of a project that is fully and accurately described (and, thus, morally specified) as producing pleasure, whether as an end in itself or as means to other ends."[48] Macedo responds that this mischaracterizes the experience of many lesbian and gay partners.[49] Bradley and George would doubtless reply that, in "nonmarital" sex acts, even if the overall goal is to realize intimacy and love, the specific aim of the sex acts *as such*—the reason the partners induce orgasm in each other, rather than engaging in other activities—is to produce pleasure. This would seem to prove too much, however. Even married heterosexuals engaging in uncontracepted sex typically do some things solely for the purpose of producing or increasing physical pleasure. Must the new natural lawyers condemn these acts as well? How detailed a sex manual, with how many subtle distinctions between permitted and forbidden acts, sequences of acts, and positions, does the new natural law theory imply?

A more coherent approach is to follow the line on homosexuality that

Thomas Aquinas took, by insisting on natural teleology. This is the move made by other Christian writers who defend the traditional position on homosexuality. From this perspective, heterosexual complementarity is taken to be a sign of God's creative design. "If we affirm a faith in a personal God who intends a purpose for us and whose creation evinces a design intelligible to reason as well as disclosed by revelation, it is only logical that we see that design manifest in the act that makes us."[50] Even a childless heterosexual marriage reflects this design, as it "remains a sign and symbol of humanity's foundational acts."[51]

The impulse reflected by this reasoning is understandable, but it ultimately rests on bad theology as well as bad philosophy. The desire to see God's design in the world produces a characteristic vice, the temptation to suppress evidence that spoils the pattern we thought we saw (such as the testimony of others who do not see it or who see a different pattern). This is reflected most strikingly in the trial of Galileo: his opponents insisted that, since their understanding of the divine plan was incompatible with Copernican astronomy, the old Ptolemaic system must be the correct one. Galileo's findings have now been assimilated by the religious, but even at this late date Darwin is still giving indigestion to some. The denial that homosexual conduct produces any good beyond the gratification of sexual appetite appears at least in part to have the same source: homosexuality seems to signify a disenchanted universe, in which, for all we can tell, there is no plan or purpose at all. This disenchantment is particularly troubling in matters sexual, which many people feel a special need to integrate into a religious narrative.

It is, of course, a fallacy to think that a disenchanted view of nature is irreconcilable with belief in God. It is at least equally consistent with the Judeo-Christian tradition to consider it impious for one to presume knowledge of God's intentions in creating the universe: "Where wast thou when I laid the foundations of the earth? declare, if thou hast understanding" (Job 38:4). The theories of Galileo and Darwin and the rejection of natural teleology are all compatible with religion. There is no reason in principle why one cannot believe in God without also believing that He is a kind of cosmic Kilroy, who feels impelled to leave his initials carved on every tree. However, these theories do place greater demands on religious faith than their predecessors. They demand that faith stand on its own bottom, rather than leaning on comforting hints drawn from observed phenomena. And this is, perhaps, why they are resisted so fiercely. Faith is hard.

The new natural lawyers are more sophisticated than their predecessors, but they, too, appear to fall into the trap of imputing divine intentions to natural phenomena. Moreover, judged by the standards implicit in their own work, their arguments about homosexuality are not only mistaken, but positively destructive. If they are in error, then the prevalence of this kind of error is itself an obstacle to the realization of self-evident goods and harms innocent people. They may well be right that marriage is a noninstrumental good. They have not, however, shown that the good they are describing is necessarily heterosexual or that it has any intrinsic relation to sexual acts of the procreative kind. And if they haven't been able to show this, it seems most unlikely that other, less philosophically sophisticated efforts can succeed.

· CHAPTER FIVE ·

The Homosexual Movement

THE RAMSEY COLLOQUIUM

The Ramsey Colloquium, a group of Jewish and Christian scholars that meet periodically to discuss public policy issues from a biblical perspective, offers its views on the increasingly visible gay and lesbian rights movement. The colloquium identifies the movement with the sexual revolution of the past several decades and argues that it shares many of the latter's harmful effects. After defending "the heterosexual norm," the colloquium responds to several specific claims of the homosexual movement.

I. The New Thing

Homosexual behavior is a phenomenon with a long history, to which there have been various cultural and moral responses. But today in our public life there is something new, a *novum,* which demands our attention and deserves a careful moral response.

The new thing is a movement that variously presents itself as an appeal

This chapter first appeared in *First Things: A Monthly Journal of Religion and Public Life* 41 (March 1994). *First Things* is a monthly journal published in New York City by the Institute on Religion and Public Life. Reprinted by permission; with minor revisions.

The Ramsey Colloquium: Hadley Arkes, Amherst College; Matthew Berke, *First Things;* Gerard Bradley, Notre Dame Law School; Rabbi David Dalin, University of Hartford; Ernest Fortin, Boston College; Jorge Garcia, Rutgers University; Rabbi Marc Gellman, Hebrew Union College; Robert George, Princeton University; Rev. Hugh Haffenreffer, Emanuel Lutheran Church, Hartford, CT; John Hittinger, College of Saint Francis; Russell Hittinger, Catholic University of America; Robert Jenson, St. Olaf College; Gilbert Meilaender, Oberlin College; Jerry Muller, Catholic University of America; Fr. John Neuhaus, Institute on Religion and Public Life; Rabbi David Novak, University of Virginia; James Nuechterlein, *First Things;* Max Stackhouse, Princeton Theological Seminary; Philip Turner, Berkeley Divinity School, Yale University; George Weigel, Ethics and Public Policy Center; Robert Wilken, University of Virginia.

for compassion, as an extension of civil rights to minorities, and as a cultural revolution. The last of these seems to us the best description of the phenomenon; indeed, that is what its most assertive and passionate defenders say it is. *The Nation*, for example, asserts (May 3, 1993):

> All the crosscurrents of present-day liberation struggles are subsumed in the gay struggle. The gay movement is in some ways similar to the moment that other communities have experienced in the nation's past, but it is also something more, because sexual identity is in crisis throughout the population, and gay people—at once the most conspicuous subjects and objects of the crisis—have been forced to invent a complete cosmology to grasp it. No one says the changes will come easily. But it's just possible that a small and despised sexual minority will change America forever.

Although some date "the movement" from the "Stonewall Riot" of June 1969, we have more recently witnessed a concerted and intense campaign, in the media and in leading cultural institutions, to advance the gay and lesbian cause. Despite the fact that the Jewish and Christian traditions have, in a clear and sustained manner, judged homosexual behavior to be morally wrong, this campaign has not left our religious communities unaffected. The great majority of Americans have been surprised, puzzled, shocked, and sometimes outraged by this movement for radical change. At the same time, the movement has attracted considerable support from heterosexual Americans who accept its claim to be the course of social justice and tolerance.

We share a measure of ambivalence and confusion regarding this remarkable insurgency in our common life. We do not present ourselves as experts on the subject of homosexuality. We are committed Christians and Jews, and we try to be thoughtful citizens. In this statement, we do our best to respond to the claims made by the gay and lesbian movement and to form a moral judgment regarding this new thing in our public life.

We are not a "representative group" of Americans, nor are we sure what such a group would look like. No group can encompass the maddening and heartening diversity of sex, race, class, cultural background, and ideological disposition that is to be found among the American people. We are who we are. As such, we offer this product of our study, reflection, and conversation in the hope that others may find it helpful.

Our aim is to present arguments that are public in character and accessible to all reasonable persons. In doing so, we draw readily on the religious and moral traditions that have shaped our civilization and our own lives.

We are confident that arguments based, inter alia, on religious conviction and insight cannot legitimately be excluded from public discourse in a democratic society.

In discussing homosexuality, homosexuals, and the gay and lesbian movement, it is necessary to make certain distinctions. Homosexuality is sometimes considered a matter of sexual "orientation," referring to those whose erotic desires are predominantly or exclusively directed to members of the same sex. Many such persons live lives of discipline and chastity. Others act upon their homosexual orientation through homogenital acts. Many in this second group are "in the closet," although under the pressure of the current movement, they may be uneasy about that distinction between public and private. Still another sector of the homosexual population is public about its orientation and behavior and insists that a gay "lifestyle" be not simply tolerated, but affirmed. These differences account for some of the tensions within the "movement." Some aim at "mainstreaming" homosexuality, while others declare their aim to be cultural, moral, and political revolution.

We confront, therefore, a movement of considerable complexity, and we must respect the diversity to be found among our homosexual fellow citizens and fellow believers. Some want no more than help and understanding in coping with what they view as their problem; others ask no more than that they be left alone.

The new thing, the *novum,* is a gay and lesbian movement that aggressively proposes radical changes in social behavior, religion, morality, and law. It is important to distinguish public policy considerations from the judgment of particular individuals. Our statement is directed chiefly to debates over public policy and what should be socially normative. We share the uneasiness of most Americans with the proposals advanced by the gay and lesbian movement, and we seek to articulate reasons for the largely intuitive and pre-articulate anxiety of most Americans regarding homosexuality and its increasing impact on our public life.

II. New Thing/Old Thing: The Sexual Revolution

While the gay and lesbian movement is indeed a new thing, its way was prepared by, and it is in large part a logical extension of, what has been called the "sexual revolution." The understanding of marriage and family once considered normative is very commonly dishonored in our society and, too frequently, in our communities of faith. Religious communities and leaderships have been, and in too many cases remain, deeply complicit in the demeaning of social norms essential to human flourishing.

Thus moral criticism of the homosexual world and movement is unbalanced, unfair, and implausible if it is not, at the same time, criticism of attitudes and behaviors that have debased heterosexual relations. The gay and lesbian insurgency has raised a sharp moral challenge to the hypocrisy and decadence of our culture. In the light of widespread changes in sexual mores, some homosexuals understandably protest that the sexual license extended to "straights" cannot be denied to them.

We believe that any understanding of sexuality, including homosexuality, that makes it chiefly an arena for the satisfaction of personal desire is harmful to individuals and society. Any way of life that accepts or encourages sexual relations for pleasure or personal satisfaction alone turns away from the disciplined community that marriage is intended to engender and foster. Religious communities that have in recent decades winked at promiscuity (even among the clergy), that have solemnly repeated marriage vows that their own congregations do not take seriously, and that have failed to concern themselves with the devastating effects of divorce upon children cannot with integrity condemn homosexual behavior unless they are also willing to reassert the heterosexual norm more believably and effectively in their pastoral care. In other words, those determined to resist the gay and lesbian movement must be equally concerned for the renewal of integrity, in teaching and practice, regarding "traditional sexual ethics."

It is a testimony to the perduring role of religion in American life that many within the gay and lesbian movement seek the blessing of religious institutions. The movement correctly perceives that attaining such formal approbation—through, for example, the content and style of seminary education and the ordination of practicing homosexuals—will give it an effective hold upon the primary institutions of moral legitimation in our popular culture. The movement also correctly perceives that our churches and synagogues have typically been inarticulate and unpersuasive in offering reasons for withholding the blessing that is sought.

One reason for the discomfort of religious leaders in the face of this new movement is the past and continuing failure to offer supportive and knowledgeable pastoral care to persons coping with the problems of their homosexuality. Without condoning homogenital acts, it is necessary to recognize that many such persons are, with fear and trembling, seeking as best they can to live lives pleasing to God and in service to others. Confronted by the vexing ambiguities of eros in human life, religious communities should be better equipped to support people in their struggle, recognizing that we all fall short of the vocation to holiness of life.

The sexual revolution is motored by presuppositions that can and ought to be effectively challenged. Perhaps the key presupposition of the revolution is that human health and flourishing require that sexual desire, understood as a "need," be acted upon and satisfied. Any discipline of denial or restraint has been popularly depicted as unhealthy and dehumanizing. We insist, however, that it is dehumanizing to define ourselves, or our personhood as male and female, by our desires alone. Nor does it seem plausible to suggest that what millennia of human experience have taught us to regard as self-command should now be dismissed as mere repression.

At the same time that the place of sex has been grotesquely exaggerated by the sexual revolution, it has also been trivialized. The mysteries of human sexuality are commonly reduced to matters of recreation or taste, not unlike one's preferences in diet, dress, or sport. This peculiar mix of the exaggerated and the trivialized makes it possible for the gay and lesbian movement to demand, simultaneously, a respect for what is claimed to be most importantly and constitutively true of homosexuals and a tolerance for what is, after all, simply a difference in "lifestyle."

It is important to recognize the linkages among the component parts of the sexual revolution. Permissive abortion, widespread adultery, easy divorce, radical feminism, and the gay and lesbian movement have not by accident appeared at the same historical moment. They have in common a declared desire for liberation from constraint—especially constraints associated with an allegedly repressed culture and religious tradition. They also have in common the presuppositions that the body is little more than an instrument for the fulfillment of desire and that the fulfillment of desire is the essence of the self. On biblical and philosophical grounds, we reject this radical dualism between the self and the body. Our bodies have their dignity, bear their own truths, and are participant in our personhood in a fundamental way.

This constellation of movements, of which the gay movement is part, rests upon an anthropological doctrine of the autonomous self. With respect to abortion and the socialization of sexuality, this anthropology has gone a long way toward entrenching itself in the jurisprudence of our society as well as in popular habits of mind and behavior. We believe it is a false doctrine that leads neither to individual flourishing nor to social well-being.

III. The Heterosexual Norm

Marriage and the family—husband, wife, and children, joined by public recognition and legal bond—are the most effective institutions for the rearing of children, the directing of sexual passion, and human flourishing in community. Not all marriages and families "work," but it is unwise to let pathology and failure, rather than a vision of what is normative and ideal, guide us in the development of social policy.

Of course, many today doubt that we can speak of what is normatively human. The claim that all social institutions and patterns of behavior are social constructions that we may, if we wish, alter without harm to ourselves is a proposal even more radical in origin and implication than the sexual revolution. That the institutions of marriage and family are culturally conditioned and subject to change and development no one should doubt, but such recognition should not undermine our ability to discern patterns of community that best serve human well-being. Judaism and Christianity did not invent the heterosexual norm, but these faith traditions affirm that norm and can open our eyes to see in it important truths about human life.

Fundamental to human life in society is the creation of humankind as male and female, which is typically and paradigmatically expressed in the marriage of a man and a woman who form a union of persons in which two become one flesh—a union that, in the biblical tradition, is the foundation of all human community. In faithful marriage, three important elements of human life are made manifest and given support.

1. *Human society extends over time; it has a history.* It does so because, through the mysterious participation of our procreative powers in God's own creative work, we transmit life to those who will succeed us. We become a people with a shared history over time and with a common stake in that history. Only the heterosexual norm gives full expression to the commitment to time and history evident in having and caring for children.
2. *Human society requires that we learn to value difference within community.* In the complementarity of male and female we find the paradigmatic instance of this truth. Of course, persons may complement each other in many different ways, but the complementarity of male and female is grounded in, and fully embraces, our bodies and their structure. It does not sever the meaning of the person from bodily life, as if human beings were simply desire, reason, or will. The complementarity of male and female invites us to learn to accept and affirm the natural world from which we are too often alienated.

   Moreover, in the creative complementarity of male and female we are directed toward community with those unlike us. In the community between male and female, we do not and cannot see in each other mere reflections of ourselves. In learning to appreciate this most basic difference, and in forming a marital bond, we take both difference and community seriously. (And ultimately, we begin to be prepared for communion with God, in Whom we never find simply a reflection of ourselves.)

3. *Human society requires the direction and restraint of many impulses.* Few of those impulses are more powerful or unpredictable than sexual desire. Throughout history societies have taken particular care to socialize sexuality toward marriage and the family. Marriage is a place where, in a singular manner, our waywardness begins to be healed and our fear of commitment overcome, where we may learn to place another person's needs rather than our own desires at the center of life.

Thus, reflection on the heterosexual norm directs our attention to certain social necessities: the continuation of human life, the place of difference within community, the redirection of our tendency to place our own desires first. These necessities cannot be supported by rational calculations of self-interest alone; they require commitments that go well beyond the demands of personal satisfaction. Having and rearing children is among the most difficult of human projects. Men and women need all the support they can get to maintain stable marriages in which the next generation can flourish. Even marriages that do not give rise to children exist in accord with, rather than in opposition to, this heterosexual norm. To depict marriage as simply one of several alternative "lifestyles" is seriously to undermine the normative vision required for social well-being.

There are legitimate and honorable forms of love other than marriage. Indeed, one of the goods at stake in today's disputes is a long-honored tradition of friendship between men and men, women and women, women and men. In the current climate of sexualizing and politicizing all intense interpersonal relationships, the place of sexually chaste friendship and of religiously motivated celibacy is gravely jeopardized. In our cultural moment of narrow-eyed prurience, the single life of chastity has come under the shadow of suspicion and is no longer credible to many people. Indeed, the nonsatisfaction of sexual "needs" is widely viewed as a form of deviance.

In this context it becomes imperative to affirm the reality and beauty of sexually chaste relationships of deep affectional intensity. We do not accept the notion that self-command is an unhealthy form of repression on the part of single people, whether their inclination be heterosexual or homosexual. Put differently, the choice is not limited to heterosexual marriage, on the one hand, or relationships involving homogenital sex, on the other.

IV. The Claims of the Movement

We turn our attention now to a few of the important public claims made by gay and lesbian advocates (even as we recognize that the movement is not monolithic). As we noted earlier, there is an important distinction between those who wish to "mainstream" homosexual life and those who aim at restructuring culture. This is roughly the distinction between those who seek integration and those who seek revolution. Although these different streams of the movement need to be distinguished, a few claims are so frequently encountered that they require attention.

Many gays argue that they have no choice, that they could not be otherwise than they are. Such an assertion can take a variety of forms—for example, that "being gay is natural for me" or even that "God made me this way."

We cannot settle the dispute about the roots—genetic or environmental—of homosexual orientation. When some scientific evidence suggests a genetic predisposition for homosexual orientation, the case is not significantly different from evidence of predispositions toward other traits—for example, alcoholism or violence. In each instance, we must still ask whether such a predisposition should be acted upon or whether it should be resisted. Whether or not a homosexual orientation can be changed—and it is important to recognize that there are responsible authorities on both sides of this question—we affirm the obligation of pastors and therapists to assist those who recognize the value of chaste living to resist the impulse to act on their desire for homogenital gratification.

The Kinsey data, which suggested that 10 percent of males are homosexual, have now been convincingly discredited. Current research suggests that the percentage of males whose sexual desires and behavior are exclusively homosexual is as low as 1 percent or 2 percent in developed societies. In any case, the statistical frequency of an act or desire does not determine its moral status. Racial discrimination and child abuse occur frequently in society, but that does not make them "natural" in the moral sense. What is in accord with human nature is behavior appropriate to what we are meant to be—appropriate to what God created and calls us to be.

In a fallen creation, many quite common attitudes and behaviors must be straightforwardly designated as sin. Although we are equal before God, we are not born equal in terms of our strengths and weaknesses, our tendencies and dispositions, our nature and nurture. We cannot utterly change the hand we have been dealt by inheritance and family circumstances, but we are responsible for how we play that hand. Inclination and temptation are not sinful, although they surely result from humanity's fallen condition. Sin occurs in the joining of the will, freely and knowingly, to an act or way of life that is contrary to God's purpose. Religious communities in particular must lovingly support all the faithful in their struggle against temptation, while at the same time insisting that precisely for their sake we must describe as sinful the homogenital and extramarital heterosexual behavior to which some are drawn.

Many in our society—both straight and gay—also contend that what people do sexually is entirely a private matter and no one's business but their own. The form this claim takes is often puzzling to many people—and rightly so. For what were once considered private acts are now highly publicized, while, for the same acts, public privilege is claimed because they are private. What is confusedly at work here is an extreme individualism, a claim for autonomy so extreme that it must undercut the common good.

To be sure, there should in our society be a wide zone for private behavior, including behavior that most Americans would deem wrong. Some of us oppose antisodomy statutes. In a society premised upon limited government there are realms of behavior that ought to be beyond the supervision of the state. In addition to the way sexual wrongdoing harms character, however, there are often other harms involved. We have in mind the alarming rates of sexual promiscuity, depression, and suicide, and the ominous presence of AIDS within the homosexual subculture. No one can doubt that these are reasons for public concern. Another legitimate reason for public concern is the harm done to the social order when policies are advanced that would increase the incidence of the gay lifestyle and undermine the normative character of marriage and family life.

Since there are good reasons to support the heterosexual norm, since it has been developed with great difficulty, and since it can be maintained only if it is cared for and supported, we cannot be indifferent to attacks upon it. The social norms by which sexual behavior is inculcated and controlled are of urgent importance for families and for the society as a whole. Advocates of the gay and lesbian movement have the responsibility to set forth publicly their alternative proposals. This must mean more than calling for liberation from established standards. They must clarify for all of us how sexual mores are to be inculcated in the young, who are particularly vulnerable to seduction and solicitation. Public anxiety about homosexuality is preeminently a concern about the vulnerabilities of the young. This, we are persuaded, is a legitimate and urgent public concern.

Gay and lesbian advocates sometimes claim that they are asking for no more than an end to discrimination, drawing an analogy with the earlier civil rights movement that sought justice for black Americans. The analogy is unconvincing and misleading. Differences of race are in accord with—not contrary to—our nature, and such differences do not provide justification for behavior otherwise unacceptable. It is sometimes claimed that homosexuals want only a recognition of their status, not necessarily of their behavior. But in this case, the distinction between status and behavior does not hold. The public declaration of status ("coming out of the closet") is a declaration of intended behavior.

Certain discriminations are necessary within society; it is not too much to say that civilization itself depends on the making of such distinctions (between, finally, right and wrong). In our public life, some discrimination is in order—when, for example, in education and programs involving young people the intent is to prevent predatory behavior that can take place under the guise of supporting young people in their anxieties about their "sexual identity." It is necessary to discriminate between relationships. Gay and lesbian "domestic partnerships," for example, should not be socially recognized as the moral equivalent of marriage. We note again that marriage and the family are institutions necessary for our continued social well-being and, in an individualistic society that tends to liberation from all constraint, they are fragile institutions in need of careful and continuing support.

V. Conclusion

We do not doubt that many gays and lesbians—perhaps especially those who seek the blessing of our religious communities—believe that theirs is the only form of love, understood as affection and erotic satisfaction, of which they are capable. Nor do we doubt that they have found in such relationships something of great personal significance, since even a distorted love retains traces of love's grandeur. Where there is love in morally disordered relationships we do not censure the love. We censure the form in which that love seeks expression. To those who say that this disordered behavior is so much at the core of their being that the person cannot be (and should not be) distinguished from the behavior, we can only respond that we earnestly hope they are wrong.

We are well aware that this declaration will be dismissed by some as a display of "homophobia," but such dismissals have become unpersuasive and have ceased to intimidate. Indeed, we do not think it a bad thing that people should experience a reflexive recoil from what is wrong. To achieve such a recoil is precisely the point of moral education of the young. What we have tried to do here is to bring this reflexive and often prearticulate recoil to reasonable expression.

Our society is, we fear, progressing precisely in the manner given poetic expression by Alexander Pope:

> Vice is a monster of so frightful mien,
> As to be hated needs but to be seen;
> Yet seen too oft, familiar with her face,
> We first endure, then pity, then embrace.

To endure (tolerance), to pity (compassion), to embrace (affirmation): that is the sequence of change in attitude and judgment that has been advanced by the gay and lesbian movement with notable success. We expect that this success will encounter certain limits and that what is truly natural will reassert itself, but this may not happen before more damage is done to innumerable individuals and to our common life.

Perhaps some of this damage can be prevented. For most people marriage and family is the most important project in their lives. For it they have made sacrifices beyond numbering; they want to be succeeded in an ongoing, shared history by children and grandchildren; they want to transmit to their children the beliefs that have claimed their hearts and minds. They should be supported in that attempt. To that end, we have tried to set forth our view and the reasons that inform it. Whatever the inadequacies of this declaration, we hope it will be useful to others. The gay and lesbian movement, and the dramatic changes in sexual attitudes and behavior of which that movement is part, have unloosed a great moral agitation in our culture. Our hope is that this statement will contribute to turning that agitation into civil conversation about the kind of people we are and hope to be.

· CHAPTER SIX ·

A Reply to the Ramsey Colloquium

THOMAS WILLIAMS

Thomas Williams, assistant professor of philosophy at the University of Iowa, responds to the arguments of the Ramsey Colloquium in the previous essay. Specifically, Williams denies that homosexual people must embrace the false and dangerous claims of the sexual revolution, and he contends that the Ramsey Colloquium's arguments for the normative status of heterosexual marriage provide no grounds for condemning all homosexual activity. Williams also argues that the Ramsey Colloquium's position depends on several false dichotomies and a mistaken notion of friendship and chastity.

. . . . .

In the essay titled "The Homosexual Movement," the members of the Ramsey Colloquium offer little direct criticism of homosexuality or of the movement that defends it. Instead, they first criticize the sexual revolution and then defend what they call "the heterosexual norm." These two strategies are supposed to amount to criticisms of the homosexual movement, since that movement allegedly embraces the false and dangerous claims of the sexual revolution and attacks the heterosexual norm. In the first section of this chapter, I argue that the homosexual movement is not in fact committed to the false and dangerous claims of the sexual revolution; in the second section, I show that the authors' defense of the heterosexual norm in no way implies a condemnation of homosexuality. I then go on to offer more general criticisms of their paper: in the third section, I try to expose some of the false dichotomies that underlie the authors' thinking; and in the fourth section, I discuss their mistaken understanding of friendship and chastity.

Deserters from the Sexual Revolution

The authors begin by criticizing the "homosexual movement" indirectly—as part of a larger phenomenon, the sexual revolution. In this section, I shall consider three of their criticisms of the sexual revolution. For the sake of argument, I shall simply admit that the views the authors discuss are in fact false and dangerous; but in each case, I shall argue that homosexuals need not endorse them. So if those views are indeed part of the sexual revolution, homosexuals can simply be deserters.

The Demeaning of Heterosexual Marriage

The argument: According to the authors, the sexual revolution dishonors and demeans the traditional understanding of marriage and the family. That traditional understanding, they argue, protects norms that are "essential to human flourishing," and so the sexual revolution is a threat to human flourishing. Since the homosexual movement agrees with this attack on heterosexual marriage, it too is a threat to human flourishing.

My response: It seems clear to me that the sexual revolution has indeed been aimed at undermining the traditional understanding of marriage and the family. But it seems equally clear that homosexuals need not go along with the sexual revolution on this point. Admittedly, there are homosexuals who talk about attacking the very institution of marriage. But as far as I can tell, they are a small and radical minority. Most homosexuals seem to agree that heterosexual marriage is a wonderful thing and that forces in society that make it difficult for marriages to endure and flourish are to be deplored and resisted.

Hedonism and Selfishness

The argument: According to the authors, "any understanding of sexuality . . . that makes it chiefly an arena for the satisfaction of personal desire is harmful to individuals and society." Since the sexual revolution "accepts or encourages sexual relations for pleasure or personal satisfaction alone," it is harmful to individuals and society. And since the homosexual movement endorses the hedonism and selfishness of the sexual revolution, it too is harmful.

My response: Once again, it seems plausible to suppose that the sexual revolution really does accept and encourage sexual relations for the sake of pleasure and personal satisfaction alone, but it also seems clear that homosexuals need not go along with the sexual revolution on this point. There is nothing intrinsic to homosexuality that prevents homosexuals from seeking more than just personal satisfaction in sexual relations. In fact, many homosexuals are drawn precisely to that "disciplined community that marriage is intended to engender and foster." Perversely enough, the pressures placed upon homosexuals by the authors and other like-minded people make it difficult for homosexuals to develop and sustain such community—make it, in fact, *impossible* for such community to have any recognized social standing—and therefore contribute to the idea that homosexual sex cannot be anything more than a means of achieving pleasure and personal satisfaction.

The Rejection of Restraint

The argument: According to the authors, "Perhaps the key presupposition of the [sexual] revolution is that human health and flourishing require that sexual desire, understood as a 'need,' be acted upon and satisfied. Any discipline of denial or restraint has been popularly depicted as unhealthy and dehumanizing. We insist, however, that it is dehumanizing to define ourselves . . . by our desires alone." The homosexual movement, they imply, shares this rejection of all restraint, and so it too is dehumanizing.

My response: To this argument I will respond, not by saying that homosexuals can be deserters from the sexual revolution on this point, but by saying that the sexual revolution does not involve any such claim. Perhaps some enthusiasts with more rhetorical fervor than common sense might have said that all restraint is unhealthy, but even the most superficial examination shows just how foolish such a view would be. Obviously I should not hit someone whenever I feel like it; if I did, I might harm an innocent person or fail in the respect due even to a guilty person. Obviously I should not eat whenever I feel like eating; if I did, I would soon grow fat and sluggish and render myself unfit for the ordinary business of life. Obviously I should not take off from work whenever I feel like goofing off; if I did, I would be cheating my students and colleagues and developing bad habits that would frustrate my own goals as a scholar and teacher. And obviously I should not have sex whenever I happen to feel aroused; no one could sensibly think that I should. There are often good reasons not to act on a desire I happen to have, and sexual desires are no different from other desires in that respect.

So of course I admit that there are often good reasons for us not to act on our sexual desires. The real dispute is not over whether there are sometimes good reasons for restraining sexual desire, but over what exactly should count as good reasons. According to the members of the Ramsey Colloquium, the fact that a sexual desire is *homosexual* desire is, *in and of itself,* a good reason not to act on it. In the next section, I examine the arguments for this claim.

What Is Normative about the Heterosexual Norm?

The authors do not actually argue directly that there is always good reason to restrain homosexual desire *simply because* it is homosexual. Instead, they argue for what they call "the heterosexual norm." Heterosexual marriage is normative, they contend, because it manifests and supports three important elements of human life. Let's look at each in turn.

The Commitment to Time and History

The argument: "*Human society extends over time; it has a history.* It does so because, through the mysterious participation of our procreative powers in God's own creative work, we transmit life to those who succeed us. . . . Only the heterosexual norm gives full expression to the commitment to time and history evident in having and caring for children."

My response: That last sentence hides a crucial ambiguity. It might easily be taken to mean that a commitment to time and history is evident *only* in the bearing and rearing of children. After all, when explaining what they mean by saying that "human society extends over time" and "has a history," the authors refer only to procreation. And so they seem to be inviting us to reason in something like the following way: "Human society has a historical dimension because it involves the bearing and rearing of children. Homosexuals as such do not procreate, and so they do not exhibit any commitment to time and history."

If we construe their argument in this way, it clearly fails. People contribute to the historical dimension of human society in many ways, of which the bearing and rearing of children is only one. Consider, for example, a rabbi who passes along centuries of hard-won wisdom, a scientist who builds on the accomplishment of her predecessors and trains others to carry on her work, or a judge who has great respect for the precedents of the past while carefully applying them to changing circumstances. We need not check on whether these people are also parents in order to know that they have a deep commitment to time and history.

There is a second way to interpret their argument. Note that in the last sentence I quoted above, they say that only the heterosexual norm gives *full* expression to the historical dimension of human society—thus leaving themselves room to acknowledge that there are other, less satisfactory ways to express the commitment to time and history. Now, if we assume that they are indeed willing to acknowledge that fact, we can restate their argument as follows: "Of course there are many ways in which people express their commitment to time and history. But procreation is the best way—in fact, the only fully adequate way—in which to express that commitment.

Homosexuals as such do not procreate, and so their commitment to time and history is, at best, inadequate."

Unfortunately, if this argument works against homosexuality, it works just as well against celibacy. Celibates do not procreate either; if procreation is the only fully adequate way in which to express a commitment to time and history, celibacy will be every bit as objectionable as homosexuality. We know that the members of the Ramsey Colloquium do not object to celibacy; indeed, they express concern over the fact that "the place of . . . religiously motivated celibacy is gravely jeopardized." So if they want to be consistent, they cannot hold that procreation is the only fully adequate way in which to express a commitment to time and history. And once they give up that premise, this argument against homosexuality collapses.

The Value of Complementarity

The argument: "Human society requires that we learn to value difference within community," and only the heterosexual norm adequately values the complementarity that needs to be taken seriously if we are to have genuine and fulfilling human community.

Now there is an obvious objection to this argument. One might very well ask, "But aren't there all sorts of differences? Why think that the complementarity of male and female is somehow paradigmatic?" The authors are aware of this objection and try to forestall it. "Of course," they say, "persons may complement each other in many different ways, but the complementarity of male and female is grounded in, and fully embraces, our bodies and their structure."

My response: Obviously the authors are correct in holding that in heterosexual relationships there can be both spiritual and physical complementarity, while in homosexual relationships there can only be spiritual complementarity. But why is physical complementarity essential? The authors offer two reasons. The first is that physical complementarity contributes to the important goal of teaching us to value difference. "[I]n the creative complementarity of male and female we are directed toward community with those unlike us. In the community between male and female, we do not and cannot see in each other mere reflections of ourselves."

If they mean to imply that the partners in a homosexual couple do see in each other mere reflections of themselves, they are wildly mistaken. For example, suppose I am attracted to a woman who mirrors practically all of my important qualities. Like me, she is a Southerner, a philosopher, an Episcopalian, and a musician; she agrees with my fundamental political views and shares my basic outlook on life. We might well be inclined to say that I see in her a mere reflection of myself, notwithstanding the fact that she is a woman and I am a man. But suppose instead that I am attracted to a man who is from California, is a chemist, holds no particular religious beliefs, and can barely carry a tune, someone whose political opinions I find consistently perverse and who often disagrees with me on matters I think are important. It would be foolish to say that I see in him a mere reflection of myself, simply because we are both men. As this example shows, physical complementarity does not guarantee that we will be "directed toward community with those unlike us," and the absence of that complementarity does not prevent us from learning to value difference—if it did, celibacy would be just as immoral as homosexuality, since celibate people do not seek physical complementarity with anyone either. So the authors' first argument that physical complementarity is necessary clearly fails.

According to their second argument, a relationship that lacks this physical complementarity denigrates the body and treats people as if they were purely spiritual beings. The authors imply that if I value another man, who is not physically complementary to me in the way that a woman is, I am somehow "sever[ing] the meaning of the person from bodily life" and acting "as if human beings were simply desire, reason, or will."

This implication is clearly false, however, as we can see by considering three different ways in which I might value another man. First, I might simply be physically attracted to him. In that case, I am clearly not treating him as if he were simply desire, reason, or will; on the contrary, I am valuing him *precisely because of* his bodily life—I "want his body," as we might say.

Second, suppose I am in love with a man. It would no longer be true to say simply that I want his body; rather, I want *him*, the whole person. I cannot separate his body from his desire, reason, and will; I do not see him as bits and pieces of which I desire some and disparage others. In fact, in this case I am especially likely to see his bodily life as intimately bound up with his spiritual features: his smile, for example, reminds me of his wonderful sense of humor.

The third possibility is that I value the man simply as a non-sexual friend. Perhaps here we might think I am separating his desire, reason, and will from his bodily life, but such a conclusion seems to overstate the case. For if such a friendship must be said to denigrate the body, then celibate people are constantly treating everyone they meet as disembodied spirits. So they should come in for an even greater share of condemnation from the Ramsey Colloquium than homosexuals do—a conclusion that the authors ought to find disquieting.

Note, by the way, how the authors' arguments have shifted. In much of their paper, they write as if homosexual activity invariably treats people as sheerly physical beings; here they are arguing that it treats people as disembodied spirits. The two charges are inconsistent, and both are unfounded. No doubt homosexuals sometimes treat sex as if it were nothing but a physical event; but then, so do heterosexuals. Perhaps homosexuals sometimes treat sex as if it were detachable from their bodily existence (although I have trouble understanding exactly why two disembodied spirits would bother to have sex with each other), but if homosexuals are capable of doing this, so are heterosexuals. Moreover, even if homosexual sex *can* embody "a radical dualism between the self and the body," it *need not* do so. And so an argument against such a dualism is neither an argument against homosexual sex nor a defense of heterosexual sex as normative.

The Importance of Restraint

The argument: "Human society requires the direction and restraint of many impulses." In a faithful heterosexual marriage, "our waywardness begins to be healed and our fear of commitment overcome . . . [and] we may learn to place another's needs rather than our own desires at the center of life."

My response: Obviously the partners in a faithful homosexual couple are also restraining their impulses; they have presumably overcome their fear of commitment, and each can learn to place the other's needs at the center of life. Even in a non-sexual friendship, each friend will gladly put the needs of his or her friend at the center of life. Good teachers will often give more weight to a student's needs than to their own interests; good legislators act primarily for the well-being of their constituents rather than for their own individual well-being. So there are many relationships in which we must redirect "our tendency to place our own desires first"; most of us are involved in several such relationships at any given time. Heterosexual marriage is not the only, or even the primary, domain in which we restrain our impulses in the interest of others.

False Dichotomies

Much of the argument in "The Homosexual Movement" rests on false dichotomies, and those false dichotomies in turn rest on an impoverished view of human nature. What is perhaps most striking in all of this is the authors' view—which is implied rather than expressed—that human beings are motivated almost exclusively by selfish concerns. They come very close to suggesting that people need to be socially pressured into marrying and starting families lest they be so relentlessly selfish that society collapse under the weight of conflicting egoisms. And thus the authors arrive at their first false dichotomy: either heterosexual marriage on the one hand, or rampant selfishness on the other.

This dichotomy, as I have said, arises from a false view of human nature. Human beings are simply not exclusively selfish, and so they do not need to be pressured into marriage in order to be saved from their egoism and individualism. Love of parents and friends is every bit as spontaneous as love of self. A person who finds no happiness in the happiness of others is not a typical specimen of humanity, but a sociopathic freak.

It is surely true that no marriage can be successful unless each partner treats the other's happiness as being just as important as his or her own. But if human nature were as selfish as the authors seem to think, no one would ever want to get married in the first place, and all those marriages into which people were forced for their own good would have no chance of succeeding. In reality, of course, people sometimes fall in love; when they do, they come to care deeply about the happiness and well-being of the persons with whom they are in love. And homosexuals are just as apt to fall in love as heterosexuals are.

A lively concern for the welfare of others is therefore as much a feature of human nature as is a lively concern for self-interest. But even if it were not, this first dichotomy—either heterosexual marriage or rampant selfishness—would still be a false one, since heterosexual marriage is not the only arena in which unselfishness can be cultivated. I can cultivate unselfishness not only as a husband, but also as a friend, as a teacher, and as a son. Indeed, if I cannot see past my own narrow self-interest, I will be a dismal failure in all of these relationships. As they do so often in their paper, the authors are confusing what is useful with what is necessary, what is good with what is mandatory. Heterosexual marriage is a useful forum in which to cultivate one's concern for the well-being of another, and for that reason (among many others), it is a good thing. But heterosexual marriage is not necessary for the cultivation of concern for others, and so it is in no sense mandatory. We are not limited to a choice between heterosexual marriage and rampant egoism.

Second, the authors consistently write as if self-interest were opposed to morality; but this dichotomy is also an illusion. Self-love, properly understood, is not the enemy of morality, but one of its greatest supports. Now proper self-love does not mean gratifying every desire one happens to have; it involves careful attention to what will make one happy over the long haul. The authors paint a picture of homosexuals as living for the moment, slavishly gratifying every desire as it arises, whereas heterosexuals (married heterosexuals, at any rate) have settled down to a disciplined life of "self-command" that looks past momentary gratification and values human flourishing over time. Here is a third false dichotomy. Homosexuality does not automatically incapacitate people for pursuing long-term well-being at the sacrifice of short-term pleasure. Homosexuals are just as capable of proper self-love as anyone else.

Since the authors see human beings as basically selfish and shortsighted, they are naturally inclined to see the unselfishness and long-term commitment of marriage as an extraordinarily difficult business. They repeatedly emphasize that "marriage and the family . . . are fragile institutions in need of careful and continuing support" and that "having and rearing children is among the most difficult of human projects." Now I agree that *any* sustained course of action will encounter difficulties, and marriage is surely an especially demanding relationship. I even agree that the institutions of marriage and family need support and that such support is a legitimate end of public policy. But the authors want to claim even more than this. Marriage is *so* fragile, they say, that it is not enough for public policy to support marriage; it must also actively suppress homosexual relationships. Thus they arrive at their fourth false dichotomy: either we tolerate homosexuality and thereby show indifference to attacks on marriage, or else we support marriage and therefore condemn homosexuality.

Nonsense. Society has no more business condemning homosexuality in order to buttress marriage than condemning celibacy in order to ensure the preservation of the species. The two cases make a useful analogy here. Our society rightly permits celibacy, even though of course the preservation of the species is a morally important goal. Why? Because we recognize that celibate people contribute to the well-being of society in other ways and that most people are going to want to get married even though celibacy is an available option. (The usual reaction to a celibate person, after all, is not, "How come *he* gets to be celibate and I don't?") By exactly the same reasoning, society would be perfectly justified in permitting homosexual relationships, even though of course traditional marriages and families are morally important. Why? Because we should recognize that homosexual people—even homosexual *couples*—contribute to the well-being of society in other ways and that most people are going to want to get married to persons of the other sex even if homosexual relationships are an available option. Most people are, after all, heterosexual; tolerance of homosexuality will not lead people to flee in droves from the institution of marriage any more than tolerance of celibacy does.

The alternatives before us are not so stark as the authors would have us believe. Heterosexual marriage is not the only relationship in which selfishness gives way to a concern for others. The pursuit of self-interest is not the deadly enemy of morality. Homosexuality is not incompatible with proper self-love. Tolerance of homosexuality is no threat to heterosexual marriage or to the socially important ends that heterosexual marriage serves. The authors can justify their position only by setting up one false dichotomy after another. Such simplistic thinking may be rhetorically effective, but it is philosophically bankrupt.

Friendship and Chastity

In this last section, I want to try to figure out what the authors mean when they claim that the sexual revolution, and in particular the homosexual movement, involves an attack on friendship. They say that "[i]n the current climate of sexualizing and politicizing all intense interpersonal relationships, the place of sexually chaste friendship . . . is gravely jeopardized," and they insist that we must "affirm the reality and beauty of sexually chaste relationships." Now unless we know what is meant by calling a friendship "sexually chaste," we cannot know whether to agree that sexually chaste friendships are a good thing; nor can we evaluate the charge that the homosexual movement involves an attack on such friendships.

As a first guess, we might apply the word "chaste" to any friendship that does not involve sexual interaction. But that is far too broad a use of the word. Suppose we are talking about two friends who are not sexually attracted to each other in the first place. It seems odd to describe their friendship as "chaste"; for we usually think of chastity as the virtue that restrains sexual desire, and these friends do not have the desires that chastity is supposed to restrain.

Or so we might think. But some philosophers say that those who have a virtue do indeed lack any desire to act against that virtue: the truly honest person is not the one who struggles not to lie, but the one who is not even tempted to lie. And so, to these philosophers at least, it might seem appropriate to describe such a friendship as "sexually chaste" *precisely because* the friends have no desire to have sex with each other. But such an argument misses my point. Truly honest people are not even tempted to lie because they value honesty so highly that dishonesty seems simply repulsive to them. In this example, though, the friends are free from the temptation to have sex with each other, not because they value chastity so highly, but because they happen not to be sexually attracted to each other. The nonsexual character of their friendship is merely evidence of the current state of their hormones, not of their deepest ethical commitments. So if by "sexually chaste friendship" the authors mean any friendship that does not involve sexual interaction, they are misusing the word "chaste."

Perhaps, though, they mean a friendship in which the two friends are sexually attracted to each other but do not act on that attraction because they are committed to an ideal of chastity that would be violated if they had sexual relations. Is such restraint admirable and praiseworthy? Not necessarily. We must examine the reasons behind the restraint. There are some obvious reasons: one or both of the friends might be married to someone else, for example. And there are many less obvious reasons that might be quite good ones. Suppose any sexual relationship between them would be only a temporary fling, and they do not wish to invest so much of themselves in something that cannot last. Or suppose one of them simply thinks he cannot become the kind of person he is striving to become if he gets sexually involved with the other—he fears that his moral sensibilities will be coarsened, that his religious faith will be weakened, or that his professional effectiveness will be undermined.

If this is the sort of friendship the authors have in mind, then they are using the word "chaste" properly, but the charge that the homosexual movement involves an attack on chaste friendship becomes patently slanderous. Homosexuals are not suggesting that people cheat on their spouses, violate their religious vows, or even just settle for less than the very best in their lives, simply in order to have sex with (apparently) as many of their friends as possible.

Now suppose that the two friends would be breaking no promises and violating no commitments if they became sexually involved. Suppose also that their relationship would not interfere with their pursuit of excellence—that in fact it would permit both of them to lead richer, better, nobler lives. Why should they then maintain a "sexually chaste friendship," when both reason and desire press them to become sexually involved, and no reason holds them back?

The authors offer no good reason for anyone to refrain from homosexual sex simply because it is homosexual, and yet they think people should "experience a reflexive recoil" from homosexual sex. Recoiling from something for no good reason is a sign not of virtue, but of neurosis. Anorexia is not temperance, and neurotic loathing of a certain kind of sex is not chastity. If this is what they mean by "sexually chaste friendship"—a friendship in which the friends "experience a reflexive recoil" from a sexual relationship that they deeply desire and from which there is no good reason to refrain—then the authors are again misusing the word "chaste."

Furthermore, sexually "chaste" friendship of this sort is not desirable in the least. To the extent that the homosexual movement involves an attack on this sort of "chastity," it is a movement toward sanity, and homosexuals—and everyone else—would do well to embrace it.

· CHAPTER SEVEN ·

The Bible on Homosexuality

Ethically Neutral

DANIEL A. HELMINIAK

Daniel A. Helminiak, a theologian and author of What the Bible Really Says about Homosexuality, *argues that a historical-critical reading of the Bible fails to support the blanket condemnation of homosexuality traditionally attributed to it. Focusing on a passage in Paul's letter to the Romans as the key text, Helminiak argues that the vocabulary of the passage, the structure of the passage, and the overall argument of Romans all indicate that Paul viewed homosexual relations as ethically neutral.*

· · · · ·

The Bible provides the ultimate condemnation of homosexuality—or at least this is what some people claim. The more accurate statement is this: the Bible can supply the ultimate rationalization for people who want to condemn homosexuality. Just as the Bible was used to justify slavery, the Bible can be used to oppress gay and lesbian people. Quote the Bible, and supposedly all discussion is to cease. But not all Christians take the Bible to condemn same-sex acts.

The Historical-Critical Method and Biblical Inerrancy

In the late nineteenth century, as part of the new philological study of the Greek and Latin classics,[1] a new way of reading the Bible emerged. This new way is called the "historical-critical method." It is "historical" because it insists on reading the ancient texts in the context of their own time and place. What a text meant to its original author, as best as can be determined, is taken to be what the text means. This method is "critical" because it asks questions of the text; it investigates things that strike the contemporary mind as peculiar; it challenges inconsistencies; it demands a coherent explanation for a proposed interpretation. "Critical" is not used in the popular sense of finding fault with things, but in a technical sense as in the phrase "critical thinking."

All the mainline Christian churches endorse the historical-critical method. This is not to say that they always agree with, or are happy with, the conclusions that result from applying it. The conclusion regarding homosexuality is only one case in point. Other examples would be the role of women in church and society, the origins of the eucharistic ritual, the authority structure in the ancient Christian community, the intent of Jesus' teaching on divorce, or Jesus' self-awareness as "Son of God." Applying the historical-critical method sometimes turns things upside down. No wonder conservative Christians are reacting vigorously.

The historical-critical method is fully compatible with the belief that the Bible is inspired by God and is therefore free from error. These matters of inspiration and inerrancy are not at stake in this discussion. Although the various churches would understand these matters differently, no denomination would outright deny them. Not their inspiration and inerrancy, but the meaning of the texts is the point of debate. For if the Bible is inspired and inerrant, it is precisely the intended meaning of the text that is inspired and inerrant. Determining the intended meaning is the crucial issue.

Bible Texts on Homogenitality

Read against their original historical situations and interpreted according to the minds of the original authors, the Bible texts do not condemn homosexuality as we understand it today. In fact, even the term "homosexuality" is misleading in this discussion. The Bible's concern is about same-sex acts, what has been called "homogenitality." The Bible texts show no awareness of homosexuality, the psychological disposition that inclines people to be emotionally and erotically attracted to people of their own sex. The elaboration of sexual orientation as a permanent personality trait is a development of our own day. Now, this fact alone should make one wary of reading the biblical texts as if they were addressing today's questions about homosexuality. Nonetheless, even as regards only homogenitality, a historical-critical reading shows that the Bible offers no ethical condemnation.

The Bible actually addresses homogenitality in only five texts.[2] Still, there is no room here to treat each in detail. After a brief statement about the other texts, this chapter will focus on Romans 1:26–27 as an extended example of historical-critical interpretation.

First, the story of Sodom in Genesis 19:1–11 is said to condemn homosexuality. The men of Sodom wanted "to know" (that is, have sex with) two angelic visitors, whom the just man, Lot, took into his house as guests for the night. Because of this attempted male rape, people say that the sin of Sodom was homosexuality. But attention to the whole story makes clear that the male rape was only one facet of the real sin, namely, the inhospitality and hard-heartedness of the Sodomites. Ezekiel 16:48–49 says so outright and accuses the Sodomites of pride, excess, and unwillingness to aid the poor and needy. Wisdom 10:8 faults Sodom for rejecting wisdom, and Wisdom 19:13, for the hatred of strangers and the enslavement of guests. Sirach 16:8 accuses Sodom of insolence. Even Jesus (Matt. 10:5–15) compared Sodom to the towns that would not welcome his missionary apostles. None of the explicit biblical references to Sodom names homosexuality as its sin. It is unbiblical to see homosexuality everywhere Sodom gets a biblical mention.

Second, Leviticus 18:22 states, "You shall not lie with a male as with a woman; it is an abomination." Leviticus 20:13 adds the punishment: "they shall be put to death." "Abomination" sounds bad in English, but the Hebrew "*toevah*" could also be translated as uncleanness, impurity, or religious/ritual taboo. In question are certain practices that disqualified a person from participating in religious ceremonies—like eating pork or shellfish, touching a dead body, and having a menstrual flow or a seminal emission. The ancient Israelites enforced certain practices to keep themselves distinct from the surrounding Gentile tribes. Even today, traditional Jews observe kosher laws and wear a yarmulke in public. Supposedly, male-male sex was a practice among the ancient Canaanites, so to engage in it was to identify with them and, as it were, deny one's Jewish affiliation. Hence, the act represented apostasy and merited severe punishment. A contemporary parallel would be the Roman Catholic who used to be thought guilty of mortal sin, and so liable to hell, eternal death, for eating meat on Friday. The offense was against one's Catholicism and had nothing to do with the moral status of vegetarianism. Thus, although Leviticus clearly forbids male-male sex (it says nothing of lesbianism), the reason for forbidding it is irrelevant today. Few today are concerned about appearing to be Canaanite. So crying "Abomination!" to condemn homosexuality is wrongheaded and anachronistic.

Third and fourth are 1 Corinthians 6:10 and 1 Timothy 1:10, and these are the most difficult of all the texts to interpret. Both are Christian Scriptures, and both turn on one and the same obscure Greek term "*arsenokoitai.*"[3] 1 Corinthians 6:10 says that *arsenokoitai,* among others, will not enter the Reign of God, and 1 Timothy 1:10 says that it was against *arsenokoitai* that the law was written. The meaning of this term is highly debated, for it occurs nowhere in earlier documents, and its inclusion in a list of sinners hardly helps explain its meaning. It is clear that the term refers to men (*arsen*) but is not applicable to women, so it could not accurately be translated as "homosexuals" unless "male" is specified. And it is clear that it implies some kind of sexual penetration (*koite*). But what exactly this term includes, even whether it is restricted to homogenital acts, is uncertain. In light of the tolerant and calculated teaching in Romans, summarized below, it is dishonest to cite *arsenokoitai* to indiscriminately condemn all expressions of male homogenitality.

The Bible's Supposed Overall Teaching

Before we turn to the text in Romans, one other argument needs to be addressed. Losing the argument on the basis of individual biblical texts, fundamentalists have begun to appeal to the Bible as a whole to make their case. They argue that, wherever the Bible mentions sex in a positive light, it proposes an ideal of heterosexual marriage. Therefore, they conclude, the Bible is opposed to homosexuality. The popular formulation runs, "God created Adam and Eve, not Adam and Steve." But the argument is flawed on both biblical and logical grounds.

This argument presumes that the biblical authors who wrote about Adam and Eve or about heterosexual marriage had in the back of their minds a concern about sexual orientation. But there is no evidence whatsoever to support such a concern in those ancient texts. Sexual orientation is a recent preoccupation. In themselves, those texts cannot legitimately be taken as making a point about sexual orientation. They simply do not consider the matter; they express no opinion about it.

And the argument about Adam and Eve depends on a glaring logical flaw. It is called the "*ad ignorantiam* argument"—argument based on what is *not* known. This argument supposes that, because the Bible talks about heterosexual marriage and not about homosexual relationships, the Bible must be opposed to homosexuality. But one cannot know what the Bible or anyone thinks by appealing to what is not said. Following this mistaken logic, the Bible must also be opposed to automobiles, computers, and open-heart surgery. The Bible must be opposed to anything about which it does not speak positively. Obviously, such conclusions are absurd. No matter how convincingly it is argued that the Bible endorses heterosexual marriage, it simply does not and never will follow that the Bible therefore condemns homosexuality.

The Letter to the Romans

The fifth and final biblical reference to homogenitality is in chapter 1 of St. Paul's letter to the Romans. This Christian text is the Bible's longest statement about homogenitality, and it is supposed to be the most damning. But precisely because it is long, it provides ample material for analysis. This analysis shows that, far from condemning homogenitality, the apostle Paul actually believed the matter is ethically neutral.[4] The relevant verse, 27, with its surrounding context, follows:

> [18]For the wrath of God is revealed from heaven against all ungodliness (*asebeian*) and wickedness [*adikia*] of those who by their wickedness [*adikia*] suppress the truth. [19]For what can be known about God is plain to them, because God has shown it to them. [20]Ever since the creation of the world his eternal power and divine nature, invisible though they are, have been understood and seen through the things he has made. So they are without excuse; [21]for though they knew God, they did not honor him as God or give thanks to him, but they became futile in their thinking and their senseless minds were darkened. [22]Claiming to be wise, they became fools; [23]and they exchanged the glory of the immortal God for images resembling a mortal human being or birds or four-footed animals or reptiles.
>
> [24]Therefore God gave them up in the lusts [*epithemiais*] of their hearts to impurity [*akatharsian*], to the degrading [*atimazesthai*] of their bodies among themselves, [25]because they exchanged the truth about God for a lie and worshipped and served the creature rather than the Creator, who is blessed forever! Amen.
>
> [26]For this reason God gave them up to degrading [*atimias*] passions [*pathe*]. Their women exchanged natural intercourse for unnatural [*para physin*], [27]and in the same way also the men, giving up natural intercourse with women, were consumed with passion [*orexei*] for one another. Men committed shameless [*aschemosynen*] acts with men and received in their own persons the due penalty for their error.
>
> [28]And since they did not see fit to acknowledge God, God gave them up to a base mind and to things that should not be done [*ta me*

kathekonta]. [29]They were filled with every kind of wickedness [*adikia*], evil, covetousness, malice. Full of envy, murder, strife, deceit, craftiness, they are gossips, [30]slanderers, God-haters, insolent, haughty, boastful, inventors of evil, rebellious toward parents, [31]foolish, faithless, heartless, ruthless. [32]They know God's decree, that those who do such things deserve to die—yet they not only do them but even applaud those who practice them.

Three interlocking considerations support the claim that Paul teaches in Romans that homogenitality is ethically neutral. First, the vocabulary used to describe male-male sex refers to reputation and public opinion, social expectations, and not to ethics. Paul understands homogenitality as a matter of purity or cleanness, as prescribed in the Jewish Law. Second, the structure of the passage deliberately contrasts the purity issue with another issue, morality or ethics. Third, the overall argument of Romans uses those two issues to teach that the ethical remains relevant to Christianity but the purity matter does not. In summary, Paul understands the objection to male-male sex to be a purity requirement of the Jewish Law. His considered opinion is that Jewish purity requirements are not binding on Christians.

The Vocabulary of Paul

Paul uses three terms to describe the sexual acts: "*para physin,*" "*atimia,*" and "*aschemosyne.*" None has ethical weight in Paul's usage.

Para physin is translated as "unnatural" and has thus influenced centuries of Western usage—for example, talk of "unnatural" vice. But this is a mistranslation, pure and simple. In fact, *para physin* is a technical term in Stoicism, a philosophy prevalent in the Roman Empire in the early centuries of Christianity. Other Stoic terms also occur in Romans. Paul undoubtedly knew of Stoicism and was probably throwing around some technical terminology to impress his Romans readers. Paul was trained in rhetoric; he knew how to win over and convince an audience. As a Stoic term, *para physin* is correctly translated "contrary to nature" or "unnatural." But Paul did not understand Stoic philosophy. Translated as Paul meant it, the term should read "atypical."[5]

The Stoics had achieved an abstract understanding of nature, *physis,* as in the phrase "Nature and Nature's Laws." Paul's use of the term "*physis*" is never abstract. For Paul, "nature" means the kind or type or character of this or that thing; Paul's is a concrete understanding (Gal. 2:14; 1 Cor. 11:14; Rom. 2:14, 27). So whereas for the Stoics *para physin* would mean "beyond the natural," for Paul it would mean "*beyond the typical*," that is, "unusual" or "unexpected."

Paul's usage in Romans 11:24 confirms this interpretation beyond doubt. There, Paul says that God acted *para physin* in grafting the "wild stock" of the Gentiles into the "cultivated stock" of the Jews. Such an act is unusual; it is not the standard agricultural practice. If Paul's use of *para physin* is to be translated as "unnatural," then Paul believed that God acts contrary to nature—which is absurd. God is the author of nature, and this is the very point that the Stoics would make and that Paul failed to grasp in their terms. More than this, in this very same verse, Paul also uses the complementary Stoic term "*kata physin*," according to nature, and Paul plays these two terms back and forth off each other. His word game demonstrates clearly that he did not understand the Stoic sense of these words. For Paul, *para physin* meant "atypical."

Now, that is precisely how he described male-male sex in Romans 1. There is no ethical condemnation in Paul's usage.

Next, consider *atimia*. Literally, the term means without honor, hence the translation "degrading." But dishonor or degradation refers to a person's standing in the eyes of others. In itself, it does not imply an ethical or moral judgment. In fact, in 2 Corinthians 6:8 and 11:21, Paul uses this very term to describe himself, held in disrepute for preaching Christ. Clearly, the term implies no ethical condemnation. Other Pauline usages unanimously confirm this conclusion (1 Cor. 11:14; Rom. 9:21; 2 Tim. 2:20).

A standard objection to this analysis of *atimia* is to find an instance where the dishonor in question attaches to an act that is obviously wrong. Then it is argued that "dishonorable" means "wrong." But this objection muddles the matter. It fails to distinguish between the act, which might be right or wrong, and the reputation that accrues to the act, which might itself be positive or negative, and these combinations could change, depending on the audience. But in whatever case, the public reaction cannot be taken to be the same thing as the ethical status of the act. *Atimia* clearly refers to a negative judgment in the arena of public opinion. This is what "dishonorable" or "degrading" means. The ethical status of the act is another thing. An act may well have been dishonorable, say, among the Jews but hardly at all dishonorable, say, among the Greeks and Romans—all of which should make one begin to wonder what Paul was up to in this passage addressed to the Romans.

Finally, consider *aschemosyne*. This is an adjective that translates as "shameless" or "shameful." The King James Version says "unseemly."

These translations already suggest that *aschemosyne* is a parallel to *atimia.* Both indicate negative public opinion.

Aschemosyne is not widely used in the Christian Scriptures. It occurs as an adjective in only one other place, and there it refers to one's being seen naked (Rev. 16:15). A nominal form of this same word occurs in 1 Corinthians 12:23 and refers simply to the genitals. And a verbal form occurs in 1 Corinthians 7:36, a passage whose meaning is highly debated. In all these places, the word involves something sexual. But unless one thinks that having genitals or being naked is itself somehow wrong, this word carries no ethical connotation. A final verbal usage occurs in the famous passage on love in 1 Corinthians 13:5: love is not "rude." This instance confirms the nonethical meaning of this word.

So in Paul's usage, none of the three terms that describe the sexual acts in Romans 1 carries an ethical implication. Therefore, Paul is not saying that those acts are wrong; he is saying that they are unusual and do not enjoy social approval.

Critics of this interpretation would have to show that, contrary to the evidence just presented—and there is no other evidence; every Pauline occurrence has been listed—somehow Paul still intended condemnation by those terms. The assertion would be that, despite Paul's consistent usage elsewhere, when he speaks of homogenitality, his words have a negative ethical implication. But obviously, such an assertion just begs the question. Likewise, it would not be enough to find one ambiguous case or another where one could link those terms with an ethical wrong. One would have to show that Paul's ordinary usage of those terms implies ethical condemnation. One or another ambiguous usage would only show that this interpretation, like almost any interpretation of any text, is not absolutely cut-and-dried. But even such ambiguity would not rule out an ethically neutral interpretation as an honest possibility. Besides, Paul's usage is not ambiguous. Only in 1 Corinthians 7:36 is the exact implication of *aschemosyne* debated, and overall, *aschemosyne* is simply not an ethical term.

The ethical neutrality of the three descriptors that Paul uses clarifies the significance of the nouns in the passage.

Epithemia simply means "desire"; the term in itself is neutral. Paul uses this word positively in 1 Thessalonians 2:17 and in Philippians 1:23 to name his longing to be with his fellow Christians and to be with Christ. To make clear that a negative meaning is intended, Colossians 3:5 adds an adjective: "*evil* desires." "Lusts" in Romans 1:24 is an unwarranted negative translation of *epithemia.*

Pathos simply means "sexual desire" or "passion." Though it may be used in a negative sense, its core meaning is neutral. Besides, the *pathe* in question in Romans 1:26 is explicitly described as dishonorable, not as wrong.

The same holds for *orexis.* It is a synonym for *pathe,* and it occurs nowhere else in the Christian Testament. Its intent must be determined by the descriptors in the passage—ethically neutral.

If Paul had wanted to use condemning terms to describe homogenitality, he could easily have done so. Before and after the verses on sex, Paul does use such terms: "*asebeia,*" "*adikia,*" and "*ta me kathekonta*" (another technical Stoic term that implies ethical wrong-doing). Isn't it strange that, describing sexual acts that supposedly subvert the whole order of creation and are supposedly the paradigmatic symbol for rebellion against God,[6] Paul does not call them "ungodly" or "wicked" or "evil"? Could this discrepancy be accidental? By no means. Paul deliberately describes homogenitality in terms of Jewish impurity—socially disdained, looked down upon, outside expected parameters. Impurity is precisely what he is talking about. He says so outright in verse 24: "God gave them up . . . to impurity."

Of course, it is true that Paul usually uses *akatharsia* (impurity, uncleanness) in the Christian, and not the Jewish, sense (1 Thess. 2:3, 4:3–8; 2 Cor. 12:21; Gal. 5:19; Eph. 5:3, 5; Col. 3:5–6). For Jesus and his followers, true uncleanness is corruption of the heart, sinfulness (Matt. 5:8, 15:10, 18–20). Nonetheless, in contexts that refer to the Jewish Law (Matt. 23:27; Acts 10:14, 28, 11:8), the Christian Testament continued to use this term and its cognates in the Jewish sense—just as Paul did in Romans 1:24 (and probably also in 6:19). Paul explicitly describes the impurity in question as the dishonoring kind: *akatharsian tou atimazesthai.*

Only in Romans 14 does Paul finally come clean on his full teaching about impurity. He is a skilled teacher and a trained rhetorician. Throughout Romans, step by step, he leads his readers from a Jewish to a Christian understanding of the matter. Attention to the structure of 1:18–32 and to the overall argument of Romans substantiates this claim—as shown below. But attention only to the vocabulary that Paul uses to describe homogenital acts already makes clear that he is intending no ethical condemnation.

The Structure of the Passage

Paul begins Romans 1:18–32 by pointing out the guilt of people who know God but do not honor God. Then he indicates two results of that idolatry: impurity and real wrongs. That is, Paul's presentation falls into two parts, verses 24–27 and verses 28–32. One of the biggest mistakes people make in interpreting this passage is to run the whole together. Then all the wicked things listed in the latter part can be applied to the homogenitality treated in the first part. But the division into two sections is lucid.

The difference in vocabulary already indicates a deliberate contrast in Paul's presentation. In addition, Paul uses a repeated phrase to break up his presentation: "God gave them up." Of course, this phrase occurs three times, but attention to Paul's argument shows that, deliberately or not, he got sidetracked in verse 25 and had to refocus his argument by repeating his phrase in verse 26. Paul often digresses in his letters and turns to proclaiming the praises of God (Rom. 9:5, 11:33–36; Gal. 1:5; Phil. 4:20). Such digression is what happened here. The subject matter of verse 24, dishonoring, is the same as that of verse 26. So verses 24–27 constitute a single section. Moreover, Paul begins verse 28 with "And." Obviously, he intends to signal the introduction of something new. His summary of his basic argument—"since they did not see fit to acknowledge God, God gave them up"—reinforces the realization that he is introducing a second theme. Finally, the very topics Paul announces for these two sections show explicit contrast: "impurity" (verse 24), on the one hand, and "a debased mind and things not to be done" (verse 28), on the other hand. Clearly, Paul is sorting out two different effects of disregard for the God of Israel.

These analyses already make clear that Paul is not condemning homogenitality in Romans 1. One further consideration can even explain, then, why he mentioned it.

The Overall Argument of Romans

Paul is writing to a Christian community that he hopes to visit. If he wants to be welcome, he needs to ingratiate himself to everyone—without compromising his teaching. But the Roman community, like all the early Christian communities, included Jewish converts and Gentile converts, and they were at one another's throats (Acts 10, 15; Gal. 2). The point of contention was whether or not a Gentile convert had first to become a Jew before becoming a Christian. Said otherwise, did Christian males need to be circumcised? Did Christians have to obey the Jewish Law? Paul was noted for his negative answer to these questions. Along with Jesus, Paul insisted that righteousness before God does not require following the purity requirements of the Jewish Law.

Paul began his letter by seeking the goodwill of the Jewish converts. In fact, seeming to side with their prejudice, he was saying with them, "The Gentiles are a dirty lot!" For this ploy to work, Paul had to be circumspect at first about his position. He phrased it in terms that would let the Jewish Christians think they heard what they wanted to hear. This is where his reference to unusual, dishonorable, and unseemly desires and sexual passion comes in. Evidently, Paul expressed very carefully what he meant, as has been shown. But what his audience heard might be another matter. Paul's rhetorical strategy required some degree of ambiguity.

Paul was deliberately baiting the Jewish Christians. And he quickly turned the tables on them. By chapter 2, he already insists that they have nothing to brag about; they are as sinful as anybody else. By chapter 12, he protests that all Christians, though different members, make up one body in Christ. Differences in faith and gifts must not splinter the community. He had already dealt with the easier matter, circumcision, in 2:29: "real circumcision is a matter of the heart—it is spiritual, not literal." By chapter 14, he confronts the toughest question head on: foods are neither clean nor unclean. Still, in all things, conscience and charity—purity of heart—must prevail.

Paul begins Romans with mention of sexual mores as a relatively safe example of Jewish purity requirements. The Gentiles would not have been offended. The whole ancient world was aware of the Jewish peculiarity on this matter, and Gentiles just shrugged it off. Paul mentioned Jewish prejudice regarding homogenitality precisely to dismiss it as irrelevant in Christ.

Patently, a Jewish-Gentile polemic is at stake in Romans. With a double entendre, verse 1:16 announces that Paul will address the Jews first and then the Gentiles. Verse 2:1 alludes to the Jews, and 2:17 addresses them directly. By 9:4, Paul turns from the Jews and speaks of them in the third person. By 11:11, he is speaking about the Gentiles but only in the third person. Then, in 11:13, he addresses the Gentiles directly, enjoining them, too, not to boast and to respect the Jews.

Summary on Romans and Conclusion

The letter to the Romans is Paul's plea to the early Christians to stop bickering over insignificant differences. In recent centuries and especially in our own day, his plea continues to go unheard. Among those insignificant differences are sexual ones, including—in Paul's considered opinion—the homogenitality mentioned in Romans 1:27. Three considerations converge to support this interpretation: Paul's vocabulary, the structure of the passage, and the overall argument of Romans. This reading places Romans in its original historical context and understands it according to the mind of Paul. Paul teaches that, in itself, homogenitality is an ethically neutral matter.

Of course, this interpretation is new. Its conclusion radically challenges standard beliefs. Careful as they are, scholars are wary of endorsing it too quickly. The tendency is still to read Paul as if he were a Greco-Roman philosopher or Hellenistic Jew—like Philo, Josephus, or Seneca. Yet even such scholars as Victor Paul Furnish[7] and Bernadette Brooten[8] insist that the biblical answers do not apply to today's questions. Across the board, the biblical authors were simply not talking about homosexuality as we now understand it. Those who see condemnation in the Bible are reading their own prejudgments into it.

· CHAPTER EIGHT ·

Romans 1:26–27 and Biblical Sexuality

THOMAS E. SCHMIDT

Thomas E. Schmidt, a New Testament scholar and author of Straight and Narrow? Compassion and Clarity in the Homosexuality Debate, *challenges "revisionist" interpretations of the Bible like Daniel Helminiak's in the previous essay. Like Helminiak, Schmidt focuses on Paul's letter to the Romans. Unlike Helminiak, he argues that the historical-critical method affirms the traditional interpretation of the Bible on homosexuality. According to Schmidt, Paul's treatment of same-sex relations stems from the Creation-based view of marriage emphasized consistently throughout the Bible.*

· · · · ·

Are we proponents of exclusive heterosexuality merely attempting to top off a bucket full of bigotry with a handful of verses? There are, after all, only a few texts, mere droplets next to the deluge of love and justice in the Bible. And in recent decades, the traditional interpretation of even those few verses has been challenged by a growing number of revisionist writers whose findings purportedly contrast an enlightened historical-critical method to outmoded "literal" interpretations.

The purpose of this chapter is to demonstrate that responsible use of the historical-critical method affirms a traditional reading of the biblical material; that the proscription of homosexuality does not depend, ultimately, on a list of proscribed activities, but on the pervasive and coherent biblical affirmation of marriage; that the central proscription, Romans 1:26–27, is an inference from Paul's Creation-based view of marriage; and that this and other references to same-sex relations constitute a consistent biblical prohibition of conduct that includes what we refer to today as "homosexual acts."[1]

Genesis 1–2 and Biblical Sexuality

The Genesis narrative is indisputably normative for Jewish and Christian sexuality. Subsequent moral teaching is entirely consistent with, and in several key texts explicitly dependent on, the Genesis description of marital union between male and female (Matt. 19:1–12; 1 Cor. 6:12–20; *Babylonian Talmud, Tractate Sanhedrin.* 58a). Of course, the author of the Creation account does not consciously exclude same-sex relations, but the text contains affirmations that ground later biblical claims for heterosexual exclusivity.

First, *reproduction is good.* On the heels of the command for humans to multiply is the divine proclamation of all that was created as "very good" (Gen. 1:28–31). From this point, the Bible assumes the goodness of reproduction, perhaps most clearly in the promised blessing to Abraham that God will make him "exceedingly numerous" (Gen. 17:2). In Israel, to bear children is to know a blessing from God (Ps. 127:3). It is through reproduction that God begins to provide salvation, focusing first on the covenant with Israel, then on the Messiah "come in the flesh" (1 John 4:2), and finally on the perfected community of the New Jerusalem (Rev. 21–22). At that point, salvation is accomplished, so marriage discontinues (Mark 12:25) and, with it, presumably sex and reproduction—not because these things are bad, but because they have achieved their purpose. Indeed, it is through sexual reproduction that humanity participates in the generative capacity of God, the ability to create new creatures to love. Reproduction, then, is not an incidental outcome of the pleasure of sex; rather, sexual pleasure is an integral part of the human privilege to love as God loves.

Second, *sex is good.* The fact that the man rejoices at the gift of the woman with whom he becomes one flesh and the fact that the two are unashamed in their nakedness (Gen. 2:23–25) imply that the process by which children are produced is not a shameful necessity, but a beautiful experience. The Bible rejects asceticism, which in the New Testament period discounted the body as the demeaned half of a mistaken dualism. Whether ascetic or licentious, any manifestation of dualism runs counter to the biblical view that each person is an *embodied soul* for whom the good of physical existence, including sexual identity, goes back before the Fall and forward beyond the Resurrection. The ancient Gnostics misunderstood this and attempted to make sexuality transcend the body and its procreative potential. Recent revisionists employ disturbingly similar logic in their appeal to ideals of interpersonal relations as the basis of sexual morality.

Third, *marriage is good.* This is implied in Genesis, assumed throughout the Old Testament, and reiterated by both Jesus and Paul, who both cite Genesis. In Matthew 19:1–12, God's original intent for marriage is described as a union rather than a contract—in chemical terms, a solution rather than a mixture. Paul likewise affirms marriage as an indissoluble union in 1 Corinthians 6–7, although he quotes Genesis to discourage fornication rather than divorce. What is common to the understanding of Genesis in Jesus and Paul is the implication that marriage is lifelong because it involves a profound bond between two people.

Fourth, *male and female are necessary counterparts.* Humanity is created male and female (Gen. 1:27). Adam is not given a mirror-image companion, he is given a "partner" (Gen. 2:18), and he delights in her "correspondence" to him (Gen. 2:23), which resides in both her likeness (human) and her difference (female). The pair are, literally and figuratively, made for each other. Because union is the remedy of incompleteness ("for this reason," Gen. 2:24), humans possess a drive to "leave and cleave" in marriage.

These statements are not explicated within the Bible, but reasonable implications may be derived from them. What I am *not* confident can be derived from them is a definition of Creation "in God's image" as either sexual differentiation or human fellowship. It seems more natural to understand God's action here as creating a counterpart with whom God can communicate. In relation to Creation, humanity acts as *steward* for God, exercising "dominion" (verse 28). It is necessary that humans "be fruitful and multiply" in order for there to be enough humans to exercise stewardship; hence, sexes are necessary; hence, "male and female" (verse 27). But the crucial implication of the passage does not hinge on the precise meaning of "image." What is crucial is that sexual differentiation is good, and it is good because the union of the corresponding sexes remedies their incompleteness apart from each other. Furthermore, their correspondence is not limited to the social or spiritual dimension, although that is important: the woman is "helper" and "partner" (Gen. 2:18). But to leave the relationship at that level would be an abstraction utterly foreign to the context and to the biblical understanding of a human being as an *embodied soul.* The fit between the two is in fact described in *physical* terms ("bone of my bones," "become one flesh" [2:23–24]). The pair are complete counterparts, including their physical natures.

These affirmations reveal that the biblical norm of heterosexuality involves responsibility toward the embodied self and toward the family. Biblical morality is not, as some revisionists suggest, merely a mechanism for protection of male power and property or for the preservation of Jewish purity. As I will demonstrate below, the proscription of same-sex acts derives directly from the biblical norm of marriage. That is, whether such acts are termed impure, or abominable, or nonconsensual, or lustful, or none of these, they constitute intrinsic violations of the plan of God, present from Creation, for the lifelong union of husband and wife.

Romans 1:26–27: Context and Content

> For this reason God gave them up to degrading passions. Their women exchanged natural intercourse for unnatural, and in the same way also the men, giving up natural intercourse with women, were consumed with passion for one another. Men committed shameless acts with men and received in their own persons the due penalty for their error. (Rom. 1:26–27)

L. William Countryman advances some new exegetical arguments against the traditional view that Paul proscribes all forms of homosexual practice.[2] Countryman's position, briefly put, is that Paul in Romans 1 portrays same-sex relations as *impure* for the purposes of his argument, but since the gospel releases Gentiles from the purity code, Paul cannot be said to describe same-sex relations as *sinful.* I will demonstrate on contextual and linguistic grounds that Paul does describe same-sex relations as sinful and that his understanding is grounded in a Creation-based view of marriage.

The Structure of Paul's Argument

Countryman maintains that Paul's purpose in Romans 1 is to describe the result of the Gentiles' decision not to worship the true God, but he wants to do this in such a way that the Jewish segment of his audience will be "set up" for the next chapter. Same-sex relations are an appropriate choice as the prime illustration of Gentile uncleanness because while such behavior is repulsive to Jews, Gentiles will merely consign this repulsion to Jewish peculiarity and not associate it with sin. Thus, while the Jewish portion of Paul's audience is drawn in to his argument, the Gentile readers are not alienated because they "already know where he stands on the whole issue of purity."[3]

There are several flaws in this representation of Paul's design that bear mentioning before proceeding to a consideration of specific vocabulary. First, it is a mistake to operate under the assumption that Gentiles universally accepted same-sex relations, especially those resembling homosexuality as we know it today. Where sex between males in Greek society found approval, it was heavily qualified by limitation to those who were among the social elite, who had sex with boys between twelve and seventeen years of age, who took only the active role in intercourse, and who abandoned the behavior in favor of heterosexual relations as they matured. Some prominent Greek writers, notably Plato, condemn same-sex activity on the ground that it is not directed toward procreation. The early Romans legislated against pederasty and relations between adult males, but gradually under Greek influence, Romans accepted pederasty as an alternative means of sexual gratification for freemen. Nero himself numbered among his consorts both a castrated boy and an adult male—facts undoubtedly well known to Paul's Roman audience. Such behavior was not, however, without strong critics, among them Paul's contemporaries Seneca and Plutarch. Finally—and this is highly important—sex between females was almost always and everywhere strongly condemned. Since Paul's first reference in the passage is to relations between females, and since he then makes a link to relations of mutual desire between males, it would be impossible for any Gentile to limit the application of Paul's words to pederasty, much less find approval or neutrality in those words.

The second problem is chronological. Paul had, of course, not yet visited Rome. It is unreasonable to expect that the Romans, even if they did know by hearsay Paul's stance with regard to purity, would extrapolate from what he says about food to specifics of sexual morality. Moreover, it is highly unlikely that Paul, after the problems he has just had with the Corinthians, would take such knowledge for granted. When he does discuss food purity in Romans 14, his lengthy comments suggest that he assumes little prior understanding of his position. Furthermore, since he makes no connection in chapter 14 between food and sex, we can hardly expect his audience to read such a connection back into chapter 1.

The immediate context supplies further evidence that Paul equally condemns same-sex relations and the other behaviors that he mentions in verses 28–32. The section (Rom. 1:18–32) is clearly a unit, introduced by reference to "the wrath of God . . . against all ungodliness and wickedness." The threefold idolatrous "exchange" (verses 23, 25, 26) is followed in each instance by the words "God gave them up" (verses 24, 26, 28), and these subsections are joined by simple correlative conjunctions. If Paul intends his audience to perceive a distinction between sin and same-sex acts, his structure of the passage certainly does not help to do so.

Vocabulary and Sin in Romans 1:24–28

The main problem that Countryman attempts to solve by his analysis and translation of Romans 1:24–32 is the apparent carryover here of an Old

Testament purity ethic that is contrary to Paul's thought elsewhere. In order to maintain the consistency of Paul's definition of sexual sin as "intent to harm,"[4] Countryman argues that Paul carefully avoids his usual vocabulary for sin when describing homosexual acts in Romans 1:24–28, employing in its place the language of ritual impurity. This means that Countryman's argument depends not on a general impression, but on the viability of each key term. In other words, if a single term in Romans 1:24–28 that makes reference to same-sex relations is linked unequivocally to sin, Countryman's thesis is refuted. In fact, *every* term is linked to sin. A few examples will suffice to show the difference between Countryman's approach and one that respects historical-critical methodology in the interpretation of ancient texts.

In verses 24, 26, and 27, three words appear ("*epithymia,*" "*pathos,*" "*orexis,*" respectively) to denote the inclination of the will that leads to same-sex relations. While most translations, like the New Revised Standard Version (NRSV), use words like "lust" to convey the meaning of these terms, Countryman argues for a "neutral" translation like "desires." He grants that Paul, like the Stoics, employs *epithymia* for the most part in a negative sense but argues on the basis of a single reference, 1 Thessalonians 2:17 (Paul's "desire" to see the church), that the word *could* have a positive meaning and that we should at least render it neutral so as not to decide prematurely the question of Paul's evaluation of homosexuality. There is, however, no justification for such special pleading. The undisputed letters of Paul contain nine other instances of *epithymia,* only two of which allow for a positive connotation (1 Thess. 2:17 and Phil. 1:23, Paul's "desire" to be with Christ). This in itself is hardly a compelling statistic, but the more significant consideration is that these two instances occur in the context of autobiographical narrative, while the other seven—like Romans 1:24—occur in the context of moral argument. Four of these, significantly, occur in Romans. The number of supporting instances is doubled by factoring in the rest of the Pauline corpus, and it is tripled by factoring in the rest of the New Testament. Particular attention must be given to the other occurrences in Romans, with special reference to the link between *epithymia* and Paul's vocabulary of sin, especially physical sin. In 6:12, Paul commands, "do not let *sin* exercise dominion in your *mortal bodies,* to make you obey their passions." In 7:7–8, we read, "I would not have known *sin.* I would not have known what it is to *covet.* . . . But *sin,* seizing an opportunity in the commandment, produced in me all kinds of *covetousness.*" In 13:14, Paul commands, "make no provision for the *flesh,* to gratify its *desires.*"

Perhaps even more telling than these instances is the use of *epithymia* in an explicit reference to sexual sin that contains echoes of Romans 1 in its comparison to the Gentile world. In 1 Thessalonians 4:5–6, Paul commands believers to express their sexuality "not with lustful passion [*pathei epithymias*] like the Gentiles who do not know God." There can be no doubt of the equation between *epithymia* and sexual sin here: Paul has just specified a proscription of *porneia* (verse 3), and *pathei epithymias* is defined by the command in verse 5 not to "wrong" or "exploit." Significantly, the latter word contains the very stem from which hangs Countryman's own argument[5] that Paul redefines "uncleanness" as "greed." If greed is sin, and Paul here equates *epithymia* with greed, the conclusion seems inescapable that in an explicit discussion of sexual ethics, Paul equates *epithymia* with sin.

In verses 26–27, Paul uses two other terms for same-sex "passions" (NRSV), "*pathos*" and "*orexis.*" Once again, Countryman maintains that these words can be understood in a positive sense. As in the case of *epithymia,* this statement is technically true but actually quite misleading in light of pertinent occurrences of the word. There are only two other instances of *pathos* in the New Testament. The first of these, 1 Thessalonians 4:5, was quoted above and clearly denotes sinful action. The other instance is the vice list of Colossians 3:5. The related word "*pathema*" is often used in the New Testament of sufferings endured by believers or by Christ. On the two occasions when *pathema* is used in an ethical context, however, the association with sin is unmistakable. Romans 7:5 states that "while we were living in the flesh, our *sinful passions* [*ta pathemata ton harmartion*] . . . were at work in our members." Galatians 5:24 lauds those who "have crucified the *flesh* with its *passions* and *desires*" [*pathemasin kai epithymiais*]. Clearly, the evidence, particularly from the Pauline corpus, constitutes a compelling case for the association of *pathos* with sin in Romans 1:26.

In verse 27, Paul employs *orexis* to describe the desire of males for one another. This is the only New Testament occurrence, but the verb "*oregesthai*" is used in an ethical context once (1 Tim. 6:10) in a warning about "eagerness" for wealth. Philo employs *orexis* fourteen times, always negatively, and twice in discussions of sexual desire (*Deus.* 113; *Dec.* 123). The Septuagint also supports this sense (e.g., Sir. 18:30, 23:6; 4 Macc. 1:33, 35). The verb that "*orexis*" modifies, translated "consumed," has a similar connotation of sinful burning (Sir. 23:15; Philo *Dec.* 49; *Gig.* 34).

As in the case of *epithymia* and *pathos,* analysis of *orexis* disallows the "neutral" sense that Countryman justifies only by appeal to scattered references in very different contexts. But the vast majority of the evidence, and that in contexts similar to that of Romans 1, demonstrate overwhelmingly that the words employed by Paul in Romans 1:24–27 for the inclination of the will toward same-sex relations are not only pejorative in their connotations but clearly and consciously linked to sin. There is warrant to support translation by a strong English word like "lust."

The same analysis of vocabulary yields the same result for each of eight terms in the passage that Countryman attempts to "neutralize." True, Paul does not use the word "sin" itself in verses 26–27, but it is misleading to infer that Paul is thereby avoiding the connotation of sin with regard to homosexuality: the word "sin" does not occur anywhere in the first two chapters of Romans, but the description of sin is clearly the point. Even if a closed "sin vocabulary" could be substantiated in general terms, we should not expect to find elements of it in every passage, much less a two-verse statement on a topic not treated by Paul elsewhere. Indeed, Paul is probably choosing expressions peculiarly suited to the Gentile world in order to expose the sinfulness of that world in its own terms. Romans 1:26–27, far from being an exception to Paul's horror of sin, is in fact a prime and specific example.

The thesis that Paul regards homosexuality as impure but not sinful is unsupportable. What, then, is his point, and why does he employ homosexuality as an example of sexual sin? Closer inspection of another key term in the passage points toward an answer.

"Unnatural" (*Para physin*) in Paul's Understanding

Much discussion of the term "*para physin*" in Romans 1:26, usually translated "unnatural," has been generated by John Boswell's argument that the expression means "beyond nature" with no connotation of immorality. Countryman and Daniel Helminiak follow this view, citing "neutral" Pauline usage of *physis, physikos* in other contexts as evidence that same-sex relations among the Gentiles were not wrong, but merely "outside the ordinary" or "unusual."[6]

Boswell moves in a different direction by maintaining that Romans 1:26–27 describes individual heterosexuals who occasionally deny their own "natures" by performing homosexual acts.[7] One major weakness of this interpretation is its assumption that individual action is in view; that is, each same-sex act involves an "exchange" (verse 26) of that person's true nature for a false nature. This interpretation not only introduces a debatable modern concept of "nature" but also misses the point of the entire section, verses 18–32. Here, Paul is describing, not individual actions, but the *corporate* rebellion of humanity against God and the kinds of behavior that result. This is clear when we consider the word "exchange," which appears twice in the passage (verses 23, 25) to denote the movement from worship of God to worship of images. It is ludicrous to suppose that each Gentile reinvents idolatry; rather, Paul is describing the sweep of history.

Then the word "exchange" appears again in verse 26, this time to describe same-sex relations. The point is that same-sex relations are a specific falsification of right behavior (immorality), made possible by the general falsification of right thinking about God (idolatry). Paul's concern is not with individuals who deny their true selves, but with humanity that, first generally, now specifically (and sexually), replaces a truth with a falsehood.

Countryman grants that Paul is describing what we would call "homosexuality," but he insists on a neutral meaning for *para physin.* This is not possible given how Paul's contemporaries used the contrast *kata physin/para physin* ("according to nature/against nature") in relevant contexts. A few examples will suffice to demonstrate that Paul's terminology in Romans 1 was thoroughly consistent with his contemporaries' usage. Plato writes that "when male unites with female for procreation the pleasure experienced is held to be due to nature, but contrary to nature (*para physin*) when male mates with male or female with female, and that those first guilty of such enormities were impelled by their slavery to pleasure" (*Laws,* 636C). Plutarch (c. A.D. 100) contrasts "natural" love between men and women with "union contrary to nature with males," and a few lines later, he repeats that those who "consort with males" do so *para physin* (*Erot.,* 751C, E). In *Abr.,* 135, Philo remarks that the men of Sodom "threw off from their necks the law of nature" to mount males "not respecting the common nature with which the active partner acts upon the passive." In *Spec. Leg.,* III, 37–42, he characterizes pederasty as a "transformation of the male nature" and several lines later as *para physin.* Josephus makes reference to the homosexual activity of the people of Elis and Thebes as *para physin,* a few lines later including homosexuality with incest as characteristic of the "monstrous and unnatural (*para physin*) pleasures" of the Gentiles (*Ag. Ap.,* 2.273–275). Thus, notwithstanding the different sense given to *physis, physikos* by Paul in other places, the specific expression "*para physin*" has an unmistakably pejorative connotation in contexts similar to Romans 1.

Now we approach the crucial question of the basis for Paul's condemnation of same-sex relations. What appears to be the case is that many Jews of Paul's time melded the *kata physin/para physin* distinction with their notions of Creation and Fall. This is most clearly the case in Wisdom 13–14, which is often cited for its similarities to Romans 1:

> For all people who were ignorant of God were foolish by nature; and they were unable from the good things that are seen to know the one who exists, nor did they recognize the artisan while paying heed to his works (13:1). . . . Therefore those who lived unrighteously, in a

> life of folly, you tormented through their own abominations (12:23). . . . For the idea of making idols was the beginning of fornication, and the invention of them was the corruption of life (14:12). . . . For they . . . no longer keep either their lives or their marriages pure, but they . . . grieve one another by adultery, and all is a raging riot of blood and murder, theft and deceit, corruption, faithlessness, tumult, perjury, confusion over what is good, forgetfulness of favors, defiling of souls, sexual perversion, disorder in marriages, adultery, and debauchery. For the worship of idols not to be named is the beginning and cause and end of every evil (14:23–27).

The supposition that Paul is familiar with this text further undermines the "neutrality" of his reference to sexual conduct in Romans 1. But whether or not we suppose direct dependence, there can be little doubt that Paul is thinking of Genesis and humanity's corporate rebellion against the Creator. Granted, Paul does not *quote* Genesis, but the passage is filled with allusions to humanity's Creation and Fall. "Ever since the creation," verse 20 begins, God's power has been evident in "the things he has made." The fall involved a temptation toward knowledge; hence, "claiming to be wise, they became fools" (verse 23). God is called "Creator" (verse 25). Then, in verses 26–27, Paul departs from the usual "woman/man" (cf. 1 Cor. 11:11–13; Rom. 7:2–3) for "female/male" (as in LXX Gen. 1:27—and elsewhere in the New Testament only in Gal. 3:28). Moreover, the unusual sequence from female to male may allude to the fact that the woman fell first (cf. 1 Tim. 2:14).

Paul's reliance on Genesis has important implications. Many revisionists have argued that Paul knew only pederasty and would not have been so harsh had he observed modern, consensual homosexual partnerships between adults. But Paul's line of argument does not derive from empirical research on Gentile sexual practices; rather, he is paraphrasing the Genesis account of humanity's corporate rebellion and its result. Why same-sex relations? If we follow the Genesis narrative, we see that, well before the famous incident in chapter 19, Sodom becomes a paradigm for the equation of idolatry and wickedness (Gen. 13:13, 18:20; cf. Gen. 10:19 where Sodom is linked to the Canaanites). This is not a story of pederasty, nor are the proscriptions of same-sex relations in Leviticus 18:22, 20:13, which derive from a similar view of Canaanite sexual practices—and from which Paul takes the compound word for same-sex practice used in 1 Corinthians 6:9, 1 Timothy 1:10. The Sodom narrative is, rather, a story of deviation from the sexual norm of marriage, one sin of many caused by idolatry. Notwithstanding the obscuring complications offered by revisionists, Paul's line of argument in Romans 1 involves a simple paraphrase of Genesis: into the mental vacuum left by the Fall, rebellious humanity invents idols; and into the moral vacuum left by such empty worship, rebellious humanity inverts sexuality, then corrupts relationships (Rom. 1:29–32).

Now we come to the heart of the matter. It is essential to understand that what Paul is stating here is unusual—probably unique. Unlike some of his contemporaries, Paul is not interested in active/passive roles or male progeniture, nor does his statement apply only to pederasty. Instead, he begins with reference to women, establishes a link to male same-sex relations, and then uses terminology denoting mutual desire: they were "consumed with passion for one another." When Paul places such a statement in a passage filled with allusions to the Creation narrative, we can be sure that he does not view the matter as a mere expression of popular custom, but as a norm originating "in the beginning." He understands that the complementary sexualities of male and female have moral implications, which Paul conveys here by the term "natural." He understands, further, that the desire of female for female or male for male dishonors this arrangement by substituting an untruth for the truth. He understands, finally, that this untruth may involve two members of either sex acting in consent to satisfy desire. In this, Paul expresses a principle that applies equally—perhaps even better—to the most common forms of same-sex practice in our own day than to those of the first century.

Summary and Conclusion

The affirmation of marriage in Genesis involves a union of sexually differentiated persons. The structure of Paul's argument and the particular vocabulary employed for same-sex relations in Romans 1:18–32 unequivocally connect this behavior to sin. Paul's proscription is grounded in the law, particularly the Creation account, which views same-sex relations as a violation of marriage akin to adultery.

A fuller analysis could demonstrate the connection and relevance of corollary texts such as Genesis 19, Leviticus 18:22, 20:13, 1 Corinthians 6:9, 1 Timothy 1:10, 2 Peter 2:6–7, and Jude 7. A variety of practices and motivations for same-sex relations are evident in the biblical texts, including rape, prostitution, pederasty, and relationships of mutual consent. Some references are more general and may be applied to different practices. Revisionist attempts to isolate each text and show its dissimilarity to modern practice fail both because some texts defy such limitations and because details of practices and motivations miss the point.

The point is simple, and it runs like a red thread through all the passages. The point is marriage. When biblical writers evaluate any same-sex act—with angels, with prostitutes, with boys, with mutually consenting adults—in relation to the marital union of male and female, they find that it falls short of the plan of God present from Creation. As revisionists have rightly pointed out, it is inappropriate to call such an act "impure" or "disgusting." But as revisionists have refused to recognize, the Bible clearly calls such an act "wrong."

That is not to say that the discussion of modern morality ends here: the exegete may serve only to narrow and deepen the channel to the hermeneutical swamp beyond. Revisionists may be faced with the difficult and (in some circles) unpopular choice to reject the sexual morality of the Bible, but this choice has far more integrity than does the attempt to make the Bible say something other than what it says.

· PART TWO ·

Science and Identity

· CHAPTER NINE ·

The Origins of Sexual Orientation

Possible Biological Contributions

WILLIAM BYNE AND MITCHELL LASCO

William Byne, a neuroanatomist and psychiatrist at Mount Sinai Medical Center in New York, and Mitchell Lasco, a Ph.D. candidate in psychological development at New York University, explore three different models for conceptualizing the role of biology in sexual orientation formation: the "permissive" model, in which biological factors simply provide the neural machinery through which sexual orientation is inscribed by early childhood experience; the "indirect" model, in which biological factors influence sexual orientation through some intermediate factor such as personal temperament (cf. the following essay by Daryl J. Bem); and the "direct" model, in which biological factors directly organize the brain circuits that mediate sexual orientation. Byne and Lasco then review some of the recent biological research—which has been both widely publicized and widely misunderstood—in light of these models.

· · · · ·

Because we are biological beings, all our thoughts, actions, and emotions must have a biological substrate at some fundamental level. Thus, we should not ask if sexual orientation is biological. We should not even ask if it is *primarily* biological. How could biological and psychosocial factors be teased apart, and what units of measurement would allow them to be assessed and weighed against one another to determine which is more important? From a scientific perspective, it would be more productive to ask about the alternative pathways through which biological and experiential factors might interact to influence sexual orientation.

The goal of this chapter is to review recent biological research into the origins of sexual orientation. We will begin by considering three simple models for conceptualizing the possible contributions of biological factors, as well as the ways in which these factors may influence and interact with psychological and social factors.

Models

Figure 9.1 illustrates what we refer to as the "model of permissive biological effects." In this model, biology primarily provides the neural machinery through which sexual orientation is inscribed by formative experience. Biology could also delimit the period during which the relevant formative experience must occur. For example, many songbirds must learn their species' song by hearing it during a restricted period of early development.[1] While the song is clearly acquired through experience, biology determines the period during which that experience must occur. Once a particular song has been learned, that is the bird's song for life. It will not be able to unlearn that song or to learn another. By giving this example, we do not want even to imply that sexual orientation might be acquired by simple mimicry. Instead, we are merely suggesting that a particular experience or set of experiences might have a greater or lesser impact on sexual orientation depending on the developmental period (e.g., state of psychological

FIGURE 9.1
Model of Permissive Biological Effects

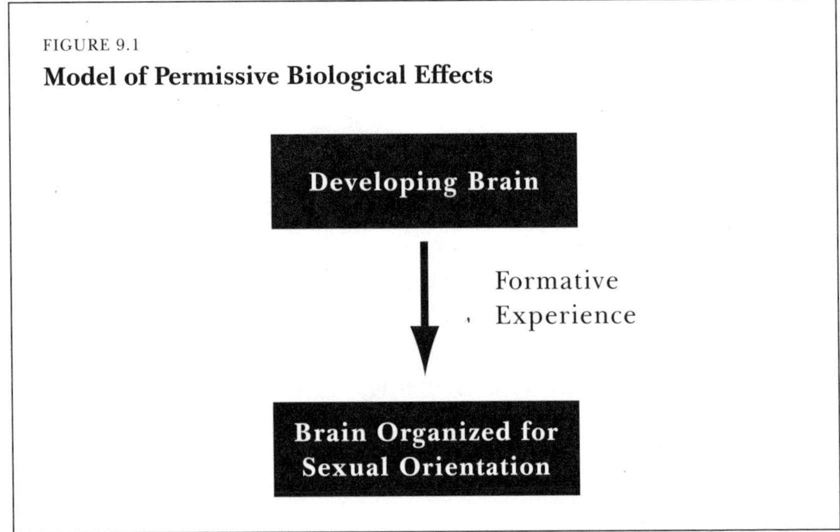

and/or biological readiness) during which it occurs. Furthermore, the example shows that phenomena acquired through experience may, nonetheless, be immutable. Thus, the fact that sexual orientation is impervious to change does not militate against the significance of formative experience.

"Formative experience" can be defined as the subjective internalization of one's interactions with the environment. Internalization includes the perception of the environment and the interpretation and integration of ongoing experience in the contexts of the moment and of one's life history. Each formative experience changes the individual so that the next interaction with the environment will be different. The individual is not passive in this process but, instead, repeatedly provokes responses from the environment and changes the environment in the process. As described by Graeme Hanson and Lawrence Hartmann, this back-and-forth results in continuing, evolving, and interacting cycles of mutual influence between the individual and the environment.[2] Behavior is the most easily measured part of this cycle, but from the perspective of the model of permissive biological effects, perceptions, cognitions, and fantasies would be more salient. If this model is correct, attempts to find the origins of sexual orientation by analyzing purely environmental and behavioral measures alone are unlikely to be successful. What the developing individual brings to his or her environment needs to be included in the analysis. The relevant individual differences would include temperamental, cognitive, and emotional differences as well as the individual contexts in which these differences are expressed.

The contribution of individual differences, some of which may be constitutional, is addressed in what we call the "model of indirect biological effects (Figure 9.2). According to this model, biological factors would influence sexual orientation only indirectly. The more direct action of biological factors would be on some intermediate factor such as temperament or other personality traits. These traits would then influence how one experiences, interacts with, and modifies the environment from the moment of birth in shaping the relationships and experiences that influence how sexual orientation develops. This model is similar to the model of permissive biological effects, but goes beyond that model in suggesting that the relevant formative experiences may, themselves, be strongly affected by biologically influenced personality variables.

Most biological research into sexual orientation has been premised on what we call the "model of direct biological effects" (Figure 9.3). We call this model "direct" because the arrow of causation goes directly from biological factors to sexual orientation. That is, the actions of biological factors such as genes or hormones would directly influence the organization

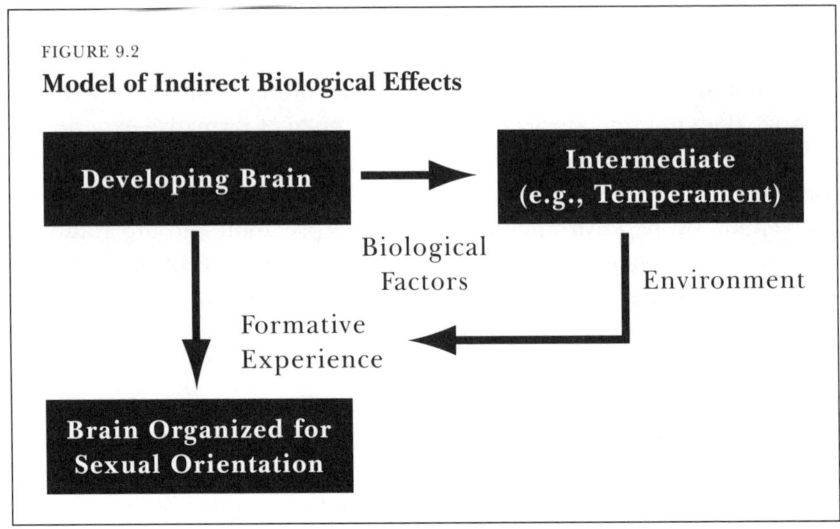

FIGURE 9.2
Model of Indirect Biological Effects

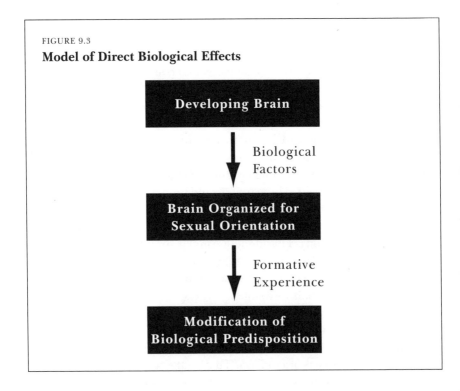

FIGURE 9.3
Model of Direct Biological Effects

Developing Brain

Biological
Factors

Brain Organized for
Sexual Orientation

Formative
Experience

Modification of
Biological Predisposition

of the hypothetical brain circuits that mediate sexual orientation. According to this model, the brain would have an intrinsic (i.e., constitutional) sexual orientation or predisposition toward one orientation or another. This constitutional orientation or predisposition could nonetheless be subsequently modified by experience. Sandor Rado endorsed a direct model when he articulated the psychoanalytic view in 1969: "We assume that heterosexuality is the biological norm and unless interfered with all individuals are heterosexual."[3] Subsequently, the sexologist John Money speculated that some individuals may be born with homosexual brains—perhaps due to an error of sexual differentiation.[4] In many such cases, however, Money suggested that social factors may override the biological predisposition. More recently, some gay rights activists have maintained that, by bolstering the argument that sexual orientation is not chosen, the biological evidence will enhance society's tolerance of homosexuality, making a variety of social and political goals more easily attainable. However, to be strong, arguments for the rights of gay men and lesbians should be cast in terms of justice, privacy, equality, and liberty, not in terms of lack of choice or genetic determinism.

The existing biological data relevant to sexual orientation are equally compatible with both the direct and indirect models. The distinction between these models can be appreciated by considering how they lead to different interpretations of three of the more robust findings in the sexual orientation literature. The first of these findings is that the propensity to engage in rough-and-tumble play appears to be influenced by prenatal exposure to male hormones. This finding holds across species and laboratories and may even apply to humans.[5] Second, compared to heterosexual men, more, but not all, homosexual men recall a childhood aversion to competitive rough-and-tumble play.[6] Third, compared to heterosexual men, more, but not all, homosexual men recall their fathers as having been distant or rejecting.[7]

In a direct model interpretation, the aversion to rough-and-tumble play is merely the childhood expression of a brain that has been prewired for homosexuality. This is the position of the analyst Richard Isay,[8] who suggests that biological factors wire the brain for sexual orientation and consequently reverse the polarity of the Oedipal complex. In addition to shunning rough-and-tumble play, prehomosexual boys would be erotically interested in their fathers during the Oedipal period. Fathers might recoil from their prehomosexual sons' gender nonconformity or sexual inclinations. Even if the father did not recoil, Isay speculates that in adulthood gay men might nevertheless recall their fathers as having been cold or distant in order to avoid conscious awareness of their earlier sexual attraction to them.

Alternatively, an indirect model interpretation postulates that the biologically influenced aversion to rough-and-tumble play does not imply prewiring for homosexuality at all. Instead, such an aversion would become a potent factor predisposing to homosexual development only in particular environments—perhaps where it is stigmatized as "sissy" behavior and causes the boy to see himself as different from his father and male peers.[9] In this scenario, the father's withdrawal from his son would contribute to, rather than result from, his homosexuality. Importantly, the aversion to rough-and-tumble play would arguably have different consequences in environments where it is accepted, perhaps making no contribution to sexual orientation at all.

By giving this example, we do not wish to imply that a distant or rejecting father is a feature of all or even the majority of pathways to male homosexuality. Based on the indirect model, one might conjecture how any number of temperamental variants could influence sexual orientation. A given variant might predispose to homosexuality in one environment and to heterosexuality in another, while making no contribution to sexual orientation in others. To the extent that the indirect model approximates reality, the search for predisposing biological factors will result in incomplete and possibly misleading findings until their interactions with environmental factors are taken into account and controlled for in adequate longitudinal studies. Such studies would need to assess temperaments, cognitions, fantasies, contexts, and internalized (i.e., subjective) experiences, in addition to biological factors and objective behavioral and environmental variables.

Biological Theory

The Prenatal Hormone Hypothesis

Because of the difficulties in conceptualizing and executing research premised on the indirect model, most biological research into sexual orientation has been premised on the Direct Model paradigm. This is especially true of research in the disciplines of endocrinology and neuroanatomy, most of which has been guided by the prenatal hormonal hypothesis. According to this hypothesis, the brain of a fetus has the potential to develop as either male or female. In rats, we know that sex differences arise from variances in early exposure to androgens (the so-called male hormones) and their metabolites. Either genetic sex will develop a male-typical brain if exposed to male hormones in early development, and, conversely, either genetic sex will develop a female-typical brain if not exposed to these hormones at the right time.[10]

Some proponents of this hypothesis suggest that sexual orientation is simply a sexually dimorphic brain function. By "sexually dimorphic," we mean having two forms, one of which is associated with heterosexual men and the other with heterosexual women. This assumption leads researchers to try to define two archetypes for the human brain or its components: a female type that would be shared by heterosexual women and gay men and drive sexual attraction to men, and a male type that would drive sexual attraction to women. Thus, homosexuality is sometimes conceptualized as a condition of "central nervous pseudohermaphroditism."[11] The assumption that homosexuality results from a sex-reversed or an incompletely sexually differentiated brain is referred to in this chapter as the "intersex assumption." This assumption appears to be culture bound. For example, not all cultures have associated homosexuality with gender atypicality.[12]

The prenatal hormonal hypothesis of sexual orientation draws heavily on the observation that experimenters can elicit a female mating posture (i.e., lordosis or saddle back) from genetically male rats by inducing a deficiency of male hormones during a critical early phase of brain development. Conversely, male mating behavior (i.e., mounting) is shown by female rats that were exposed to androgens at an early stage.[13]

There are major problems in extrapolating from these findings to sexual orientation in humans. First, in the paradigm of the neuroendocrine laboratory, the male rat that shows lordosis when mounted by another male is considered the homosexual. Importantly, however, lordosis is little more than a reflex. The male rat that displays lordosis when mounted by another male will also display the posture if its back is stroked by a researcher. We cannot deduce anything about sexual motivation in the male that exhibits this posture. Ironically, however, the male that does display sexual motivation in this paradigm—the mounter—escapes scientific scrutiny and labeling, as does the female that displays lordosis when mounted by another female. As the psychoanalyst Diana Miller puts it, "There simply are no gay rat couples in the neuroendocrine laboratory."[14]

We certainly do not believe that when two people of the same sex engage in sexual intercourse, only one of them is homosexual, depending on who takes what positions. Human sexual orientation is defined not by motor patterns during copulation, but by erotic responsiveness and self-identification. It is unlikely that prenatal hormones influence phenomena as complex as human sexual orientation in the same direct way they organize the motor components of the mating behaviors of rats.

Some researchers have begun to acknowledge the problem of equating behaviors in rodents with sexual orientation and have thus begun to employ a variety of strategies to actually assess partner preference in animals. Even these studies may have little relevance to human sexual orientation. In order for the genetic male rodent to behave as a female, with respect to either partner preference or lordosis behavior, he must be exposed to extreme hormonal abnormalities that are unlikely to occur outside the neuroendocrine laboratory. Not only must he be castrated as a neonate, depriving him of androgens, but in order to activate the display of female-typical behaviors and preferences, he must also be injected with estrogens in adulthood.[15] It is difficult to see how this situation has any bearing on human sexual orientation when gay men and lesbians have hormonal profiles that are indistinguishable from those of their heterosexual counterparts.[16] Nor do the vast majority of homosexuals exhibit stigmata indicative of sexually atypical prenatal hormone levels.

A final problem for much neurobiological research into sexual orientation is that it assumes the existence of sex differences in the human brain in circuits believed to be involved in sexual orientation.[17] Despite dozens of inadequately corroborated reports of sex differences in the human brain over the past 150 years, all we can say with confidence is that the human brain tends to be slightly larger in men than in women.[18] Even if other sex differences can be demonstrated convincingly, it would be naive to merely assume that they have anything to do with sexual orientation based on our current understanding of the brain. At present, we simply do not know how or where sexual orientation is represented in the brain.

Biological Evidence

Neuroendocrinology

In addition to influencing mating behaviors, androgen activity in the developing rodent brain determines the signal relayed to the pituitary gland in response to high blood levels of estrogen—one of the so-called female hormones. If rats experience high androgen levels at a certain early stage of development (as normal males do), the adult brain will respond to estrogen by directing the pituitary gland to decrease its secretion of luteinizing hormone (LH). If the rodent brain has been deprived of these high androgen levels (as normal females are), it will subsequently respond to high levels of estrogen by directing the pituitary to produce more LH—a positive feedback cycle required for normal ovulation and fertility.

Two laboratories have published evidence suggesting that gay men exhibit femalelike patterns of LH secretion in response to estrogen injections.[19] While these studies assume that the brain regulates LH release in primates the same way it does in rodents, there is much evidence against that view.

In primates, the brain mechanism regulating LH appears to be the same in both sexes rather than taking two sexually distinct forms, as it does in rodents.[20] (Women and men have different patterns of LH secretion, of course, but that is because LH secretion is regulated differently by testes and ovaries. In other words, LH secretion seems to differ between men and women not because they have different brains, but because they have different gonads. Male and female rodents have different brains in addition to having different gonads.) Consequently, there is little reason to believe that the brain mechanism for regulating LH secretion should be atypical in homosexual men. If this mechanism is the same in men and women, then one cannot logically suggest that it should be feminized in gay men. In the absence of a sex difference, the concept of "typical of the other sex" becomes meaningless.

Brain Anatomy

Since roughly 1974, sex differences have been confirmed in the size of several brain structures in a variety of laboratory animals. These findings have generated speculation concerning the existence of parallel differences in the human brain associated not only with sex but also with sexual orientation. Most research in this area has been premised on the intersex assumption; and typically proceeds by first trying to identify sex differences and then seeing if any alleged sex difference is either sex-reversed or incompletely differentiated in homosexuals.

Hypothalamus

Most of the structural sex differences identified to date involve specific cell groups within a broad region of the rodent hypothalamus that participates in regulating a variety of functions including sexually dimorphic copulatory behaviors. Like the sex differences in copulatory behaviors, several of the structural sex differences in the rodent brain have been demonstrated to develop in response to sex differences in early androgen exposure: high androgen levels at the appropriate time lead to male-typical structures, while low levels lead to female-typical structures. Consequently, the behavioral sex differences are thought to be mediated, at least in part, by the structural differences.

The best-studied anatomical sex difference in the rodent brain involves a cell group that straddles the medial preoptic and anterior regions of the hypothalamus. In the rat, where it was initially described, this structure is five to eight times larger in males than in females and is called the "sexually dimorphic nucleus of the preoptic area" (SDN-POA).[21]

Damage to the preoptic region of the brain has been demonstrated to decrease mounting behavior in a variety of laboratory species, while electrical stimulation of the region elicits mounting behavior. These observations, and the finding that the size of the SDN-POA correlates positively with mounting frequencies in rats, have established the belief that the preoptic area participates in regulating male sex behavior.[22]

Interstitial Nuclei. Speculation that the SDN-POA may be involved in the regulation of reproductive behavior in male rats has stimulated considerable interest in finding a comparable nucleus in humans. Four candidates have been identified and designated as the interstitial nuclei of the anterior hypothalamus (INAH1, INAH2, INAH3, and INAH4). Measurement of these nuclei by different laboratories has generated inconsistent results.[23] Nevertheless, two studies are in agreement in finding the INAH3 to be larger in men than in women. One of these, the highly publicized study conducted by Simon LeVay, also reported that in homosexual men the INAH3 was as small as in women.[24]

LeVay's study has been widely interpreted as strong evidence that the size of the INAH3 determines or influences sexual orientation. The common criticisms that his study is invalid because of inadequate sexual histories and small sample sizes are not very convincing. These factors would have actually decreased, rather than increased, the probability of obtaining statistically significant results. As reviewed elsewhere, a variety of more valid criticisms detract from the study.[25] Only three of these will be considered here.

First, the finding has not been corroborated, and studies based on measurements of human brain structures have a dismal record of replicability. In light of this track record, Heino Meyer-Bahlburg suggested at the 1993 annual meeting of the American Psychiatric Association that, as a rule of thumb, no such study should be accepted until it has been replicated three times over—provided that there are no intervening failures of replication.[26] To date, no report of a difference in the structure of the human brain associated with either sex or sexual orientation has met this criterion.

Second, all of the brains of gay men came from persons with AIDS. This is relevant because, at the time of death, virtually all men with AIDS have decreased testosterone levels as the result of AIDS itself or of the side effects of particular treatments. In some laboratory animals, the size of a structure comparable to the SDN-POA of rats varies with the amount of testosterone in the animal's circulation. Thus, it is possible that the effects on the size of the INAH3 that were attributed to sexual orientation were actually due to the hormonal abnormalities associated with AIDS. The inclusion in this study of a few brains from heterosexual men with AIDS did not constitute an adequate control to rule out this possibility.

Third, much speculation concerning the function of the INAH3 is based on the assumption that it is the homologue of the rat's SDN-POA. But the function of the rat's SDN-POA has eluded researchers for years. In fact, the SDN-POA can be totally destroyed without any discernible effect on the mounting behavior of male rats. While brain damage in the vicinity of the SDN-POA does decrease mounting behavior, the precise site of the effective damage appears to be above the SDN-POA itself. Similarly, it has been claimed that damage to the preoptic area causes male monkeys to become apparently indifferent to sex with female monkeys. But the data are more complex. Though they decreased the frequency of copulatory behavior in male monkeys, preoptic lesions did not eliminate it entirely. Moreover, the lesions actually appeared to increase the frequency with which males would press a lever for access to females.

The Suprachiasmatic Nucleus (SCN). In contrast to the INAH3, this nucleus has been reported to be larger in homosexual men than in heterosexuals.[27] This study has yet to be replicated and also relied on the brains of homosexual men with AIDS and is thus subject to many of the same criticisms as LeVay's study of the INAH3. Unlike the INAH3, however, the size of the SCN was not found to vary with sex. Furthermore, the SCN is not believed to be directly involved in the regulation of sexual behaviors. Thus, if the dimorphism proves to be replicable, it will not lend support to the notion that sexual orientation reflects the sexually differentiated state of the brain. Alternative explanations will have to be considered.

The Brain Commissures

In addition to the hypothalamus, researchers have begun to seek sex and sexual orientation differences in the brain commissures, the bundles of fibers that interconnect the left and right halves of the brain. These studies and their rationale are critiqued more fully elsewhere.[28] Briefly, one as yet uncorroborated study, which examined the brains of gay men with AIDS, reported the anterior commissure (AC) to be larger in women and homosexual men than in heterosexual men. Even though there was a statistical difference between these groups in the average size of the AC, the size of the AC of twenty-seven out of thirty homosexual men fell within the range established by thirty heterosexual men. Thus, even if this study proves replicable, the size of the AC alone would tell us nothing about an individual's sexual orientation. Moreover, the only other laboratory to examine the AC for sex differences reported a tendency for it to be larger in men than in women.

There has also been speculation that the morphology of the corpus callosum may be sex reversed in homosexuals; however, no sex difference has been consistently reported in the callosum even though approximately three dozen studies have looked for one. Moreover, a meta-analysis conducted on forty-nine of these studies found no evidence for a main effect of sex on any aspect of callosal morphology.[29]

The Genetic Evidence

Like the neuroendocrinological research, some genetic studies have also been premised on the intersex assumption. These include attempts to show that homosexuals have opposite sex chromatin in their cells[30] and studies seeking to link homosexuality with genetically controlled aberrations in the process of sexual differentiation.[31] None of those studies have met with success. Importantly, however, some recent genetic studies are not necessarily committed to the intersex assumption and may open the door to consideration of more diverse and complex pathways to sexual orientations.

Several studies suggest that the brothers of homosexual men are more likely to be homosexual than are men without gay brothers,[32] but they are not really helpful in distinguishing between genetic and environmental influences because most related individuals share environmental variables as well as genes. Disentangling genetic and environmental influences requires adoption studies.

The only heritability study of homosexuality that included an adoption component was the highly publicized study of J. Michael Bailey and Richard Pillard.[33] This study suggested a significant environmental contribution to the development of sexual orientation in men, in addition to a moderate genetic influence. This study assessed sexual orientation not only in identical and fraternal twins, but also in nontwin biological brothers and unrelated adopted brothers of gay men. If there were no environmental effect on sexual orientation, then the rate of homosexuality among adopted brothers should be equal to the base rate of homosexuality in the population, which recent studies place at somewhere between 2 and 5 percent. The fact that the observed concordance rate was 11 percent (two to five times higher than expected given the estimates) suggests a major environmental contribution—especially when we consider that the rate for homosexuality among nontwin biological brothers was 9 percent. If the concordance rate for homosexuality among nontwin brothers is the same whether or not the brothers are biologically related, then the concordance rate cannot be explained genetically.

The concordance rate for identical twins (52 percent) was, however, much higher than the rate for fraternal twins (22 percent). The higher concordance rate in the identical twins is consistent with a genetic effect because identical twins share all of their genes, while fraternal twins, on average, share only half of their genes. Nevertheless, the increased concordance rate in identical twins cannot be attributed entirely to increased gene sharing. When considered together, the data from the twins and the data from the adopted brothers suggest that the increased concordance in identical twins is due to the combination of both genetic and environmental influences. Further, the combined effect of genetic and environmental influences might not simply be their sum; instead, these factors could interact in a nonadditive or synergistic manner. In our opinion, the most interesting and consistent finding of the recent heritability studies is that, despite sharing both their genes and familial environments, approximately half of the monozygotic twins were nonetheless discordant for sexual orientation. This finding, which has been consistent across studies,[34] underscores just how little we actually know about the origins of sexual orientation.

Of all the recent biological studies, the genetic linkage study by Dean Hamer's group is the most complex conceptually, and the most likely to be misinterpreted—especially by those unfamiliar with the rationale of genetic linkage studies.[35] Briefly, this study presented statistical evidence that genes influencing sexual orientation may reside in the q28 region of the X chromosome. Contrary to popular belief, the study did not discover any particular genetic sequence associated with homosexuality. Also, a Canadian team has been unable to duplicate the finding using a comparable experimental design.[36]

While some authors have recently speculated about the existence of "genes for homosexuality," genes in themselves cannot directly specify any behavior or psychological phenomenon. Instead, genes direct a particular pattern of RNA synthesis that in turn specifies the production of a particular protein that in turn may influence behavior. There are necessarily many intervening pathways between a gene and a specific behavior and even more intervening variables between a gene and a pattern that involves both thinking and behaving. The term "homosexual gene" is, therefore, without meaning, unless one proposes that a particular gene, perhaps through a hormonal mechanism, organizes the brain specifically to support the desire to have sex with people of the same sex. No one has, however, presented compelling evidence in support of such a simple and direct link between genes and sexual orientation. As discussed by Terry R. McGuire, the process of growing from a single cell to a functional adult is chaotic and dynamic. It is possible that behavior, in general, and sexual orientation, in particular, involve idiosyncratic processes. In development, minor events (genetic, environmental, and experiential) can be amplified to have major effects.[37]

Importantly, "homosexual genes" are not required for homosexuality to be heritable. This is because heritability has a precise technical meaning and merely reflects the degree to which a given outcome is linked to genetic factors. It says nothing about the nature of those factors nor about their mechanism of action. Homosexuality would be heritable even if genes worked through a very indirect mechanism, such as that outlined in our model of indirect biological effects.

Summary

To sum up, the current genetic, hormonal, and neuroanatomical evidence on human sexual orientation is inconclusive. That does not suggest that biology is irrelevant, just that the precise contribution made by any biological factor has yet to be determined. While it is conceivable that the role of some biological factors may be direct, it is equally plausible that the primary influence of biological factors is on temperament, which in turn influences the way sexual orientation unfolds in the context of individual learning and experience. There may be no set of biologically influenced temperamental or personality traits that inevitably leads to homosexuality. If not, as we have emphasized previously, the search for predisposing biological factors will result in inconclusive and potentially misleading findings until their interactions with environmental factors are taken into account and are controlled for in adequate longitudinal studies.

· CHAPTER TEN ·

The Exotic-Becomes-Erotic Theory of Sexual Orientation

DARYL J. BEM

Daryl J. Bem, professor of psychology at Cornell University, presents a developmental theory of erotic/romantic attraction in which biological variables (such as genes) do not code for sexual orientation per se, but instead, for childhood temperaments that influence a child's preferences for sex-typical or sex-atypical activities and playmates. These preferences lead children to feel different from opposite- or same-sex peers—to perceive them as unfamiliar and exotic. This feeling of difference, in turn, produces heightened nonspecific physiological arousal that subsequently gets eroticized to that same class of unfamiliar peers: exotic becomes erotic. Bem also analyzes the concept of sexual orientation and discusses the politics of his theory.

· · · · ·

The question "What causes homosexuality?" is both politically suspect and scientifically misconceived. Politically suspect because it is so frequently motivated by an agenda of prevention and cure. Scientifically misconceived because it presumes that heterosexuality is so well understood—so obviously the "natural" evolutionary consequence of reproductive advantage—that only deviations from it are theoretically problematic. Accordingly, the theory described in this article addresses the question "What causes sexual orientation?" and proposes the same basic account for both opposite-sex and same-sex desire. In particular, Figure 10.1 displays the proposed temporal sequence of events that leads to sexual orientation for most men and

This article is a revised and much-shortened version of Daryl J. Bem, "Exotic Becomes Exotic: A Developmental Theory of Sexual Orientation," *Psychological Review* 103(1996): 320–335.

FIGURE 10.1

The Temporal Sequence of Events Leading to Sexual Orientation for Most Men and Women in a Gender-Polarizing Culture

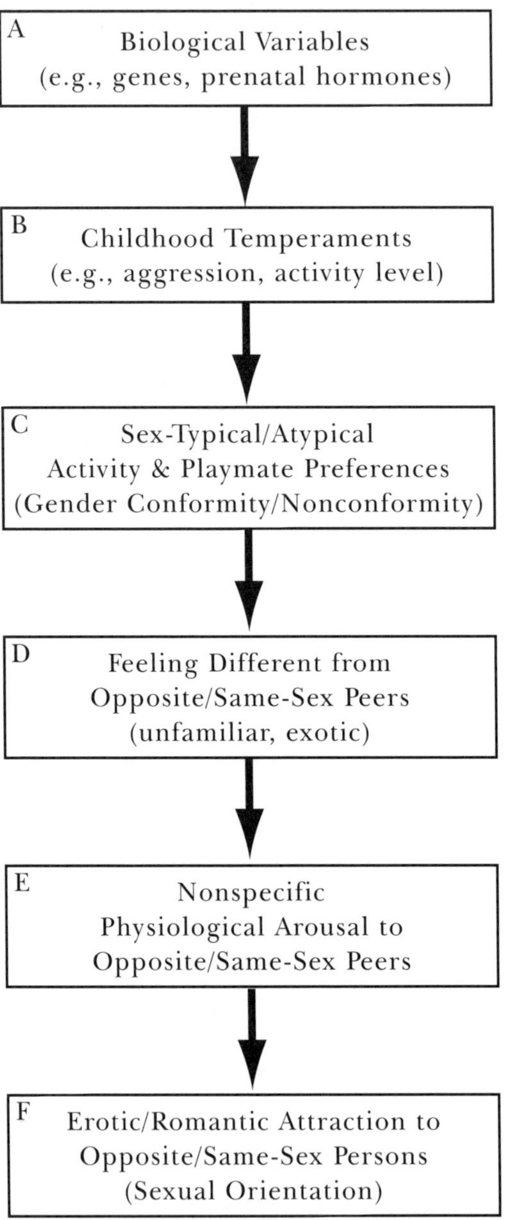

women in a gender-polarizing culture like ours—a culture that emphasizes the differences between the sexes by pervasively organizing both the perceptions and realities of communal life around the male/female dichotomy. The sequence begins at the top of the figure with biological variables (labeled *A*) and ends at the bottom with erotic/romantic attraction (*F*).

A → *B:* Biological variables such as genes or prenatal hormones do not code for sexual orientation per se, but for childhood temperaments, such as aggression or activity level.

B → *C:* Children's temperaments predispose them to enjoy some activities more than others. One child will enjoy rough-and-tumble play and competitive team sports (male-typical activities); another will prefer to socialize quietly or play jacks or hopscotch (female-typical activities). Children will also prefer to play with peers who share their activity preferences. Children who prefer sex-typical activities and same-sex playmates are referred to as "gender conforming"; children who prefer sex-atypical activities and opposite-sex playmates are referred to as "gender nonconforming."

C → *D:* Gender-conforming children will feel different from opposite-sex peers, perceiving them as unfamiliar and exotic. Similarly, gender-nonconforming children will perceive same-sex peers as unfamiliar and exotic.

D → *E:* These feelings of unfamiliarity produce heightened physiological arousal. For the male-typical child, it may be felt as antipathy toward girls; for the female-typical child, it may be felt as timidity or apprehension in the presence of boys. A particularly clear example is provided by the "sissy" boy who is taunted by male peers for his gender nonconformity and, as a result, is likely to experience the strong physiological arousal of fear and anger in their presence. The theory claims, however, that every child, conforming or nonconforming, experiences heightened nonspecific physiological arousal in the presence of peers from whom he or she feels different. In this most common case, the arousal will not necessarily be affectively toned or consciously felt.

E → *F:* This physiological arousal is transformed in later years into erotic/romantic attraction. Steps *D* → *E* and *E* → *F* thus encompass specific psychological mechanisms that transform exotic into erotic (*D* → *F*). For brevity, the entire sequence outlined in Figure 10.1 will be referred to as the "EBE (exotic becomes erotic)" theory of sexual orientation.

As noted above, Figure 10.1 does not describe an inevitable, universal path to sexual orientation but, rather, the most common path followed by men and women in a gender-polarizing culture like ours. Individual variations, alternative paths, and cultural influences on sexual orientation are discussed later in the chapter.

Evidence for the Theory

Evidence for EBE theory is organized into the following narrative sequence: gender conformity or nonconformity in childhood is a causal antecedent of sexual orientation in adulthood ($C \rightarrow F$). This is so because gender conformity or nonconformity causes a child to perceive opposite- or same-sex peers as exotic ($C \rightarrow D$), and the exotic class of peers subsequently becomes erotically or romantically attractive to him or her ($D \rightarrow F$). This occurs because exotic peers produce heightened physiological arousal ($D \rightarrow E$) which is subsequently transformed into erotic/romantic attraction ($E \rightarrow F$). This entire sequence of events can be initiated, among other ways, by biological factors that influence a child's temperaments ($A \rightarrow B$), which, in turn, influence his or her preferences for gender-conforming or gender-nonconforming activities and peers ($B \rightarrow C$).

Gender Conformity or Nonconformity in Childhood Is a Causal Antecedent of Sexual Orientation ($C \rightarrow F$)

In a study designed to test hypotheses about the development of sexual orientation, researchers conducted intensive interviews with approximately 1,000 gay men and lesbians and with 500 heterosexual men and women in the San Francisco Bay Area. The study (hereinafter, the San Francisco study) found that childhood gender conformity or nonconformity was not only the strongest, but also the only significant, childhood predictor of later sexual orientation for both men and women. As Table 10.1 shows, the effects were large and significant.[1]

TABLE 10.1

Percentage of Respondents Reporting Gender-Nonconforming Preferences and Behaviors During Childhood

	Men		*Women*	
Response	*Gay* (n=686)	*Heterosexual* (n=337)	*Lesbian* (n=293)	*Heterosexual* (n=140)
Had not enjoyed sex-typical activities	63	10	63	15
Had enjoyed sex-atypical activities	48	11	81	61
Atypically sex-typed (masculinity/femininity)	56	8	80	24
Most childhood friends were opposite sex	42	13	60	40

Note: All chi-square comparisons between gay and heterosexual subgroups are significant at $p < .0001$.

For example, gay men were significantly more likely than heterosexual men to report that as children they had not enjoyed boys' activities (e.g., baseball and football), had enjoyed girls' activities (e.g., hopscotch, playing house, and jacks), and had been nonmasculine. These were the three variables that defined gender nonconformity in the study. Additionally, gay men were more likely than heterosexual men to have had girls as childhood friends. The corresponding comparisons between lesbian and heterosexual women were also large and significant.

It is also clear from the table that relatively more women than men had enjoyed sex-atypical activities and had opposite-sex friends during childhood. (In fact, more heterosexual women than gay men had enjoyed boys' activities as children—61 percent versus 37 percent, respectively.)

Many other studies have also shown that gay men and lesbians are more likely than heterosexual men and women to have gender-nonconforming behaviors and interests in childhood, including some studies that began with children and followed them into adulthood. The largest of these reported that approximately 75 percent of gender-nonconforming boys became bisexual or homosexual in adulthood, compared with only 4 percent of gender-conforming boys.[2]

Gender Conformity and Nonconformity Produce Feelings of Being Different from Opposite- and Same-Sex Peers, Respectively ($C \rightarrow D$)

EBE theory proposes that gender-nonconforming children will come to feel different from their same-sex peers. In the San Francisco study, 70 percent of gay men and lesbians reported that they had felt different from same-sex peers in childhood, compared with only 38 percent and 51 percent of heterosexual men and women, respectively ($p < .0005$ for both gay/heterosexual comparisons). They further reported that they had felt this way throughout childhood and adolescence.

When asked in what way they had felt different from same-sex peers, gay men were most likely to say that they did not like sports; lesbians were most likely to say that they were more interested in sports or were more masculine than other girls. In contrast, those heterosexual men and women who had felt different from their same-sex peers typically cited differences unrelated to gender, such as being poorer, more intelligent, or more introverted. Heterosexual women frequently cited differences in physical appearance.

Exotic Becomes Erotic ($D \rightarrow F$)

The heart of EBE theory is the proposition that individuals become erotically or romantically attracted to those who were unfamiliar to them in childhood. We have already seen some evidence for this in Table 10.1: those who played more with girls in childhood, gay men and heterosexual women, preferred men as sexual/romantic partners in later years; those who played more with boys in childhood, lesbian women and heterosexual men, preferred women as sexual/romantic partners in later years. Moreover, it has long been known that childhood familiarity is antithetical to later erotic or romantic attraction. For example, Westermarck observed over a century ago that married couples who had been betrothed in childhood experienced problematic sexual relationships when the girl had been taken in by the future husband's family and treated like one of the siblings.

A contemporary example is provided by children on Israeli kibbutzim, who are raised communally with age-mates in mixed-sex groups and exposed to one another constantly during their entire childhood. Sex play is not discouraged and is quite intensive during early childhood. After childhood, there is no formal or informal pressure or sanction against heterosexual activity within the peer group from educators, parents, or members of the peer group itself. Yet despite all this, there is a virtual absence of erotic attraction between peer group members in adolescence or adulthood. A review of nearly 3,000 marriages contracted by second-generation adults in all Israeli kibbutzim revealed that there was not a single case of an intrapeer group marriage.[3]

The Sambian culture in New Guinea illustrates the phenomenon in a homosexual context. Sambian males believe that boys cannot attain manhood without ingesting semen from older males. At seven years of age, Sambian boys are removed from the family household and initiated into secret male rituals, including ritualized homosexuality. For the next several years, they live in the men's clubhouse and regularly fellate older male adolescents. When they reach sexual maturity, they reverse roles and are fellated by younger initiates. During this entire time, they have no sexual contact with girls or women. And yet, when it comes time to marry and father children in their late teens or early twenties, all but a small minority of Sambian males become exclusively heterosexual. Although Sambian boys enjoy their homosexual activities, the context of close familiarity in which it occurs apparently prevents the development of strongly charged homoerotic feelings.[4]

How Does Exotic Become Erotic? ($D \rightarrow E \rightarrow F$): The Extrinsic Arousal Effect

In his first-century Roman handbook, *The Art of Love,* Ovid advised any man who was interested in sexual seduction to take the woman in whom he was interested to a gladiatorial tournament, where she would more easily be aroused to passion. He did not say why this should be so, however, and it was not until 1887 that an elaboration appeared in the literature:

> Love can only be excited by strong and vivid emotion, and it is almost immaterial whether these emotions are agreeable or disagreeable. The Cid wooed the proud heart of Donna Ximene, whose father he had slain, by shooting one after another of her pet pigeons.[5]

A contemporary explanation of this effect is that it is a special case of the two-factor theory of emotion. That theory states that the physiological arousal of our autonomic nervous system provides the cues that we are feeling emotional but that the more subtle judgment of which emotion we are feeling often depends on our cognitive appraisal of the surrounding circumstances. Thus, the experience of passionate love or erotic/romantic attraction results from the conjunction of physiological arousal and the cognitive causal attribution (or misattribution) that the arousal has been elicited by the potential lover.[6]

There is now extensive experimental evidence that an individual who has been physiologically aroused will show heightened sexual responsiveness to an appropriate target stimulus. In one set of studies, male participants were physiologically aroused by running in place, by hearing an audiotape of a comedy routine, or by hearing an audiotape of a grisly killing. They then viewed a taped interview with a physically attractive woman. Finally, they rated the woman's attractiveness, sexiness, and the degree to which they would like to date or kiss her. No matter how the arousal had been elicited, participants were more erotically responsive to the attractive woman than were control participants who had not been aroused.[7]

This extrinsic arousal effect can also be detected physiologically. In a pair of studies, men or women watched a sequence of two videotapes. The first portrayed either an anxiety-inducing or nonanxiety-inducing scene; the second videotape portrayed a nude heterosexual couple engaging in sexual foreplay. Preexposure to the anxiety-inducing scene produced greater penile tumescence in men and greater vaginal blood volume increases in women in response to the erotic scene than did preexposure to the nonanxiety-inducing scene.[8]

In short, physiological arousal, regardless of its source or affective tone, can subsequently be experienced cognitively, emotionally, and physiologically as erotic/romantic attraction. At that point, it *is* erotic/romantic attraction. The pertinent question, then, is whether this effect can account for the link between the hypothesized "exotic" physiological arousal in childhood and the erotic/romantic attraction later in life. One difficulty is that the effect occurs in the laboratory over brief time intervals, whereas the proposed developmental process spans several years. The time gap may be more apparent than real, however. As noted earlier, an individual's sense of being different from same- or opposite-sex peers is not a one-time event, but a protracted and sustained experience throughout the childhood and adolescent years. This implies that the arousal will also be present throughout that time, ready to be converted into erotic or romantic attraction whenever the maturational, cognitive, and situational factors coalesce to provide the defining moment.

In fact, the laboratory experiments may actually underestimate the strength and reliability of the effect in real life. In the experiments, the arousal is deliberately elicited by a source extrinsic to the intended target, and there is disagreement over whether the effect even occurs when participants are aware of that fact. But in the real-life scenario envisioned by EBE theory, the physiological arousal is genuinely elicited by the class of individuals to which the erotic/romantic attraction develops. The exotic arousal and the erotic arousal are thus likely to be subjectively indistinguishable to the individual.[9]

The Biological Connection: $(A \rightarrow F)$ versus $(A \rightarrow B)$

In recent years, researchers, the mass media, and segments of the lesbian/gay/bisexual community have rushed to embrace the thesis that a homosexual orientation is coded in the genes or determined by prenatal hormones and brain neuroanatomy. In contrast, EBE theory proposes that biological factors influence sexual orientation only indirectly, by intervening earlier in the chain of events to determine a child's temperaments and subsequent activity preferences.

One technique used to determine whether a trait is correlated with an individual's genotype (inherited characteristics) is to compare monozygotic (identical) twins, who share all their genes, with dizygotic (fraternal) twins, who, on average, share only 50 percent of their genes. If a trait is more highly correlated across monozygotic pairs of twins than across dizygotic pairs, this provides evidence for a correlation between the trait and the genotype. Using this technique, researchers have recently reported evidence for a correlation between an individual's genotype and his or her sexual orientation. For example, in a sample of gay men who had male twins, 52 percent of monozygotic twin brothers were also gay compared with only 22 percent of dizygotic twin brothers. In a comparable sample of lesbians, 48 percent of monozygotic twin sisters were also lesbian compared with only 16 percent of dizygotic twin sisters. A more systematic study of nearly 5,000 twins who had been drawn from a twin registry confirmed the genetic correlation for men but not for women.[10]

But these same studies provide even stronger evidence for the link proposed by EBE theory between an individual's genotype and his or her childhood gender nonconformity—even when sexual orientation is held constant. For example, in the 1991 twin study of gay men, the correlation on gender nonconformity in which both brothers were gay was .76 for monozygotic twins but only .43 for gay dizygotic twins, implying that gender conformity is significantly correlated with the genotype. Childhood gender nonconformity was also significantly correlated with the genotype for both men and women in the large twin registry study, even though sexual orientation itself was not correlated for the women. These studies are thus consistent with the link specified by EBE theory between the genotype and gender nonconformity ($A \rightarrow C$).

EBE theory further specifies that this link is composed of two parts; a link between the genotype and childhood temperaments ($A \rightarrow B$) and a link between those temperaments and gender nonconformity ($B \rightarrow C$). The temperaments most likely to be involved are aggression—and its benign cousin, rough-and-tumble play—and activity level. There is now substantial evidence that boys' play shows higher levels of rough-and-tumble play and activity than girls' play, that gender-nonconforming children of both sexes are sex-atypical on both traits, and that both traits are significantly correlated with the genotype.[11]

In addition to these empirical findings, there are, I believe, conceptual grounds for preferring the EBE account to the competing hypothesis that there is a direct link between biology and sexual orientation. First, no theoretical rationale for a direct link between the genotype and sexual orientation has been clearly articulated, let alone established. At first glance, the theoretical rationale would appear to be nothing less than the powerful and elegant theory of evolution. The belief that sexual orientation is coded in the genes would appear to be just the general case of the implicit assumption, mentioned in the introduction, that heterosexuality is the obvious "natural" evolutionary consequence of reproductive advantage. But if that is true, then a homosexual orientation is an evolutionary anomaly that requires an explanation of how lesbians and gay men would pass on their "homosexual genes" to successive generations. Although several hypothetical scenarios have been suggested, they have been faulted on both theoretical and empirical grounds.[12]

But the main problem with the direct-link hypothesis is that it fails to spell out any developmental process through which an individual's genotype actually gets transformed into his or her sexual orientation—which is precisely what EBE theory attempts to do. It is not that an argument for a direct link has been made and found wanting; it is that it has not yet been made.

I am certainly willing to concede that heterosexual behavior is reproductively advantageous, but it does not follow that it must therefore be sustained through genetic transmission. In particular, EBE theory suggests that heterosexuality is the most common outcome across time and culture because virtually all human societies polarize the sexes to some extent, setting up a sex-based division of labor and power, emphasizing or exaggerating sex differences, and, in general, superimposing the male/female dichotomy on virtually every aspect of communal life. These gender-polarizing practices ensure that most boys and girls will grow up seeing the other sex as unfamiliar and exotic—and, hence, erotic.

The more general point is that as long as the environment supports or promotes a reproductively successful behavior sufficiently often, it will not necessarily get programmed into the genes. For example, it is presumably reproductively advantageous for ducks to mate with other ducks, but as long as most baby ducklings first meet—and get imprinted on—other ducks, evolution can simply implant the imprinting process itself into the species rather than the specific content of what, reproductively speaking, needs to be imprinted. Analogously, because most cultures ensure that the two sexes will see each other as exotic, it would be sufficient for evolution to implant exotic-becomes-erotic processes into our species rather than heterosexuality per se. In fact, ethological studies of birds show that an exotic-becomes-erotic mechanism is actually a component of sexual imprinting. If ducks, which are genetically free to mate with any moving object, have not perished from the earth, then neither shall we.[13]

In general, any biological factor that correlates with one or more of the intervening processes proposed by EBE theory could also emerge as a correlate of sexual orientation. Even if EBE theory turns out to be wrong, the more general point, that a mediating personality variable could account for observed correlations between biological variables and sexual orientation, still holds.

Individual Variations and Alternative Paths

As noted earlier, Figure 10.1 is not intended to describe an inevitable, universal path to sexual orientation but only the path followed by most men and women in a gender-polarizing culture. Individual variations can arise in several ways. First, different individuals might enter the EBE path at different points in the sequence. For example, a child might come to feel different from same-sex peers not because of a temperamentally induced preference for gender-nonconforming activities, but because of an atypical lack of contact with same-sex peers or a physical disability. In general, EBE theory predicts that the effect of any childhood variable on an individual's sexual orientation depends on whether it prompts him or her to feel more similar to or more different from same-sex or opposite-sex peers.

Individual variations can also arise from differences in how individuals interpret the "exotic" arousal emerging from the childhood years, an interpretation that is inevitably guided by social norms and expectations. For example, girls might be more socially primed to interpret the arousal as romantic attraction, whereas boys might be more primed to interpret it as sexual arousal. Certainly, most individuals in our culture are primed to anticipate, recognize, and interpret opposite-sex arousal as erotic or romantic attraction and to ignore, repress, or differently interpret comparable same-sex arousal. In fact, the heightened visibility of gay men and lesbians in our society is now prompting individuals who experience same-sex arousal to recognize it, label it, and act on it at earlier ages than in previous years.[14]

In some instances, the EBE process itself may be supplemented or even superseded by processes of conditioning or social learning, both positive and negative. Such processes could also produce shifts in an individual's sexual orientation over the life course. For example, the small number of bisexual respondents in the San Francisco study appeared to have added same-sex erotic attraction to an already established heterosexual orientation after adolescence. Similar findings were reported in a more extensive study of bisexual individuals, with some respondents adding heterosexual attraction to a previously established homosexual orientation. This same study also showed that different components of an individual's sexual orientation need not coincide; for example, some of the bisexual respondents were more erotically attracted to one sex but more romantically attracted to the other.[15]

Finally, some women who would otherwise be predicted by the EBE model to have a heterosexual orientation might choose for social or political reasons to center their lives around other women. This could lead them to avoid seeking out men for sexual or romantic relationships, to develop affectional and erotic ties to other women, and to self-identify as lesbians or bisexuals. In general, issues of sexual orientation identity are beyond the formal scope of EBE theory.

Deconstructing the Concept of Sexual Orientation

Nearly fifty years ago, Alfred Kinsey took a major step in deconstructing or redefining the concept of sexual orientation by construing it as a bipolar continuum, ranging from exclusive heterosexuality, through bisexuality, to exclusive homosexuality. Because many of the studies cited in this chapter have selected their respondents on the basis of Kinsey-like scales, EBE theory has necessarily been couched in that language: but the theory itself is not constrained by such bipolar dimensions. In fact, Figure 10.1 actually treats sexual orientation as two separate dimensions—a heteroerotic dimension and a homoerotic dimension—and EBE theory describes the processes that determine an individual's location on each of the two dimensions.

Conceptually, the two paths are independent, thereby allowing for a panoply of individual differences, including several variants of bisexuality (e.g., being erotically attracted to one sex and romantically attracted to the other). Empirically, however, the two dimensions are likely to be negatively correlated in a gender-polarizing culture in which most individuals come to be familiar with one sex while being estranged from the other. EBE theory predicts that this should be especially true for men in American society because, as shown in Table 10.1, boys are less likely than girls to have childhood friends of both sexes. This prediction is supported in a survey of a national probability sample of Americans. When asked to whom they were sexually attracted, men were likely to report that either they were exclusively heterosexual or exclusively homosexual. In contrast, women were more likely to report that they were bisexual than that they were exclusively homosexual.[16]

Culture influences not only the structure and distribution of sexual orientation in a society, but also how its natives, including its biological and behavioral scientists, conceptualize sexual orientation. Like the natives of any gender-polarizing culture, we have learned to look at the world through the lenses of gender, to impose the male/female dichotomy on virtually every aspect of life, especially sexuality. Which brings us to the most deeply embedded cultural assumption of all: that sexual orientation is necessarily based on sex. As Sandra Bem remarked,

> I am not now and never have been a "heterosexual." But neither have I ever been a "lesbian" or a "bisexual." . . . The sex-of-partner dimension implicit in the three categories . . . seems irrelevant to my own particular pattern of erotic attractions and sexual experiences. Although some of the (very few) individuals to whom I have been

> attracted . . . have been men and some have been women, what those individuals have in common has nothing to do with either their biological sex or mine—from which I conclude, not that I am attracted to both sexes, but that my sexuality is organized around dimensions other than sex.[17]

This statement also suggests the shape that sexual orientation might assume in a nongender-polarizing culture, a culture that did not systematically estrange its children from either opposite-sex or same-sex peers. Such children would not grow up to be asexual; rather, their erotic and romantic preferences would simply crystallize around a more diverse and idiosyncratic variety of attributes. Gentlemen might still prefer blonds, but some of those gentlemen (and some ladies) would prefer blonds of any sex. In the final deconstruction, then, EBE theory reduces to but one "essential" principle: exotic becomes erotic.

A Political Postscript[18]

Biological explanations of homosexuality have become more popular with the public in the 1990s, and many members of the lesbian/gay/bisexual community welcome this trend. For example, *The Advocate*, a national gay and lesbian newsmagazine, reported that 61 percent of its readers believed that "it would mostly help gay and lesbian rights if homosexuality were found to be biologically determined."[19]

Because EBE theory proposes that an individual's sexual orientation is more directly the result of childhood experiences than of biological factors, it has prompted concerns that it could encourage an antigay agenda of prevention and "cure." In particular, the theory appears to suggest that parents could prevent their gender-nonconforming children from becoming gay or lesbian by encouraging sex-typical activities and same-sex friendships and by discouraging sex-atypical activities and opposite-sex friendships.

Of course, our society hardly needed EBE theory to suggest such a strategy. The belief that childhood gender nonconformity leads to later homosexuality is already so widely believed that many parents (especially fathers) already discourage their children (especially sons) from engaging in gender-nonconforming behaviors lest they become homosexual. And, if EBE theory is correct in positing that both homosexuality and heterosexuality derive from the same childhood processes, then it is clear that a gender-polarizing society like ours is already spectacularly effective in producing heterosexuality: 85–95 percent of all men and women in the United States are exclusively heterosexual.

But this same figure suggests that those children who continue to express sex-atypical preferences despite such cultural forces must have their gender nonconformity strongly determined by their basic inborn temperaments—as EBE theory proposes. Forcing such children to engage exclusively in sex-typical activities is unlikely to diminish their feelings of being different from same-sex peers and, hence, is unlikely to diminish their subsequent erotic attraction to those peers.

Empirical support for this hypothesis emerges from the longitudinal study of gender-nonconforming boys, cited earlier. About 27 percent of these boys had been entered by their parents into some kind of therapy, including behavioral therapy specifically designed to prevent a homosexual orientation from developing. Compared with parents of other gender-nonconforming boys, these parents were more worried about their sons' later sexuality, which suggests that they probably tried to discourage their sons' gender nonconformity in many other ways as well. All of this effort was for naught: 75 percent of their sons emerged as homosexual or bisexual, slightly more than the percentage of boys whose more laid-back parents had not entered them into therapy.[20] In the context of our society's current gender-polarizing practices, then, EBE theory does not provide a successful strategy for preventing gender-nonconforming children from becoming homosexual adults.

In general, I suggest that biological explanations of homosexuality are no more likely to promote gay-positive attitudes and practices than experienced-based explanations. For example, whenever new evidence for a "gay gene" is announced in the media, the researchers receive inquiries about techniques for detecting pregay children before they are born—presumably so that such children could be aborted. This chilling prevention strategy should disabuse us of the optimistic notion that biological explanations of homosexuality necessarily promote tolerance. Historically, of course, biological theories of human differences have tended to produce the least tolerant attitudes and the most conservative, even draconian, public policies—as in Nazi Germany.

Even more generally, I do not believe that attitudes toward homosexuality are substantially influenced by beliefs about causality; on the contrary, I believe that an individual's beliefs about causality are influenced by his or her preexisting attitudes toward homosexuality: people tend to find most credible those beliefs that best rationalize their attitudes. In short, EBE theory does not threaten the interests of the lesbian/gay/bisexual community any more than does a biological theory.

· CHAPTER ELEVEN ·

The Ethical Relevance of Scientific Research on Sexual Orientation

EDWARD STEIN

Edward Stein, who teaches philosophy and lesbian and gay studies at Yale University, argues that research into the origin of sexual orientation is irrelevant to the case for lesbian and gay rights. Many claim that establishing a "biological basis" for homosexuality would show that gays and lesbians deserve protected group status, or that homosexuality is not a choice, or that homosexuality is "natural" in some relevant sense. Stein examines and rebuts each of these claims, as well as the claim that arguments linking gay and lesbian rights to biology ought to be embraced on pragmatic grounds. He then briefly considers the question of what kind of arguments are *relevant to lesbian and gay rights.*

· · · · ·

> We are interested in obtaining rights for our respective minorities as Negroes, as Jews, and as Homosexuals. Why we are Negroes, Jews or Homosexuals is totally irrelevant, and whether we can be changed to Whites, Christians or heterosexuals is equally irrelevant.
>
> —Franklin E. Kameny, "Speech to the New York Mattachine Society," July 1964[1]

These days, there is quite a bit of scientific research that attempts to answer the question why some people are gay or lesbian and others are not.[2] In

This article is a slightly modified excerpt from "The Relevance of Scientific Research on Sexual Orientation to Lesbian and Gay Rights," *Journal of Homosexuality* 27 (1994); 269–308; simultaneously published in Timothy F. Murphy, ed., *Gay Ethics: Controversies in Outing, Civil Rights and Sexual Science* (Haworth Press, 1994). It is reprinted here with the permission of Haworth Publishing and the author. Some notes have been deleted, some notes have been added, and the notes have been renumbered, in addition to minor editorial revisions.

this essay, I am concerned with the ethical relevance (if any) of such research, in particular, with whether this research is relevant to questions concerning lesbian and gay rights. I argue that the case for lesbian and gay rights is to be made independent of any theory of the origins of sexual orientations. I examine the arguments that people make (at least implicitly) for connecting scientific research concerning sexual orientations to lesbian and gay rights, and I find that these arguments are not up to the task.[3]

Can Scientific Research Advance Lesbian and Gay Rights?

People who think discovering a cause for homosexuality has good moral and political implications for lesbian and gay rights have various arguments in mind for their view, but these arguments seem to have the same general structure. In its schematic form, the argument is as follows:

1. Homosexuality has a biological basis.[4]
2. If homosexuality is biological, then ________.
3. If ________, then lesbian and gay men deserve rights, protection against discrimination, and so forth.
4. Therefore, lesbians and gay men deserve rights, protection against discrimination, and so forth.

The different versions of the argument result from different ways of filling in the blanks. I will consider various ways of doing so in the following subsections.

Protected Group Status

One way to fill in the blanks in the above argument involves the notion of protected groups. In the United States, various categories of people are singled out as warranting special protection against discrimination. For example, race, sex, gender, religious affiliation, age, disability, nationality, and ethnic status are in various contexts singled out as protected categories. If sexual orientation deserves to be a "special status" category, then this might entail that lesbians and gay men deserve rights, and all that accompanies them.[5] Some people have argued that establishing a genetic basis for homosexuality will entail that sexual orientation should count as a protected category. The specific argument is as follows:

1. Homosexuality has a biological basis.

2a. If homosexuality has a biological basis, then sexual orientation should be a protected category.
3a. If sexual orientation is a protected category, then lesbians and gay men deserve rights, protection against discrimination, and so forth.
4. Therefore, lesbians and gay men deserve rights, protection against discrimination, and so forth.

Why should we believe premise 2a? There are, in fact, several reasons for doubting it. First, just because a category has a biological basis does not thereby entail that members of it deserve protected status; there are many categories with a biological basis that are not thought to be morally relevant categories, much less to that warrant protected status. For example, hair color has a biological basis, but people with a particular hair color do not constitute a protected category. Being a biologically based category is thus not a *sufficient* condition for being a category that deserves protected status. It is worth noting that being biologically based is not a *necessary* condition either. For example, being of a certain religious affiliation or nationality is not biologically based, but they constitute protected categories.

A friend of the "protected group" argument for lesbian and gay rights might respond to the hair-color example by pointing out that *if* people were unjustifiably discriminated against on the basis of hair color, then hair color *should* be a protected category and it should be *because* it is genetically based. Behind this response is the notion that being biologically based is not enough to make a category a protected one; there must be some *further* requirement, perhaps that the category is the basis for unjustified discrimination. While there does seem to be something right about it, the further requirement that there be "unjustified discrimination" against members of a category for that category to warrant special protection is not necessarily connected to the biologically based requirement. Any category that is the basis for unjustified discrimination—whether biologically based or not—seems a plausible candidate for a protected category. This very fact—that whether or not the category is biologically based seems to have nothing to do with whether the category should be a protected one—suggests that there is no interesting connection between the causes of sexual orientation and whether sexual orientation should be a protected category. Premise 2a is thereby undermined.

This consideration against 2a aside, there is a further problem with the protected category argument for lesbian and gay rights. Even if being gay or lesbian is biologically based, so much of what is crucial about being a bisexual, a lesbian, or a gay man would not be biologically based and hence would not be protected by the argument with premises 2a and 3a. For example, even if homosexuality is biologically based, actually engaging in homosexual acts, actually identifying as lesbian or gay, and so on, are *choices*, choices that each lesbian or gay man might well not have made (that is, he or she could have decided to be celibate and closeted). Someone who is convinced that lesbians and gay men deserve rights only because homosexuality is biologically based believes people should not be discriminated against on the basis of their biological features and on these alone. For example, if I were convinced by the protected status argument, I would think that people who had homoerotic desires should not be discriminated against on the basis of their having these desires. This is perfectly compatible, however, with my thinking that people who engage in same-sex sexual acts *are* appropriate targets of discrimination, criminal penalties, and the like. A friend of the biological argument for lesbian and gay rights might try to respond to this criticism by attempting to make a connection between being protected against discrimination because one's desire is biologically based and being protected against discrimination on the basis of behaviors that stem from biologically based desire. Without a detailed story of how it could be made, this connection seems implausible. Even if premises 1 and 2a of the protected status argument are true, there are reasons to doubt premise 3a; even if sexual orientation is a protected category, lesbian and gay rights (in any nontrivial sense of the term "rights") do not follow.

This objection to the protected status argument seems to constitute an objection to all versions of the general argument with the biological basis of homosexuality as a premise and with the claim that lesbians and gay men deserve rights and the like as the conclusion. Arguments of this form seem limited to showing that gay men and lesbians deserve rights only with respect to those attributes lesbians and gay men have in virtue of their particular biological constitution. Whether this objection applies to the other versions of the biological argument for lesbian and gay rights will be considered below.

Determinism

Another argument for lesbian and gay rights of the same general structure as the one discussed above involves determinism, the thesis that sexual orientation is not a choice. The idea behind this particular argument is that if homosexuality has a biological basis, then sexual orientation is not a choice; but if sexual orientation is not a choice, then one can hardly be punished for or discriminated against on the basis of sexual orientation. The argument goes as follows:

1. Homosexuality has a biological basis.
2b. If homosexuality has a biological basis, then sexual orientation is not a choice.
3b. If sexual orientation is not a choice, then lesbians and gay men deserve rights, protection against discrimination, and so forth.
4. Therefore, lesbians and gay men deserve rights, protection against discrimination, and so forth.

This argument suffers from one of the problems I discussed above with respect to the protected status argument: the biological basis of homosexuality at most establishes that lesbians and gay men do not have a choice in their homoerotic desires, but it leaves open that they have a choice with respect to their behavior, their public identification of their sexual orientation, and the like. If lesbians and gay men deserve rights in virtue of the truth of determinism about sexual orientation, then it would still be permissible to discriminate against people on the basis of things about which they *do* have a choice, such as sexual behavior, public sexual identity, and so on. In other words, it is consistent with determinism about sexual orientation that lesbians and gay men are discriminated against in virtue of, for example, engaging in same-sex sexual acts. This is to say that premise 3b is false.

As an analogy, consider alcoholism. Suppose, as seems to be the case, that a predisposition for alcoholism is congenital. The truth of this claim might make it morally unacceptable to discriminate against someone because she is disposed to become an alcoholic. This, however, would *not* make it morally unacceptable to discriminate against someone who actually is an "active" alcoholic, that is, who gets drunk on a regular basis. Regardless of the biological basis of alcoholism, it is morally acceptable to decide not to live with someone, not to hire her, and the like, because she is frequently under the influence of alcohol, a fact that affects her ability to behave responsibly. The point of the analogy is that even if the *disposition* to engage in a behavior is not a choice, actually engaging in that behavior may be a choice, and, thus, discrimination on the basis of whether someone actually engages in such a behavior might be acceptable.

The analogy to alcoholism shows two things. First, it makes clear that the lack of choice about falling into a category does not guarantee that people who fit that category deserve rights, protection against discrimination, and the like, merely on that basis. This objection counts against premise 3b of the determinism argument for lesbian and gay rights. Second, the analogy makes clear why 3b seems appealing at first glance. If a person has no choice whether or not she falls into a particular category, then she should not be blamed for fitting that category. Freedom from blame does not, however, entail freedom from discrimination or the receipt of special rights. Friends of the determinism argument for lesbian and gay rights seem to miss this point. Premise 3b seems plausible only if you think that the absence of blame entails rights beyond the right not to be punished. The absence of blame does not have this implication. The lack of choice about one's sexual orientation does not provide grounds for lesbian and gay rights; 3b is thus false. The determinism argument for lesbian and gay rights fails.

The objection to the determinism argument for lesbian and gay rights is that the lack of choice about one's sexual orientation does not in itself provide grounds for lesbian and gay rights, that is, 3b is false. Premise 3b is false because the lack of choice about one's sexual desires fails to include much of what should be protected under the rubric of lesbian and gay rights. So, for example, even if my desire to have sex with other men was determined biologically—and thus not a choice and thus the basis for lesbian and gay rights, protection against discrimination, and the like—my decision to actually engage in sexual acts with other men would still *not* be determined biologically, would be a choice, and thus would *not* be the basis for lesbian and gay rights, protection against discrimination, and the like. Further, even if (contrary to fact) all facets of being lesbian or gay (that is, engaging in same-sex sexual acts, identifying as lesbian or gay, etc.) were biologically determined, 3b would still be false. Determinism about all facets of sexual orientation would show the absence of blame for all facets of sexual orientation, but this would not in turn entail lesbian and gay rights, since the lack of blame is not grounds for nonnegative rights. The determinism argument for lesbian and gay rights thus fails.

Naturalness

Another argument for lesbian and gay rights of the same general structure as the arguments considered above has to do with the "naturalness" of homosexuality. Some people think that being lesbian, gay, or bisexual is in some way *un*natural, and, on that basis, they have defended discrimination against lesbians and gay men. Some friends of the biological argument for lesbian and gay rights seem to think that if they can undermine this charge of "unnaturalness" by showing a biological basis for homosexuality, they can undercut the argument for discrimination and replace it with an argument for lesbian and gay rights. This argument proceeds as follows:

1. Homosexuality has a biological basis.

2c. If homosexuality has a biological basis, then homosexuality is natural.
3c. If homosexuality is natural, then lesbians and gay men deserve rights, protection against discrimination, and so forth.
4. Therefore, lesbians and gay men deserve rights, protection against discrimination, and so forth.

The first thing to note about this argument is its use of the notoriously tricky term "natural." When opponents of lesbian and gay rights claim that lesbian and gay men are unnatural, it is quite difficult to figure out what they mean by the term. The same is true when friends of lesbian and gay rights use the term "natural" as in 2c and 3c. To clarify the notion of naturalness with respect to sexual orientation, I shall enumerate four often-used senses of the term. When people claim that homosexuality is unnatural, they are typically using the term in one of the following senses:

A (sexual) behavior is unnatural if it:
i. does not contribute to the perpetuation of the species;
ii. involves using an organ or the like for a function other than the function it was selected to perform;
iii. is not performed by (nonhuman) animals;
iv. is caused by humans, is caused artificially, is not "in nature."

All four of these senses of "unnatural" either fail to apply to homosexuality or apply to a whole range of acceptable behaviors (e.g., marriage, masturbation, contraceptive sex, skiing); as such, they are inadequate for grounding a case for discrimination against lesbians and gay men. Showing in detail that homosexuality is not unnatural in any of these senses is, however, not the point here.[6] Rather, the point is to see whether 2c and 3c are true in any sense of the term "natural." I shall argue that there are no good reasons to believe 2c is true on any but the last sense of "natural."

Perpetuation of the Species
Consider first:

2c-i. If homosexuality has a biological basis, then homosexuality contributes to the perpetuation of the species.

Problems arise at first glance because there are lots of traits that humans have in virtue of their biology that do not contribute to the survival of the species. Perhaps the most obvious example of this is genetically based impotence: this sort of impotence by stipulation has a biological basis, but it cannot contribute (at least directly) to the perpetuation of the species. The mere genetic basis of a trait does not thereby establish that the trait contributes to the survival of the species; in fact, some genetic traits do just the opposite.

This is perhaps a bit too quick. The persistence of homosexuality in the human gene pool is a problem for sociobiologists since exclusive homosexuals are not known for their reproductive success. Some sociobiologists, as an attempt to solve this problem, have argued that a gene for homosexuality is evolutionary adaptive. Although an exclusively homosexual individual would not leave any offspring of her own, her homosexuality might still be adaptive in the sense of increasing the number of copies of her genes that get into subsequent generations. Sociobiologists have tried to spin out various stories of how this might work, from lesbians and gay men who help their siblings raise their children, to queers who devote their time to the arts and sciences (rather than to reproduction) and thereby make the world a better place for future generations.[7] If, implausible as they seem, any of these sociobiological stories are true and homosexuality is adaptive, then this might help to make the case for 2c-i. This, however, is only apparent. Premise 2c-i is a conditional statement; it says *if* homosexuality has a biological basis, then homosexuality contributes to the perpetuation of the species. There are other biological theories of homosexuality on which homosexuality does not contribute to the perpetuation of the species; since one of these theories *could* be true, the conditional is false—a biological basis does not entail the perpetuation of the species although some (implausible) biological theories, if true, would. Premise 2c-i is thereby undermined.

Performing Evolutionary Selected Function

Consider next:

> 2c-ii. If homosexuality has a biological basis, then homosexuality involves using organs only for functions they were selected to perform.[8]

This is also false. A behavior can be biologically based but still involve using an organ in ways other than that for which the particular organ was selected. Suppose, for example, that the human throat was selected for the role it plays in digestion. This is perfectly consistent with the fact that the throat plays a role in speaking, a behavior that also has a biological basis, although the throat was not, by stipulation, selected for because of the role it plays in speaking. More generally, traits that are selected for are often called into play in a whole host of ways for which the trait was not originally selected and, in fact, may be used in behaviors that are not themselves selectively advantageous.[9] Premise 2c-ii is false.

Performed by Animals

Consider the third sense of "natural" that might be used to make sense of 2c, namely, that a behavior is natural if nonhuman animals do it. A friend of using the "naturalness" of homosexuality as a premise in an argument for lesbian and gay rights might try to use the existence of homosexuality in animals to show that homosexuality is natural. The resulting argument would be:

1′. There are animals who engage in homosexual behavior.
2′. Therefore, homosexuality is natural.
3c-iii. If homosexuality is natural, then lesbians and gay men deserve rights, protection against discrimination, and so forth.
4. Therefore, lesbians and gay men deserve rights, protection against discrimination, and so forth.

The first problem with this argument is that the move from 1′ to 2′ seems invalid. Animals eat conspecifics, kill other animals in painful ways, and do many other things we do not think are natural for humans. On any reading of "natural" in 2′ that is supposed to suggest "natural" for humans, the argument from 1′ to 2′ is invalid—you cannot deduce "natural for humans" from "animals do it." The move from 1′ to 2′ might be valid if "natural" is read so as not to apply to humans. But then the move from 2′ to 3c will not be valid, because "natural" in 3c clearly must apply to humans. Even if there is homosexuality in the nonhuman realm, this does not establish grounds for lesbian and gay rights.

Further, while various animals engage in sexual acts with same-sex conspecifics, it is not obvious that this should count as evidence of homosexuality. For example, various studies of animal sexual behavior count a male animal who is anally penetrated by another male as a homosexual, but they do not count as homosexual the male who does the penetrating. In contrast, in the human case, scientists count both the male who penetrates and the male who is penetrated (as well as men who engage in or desire to engage in various acts that do not involve anal penetration at all) as homosexual. Moreover, human sexual activity involves a complex array of cognitive functions—some conscious, others not—for which most animals are probably not equipped. So, while there might be parallels between certain sexual acts (that is, between physical acts involving genitals) in which humans and animals engage, we might want to count sexual acts as homosexual or heterosexual only insofar as they fit into a certain (human) cognitive framework.

Suppose, then, that "homosexual," "heterosexual," and "bisexual" are applicable only to humans; would this affect lesbian and gay rights? Opponents of lesbian and gay rights have tried to use the absence of homosexuality in animals as grounds for claiming that homosexuals are unnatural and, hence, not deserving of rights, and so forth. The argument they have in mind goes as follows:

5. There is no homosexuality in animals.
6. Therefore, homosexuality is unnatural.
7. If homosexuality is unnatural, then lesbians and gay men do not deserve rights, and so forth.
8. Therefore, lesbians and gay men do not deserve rights, and so forth.

Typically, this argument has foundered on the empirical evidence against 5. I have suggested a plausible way to defend 5: allow that there is same-sex activity among animals, but deny that there is homosexuality among animals. But this line of argument will still not help foes of lesbian and gay rights, because the same line of argument could be used to show that *heterosexuality* is unnatural as well and, hence, that heterosexuals do not deserve rights, and the like. The same reasons for thinking that there are no homosexual animals provide grounds for thinking that there are no heterosexual animals either.

Clearly, this is a reductio ad absurdum of the argument from 5, 6 and 7 to 8.

Not Artificial

Finally, consider

2c-iv. If homosexuality has a biological basis, then homosexuality exists in nature, is not artificial, is not constructed by humans.

On this sense of "natural," a biological basis for homosexuality does show that homosexuality is natural: if homosexuality has a biological basis, then human homosexuality exists in nature and is not constructed by humans. So 2c-iv is true. But will it, together with the other premises of the argument for lesbian and gay rights under consideration, suffice for such an argument? Consider this argument with reading sense iv of "natural" inserted in the relevant places:

1. Homosexuality has a biological basis.
2c-iv. If homosexuality has a biological basis, then homosexuality is not caused or made by humans, is not artificial, exists in nature, and so on.
3c-iv. If homosexuality is not caused or made by humans, is not artificial, exists in nature, and so on, then lesbians and gay men deserve rights, protection against discrimination, and so forth.
4. Therefore, lesbians and gay men deserve rights, protection against discrimination, etc.

I am assuming premise 1 is true, and I have noted that 2c-iv is true. Further, the argument for 1, 2c-iv, and 3c-iv is valid. All that remains to evaluate is 3c-iv. For reasons similar to those that undermined 3a and 3b, 3c-iv is doubtful. First, there are lots of human categories that are not artificial (that is, that exist "in nature") but that do not provide grounds for giving rights to people who fall into them (e.g., being an alcoholic or having Down's syndrome). The mere nonartificiality of a category does not ground claims for rights. Second, the aspects of homosexuality that are biologically based and thus are not caused by humans (and that exist in nature, are not artificial, etc.) include only the having of homoerotic desires, but they do not include embracing a lesbian or gay identity or entering into a lesbian or gay relationship. Queer identities and relationships are (like straight identities and relationships) made by humans, do not exist in nature, and so on, and thus they are not part of the lesbian and gay rights that come out of the argument involving 3c-iv. For 3c-iv to be true, we need to adopt a *narrow* reading of lesbian and gay rights, so narrow as to be unrecognizable as lesbian and gay rights. If we adopt a more robust sense of lesbian and gay rights, 3c-iv is implausible: the nonartificiality that homosexuality inherits in virtue of its biological basis does not provide grounds for lesbian and gay rights.

The general problem for biological arguments for lesbian and gay rights is to find some claim that will bridge the gap between the empirical claim (homosexuality has a biological basis) and the normative one (lesbian and gay men deserve rights, and the like). If the blank is filled in with an empirical claim, then 2 might be plausible, but 3 will not be (this was the case when the blank was filled in with "homosexuality is natural in the sense of not being man-made"). If the blank is filled in with a normative claim, then premise 3 might be plausible, but 2 would not be. A related problem is that even if the premises are true, the attributes lesbian and gay men have and only the behaviors (if any) in which they necessarily engage in virtue of the (supposed) biological basis of their sexual orientation are all that will be protected under this argument. At best, this will include homoerotic desires and dispositions to engage in same-sex sexual acts, a rather narrow range with respect to what we typically mean when we talk of lesbian and gay rights.

The failure of arguments from the naturalness of homosexuality to establish lesbian and gay rights does not show that homosexuality is unnatural; it only shows that finding that homosexuality has a biological basis does not establish its naturalness, in senses (i–iv). In fact, on any plausible reading of "natural," homosexuality *is* natural (although not because of its biological basis, if such a basis exists).[10] If I am right about this and if 3c were true—which it is not—then this fact might be combined with 3c to get 4, the conclusion that lesbians and gay men deserve rights, etc. But this argument for lesbian and gay rights does not require a biological basis for homosexuality.

Pragmatic Argument

Some friends of lesbian and gay rights might argue that biological arguments should be embraced even in light of my discussion above since such arguments for lesbian and gay rights seem to persuade people.[11] The idea is a *pragmatic* one: embrace the theories that help to establish lesbian and gay rights.

I do not think this general line of argument is promising. Linking lesbian and gay rights to biology seems a bad strategy even on pragmatic or political grounds. First, a biological basis for homosexuality, even if it could persuade people to favor lesbian and gay rights in the short run, might at the same time spark a call for genetic engineering to prevent homosexuality and the development of amniocentesis techniques for the detection of homosexuality so as to enable the abortion of fetuses with the strongest potential to develop into homosexuals.[12]

Second, it seems bad strategy to link lesbian and gay rights to the ups and downs of scientific research. Such research is, at best, still in its early stages, and whatever indications there may be that there is a biological explanation for sexual orientation might well turn out to be mistaken. Connecting lesbian and gay rights to science is too risky. People can be persuaded of various things by all sorts of bad arguments. That people are persuaded by biological arguments for lesbian and gay rights may suggest a public relations strategy that will be successful in the short term, but it does not suggest a strategy suited for grounding a set of rights that are deeply important and that profoundly impact the lives of many men and women. Biological sophistry is still sophistry.

Third, the pragmatic argument for lesbian and gay rights is committed to a picture of science that is potentially self-undermining. Friends of the pragmatic argument for lesbian and gay rights defend the theory that homosexuality has a biological basis because of its political effects. But if it becomes known that this is the justification for favoring one scientific theory over another, the persuasiveness of scientific theories in general—the very persuasiveness on which the pragmatic argument is based—will be undermined. In other words, although such arguments depend on the distinction between science and mere propaganda, these very arguments, if widespread, would erase this distinction.

For the three reasons I have given above, I do not think that the pragmatic version of the biological argument for lesbian and gay rights fares any better than its nonpragmatic counterparts. Scientific research concerning sexual orientation is irrelevant to lesbian and gay rights. Attempts to link the science of sexual orientation to the case for lesbian and gay rights are misguided.

The Basis of Lesbian and Gay Rights

So far, I have argued that scientific explanations of sexual orientations and desires will not be relevant to lesbian and gay rights. If my conclusion is right, one might wonder what sort of evidence and what kinds of arguments *are* relevant to this issue. My answer, once it is stated, seems obvious: the arguments and evidence that should be given are *moral* and *political* in nature. Consider, for example, the sorts of arguments that get made for equal rights for racial or religious minorities. Rather than appealing to any facts about the constitution of these types of people, these arguments involve theories of justice, rights, privacy, equality, liberty, and the like. The arguments are moral and/or political in nature. The same is true for arguments for lesbian and gay rights, protection for lesbians and gay men against discrimination, respect for queer relationships, and so on; these issues are moral in nature, and arguments for them should be cast in terms of justice, rights, privacy, equality, liberty, and the like.[13]

This is not to say that empirical considerations are *never* relevant to moral issues. For example, if you hold the view that it is wrong to cause wanton pain and suffering to any animal that can feel pain and be conscious of it, then the empirical discovery that pigs feel pain and are conscious of it would be relevant to the issue of whether the factory farming of pigs is morally acceptable. Sometimes empirical evidence is relevant to moral issues. In the particular case of lesbian and gay rights, however, empirical evidence concerning why people have the sexual orientations and desires they do is not relevant.

Despite this, empirical evidence may be of interest to some of the political goals many lesbians, gay men, and their political allies share. For instance, showing that a person's sexual orientation is determined at birth might help to convince people that it is perfectly acceptable for lesbians and gay men to teach elementary school. Or showing that determinism about sexual orientation is true might convince people of the futility of attempting to change queer people's sexual orientations. I do not mean to trivialize these possibilities and the extent to which they might be able to help forward specific parts of a gay-positive political agenda. My arguments above have, however, given us good reason to think that empirical arguments for lesbian and gay rights in general are not forthcoming. Moreover, I am concerned about linking even more specific political aims to scientific research. Lesbians and gay men should be able to teach elementary school *even if* a person's sexual orientation is not fixed until puberty.

Conclusion

How do people develop sexual orientations and desires? This is an interesting question, but not for the reasons many people think. In particular, if my arguments in this chapter are correct, the answer to this question is not relevant to the moral and political issue of lesbian and gay rights. Rather, the question is important as a part of our understanding of ourselves. Sex and sexual desire are basic and central to human nature; unlocking their mysteries through science and social science is a worthwhile project on its own merits. This research project, however, should not be pursued in a vacuum; its social implications should be considered. But the results of such research will not entail that lesbians and gay men deserve rights, privileges, or recognition. Such conclusions need to be established through moral and political arguments, not scientific ones.

· CHAPTER TWELVE ·

Diversity and Variability in Women's Sexual Identities

CARLA GOLDEN

Carla Golden, associate professor of psychology at Ithaca College, discusses the variety of ways in which college women identify their sexuality. After discussing some of the controversial issues surrounding theories of lesbian identity, Golden proceeds to present her findings from interviews with college women. These interviews suggest that there is a great deal of diversity and fluidity in women's self-defined sexual identities and that these identities are often at odds with social definitions. In her postscript, Golden criticizes the male-centeredness of some of the recent scientific research and discusses how attitudes toward female sexuality have changed on college campuses over the past decade.

· · · · ·

Psychologists and feminists alike tend to assume that most persons can be neatly categorized according to membership in one of four groups: heterosexual, homosexual, bisexual, or asexual (celibate). Furthermore, they tend to accept uncritically the notion that when a person's behavior fits into one of those four sexual preference categories, that person adopts a corresponding sexual identity to match the behavior. If such beliefs are not questioned, it seems logical to assume that a person whose sexual behavior is exclusively heterosexual would also assume a heterosexual identity and, conversely, that a person with a heterosexual identity would only engage

This chapter is reprinted with some revisions from "Diversity and Variability in Women's Sexual Identities," in the Boston Lesbian Psychologies Collective, eds., *Lesbian Psychologies: Explorations and Challenges* (Urbana: University of Illinois Press, 1987) pp. 18–34. The section titled "Postscript" was written especially for this volume.

in heterosexual behavior. The same connection between sexual behavior and sexual identity would be assumed of homosexuality as well.

The relation between sexual behavior and sexual identity may not be so clear-cut, however. For women, sexuality may be an aspect of identity that is fluid and dynamic as opposed to fixed and invariant. I came to think of women's sexuality in this way as a function of interviews and more general discussions with young college women who were exploring their sexuality. Many of these women were defining themselves as lesbians despite the fact that their current or previous sexual experience was heterosexual. I was confused by this, because I had tended to think of sex between women as rather central to the definition of lesbiansim. However, as I read more feminist literature on sexuality and spoke with women who were feminists and/or lesbians, I came to see that the definition of a lesbian is both problematic and far from unambiguous. As a psychologist, I am primarily interested in how women subjectively experience their identities and how they react when their personally constructed identities are not concordant with social definitions. Exploring these issues led me to a new view of women's sexuality.

I will review here some of the controversial definitional issues that have been identified in the feminist sexuality literature and then will present the findings from interviews with college women. These interviews suggest that there is enormous diversity and variability in women's self-defined sexual identities and that these identities are often at odds with social definitions. Finally, I will discuss how the exploration of sexuality from the perspective of a "deviant" group (i.e., lesbians) sheds some important light on the nature of women's sexuality in general.

How do feminist theorists interested in women's sexuality define lesbianism? Adrienne Rich's conception of the lesbian continuum provides an interesting introduction to the problematic nature of the term.[1] Instead of using the word "lesbianism," which for her has connotations both clinical and pejorative, Rich suggests thinking in terms of a lesbian continuum. She notes that, across history and cultures, women have in a variety of ways been primarily committed to other women, and she uses the term "lesbian continuum" to refer to the range of such women-identified experiences. That a woman has actually had, or has consciously desired, genital sexual experience with another woman is but one point on the lesbian continuum. By conceiving of lesbianism in these terms, Rich suggests that many more forms of primary intensity between and among women (including emotional bonding) can be included than would be possible with a narrower definition based solely on sexual behavior. Furthermore, according to Rich's definition, a woman need not identify herself as a lesbian in order to be considered one. By defining lesbianism in terms of primary intensity between women, she allows for women from previous historical periods to be considered as lesbians, even though at the time when they lived there may have been no cultural conception of lesbianism.

Rich's formulation holds that neither sexual relations nor sexual attraction between women is necessary for inclusion in the category "lesbian." It should be noted that such a contention is not new. In 1973, the Radicalesbians, in their "Women-Identified Women" article, focused on the political, as opposed to specifically sexual, nature of lesbianism when they defined it as "the rage of all women condensed to the point of explosion."[2] Blanche Wiesen Cook, in her *Chrysalis* article, "Female Support Networks and Political Activism," defined a lesbian as "a woman who loves women, who chooses women to nurture and support and create a living environment in which to work creatively and independently, whether or not her relations with these women are sexual."[3] Such definitions, which have de-emphasized sexual feelings and behavior, have not been uncontroversial. Not only do they suggest that with whom one has sexual relations is not critical, but they also imply that a woman who never consciously considers herself to be a lesbian may in fact be thought of as one.

Ann Ferguson has argued that defining lesbianism in such a manner incorrectly downplays the importance of sexual feelings and behavior.[4] Such a definition in effect unsexes lesbianism and makes it more agreeable to some people by diminishing what is undeniably a significant difference. Furthermore, Ferguson argues that it isn't meaningful to talk about a woman as a lesbian if she doesn't acknowledge herself to be one. She suggests that, because before the twentieth century there was no cultural conception of lesbianism, one cannot and should not attempt to consider women lesbians who did not consider themselves to be such. As an alternative, Ferguson offers the following definition: "[a] lesbian is a woman who has sexual and erotic-emotional ties primarily with women or who sees herself as centrally involved with a community of self-identified lesbians whose sexual and erotic-emotional ties are primarily with women *and* who is herself a self-identified lesbian."[5] Without de-emphasizing the role of sexual behavior, this definition includes both celibate and bisexual women as lesbians, as long as they identify themselves as such.

The issue of self-conscious acknowledgment of lesbian identity is important, especially if we are talking about contemporary women for whom a definite cultural category of lesbian exists. The issue of sexual behavior is a bit more complicated, and Ferguson's definition reflects this in her use of the word "primarily," which allows for inclusion in the category "lesbian" women whose sexual relationships are not exclusively with women. It is my observation that, within certain lesbian communities, there has tended to be more ready acceptance of celibate and of sexually inexperienced women who choose to call themselves lesbians than there has been of bisexual women who choose to identify themselves as lesbians. Thus, it seems that for some members of the lesbian community, the critical issue in determining the "legitimacy" of a woman's claim to a lesbian identity is not whether or not she is sleeping with women, but whether she is sleeping with men. This kind of thinking is problematic because women's relations to men are given greater weight than are women's own self-conscious voices.

Some have argued that attempts to define who is and who is not a lesbian will only be divisive, and it seems undeniable that, to a certain extent, it has been. Jacquelyn Zita has aptly referred to this judging and weighing of who does and does not qualify for membership as the "lesbian Olympics."[6] However, it does seem both intellectually important and socially useful for groups to define themselves. It is critical for any minority or oppressed group to break free from the confining definitions of the dominant culture and to create their own. In collectively resisting oppression, minority groups need to foster not only a positive group identity, but also a sense of the cohesiveness of the group based at least partially on shared characteristics and self-definitions.

While acknowledging that it is important for minority groups to define themselves (as opposed to being defined by the dominant group), it must be recognized that it is a sociopolitical task to do so and that there are certain limitations inherent in such an enterprise. That is, to construct a definition is to identify a set of criteria according to which individual women can be considered to fit or not. Describing a social group is quite different from the psychological task of understanding what it means to any particular woman to identify as a member of that group. In fact, the construction of a categorical definition of lesbian is bound to obscure the personal and variable meanings of lesbian identity as it is experienced by real women. I say this because sexual feelings, attractions, and behavior are not necessarily fixed and invariant with regard to the sex of the person toward whom they are directed. When definitions of lesbian are conceptualized with primary reference to sexual feelings and activities, it may be difficult (if one wishes to allow for the complexity of lived experience) to construct unambiguous criteria that would specify who does and does not belong in the category "lesbian."

A precise definition of lesbian that establishes unchanging sexual criteria according to which individual women can be judged as legitimate members of the category may not have the flexibility to account for the diversity and variability in subjectively experienced lesbian identities. One serious problem that results is that individual women may find their experience of themselves at odds with the socially constructed category, even when it emanates from the lesbian community. At this point in history, when so many women are self-consciously asking who they are and how they can understand their place in society, it is possible to explore these issues with them directly.

Between 1977 and 1983, I taught at a northeastern women's college, where I served, albeit unofficially, as a counselor to young women exploring their sexual and personal identities. For many of the women I spoke with over the years, these were times of change and transition, and among the most prominent changes were those in their sexual feelings, activities, and identities and in their sense of possibilities for the future. Although many of these young women had been sexual (in varying degrees and with different sexual object choices) before coming to college, several features of their new environment converged to make the issue of sexuality in general, and their own sexuality in particular, more salient than it had been in their high school years.

One important aspect of their new environment was that they were away from their parents and had the option of engaging in sexual relations without having to be overly concerned about their parents' discovery of their behavior. Second, they were in an all-women's environment where close connections between women were valued and where they were free to develop in ways not often matched in coeducational environments. In women's colleges, relationships between women can and do flourish; women have the opportunity to live, love, learn, work, and grow together. Although such environments are special in any historic time period, there was something unique about their atmosphere in the late-1970s through mid-1980s. As a result of the women's movement, the visibility of a small but dedicated number of feminist faculty, and the presence in the curriculum of women's studies courses, a certain self-consciousness about being women existed among a majority of the students. This consciousness gave rise to both self-exploration and a broader consideration of women's lives and possibilities, including the variety of vocational choices and sexual lifestyles available to women. Added to this was the highly visible and active Lesbian Alliance on campus. At a time when many students were having to deal with themselves as sexual beings, they were also being exposed to "out" lesbians, many of whom were in more than a few respects indistinguishable from themselves. Workshops conducted by the Lesbian Alliance did a tremendous job in raising consciousness, and they also served, for some students, to heighten questions and thinking about their own sexuality.

I had extensive contact with students who were active members of the Lesbian Alliance (and who were thus viewed as "the lesbian community" on campus), as well as with students who were not publicly affiliated with the alliance. I will articulate as well as I can from their perspective some of the ways in which these young women were defining themselves and how they made sense of their pasts, their present, and their futures.

One major distinction that emerged from interviews with women who defined themselves as lesbian was between those who felt their lesbianism was essentially beyond their control and those who felt it was self-consciously chosen. Some of these women had from an earlier age (usually between six and twelve) considered themselves to be different from other girls. Whether or not they had a label for it, they experienced themselves as different in that they felt sexually attracted to and oriented toward other girls or women. Their feelings could be independent of actual sexual experiences. In other words, they may or may not have had lesbian relationships, and they may even have had heterosexual ones, but regardless, they felt themselves to be different in that they were attracted to females. Furthermore, this was experienced either at the time or, in retrospect, as something beyond their control; these women had not chosen to be attracted to women, they just were. Some of these women offered comments to the effect that they were "born" lesbians and would spontaneously contrast themselves with women who described their lesbianism as resulting from a conscious decision. Following a distinction made by Barbara Ponse in her study of a southern lesbian community, I have characterized these women as "primary lesbians"; that is, women who from an early age have a conscious sense of difference based on sexual attraction toward members of the same sex and who do not perceive this difference to be based on any kind of conscious choice.[7]

In contrast to primary lesbians were women who could be characterized, again following the distinction made by Ponse, as "elective lesbians." For these women, their lesbian identity is perceived as consciously chosen. This is not to imply that it is strictly a political choice; for the majority, it is experienced as an erotic choice as well. Unlike primary lesbians, these women did not have a conscious sense of being different from other girls at a younger age. But in similarity with primary lesbians, their sense of identity was independent of their actual sexual history. As girls, some of these elective lesbians had crushes on other girls; they may even have engaged in sexual play and exchanges with other girls. Despite such lesbian-like experiences, they did not think of themselves as different. No one had ever labeled their behavior as deviant, and it had not occurred to them that others might consider it to be.

These women usually had some heterosexual experience as they got older, and even when they had not, they had heterosexual identities. However, regardless of their actual sexual experience, they never thought of themselves as different from the "average" female in terms of their sexual orientation. Although they may never have explicitly called themselves "heterosexuals," neither did they consider the possibility that they were anything else (much in the manner of white people who never give much explicit thought to their race). I have characterized as elective lesbians women who perceive their lesbianism as a conscious choice and who do not have a history of thinking of themselves as different from other females in the realm of sexual inclinations.

Among elective lesbians, I found two distinctive subpatterns that suggested another salient dimension of lesbian identity. Some of these women viewed their sexual attraction to women as a central, basic, and unchanging aspect of who they were, and it seemed to me that this was not merely a political stance, but a strongly experienced subjective feeling about their essential natures. In light of this sense of themselves, their past heterosexual behavior and identity presented an inconsistency. Unwilling to accept this apparent discontinuity, and given their belief in the stability and enduring quality of their sexual orientation, they repeatedly expressed the view that there was something "unreal" about their previous heterosexuality. This was reflected in their tendency to reinterpret their past history to suggest a continuity between past and present senses of self. As one women put it, "In high school when I had a steady boyfriend, the real me, the lesbian, was suppressed. I just wasn't my real self back then." For other women, their less-than-satisfactory heterosexual experiences confirmed that they had really been lesbians all along. Still others pointed to their intense friendships with girlfriends as suggestive of their true lesbian identities. Sexual feelings and behaviors were central to the lesbian identities of these women, and they believed in the essentiality of their lesbianism.

Other elective lesbians did not view their lesbianism as an essential and enduring aspect of who they were. They did not show any tendency to reinterpret their past history and did not experience dissonance or contradiction in describing themselves as lesbians with heterosexual pasts. As one woman put it quite simply, "Then I was heterosexual, and now I'm a lesbian." These women expressed the view that there was nothing inconsistent or in need of explanation about their present identity and the one they had assumed in the past. Some of these women revealed, upon questioning, that they had engaged in childhood sexual play with other girls or had had strong attachments to camp counselors and teachers but had never thought of these as lesbian feelings. Although they currently identified themselves as lesbians, they saw no reason to reconstruct their pasts as implicitly lesbian. Unlike the elective lesbians previously described, they did not view sexual attraction to women as an essential and unchanging aspect of who they were, although they strongly believed they would continue to have their primary (if not all) relationships with women. Some women said they considered themselves to be lesbians whose sexual feelings could be most accurately characterized as bisexual, or just sexual; however, these comments tended to be privately, as opposed to publicly, stated. Other lesbians in this subgroup defined themselves as lesbian and let its essentiality be assumed, while privately, they experienced their sexuality as fluid, or potentially so.

To summarize, in the sample of college women with whom I worked, one major difference that emerged was in whether their lesbianism was experienced as determined (i.e., primary) or as self-consciously chosen (i.e., elective). Another major difference had to do with whether their lesbianism was experienced as a central and enduring aspect of who they were or whether it was experienced as more fluid and dynamic in nature. These two dimensions of difference were not entirely independent of each other. Among those lesbians whose identity was a chosen one, some experienced their sexuality as essential, others as fluid; among those lesbians whose identity felt determined, sexuality was experienced as essential by definition.

With respect to these dimensions of sexuality, there appear to be some interesting age differences. I have spoken with elective lesbians in their late twenties, thirties, and forties who described shifts in their thinking about the nature of their lesbianism. Some had at an earlier age experienced their sexuality as essential and fixed, that is, invariantly focused on women, but later in the development of their lesbian identity had come to feel that their sexuality was in fact more fluid. For a few, this shift resulted from bisexual experiences later in life. Others who felt this way had continued to have relationships only with women. They attributed their earlier position to their more adamant lesbian feminist politics or to what they thought was a developmental phase many lesbians go through.

Alternatively, some elective lesbians felt that in their younger years, when they were engaged in sexual exploration and discovery, their sexuality was more fluid, but that in the context of lesbian culture and relationships, they had developed a very explicit preference for women. These women thought of their sexuality as having become more fixed as they got older. Whereas the college women with whom I worked characterized their sexuality as either fixed or fluid, some older women had experienced shifts over the life cycle in this aspect of their sexuality.

It seems that as lesbians engage in the continuing process of self-definition, their sense of the essentiality or fluidity of their sexuality may change. In contrast, the distinction between primary and elective lesbianism seems to remain more dichotomous over the course of development. Women of all ages with whom I spoke made reference to such a distinction; they tended to identify as one or the other and experienced this identification as one that was stable.

Let me return to my discussion of these differing dimensions of lesbian identity as they were experienced by the students with whom I spoke. Because some of these students discussed lesbianism and their differing experiences of it among themselves, they were often aware that not all lesbians described themselves similarly. Sometimes they had distinct opinions about themselves in relation to other lesbians who described themselves differently. For example, some women whom I have characterized as primary lesbians referred to themselves as "born" or "real" lesbians, with the implicit designation of elective lesbians as "fake."

It was not uncommon for an elective lesbian to express to me privately her speculations about whether she was "really" a lesbian. At times, she wondered whether she wasn't "really" bisexual, or even heterosexual. While some primary lesbians interpret such uncertainty as difficultly in coming out, unwillingness to give up heterosexual privilege, or internalized homophobia, it seems to me that at least some of the elective lesbian's uncertainty can be traced back to the belief within the campus lesbian community that women who choose to be lesbians are somehow less real, or less legitimate, than those who felt they had no choice about it.

Despite this belief, there did seem to me to be a tolerance within the community for differences based on primary, compared with elective, lesbianism. In contrast, the issue of whether sexuality was thought of as essential or fluid was a much more sensitive one. For example, there was a noteworthy asymmetry in the application of the concept of the fluidity of sexual attractions when discussed in relation to lesbian and heterosexual women. I spoke with more than a few lesbians who were quite intolerant of (some) heterosexual women's insistence that they simply were not sexually attracted to women and that they couldn't imagine ever feeling differently. Implied in their intolerance was the belief that, despite heavy socialization pressures, sexual attraction is never so fixed and unmalleable as to be irrevocably focused just on persons of one sex. Yet some of these same women were equally intolerant of the opposite stance, that sexual feelings could exist toward persons of either sex, when expressed by a lesbian.

The assumption was often made about lesbians who were unwilling to state that they were (forever) uninterested sexually in men, that they must be having difficulty coming out or were unwilling to accept a stigmatized identity. Sometimes they were assumed to be going through a bisexual phase, or worse yet, to be male-identified and operating under a false consciousness. The assumption that bisexuality is simply a phase in the coming-out process of lesbians, and that those who call themselves "bisexuals" are really lesbians unwilling to call themselves that, has been countered by the contention from self-proclaimed bisexuals that their lesbianism was a phase in their coming out as bisexuals.[8]

The problem with all of these assumptions is that one person or set of persons presumes an attitude of knowing and understanding the meaning of another person's experience better than the person who is herself experiencing it. In this climate, individual women may have a difficult time finding their own voices and defining their own experiences. To the extent that lesbianism is very narrowly defined, the categories will restrict, rather than give full expression to, the diversity among women who subjectively define themselves as lesbian.

The question of sexual identity and how it is formed is not well understood, but some of our psychological conceptions do not do justice to the complexity of the process. We have often simplistically assumed that people have sexual attractions to persons of one or the other sex (but not both), that they act on those exclusive attractions, and that they eventually come to adopt the identity appropriate to their sexual activities, although there may be resistance when that identity is a stigmatized one. It appears to be the case, however, that sexual feelings and activities change; they can be fluid and dynamic. Furthermore, the reality is that feelings, activities, and self-conscious identities may not at all times be congruent. It has been suggested by social psychologists that people strive for congruence between their thoughts and feelings,[9] and that, with respect to sexual identity in particular, we are motivated to achieve congruence between our feelings, activities, and self-proclaimed identities.[10] This suggestion, however, does not accord with what I observed during my six and one-half years at a women's college in the late seventies and early eighties.

What particularly struck me, among this select sample of college women, was the diversity in self-definitions and the degree of incongruence between their sexual activities and their sexual identities (as expressed both publicly and privately). Every possible permutation of feelings and activities existed within each sexual identification category. Further, I was impressed by the way in which these young women were able to tolerate the ambiguity without significant internal distress.

Let me elaborate on the observation that every possible permutation existed. Among women who identified themselves to me as lesbians, there were some whose sexual behavior was explicitly and exclusively lesbian, and some whose behavior was exclusively heterosexual or bisexual (these latter also described themselves as "political lesbians"). In addition, I spoke with sexually inexperienced women who considered themselves to be lesbians. Although no student ever self-consciously identified herself as a celibate lesbian, this is a distinct possibility and has been described by Susan Yarborough.[11] Thus, among women who call themselves lesbians, a wide range of sexual behavior is evident.

Far fewer women described themselves to me as having a bisexual identity, and those who did made it quite clear that this was a confidential disclosure. The small number of self-identified bisexuals was particularly interesting in light of the findings from a survey of sexual behavior and attitudes taken in a class I taught on the psychology of women. The survey was constructed by students in the class and administered in such a way as to ensure complete anonymity. In response to the question of how they would label their sexuality to themselves, regardless of their actual sexual experiences, 65 percent (of 95 students) identified as heterosexual, 26 percent identified as bisexual, and 9 percent identified as lesbian. When asked what their actual sexual experiences were, the responses were as follows: 72 percent heterosexual, 20 percent bisexual, 4 percent lesbian, and 4 percent lacking sexual experience. Two things are interesting about these figures. First, they reveal that the way in which women sexually identify themselves does not always coincide with their actual sexual experience. Second, although three times as many women privately considered themselves to be bisexual as contrasted with lesbian, their concerns were never publicly raised, nor were their bisexual identities ever acknowledged in class. In comparison, lesbian concerns and identities were much more visible in the classroom. It began to occur to me that acknowledging one's bisexuality, or raising such issues publicly, was as stigmatized as discussing lesbianism, if not more so.

To return to the question of the various permutations of sexual activity and identity: among those interviewed women who identified themselves to me as bisexual, some were engaged in exclusively lesbian activity, some were engaged in exclusively heterosexual activity, while others actually had bisexual experience. Some women who were sexually inexperienced considered themselves on the basis of their potential sexual behavior to be bisexual.

Finally, to complete consideration of the various permutations, consider women who identified themselves to me as heterosexual. Here, too, I found women whose current sexual behavior was exclusively lesbian (of the "I just love Mindy; I'm not a lesbian" variety), as well as those whose sexual behavior was exclusively heterosexual. A few women considered themselves to be basically heterosexual even though they had had bisexual experience. And again, some women who were sexually inexperienced nevertheless asserted that they knew they were heterosexual.

The point I wish to make by describing these combinations is not simply that one's sexual identity is not always predictable on the basis of one's sexual behavior, but rather that the assumption that we inherently strive for congruence among our sexual feelings, activities, and identities may not be warranted and that, given the fluidity of sexual feelings, permanent congruence may not be an achievable state. The women with whom I spoke were not personally distressed by the fact of discrepancies between sexual behavior and sexual identity. For example, women who identified as lesbians but found themselves to be occasionally sexually attracted to men were made more uncomfortable by the thought of what other lesbians might think than by their own fluid and changing attractions. These were women who wanted to be considered legitimate members of the lesbian community but who often felt that they were not welcome, or that if they were, they were not trusted. Although very often they felt compelled to identify themselves publicly and unequivocally as lesbians whose sexuality was stable and enduring and exclusively focused on women, they privately experienced their sexuality in a more fluid and dynamic manner. The pressure to be congruent and to proclaim an identity that was in line with their sexual activities was often more externally than internally motivated.

These women are real, not hypothetical. Although the kind of lesbian they represent did not constitute a majority of the self-defined lesbians with whom I spoke, I think that the way they experienced their identities and their relation to the community has implications for how psychologists talk about sexuality and sexual identity.

Identity is constructed both societally and psychologically; it is both a social and a personal process. The process of psychological self-definition takes place within the context of existing dominant culture definitions, as well as those that emanate from within the minority community itself. Not only are lesbians a stigmatized and oppressed group, with the result that many have internalized negative images of self, but they are also a group whose central characteristic is debatable and not altogether invariant. Hence its boundaries are more permeable than those of other minority groups. Unlike one's sex or race, which is typically both highly visible and unchanging, one's sexuality (like one's class) is less visible and not so static over the course of a lifetime. Thus, the process of lesbian identity formation is complicated not only because of homophobia, but also because of the nature of sexuality itself.

When counseling women who are engaged in the act of sexual self-definition, therapists need to be aware of the variations in the process of identity formation. On the basis of the findings presented here, it is suggested that psychologists need to take a more serious look at the assumptions inherent in the phrase "coming out." It is not uncommon to hear clinicians talk about women who are in the process of coming out, or who have difficulty with coming out, as if they know what the "right" result looks like. We should begin to question not only whether there is a "right" way to come out, but also whether there is some static end point at all. Liberal teachers and clinicians often think their appropriate role with lesbians is to help them deal with coming out, but I would urge us to think seriously about the relationship between coming out and self-definition. It seems to me that the aim ought to be to encourage each woman as she struggles to define herself. This may mean facilitating her search for authenticity, rather than assuming a fixed sexuality, as what the therapist will help her discover. If being authentic entails accepting the fluidity of one's sexual feelings and activities and identifying as a lesbian, therapists should support this rather than convey the impression that the woman is confused or unwilling to accept a stigmatized identity.

These interviews suggest that sexuality is experienced by some women (both heterosexual and lesbian) as an aspect of identity that may change over the course of their lives. Although there has not been research on this issue with male homosexuals, from reading gay male literature, speaking with a small sample of gay men, and exchanging views with therapists who work with them, my sense is that gay men do not experience their sexuality in the fluid manner that some lesbian and heterosexual women do. I have no strong data on this, but I suspect that very few gay men could be characterized as elective homosexuals. Although this observation might at first seem puzzling and lead one to wonder why the nature of sexuality would be different for women and for men, I think it becomes more understandable with reference to psychoanalytic theories of mothering that place emphasis on the primary human need for social relationship and then examine the expression of that need in terms of the infant's first love object: its mother. Specifically, object relations theory can provide the framework for understanding how the conditions of early infancy might lead women to have greater bisexual potential then men. Dorothy Dinnerstein has discussed how the first relationship with a woman establishes a homoerotic potential in women,[12] and Nancy Chodorow has elaborated on the early psychic foundations of women's homoemotional needs and capacities.[13] The writings of both of these authors can provide the basis for formulation of a new question: Why do so many women become exclusively heterosexual as opposed to bisexual or lesbian?

One of the most important insights of both feminist psychology and the women's movement is that our being born female does not mean that we automatically and naturally prefer certain roles and activities. We have recognized that the category "woman" has been socially constructed and that, societal definitions notwithstanding, women are a diverse group with interests, attitudes, and identities that do not always conform to what is traditionally considered feminine. We have long been told that we are not "real" women unless we are wives and mothers, and to counter this, feminists have been forceful and articulate in asserting that one's sex is not related in any inevitable or natural way to one's sexual preference or societal role. In a similar vein, I suggest, on the basis of my discussions with a select sample of college women, that sexual feelings or activities are not always accurately described in either/or terms, nor do they exist in a simple one-to-one relation to our sexual identities. Just as we have protested the constricting social definition of what a real woman is, precisely because it has served to oppress women and to limit the expression of our diverse potentials, so too must we be careful in our social construction of sexuality not to construct categories that are so rigid and inflexible that women's self-definitions put them at odds with the social definitions. To do so only limits the expression of the diversities and variabilities in women's sexual identities.

Postscript

In the ten years since this article was first published (1987), the political and social tenor of the times has changed, and I now teach at a coeducational college. From this different vantage point, I still see ample evidence of diversity and variability in women's sexual identities. Bisexuality is no longer as invisible as it once was, and there is an easier acknowledgment and acceptance of the fluidity of women's sexuality.

Around 1980, I observed certain tensions around difference, specifically related to one's status as a primary or elective lesbian, and around issues of sexual fluidity. Now, there seems to be less discussion and hardly any antagonism over the questions "Was I born this way?" and "Did I choose it?" In fact, many young women resist making the primary/elective distinction; they may claim *both* to be true, or they may view *neither* conception relevant to who they are. Nor is the issue of sexual fluidity so divisive. More students have taken women's studies courses, and as they have become familiar with the critique of dichotomous categories, they move away from seeing such clear distinctions between the genders or between people of different sexualities. Gender fluidities are a real part of their daily experience; as women act in ways that were once called "masculine" and men in ways that were once labeled "feminine," it is clear that behavior is not determined by sex. Fluidity of behavior, dress, hairstyle, even gender identifications is much more visible in the late 1980s and 1990s, as transgender activists have insisted that they, too, be recognized. There has been a corresponding shift away from the dichotomous racial divide of black/white to a greater recognition of ethnic diversity, so that more white students are aware of having ethnic identities, and there is a cultural space for people to identify as biracial. In my first fifteen years of teaching, no student ever identified himself or herself as biracial; in recent years, however, a number of students have done so.

In this context of multilayered identities, sexual fluidity makes a great deal of sense—at least to many women. I find that men, both gay and heterosexual, remain somewhat baffled by the concept, because they have a hard time applying it to themselves. But at the same time, they comprehend—indeed seem to be threatened by—the idea of women's sexual fluidity. More than a few heterosexual women who are also strong feminists have told me that their boyfriends are convinced that they *could be* lesbians, despite the fact that they are monogamously sexually involved with these men, and self-identify as heterosexual rather than bisexual or lesbian.

Since this article was first published, the most striking change in the diversity and variability of women's sexual identities is the greater visibility of bisexuality. In 1987, I noted that far fewer women identified themselves as bisexual than as lesbian and that women never openly identified themselves as bisexuals in class, nor did they raise bisexual issues publicly. This has changed. At times, it seems that there are more bisexual women on this private northeastern college campus than lesbians. For example, at a 1995 coming-out rally, an annual campus event, about forty students took the microphone and declared their sexual identities. Twenty were gay men, eighteen were bisexual women, and two were lesbians. It seemed that, in contrast to earlier years, the lesbians had disappeared! In 1996, there was a more balanced representation of lesbian and bisexual women (most of the men were still gay). One might attribute increased bisexual visibility to the difference in college settings, but I understand that bisexuality is increasingly evident at women's colleges as well. Furthermore, I am told by first- and second-year college students that bisexuality among girls is "in" and "trendy" at the high school level. Certainly, bisexuality is more evident in the culture at large and more scholarly attention has been paid to it.[14]

While there are many different aspects of this change upon which I could comment, what I find most interesting in light of the intolerance and tension I identified in the original essay around issues of sexual fluidity, is the apparent lack of division on this particular campus between lesbian and bisexual students. It appears to me there is an unclouded tolerance for whatever sexual decisions and choices each woman might make. I have probed for tensions around this issue, and the students have a hard time understanding what I'm asking. Why would anyone challenge or question another's decision to become involved with a person of one gender or another, they wonder? Among the lesbians with whom I've spoken, there is no claim made that the bisexuals "are really lesbians" who are unwilling to admit it or afraid to let go of heterosexual privilege. As a result, the bisexual women are fully integrated into the lesbian, gay, bisexual student organization, and there appears to be greater harmony and less debate around issues of identity than I observed on a different campus.

In contrast to the early 1980s, there now seems to be less of a need to label or to argue about who is more oppressed. In fact, lesbians for the most part agreed with the bisexual students who contended that in many ways it is *harder* to be bisexual. They pointed to the stereotypes about bisexuality, the sense that they constantly have to explain themselves to others and, most painfully, to parents who refuse to acknowledge, let alone take seriously, their same-gendered attractions and relationships.

The only evidence of intolerance for women's identification as bisexual came from "older" lesbian feminists of the 1970s, some of them on the faculty, who seemed suspicious of the reasons young women would identify as bisexual, especially if they were sexually involved with women. These lesbian feminists subscribed to the view that it was internalized homophobia and a desire not to alienate men that led so many women to identify as bisexual rather than lesbian. They expressed the attitude that these women "are lacking in politics," by which they mean a 1970s lesbian feminist politics. My own view, based both on my interactions with these young women and on research interviews with older bisexually identified women,[15] is that their bisexuality is grounded in their own authentic self-expression, born of a different, more pluralized, feminist consciousness. It is neither an attempt to placate men or their parents, nor an indication of internalized homophobia, but rather an expression of a fluid and chosen sexuality in an era where women's choices have multiplied, where some men are feminists and changing in ways that suit women, and where biological sex has been rejected as a necessary criterion for choosing a sexual partner. This development only expands the possibilities for diversity and variability in women's sexual experiences and identities.

One other development since this article was first published is worth noting: the continuing investigation of biological causes of homosexuality and the increased attention to such studies in the news media. Research on biological causation is not new, but front-page news coverage is becoming increasingly common. The three most recent and widely publicized studies of homosexuality deal with differences in the brains and/or genetic DNA markers found in gay and heterosexual men. From Simon LeVay's study of the third interstitial nucleus of the anterior hypothalamus,[16] to J. Michael Bailey and Richard Pillard's study of identical and fraternal twins,[17] to Dean Hamer's study of the DNA markers in the Xq28 region of men's X chromosome,[18] the research focuses exclusively on men and has received front-page coverage in the *New York Times* and major newsmagazines. In contrast, Bailey et al.'s study of lesbian twins and siblings[19] was reported only on the inside pages of the *New York Times.*

Further, the "major" studies are androcentric in that they use a male subject pool and, upon finding some biological basis for homosexuality, assume that it makes sense to search for something similar in women. In a more recent study that received no major news coverage at all, Stella Hu et al. included lesbians in their sample and looked at the role of Xq28 in sexual orientation.[20] In contrast to the findings with men, there was no difference in concordance rates (likelihood of sharing the Xq28 genetic marker) between lesbians who had lesbian sisters and those who had heterosexual sisters, leading the researchers to conclude that Xq28 is unrelated to sexual orientation in women. Another recent study involving lesbians was also neglected by the news media. Angela Pattatucci and Dean Hamer reported that nonheterosexual women were more likely than heterosexual women to have daughters, sisters, cousins (through a paternal uncle), and nieces who were also nonheterosexual.[21] While this "familial clustering" does not allow one to tease out environmental and biological contributing factors, neither does it allow one to claim that genetics plays a definitive role.

The most obvious problem I see with the biological literature is that it doesn't take account of women's experience. That it is often gay scientists who have adopted these biological models does not make them any less problematic, nor does it make the data from their studies any more conclusive. Since this essay first appeared, a growing body of research confirms my earlier finding that women do not necessarily experience their sexuality as biologically based or as invariantly fixed on one gender.[22] It is not rare for women to say that they *chose* to be lesbian or bisexual—as a result of exploration, exposure, the women's movement, or other transformative experiences. Even some heterosexual women see the possibility of making a choice (indeed their *heterosexuality* may be a choice) and feel that their sexual preference could change in the future. Most researchers would probably acknowledge that sexual orientation is too complex to be determined by a single gene. If more consideration were given to women and the richly textured accounts they give of their sexual identities, the role of conscious choice would be better recognized and the meaning of sexual fluidity more fully explored.

· CHAPTER THIRTEEN ·

Explaining Homosexuality

Who Cares Anyhow?

FREDERICK SUPPE

Frederick Suppe, professor of philosophy and chairperson of the History and Philosophy of Science Program at the University of Maryland at College Park, challenges the scientific legitimacy of research into the cause or origin of sexual orientation. Suppe distinguishes among various components of sexual orientation and argues that virtually all research in this area rests on a crude blurring of these components. According to Suppe, such research appears legitimate only against the backdrop of late Victorian assumptions about "normal love."

· · · · ·

John: If you got a Ph.D. in philosophy, what caused you to become a prostitute?
Hustler: Who cares? . . . Guess I was just lucky!

For more than a century, psychiatric, medical, and scientific researchers have sought to identify the causes of "deviant" sexual behavior, including homosexuality. Over 1,000 studies have been published postulating—and claiming to have established—a variety of mechanisms causing or explaining homosexuality: genetic origins; hormonal imbalances; abnormal hormonal levels during gestation resulting in the feminization of male brains or masculinization of female brains; morphological differences ranging from skeletal ratios to muscularity to body fat and even to masculine versus feminine pubic hair configurations; birth order; a variety of social learning

This manuscript is a revised and augmented version of the final section of Frederick Suppe's "Explaining Homosexuality: Philosophical Issues, and Who Cares anyhow?," co-published simultaneously in the *Journal of Homosexuality* (The Haworth Press, Inc.) Vol 27, No. 3/4, 1994, pp. 223–268; and *Gay Ethics: Controversies in Outing, Civil Rights, and Sexual Science* (ed. Timothy F. Murphy), Haworth Press, 1994.

theories focusing on the personality characteristics of parents ("male homosexuals are the product of close-binding intimate mothers and distant detached fathers"); and psychoanalytic accounts in terms of arrested psychosexual development or Oedipal fixations.[1]

I have examined most of these studies to evaluate the methodological adequacy of the research; the conceptual adequacy of the main variables, measures, or concepts used to frame research hypotheses and collect data; the appropriateness of statistical techniques used to analyze data; the extent to which the data and statistics actually support the interpretations imposed upon them; and the replicability of findings by other research studies.[2] Others have done similar evaluations for selected portions of the literature.[3] The upshot of such evaluations is that most of the science isn't very good—judged by precisely the standards prevailing in the social and biological sciences. Few studies unequivocally establish what they claim to establish. This body of literature provides a virtual encyclopedia of methodologically unsound research.

There is no consensus among philosophers as to either the nature of, or the standards of adequacy for, scientific explanation. In the social sciences, a common practice is to determine statistically what percentages of the variance in an outcome variable (here, sexual orientation) can be attributed to various putative "causes" (e.g., close-binding intimate mother with detached distant father, birth order). Each such variable is said to explain that much of the outcome variance. Variables (or combinations) that explain less than 30 percent of the outcome variance are not viewed as empirically significant.

For the range of studies postulating some sort of social, as opposed to biological, etiological mechanism, an impressive Kinsey Institute replicative study of the main competing accounts was undertaken using the most diverse and adequate research sample yet assembled.[4] This team of researchers found that the putative social causes prominent in the research literature explained, at best, minuscule amounts of the variance in sexual orientation. None of the postulated mechanisms individually or in combination came close to explaining an empirically significant portion of the variance.

Thus a century's worth of research has produced a body of research, much of which is methodologically flawed, that fails to identify any plausible mechanisms causing homosexuality. In part, this is not surprising, given how much of the research was done by psychiatrists and physicians whose clinical training leaves them untrained amateurs when it comes to scientific research methodology and practice. But it does not explain why research by trained social and biological scientists has been equally unsuccessful.

Conceptualizing Homosexuality

The most pervasive defect in the literature surveyed is a high level of conceptual confusion as to what counts as a homosexual and a heterosexual. Much of the research is grounded in equivocations among homosexuality, transsexualism, gender-role stereotype nonconformity ("sissy" boys, tomboys, effeminate males, "butch" females), and transvestism. Such equivocations are undercut by solid research demonstrating that sexual orientation and sexual identity are complex conditions involving a number of distinct dimensions.

The following distinct components of sexual identity have been identified in the literature.[5]

1. *Biological sex*: the determination whether one is male, female, or hermaphroditic,
2. *Gender identity*: one's basic conviction of being male or female,
3. *Social sex role*: extent of conformity to physical and psychological characteristics culturally associated with males and females,
4. *Sexual orientation*: consists of the following five components:
    a. *sexual behavior*: patterns of erotic bodily contact with others;
    b. *interpersonal affection patterns*: associations involving various degrees of trust, such as with friends, lovers, and marital partners;
    c. *erotic fantasy structure*: sexually arousing patterns of mental images of one or more persons engaged in physical sexual activity or in affectional relationships;
    d. *arousal cue-response patterns*: sensory cues that stimulate or inhibit erotic arousal;
    e. *self-labeling*: labels one applies to oneself such as "queer," "gay," "leatherfag," "lesbian," "bull dyke," "homosexual," "heterosexual," "transvestite," "drag queen."

These dimensions are *orthogonal* in the sense that they vary independently of one another.

How strongly or loosely these dimensions correlate with one another is an empirical, not a conceptual, matter. And the empirical evidence is that virtually every combination occurs among humans. Standard classifications of sexual variation (pejoratively called "sexual paraphilias") can be differentiated only by taking into account patterns of variation among these dimensions. Thus transsexualism is incongruence between one's biological sex and one's gender identity. Transvestism may involve incongruity between biological sex and social sex role, or it may center in a fetishistic arousal cue-response pattern, or it may be outside one's sexual identity altogether (perhaps as an occupation). Persons exclusively heterosexual in behavior may have exclusively homosexual fantasy structures (e.g., male fantasizing about having sex with another male while engaging in heterosexual coitus, perhaps as part of self-deceptive denial). And one's behavior can be exclusively homosexual while one's self-labeling is heterosexual (as reportedly is the case with many male hustlers).

The terms "heterosexual" and "homosexual" have been applied to each of these eight dimensions of sexual identity. Strictly speaking, it is conceptual confusion to conflate heterosexuality or homosexuality with biological sex, gender identity, or social sex role. The terms sometimes are appropriately applied to the various dimensions of sexual orientation. However, the following qualifications are needed: first, persons may be homosexual in some dimensions of sexual orientation, while heterosexual in others. Thus it is inappropriate to speak of one having a homosexual orientation or a heterosexual orientation *simpliciter*, except as shorthand for congruent exclusivity on all five components. Second, the most significant aspects of a sexual orientation dimension need not be gendered at all. For example, the most significant arousal cues, fantasy ingredients, and the like for an individual may not be gender correlated in any way (e.g., eroticized long hair, leather, silk, body shaving, toe sucking, scents, physical trauma such as in whipping), and in such cases, heterosexual and homosexual labels may, at best, be misleading, and in some cases, totally inappropriate.

The fact that sexual identity and sexual orientation are so multidimensional has serious implications for how sexual orientation research is conceptualized. Any reasonable attempt to study the etiology of sexual identities or orientations will have to conceptualize them multivariately, and the components of sexual orientation will have to include a much richer variety of sexual activities than just vanilla male-male, female-female, and female-male coupling patterns. Even if one limits oneself to standard variations, there are literally hundreds of different sexual identities and sexual orientations. Any simplistic heterosexual or homosexual classification does too much violence to the diversity of human sexuality to have a place in scientifically credible accounts of the etiology of sexual identity or orientation. For what it studies, then, is an artifact of crude conceptualization, and it is thus a nonexistent phenomenon.

This fact, probably more than any other, explains why so little sexual orientation variance has in fact been explained by past etiological studies. It is important to understand that past and present etiological studies are conceptually crude and inadequate relative to what is known scientifically about sexual orientation and sexual identity, not just to some abstract or ideal philosophical standard of conceptual adequacy. The conceptual crudity with which the etiological problem is conceived and the inadequate research designs that follow are unacceptable under the standards routinely achieved in the social and biological sciences.

Who Cares Anyhow?

After nearly 1,000 studies of homosexual etiology, we really haven't established much of anything positive about the causes of homosexuality. In their own characteristic ways, biological theories, social learning theories, and psychoanalytic theories all prove spectacularly unsuccessful and uninformative. Two responses to this are possible. One is the "back to the drawing board" response,[6] which treats etiology as terribly important and calls for more sophisticated rethinking of the matter and improved theories and studies. The other, which I favor, is, "Who cares anyhow?" This raises the question: Why should we be concerned about the etiology of homosexuality?

Sociology of science tells us that the basic work of science is done in small (typically 50–200 people) invisible colleges that form stable scientific communities specializing in a class of problems, usually with common methodologies.[7] These invisible colleges aggregate into larger specialties, subdisciplines, and disciplines. Invisible colleges establish their own standards of scientific quality, and those standards are monitored by the larger specialties, journal editorial boards, and the like. A complex process for credentialing scientific work thus exists.[8]

Philosophers of science tell us that research within an invisible college typically is not done in a vacuum, but rather is done against its shared background of a body of received fact and theory, background knowledge, and a research agenda informed and conditioned by various preempirical commitments and claims. Dudley Shapere discusses the role of scientific domains and background knowledge in determining what questions a science investigates.[9] Larry Laudan details the role of what he calls "research traditions" in a discipline's scientific research and further explores issues over how a science sets its cognitive goals.[10] Imre Lakatos discusses his research programs,[11] Thomas Kuhn his paradigms (now disciplinary matrices),[12] and Stephen Toulmin his intellectual and explanatory ideals[13]—all of which are claimed to strongly condition the problems a science chooses to investigate and the methodology used.

As research within an invisible college matures, we find a growing body of cumulative research output in its domain. We can characterize the health of an invisible college on the basis of the richness of its domain, the ability of later research to avoid the main weaknesses of earlier research, the growth of a literature that is getting somewhere (rather than a succession of failed attempts that lead nowhere), and the extent to which the research increasingly is driven by its growing body of findings, rather than by extrascientific assumptions or ones imported from other disciplines. To extend Lakatos's apt terminology, we can speak of the research in an invisible college as progressive or degenerating.[14]

It is useful to inquire as to the health of the various invisible colleges concerned with homosexual etiology. Since the publication of Alan Bell, Martin Weinberg, and Sue Hammersmith's 1981 study, *Sexual Preferences*, investigation into social causes of homosexuality has become moribund. When we turn to genetic accounts, we find highly discontinuous research. As J. Michael Bailey and Richard Pillard note, "very little work has been done in this area from a behavioral genetic perspective"[15]—or from any other genetical perspective for that matter. In the hormonal area, work by Dörner and colleagues garnered a lot of attention, [16] then fell by the wayside as it failed to be replicated. Simon LeVay's work[17] is by an outsider who did it as a "hobby project" diversion from his usual neuroscientific research.[18] In short, what we find are scattered episodic forays into homosexual etiology, which typically lead nowhere.

It is unclear whether there are any stable invisible colleges today concerned with homosexual etiology. But it is clear that there is little cumulative growth of a body of literature that builds upon prior successes. Moreover, we find the scattered efforts recapitulating the basic conceptual confusions that have undercut prior failed attempts at explaining homosexual etiology. If there are invisible colleges, they seem inept at learning from prior failures.

The lack of progressiveness in etiological research is reflected in the fact that the basic conceptualization of the research problems is based on extrascientific considerations, not a growing body of successful science. To see this, let us ask: What are the presuppositions that make the etiology of homosexuality seem an important scientific research question? As an outgrowth of my earlier work on homosexuality research and a debate with Robert Spitzer before the Society for Health and Human Values, I did a detailed evaluation of the American Psychiatric Association's classification of sexual disorders in DSM-III.[19] As I discovered a near-total lack of competent scientific evidence substantiating its classifications of the sexual paraphilias as mental disorders, and as I realized that precisely the same reasons used to justify the removal of homosexuality per se as a mental disorder also called for the removal of all the paraphilias as per se disorders,[20] I came to suspect that the earlier inclusion of homosexuality and the continued inclusion of the paraphilias as mental disorders were nothing more than the codification of social mores masquerading as scientific results.

Such a thesis is, of course, a historical one and to establish it requires historical analysis and evidence. In a 1987 article published in *Sexuality and Medicine*[21] I supplied that historical evidence, arguing that medico-psychiatric treatments of homosexuality, the paraphilias, and transsexualism in the twentieth century were and continue to be rooted in a late Victorian view that Jonathan Katz calls "the theory of normal love."[22] On this theory, sex-love was thought all pervasive, and so lack of erotic feeling and extreme continence were viewed as sexual aberrations. Closely allied was the idea that emotions had genders or sexes, and by the 1880s and 1890s, the dominant medical meaning of sexual normality and abnormality was the procreative versus the nonprocreative and conformity versus nonconformity to sex-role stereotypes.

The results included the hopeless confusion of homosexuality, transsexualism, effeminacy in males and masculinity in females, and other nonprocreative acts into an undifferentiated "sexual perversion" category that is still being untangled and sorted out.[23] This "theory of normal love" informs and conditions medico-scientific research even today. Witness the confusion between effeminacy and male homosexuality even in recent etiology research postulating feminized brains and the like.[24] Only with the work of the Kinsey Institute, Evelyn Hooker, and that commissioned by the National Institutes of Health's Task Force on Homosexuality—all appearing after World War II—do we find significant amounts of research on homosexuality being done outside the medico-psychiatric professions. This research either tends to be not concerned with etiology or attempts to replicate medico-scientific etiological research using nonclinical, noncriminal populations—in the process, it generally fails to confirm earlier medico-psychiatric findings.

Historically, then, the basis for viewing homosexuality as an abnormality requiring treatment or prophylactic measures has been the Victorian "theory of normal love"—for which not a shred of unbiased empirical evidence has been produced, it being a codification of a late Victorian middle-class ethos (one, incidentally, that provided a welcome climate for the ready uncritical popular acceptance of Freud's views on polymorphous sexuality). No empirically validated replacement theory or findings have been produced that propel one to view homosexuality as a condition of problematic etiology *while also* viewing the etiology of heterosexuality as unproblematic. Thus we have in the homosexuality (and other sexual variation) research an instance where the background theory/beliefs conditioning a scientific research program are extrascientific normative values, in contrast to the more legitimate scientific ones that such scholars as Shapere and Laudan stress.

In short, the available scientific evidence provides no basis for treating the etiology of homosexuality as a legitimate scientific research problem. The situation here is similar to that of left-handedness. Earlier in this century, it was widely held that right-handedness was normal and left-handedness was abnormal and inferior. Strident attempts were made in the public schools to force all children to be right-handed, and there was concern over what caused the "disease" of left-handedness. Once it was accepted that there was natural variation in which hand was one's dominant hand, the etiology of left-handedness ceased to be a serious scientific research problem.

Moreover, those who continue to insist that there is a problem of homosexual etiology rely on uncritical acceptance of a crude homosexual/heterosexual classification scheme that can be sustained only in ignorance of, or at the price of rejecting, the cumulative knowledge coming out of the more progressive portions of the sex-research area. In short, there is every indication that homosexual etiology is the province of a degenerated research agenda and thus no longer represents credible science. This is reflected in the fact that much of the biological etiological research is published in psychiatric and other such journals "inappropriate" to a progressive biological research area. Continuation of such research has little scientific merit.

Against the line I have been defending, some will argue that we need to do research on homosexual etiology in order to have data to use in for example, court cases that concern child custody by homosexuals and controversies surrounding homosexual teachers. Such data could also be used in arguments concerning gay rights and responsibilities or for those involving homosexuals in the military and the like. Several responses to this are in order. First, there is ample data demonstrating that homosexual parents are as fit as heterosexual single parents and that children raised by homosexuals are as likely to be heterosexual as those raised by heterosexuals,[25] but these data have little effect on judicial deliberations.

Second, a key reason for the limited efficacy of such research on judicial and legislative deliberations is that opponents can negate the effect of such competent research by pitting against it the hostile and incompetent "expert" pronouncements of such notoriously homophobic "authorities" as Charles Socarides. One doesn't need data, one only needs pronouncements of "experts." Expert witnesses can be impeached only on the basis of inadequate credentials, not on the scientific cogency of their views. Thus one piles a confusing welter of conflicting "expert opinions" on the hapless jury. In such circumstances of "divided opinion," the experts siding with more conservative and traditional homophobic prejudices tend to prevail. The continued status of homosexual etiology as a "legitimate scientific problem" tends to perpetuate such proceedings, as well as the continued labeling of homosexuality as a "sexual deviation" meriting study.

Third, to persist in defending the research legitimacy of homosexuality etiology for reasons outlined above is just to admit that it *is* part of a political, not a scientific, agenda. The defense of the research project thus rests on grounds no more scientific than that of the Victorian origins of the project. To the extent the research is legitimized by the political goals of its proponents, it is as a piece of social engineering rather than dispassionate science.

Who cares what causes homosexuality? Only those who subscribe to the Victorian "theory of normal love," its current-day remnants, or some moral or political agenda. But insofar as we act qua scientists, it is not I who cares—nor, I would hope, anyone with serious scientific aspirations. And qua gay, I just count myself lucky.

· PART THREE ·

Identity And History

Aristophanes' Speech from the *Symposium*

PLATO
(translation and notes by Leah Himmelhoch)

Plato's Symposium, *famous for its celebration of love, is especially noteworthy for its discussion of homoerotic love. In this selection, classicist Leah Himmelhoch translates the speech of Aristophanes, whose myth of the three primordial "genders" is widely interpreted as an ancient account of the origin of sexual orientation. For a debate on this interpretation, see the following two selections, by John Boswell and David Halperin respectively.*

· · · · ·

Translator's note: The *Symposium*, or "The Drinking Party," was written circa 384–379 B.C.E. by the Athenian philosopher Plato (c. 427–c. 348) and purports to describe events that took place many years earlier at a party thrown in honor of the playwright Agathon's first dramatic victory (c. 416 B.C.E.). The dialogue is "narrated" by Apollodorus, one of Socrates' followers, who claims that his friend Aristodemus, who was present at the celebration, conveyed the story to him. This dialogue, then, is a speech about a speech that relates still other speeches. Such a stylistic dislocation of speakers and the events they describe is a typical Platonic strategy for reminding readers to actively investigate the debates at hand, rather than to passively accept them as truth. As for the setting of the symposium itself, Agathon and his lover, Pausanias, are the hosts of the soirée, and their guests include: Phaedrus, who gives his name to another Socratic dialogue on love (the *Phaedrus*); Eryximachus, a doctor and Phaedrus's lover; the comic playwright Aristophanes; the philosopher Socrates, who becomes so absorbed in thought *en route* that he arrives late; Aristodemus, a companion of Socrates, and Apollodorus's "informant"; and, last but not least, the playboy statesman Alcibiades, who, predictably, shows up late—even later than Socrates. Parties such as this one traditionally involved heavy drinking throughout the night; however, on this occasion, the participants are all exhausted from their celebration immediately following Agathon's victory of the night before, and so they choose, instead, to talk about the nature of "Eros" (love or desire). Aristophanes is the fourth speaker, following Phaedrus, Pausanias, and Eryximachus, in that order. Aristophanes is followed by Agathon, Socrates (who dislocates his readers even further by giving a speech about a conversation he once had, with a woman, no less, named Diotima), and finally, Alcibiades, who gives a speech in praise of Socrates.

Aristophanes' Speech

(189c) "Yes indeed, Eryximachus," Aristophanes began, "I intend to give a different style of speech than you and Pausanias just did.[1] You see, in my opinion, people have altogether failed to grasp the power of Eros,[2] since, if we had grasped it, I believe that, right then and there, we would have built him the greatest temples and altars, and we would have offered him the most spectacular sacrifices. Our worship of Eros—which, if anything, ought to be especially grandiose—wouldn't be like it is now, that is, practically non-existent. I say this because, of the gods, (189d) Eros is the most charitably inclined toward mortals, insofar as he is our ally and the healer of those ills whose remedy would be the greatest blessing for the human race. I shall, therefore, endeavor to relate for your instruction a parable on 'The Power of Eros,' and you, in turn, shall be the instructors of others.

"First, you must learn about Human Nature and its anguish. For, once upon a time, our nature was not the same as it is nowadays, but quite different. Originally, humanity had three genders[3]—not just two like there are now, the Male and the Female (189e)—but a third gender as well, which shared features from both the Male and the Female, whose name alone is left to us, although it has itself vanished. Yes, in those days the *Androgyne* was part Male and part Female, both in appearance and in name.[4] Nowadays, however, androgynes exist only in name, and even then the word is used as an insult.

"Back then, everybody's shape was round, with their backs and sides forming a circle, and each person used to have four arms, and the same number of legs as arms, (190a) and two faces, alike in every way, on top of a circular neck; but there was only one head for both of these faces, which were facing in opposite directions. Each individual also had four ears, and two sets of genitalia, and so on and so forth, with everything else following just as you'd expect. And each would walk about in an upright position, just as we do now, heading whichever direction either face might wish. And whenever they would break into a run, they would somersault about like circus acrobats: launching themselves off the ground in a flurry of eight limbs, they would do flips, at which point they would be whirled swiftly about in tight-spinning cartwheels.

(190b) "There were three genders of such form and content for the following reasons: the Male was originally descended from the Sun, and the Female was born from the Earth, whereas the Androgyne, which is both Male and Female, was descended from the Moon, since the moon, too, shares characteristics from the Male and the Female.[5] Because these three genders were spherical like their parents, then, both they and their gaits were roly-poly.

"Now, these three genders were awesome in their physical might and their strength of will, and they harbored great ambitions: they dared to attack the gods, and what Homer reports about the giants Ephialtes and Otus is also told about our ancestors, who were said to have forced their ascent into Heaven, (190c) thinking they could put one over on the gods.[6] Well, Zeus and the other gods deliberated at length over an appropriate response to this affront, but they were stumped: you see, as the gods saw it, they couldn't just lightning-blast the human race into oblivion as they had the giants, because if they did this, then they would also obliterate the honors and sacrifices they were used to receiving from us. Then again, the gods couldn't let humanity run amok, either. At long last, Zeus, who had given the matter considerable thought, spoke up:

" 'I think,' he said, 'I have a cunning plan, that would allow human beings to exist, and yet put an end to their license, since they would be made considerably weaker. (190d) As of now,' he declared, 'I will slice each of them in two, and not only will both halves be diminished in strength, but they'll also be more profitable for us, since their numbers will have doubled! They'll continue to walk about upright—only now on two legs. And if they still seem to act outrageously, and they won't behave, why then,' he continued, 'I'll cut them in half yet again, so that they'll have to skitter about on one foot, as if they were trying to keep their balance on a greased wineskin.'[7]

"Once Zeus finished his pronouncement, he set about cutting mortals into two halves, just as we split apples in half when we are going to make preserves, (190e) or when someone slices a boiled egg in half with a hair. And as Zeus would halve each person, he would order Apollo to rotate each half's face and half-neck toward the incision, so that by observing his or her own severing, the newly created mortals would learn to be more orderly in future. Next, Zeus bid Apollo to heal the rest of the wound. So, Apollo set about rotating each face, and, after drawing the hide together from all around the wound's edges toward the spot we now call our belly, he bunched up the edges to form a single puckered opening; then, he tied off the opening right at the center of the stomach, just like a pouch with a drawstring, to create what we today call our belly button. Finally, Apollo smoothed out the other, numerous wrinkles (191a) that remained, and articulated our chests using the sort of tool that cobblers use when they smooth the wrinkles out of leather stretched on a last. Apollo left a few wrinkles around the navel, however, as a reminder to us of this ancient trauma.

"Now, after their nature was cut in twain, each half, out of yearning for its former self, would rush toward its other half, and the two halves would throw their arms around each other and get tangled in a close embrace, longing to meld back into their former state. As a result, they started to perish of hunger and other inactivity (191b), because they were completely unwilling to separate from one another. Moreover, whenever one of the halves would die and the other was left behind, the abandoned half would seek out another half and embrace it, regardless of whether it was half of a Female whole, or a woman, as we would call her today, or half of a Male whole. And in this way, humanity was dying out.

"Zeus, however, taking pity on mortals, devised another plan, and he moved their genitals around toward their fronts. For, until then, their genitals had been located on their backsides, (191c) and they didn't use to conceive or engender offspring in one another, but in the earth, like cicadas.[8] So, Zeus shifted their genitals to their fronts, and in this way he enabled conception to take place, through the male being *in* the female. He did this for the following reasons: so that, if a man encountered a woman in an embrace, they would reproduce and there would be children. Moreover, should a man join together with a man, the two would at least gain sexual satisfaction from the union, and they could take a break from their constant search for their missing half, turn back to business affairs, and take care of the rest of their lives.[9] (191d) Erotic attraction for one another, then, is innate to mortals, and originates from such a time and circumstances as I have just described. Eros is the reintegrator of our primal nature, ever prepared to make us one from two and to mend humanity's sundered condition.

"Each of us, then, is a broken half of a contract coin,[10] split just as flatfish are, one half of a whole;[11] and for this reason, everyone constantly seeks out his or her matching half. So, those men who are a slice of the

Male-Female whole, originally called an 'Androgyne,' are inordinately fond of women, and the majority of adulterers are descended fom this gender, (191e) as are adulterous, nymphomaniacal women.[12] Women who were sliced from a Female whole, on the other hand—they don't pay attention to men at all; rather, they are oriented more toward women, and so these women-lovers[13] are descended from this primal, Female gender. Those men who are slices from the Male whole, however, pursue Maleness, and since they are slices from the primal Male, then while they are still boys they love men, and they enjoy lying alongside men and embracing them. (192a) These are the best of the boys and adolescents, since they are the bravest and most masculine by nature. True, some say that these boys are shameless—but those who say so are lying. For such boys do not act out of shamelessness, but rather, they are motivated by daring, courage, and masculinity, cherishing that which is like themselves. Here I'll provide a sure proof that what I say is right: once these boys have grown up, they alone prove fit for politics. And when they become men, (192b) these men, in turn, become lovers of boys; it isn't in their nature to care for marriage or making babies, but they do so because they are compelled to do so by society.[14] Instead, they are content to spend their lives with one another, unmarried. Such a man, then, is altogether fond of boys and men, always welcoming what is congenial to him.

"And so, whenever a man (a boy-lover, or any sort of lover, for that matter) should encounter the person who is his 'missing' half,[15] then the two are struck dumb with a sense of loving familiarity (192c) and desire, and they are loath to be parted from one another for practically the slightest instant. These are the sort of men who spend their entire lives together; and yet, they couldn't say exactly what they want from one another, for, surely, sexual pleasure alone can't explain why either one so intensely enjoys their union. Each man's soul is clearly longing for something else—what it is, the soul cannot express, (192d) but it hints at what the lover wants with oracular ambiguity.[16] Yet, what if Hephaestus,[17] holding his tools, were to stand over the two as they lay together, and what if he were to ask: 'What do you want from one another, mortals?' And as they lay there at a loss for an answer, what if he were to ask them again, 'Come now, isn't this what you desire, to become one and the same person, so that, night and day, you'd never be apart from one another? If you desire it, (192e) I'm willing to fuse you together, so as for the two of you to be one and the same. As long as you live, you'll share life as one individual, and when you die, even dead the two of you will dwell in Hades as one person instead of two.[18] But consider whether this is your desire, and whether you would be satisfied should you obtain it.'

"Once any lover heard this, we know that no one could refuse it, nor could anyone possibly wish anything else; but, plain and simple, he would think to have finally discovered what he truly desired all along: that he and his beloved could join and be melted together, to become one from two. The root cause for this need is that our primeval nature was as I described, and we were whole then. Our desire and pursuit of the whole has a name, and that is Eros (193a).[19]

"As I keep saying, long ago we were one, but now we have been dispersed, relocated as it were, by Zeus because of our wrong-doing, just as the Arcadians were resettled by the Lacedaemonians.[20] So, the fear remains that if we aren't well behaved toward the gods, we may be split down the middle once again, and we'll go about like figures sculpted onto reliefs, sawed down the center of our noses as if we were half-dice.[21] For this reason, then, it is right and proper that every man exhort his fellows to act with the utmost piety toward the gods, so that we might avoid further punishment and obtain good fortune, with Eros as our leader and general. Therefore, let no one violate this directive, for whoever does so is hateful to the gods; but, once we abandon enmity and ally ourselves with Eros, we will each chance upon our soulmates, a blessing which few men of today experience.

"Do not interrupt me, Eryximachus, and turn my speech into a burlesque by saying that I mean Pausanias and Agathon. For perhaps they actually *are* this sort, and they are both halves of what was once a Male whole. I, at least, am talking about everyone, both men and women, because the human race would be blessed if we could each fulfill our innate desire to obtain a lover[22] of our own, and return to our original state. Moreover, if this ideal is best for humanity, it must follow that the current situation closest to this ideal is also best: to obtain a lover whose nature is most congenial to one's own. Therefore, if we are to sing praise to the god who is the cause of this, we would rightly hymn Eros, who, in our present circumstances, especially benefits us by guiding us to our kindred spirits. As for the future, so long as we maintain our piety toward the gods, Eros promises the greatest of expectations, to restore us to our original, natural state, and, once he has healed us, to make us blessed and happy.

"This, Eryximachus," Aristophanes said, "is my speech concerning Eros, which is quite different from yours. So, just as I asked you, don't poke fun at it, so that we can also hear what the rest of the party-goers will say; or, better yet, let me rephrase that: what the last two will say, since only Agathon and Socrates remain."

· CHAPTER FIFTEEN ·

Revolutions, Universals, and Sexual Categories

JOHN BOSWELL

John Boswell, a noted Yale historian until his death in 1994, offers his perspective on the so-called essentialist/constructionist debate (see the introduction to this volume). Boswell explains this debate in terms of the philosophical debate between "realists," who hold that universal categories exist whether or not humans acknowledge them, and "nominalists," who hold that universal categories are convenient social devices that humans impose upon the world. Boswell considers whether the categories of human sexuality are better captured by the realist (essentialist) or nominalist (constructionist) model. To put the question more simply: Were there gay people in the ancient world, or is gayness a uniquely modern category? To answer this question, Boswell distinguishes among three broad types of sexual taxonomy and argues that ancient texts (like Aristophanes' speech in the preceding chapter) suggest that there are indeed some constants in human sexual self-understanding throughout the ages. For a contrasting perspective on the same issues, see the following essay by David Halperin.

· · · · ·

One of the revolutions in the study of history in the twentieth century might be called "minority history": the effort to recover the histories of groups previously overlooked or excluded from mainstream historiogra-

This chapter is reprinted with revisions from "Revolutions, Universals, and Sexual Categories," *Salmagundi* No. 58-59 (Fall 1982/Winter 1983), pp. 89–113. The postscript is reprinted with revisions from *Hidden from History: Exploring the Gay and Lesbian Past* (New York: Penguin, 1990) pp. 34–36.

phy. Minority history has provoked predictable skepticism on the part of some traditional historians, partly because of its novelty—which will, of course, inevitably wear off—and partly because the attitudes that previously induced neglect or distortion of minority history still prevail in many quarters. The most reasonable criticism of minority history (aside from the objection that it is sometimes very poor scholarship, against which no discipline is proof) is that it lends itself to political use, which may distort scholarly integrity. As a point about minority history as a genre, this is not cogent: since the exclusion of minorities from much historiography prior to the twentieth century was related to or caused by concerns other than purely scholarly interest, their inclusion now, even for purely political ends, not only corrects a previous "political" distortion, but also provokes a more complete database for judgments about the historical issues involved. Such truth as is yielded by historical analysis generally emerges from the broadest possible synthesis of the greatest number of viewpoints and vantages: the addition of minority history and viewpoints to twentieth-century historiography is a net gain for all concerned.

But at a more particular level, political struggles can cause serious problems for scholars, and a curious debate now taking place among those interested in the history of gay people provides a relevant and timely example of a type of difficulty that could subvert minority history altogether if not addressed intelligently. To avoid contributing further to the undue political freight the issue has lately been forced to bear, I propose to approach it by way of another historical controversy, one that was—in its day—no less heated or urgent, but that is now sufficiently distant to be viewed with dispassion by all sides.

The conflict in question is as old as Plato and as modern as cladism, and although the most violent struggles over it took place in the twelfth and thirteenth centuries, the arguments of the ancients on the subject are still in use today. Stated as briefly and baldly as possible, the issues are these: Do categories exist because humans recognize real distinctions in the world around them, or are categories arbitrary conventions, simply names for things that have categorical force because humans agree to use them in certain ways? The two traditional sides in this controversy, which is called "the problem of universals," are "realists" and "nominalists." Realists consider categories to be the footprints of reality ("universals"): They exist because humans perceive a real order in the universe and name it. The order is present without human observation, according to realists; the human contribution is simply the naming and describing of it. Most scientists operate—tacitly—in a realist mode, on the assumption that they are discovering, not inventing, the relationships within the physical world. The scientific method is, in fact, predicated on realist attitudes. On the other hand, the philosophical structure of the modern West is closer to nominalism: the belief that categories are only the names (Latin: *nomina*) of things agreed upon by humans, and that the "order" people see is their creation rather than their perception. Most modern philosophy and language theory is essentially nominalist, and even the more theoretical sciences are nominalist to some degree: in biology, for example, taxonomists disagree strongly about whether they are discovering (realists) or inventing (nominalists) distinctions among phyla, genera, species, and so on. (When, for example, a biologist announces that bats, being mammals, are "more closely related to" humans than to birds, is he expressing some real relationship, present in nature and detected by humans, or is he employing an arbitrary convention, something that helps humans organize and sort information but that bears no "truth" or significance beyond this utility?)

This seemingly arcane struggle now underlies an epistemological controversy raging among those studying the history of gay people. The "universals" in this case are categories of sexual preference or orientation (the difference is crucial). Nominalists ("social constructionists" in the current debate) in the matter aver that categories of sexual preference and behavior are created by humans and human societies. Whatever reality they have is the consequence of the power they exert in those societies and the socialization processes that make them seem real to persons influenced by them. People consider themselves "homosexual" or "heterosexual" because they are induced to believe that humans are either "homosexual" or "heterosexual." Left to their own devices, without such processes of socialization, people would simply be sexual. The category "heterosexuality," in other words, does not so much describe a pattern of behavior inherent in human being as it creates and establishes it.

Realists ("essentialists") hold that this is not the case. Humans are, they insist, differentiated sexually. Many categories might be devised to characterize human sexual taxonomy, some more or less apt than others, but the accuracy of human perceptions does not affect reality. The heterosexual/homosexual dichotomy exists in speech and thought because it exists in reality: it was not invented by sexual taxonomists, but observed by them.[1]

Neither of these positions is usually held absolutely: most nominalists would be willing to admit that some aspects of sexuality are present, and might be distinguished, without direction from society. And most realists are happy to admit that the same real phenomenon might be described by various systems of categorization, some more accurate and helpful than others. One might suppose that "moderate nominalists" and "moderate realists" could therefore engage in a useful dialogue on those areas where they agree and, by careful analysis of their differences, promote discussion and understanding of these issues.

Political ramifications hinder this. Realism has historically been viewed by the nominalist camp as conservative, if not reactionary, in its implicit recognition of the value and/or immutability of the status quo; and nominalism has generally been regarded by realists as an obscurantist radical ideology designed more to undercut and subvert human values than to clarify them. Precisely these political overtones can be seen to operate today in scholarly debate over issues of sexuality. The efforts of sociobiology to demonstrate an evolutionary etiology of homosexuality have been vehemently denounced by many who regard the enterprise as reactionary realism, an effort to persuade people that social categories are fixed and unchangeable, while on the other side, psychiatric "cures" of homosexuality are bitterly resented by many as the cynical folly of nominalist pseudoscience: convince someone he shouldn't want to be a homosexual, persuade him to think of himself as a "heterosexual," and—presto!—he is a heterosexual. The category is the person.

Whether or not there are "homosexual" and "heterosexual" persons, as opposed to persons called "homosexual" or "heterosexual" by society, is obviously a matter of substantial import to the gay community, since it brings into question the nature and even the existence of such a community. It is, moreover, of substantial epistemological urgency to nearly all of society,[2] and the gravity and extent of this can be seen in the case of the problems it creates for history and historians.

The history of minorities poses ferocious difficulties: censorship and distortion, absence or destruction of records, the difficulty of writing about essentially personal and private aspects of human feelings and behavior, problems of definition, political dangers attendant on choosing certain subjects, and so forth. But if the nominalists are correct and the realists wrong, the problems in regard to the history of gay people are of an entirely different order: If the categories "homosexual/heterosexual" and "gay/straight" are the inventions of particular societies rather than real aspects of the human psyche, there is no gay history.[3] If "homosexuality" exists only when and where people are persuaded to believe in it, "homosexual" persons will have a "history" only in those particular societies and cultures.

In its most extreme form, this nominalist view has argued that only early modern and contemporary industrial societies have produced "homosexuality," and it is futile and misguided to look for "homosexuality" in earlier human history.

> What we call "homosexuality" (in the sense of the distinguishing traits of "homosexuals"), for example, was not considered a unified set of acts, much less a set of qualities defining particular persons, in pre-capitalist societies. . . . Heterosexuals and homosexuals are involved in social "roles" and attitudes which pertain to a particular society, modern capitalism.[4]

If this position is sustained, it will permanently alter, for better or worse, the nature and extent of minority history.

Clearly, it has much to recommend it. No characteristics interact with the society around them uniformly through time. Perceptions of, reactions to, and social response regarding blackness, blindness, left-handedness, Jewishness, or any other distinguishing (or distinguished) aspect of persons or peoples must necessarily vary as widely as the social circumstances in which they occur, and for this reason alone it could be reasonably argued that being Jewish, black, blind, left-handed, and so forth, is essentially different from one age and place to another. In some cultures, for example, Jews are categorized chiefly as an ethnic minority; in others, they are not, or are not perceived to be ethnically distinct from the peoples around them, and are distinguished solely by their religious beliefs. Similarly, in some societies, anyone darker than average is considered "black"; in others, a complex and highly technical system of racial categorization classes some persons as black even when they are lighter in color than many "whites." In both cases, moreover, the differences in attitudes held by the majority must affect profoundly the self-perception of the minority itself, and its patterns of life and behavior are in all probability notably different from those of "black" or "Jewish" people in other circumstances.

There can be no question that if minority history is to merit respect, it must carefully weigh such fundamental subtleties of context: merely cataloging references to "Jews" or to "blacks" may distort more than it reveals of human history if due attention is not paid to the meaning, in their historical setting, of such words and the concepts to which they apply. Do such reservations, on the other hand, uphold the claim that categories such as "Jew," "black," or "gay" are not diachronic and cannot, even with apposite qualification, be applied to ages and times other than those in which the terms themselves were used in precisely their modern sense? Extreme realists, without posing the question, have assumed the answer was no; extreme nominalists seem to be saying yes.

The question cannot be addressed intelligently without first noting three points. First, the positions are not in fact as clearly separable as this schema implies. It could be well argued, for example, that Robert Padgug,

Jeffrey Weeks, and others are in fact extreme *realists* in assuming that *modern* homosexuality is not simply one of a series of conventions designated under the same rubric, but is instead a "real" phenomenon that has no "real" antecedent in human history. Demonstrate to us the "reality" of this homosexuality, their opponents might legitimately demand, and prove to us that it has a unity and cohesiveness that justifies your considering it a single, unparalleled entity rather than a loose congeries of behaviors. Modern scientific literature increasingly assumes that what is at issue is not "homosexuality," but "homosexualities"; if these disparate patterns of sexuality can be grouped together under a single heading in the present, why make such a fuss about a diachronic grouping?

Second, adherents of both schools fall prey to anachronism. Nearly all of the most prominent nominalists are historians of the modern United States, modern Britain, or modern Europe, and it is difficult to eschew the suspicion that they are concentrating their search where the light is best rather than where the answers are to be found, and formulating a theoretical position to justify their approach. On the other hand, nominalist objections are in part a response to an extreme realist position that has been predicated on the unquestioned, unproven, and overwhelmingly unlikely assumption that exactly the same categories and patterns of sexuality have always existed, pure and unchanged by the systems of thought and behavior in which they were enmeshed.

Third, both extremes appear to be paralyzed by words. The nominalists are determined that the same word cannot apply to a wide range of meaning and still be used productively in scholarly discourse: in order to have meaning, "gay," for example, must be applied only as the speaker would apply it, with all the precise ramifications he associates with it. This insistence follows understandably from the implicit assumption that the speaker is generating the category himself, or in concert with certain contemporaries, rather than receiving it from a human experience of great longevity and adjusting it to fit his own understanding. Realist extremists, conversely, assume that lexical equivalence betokens experiential equality and that the occurrence of a word that "means" "homosexual" demonstrates the existence of "homosexuality," as the modern realist understands it, at the time the text was composed.

It is my aim to circumvent these difficulties as far as possible in the following remarks and my hope that in so doing, I may reduce the rhetorical struggle over "universals" in these matters and promote thereby more useful dialogue among the partisans. Let it be agreed at the outset that something can be discussed, by modern historians or ancient writers, without being named or defined. (Ten people in a room might argue endlessly about proper definitions of "blue" and "red" but could probably agree instantly whether a given object was one or the other [or a combination of both].) "Gravity" offers a useful historical example. A nominalist position would be that gravity did not exist before Newton invented it, and a nominalist historian might be able to mount a convincing case that there is no mention of gravity in any texts before Newton. "Nonsense," realists would object. "The Latin *gravitas,* which is common in Roman literature, describes the very properties of matter Newton called 'gravity.' Of course gravity existed before Newton discovered it."

Both, of course, are wrong. Lack of attention to something in historical sources can in no wise be taken as evidence of its nonexistence, and discovery cannot be equated with creations or invention. But "gravitas" does not mean "gravity"; it means "heaviness," and the two are not at all the same thing. Noting that objects have heaviness is entirely different from understanding the nature and operations of gravity. For adherents of these two positions to understand each other each would have to abandon specific nomenclature and agree instead on questions to be asked of the sources. If the proper questions were addressed, the nominalist could easily be persuaded that the sources prove that gravity existed before Newton, in the sense that the operations of the force now designated "gravity" are well chronicled in nearly all ancient literature. And the realist could be persuaded that, despite this fact, the nature of gravity was not clearly articulated—whether or not it was apprehended—before Newton.

The problem is rendered more difficult in the present case by the fact that the equivalent of gravity has not yet been discovered: there is still no essential agreement in the scientific community about the nature of human sexuality. Whether humans are "homosexual" or "heterosexual" or "bisexual" by birth, by training, by choice, or at all is still an open question.[5] Neither realists nor nominalists can, therefore, establish any clear correlation—positive or negative—between modern sexuality and its ancient counterparts. But it is still possible to discuss whether modern conceptualizations of sexuality are novel and completely socially relative, or correspond to constants of human epistemology that can be documented in the past.

To simplify discussion, three broad types of sexual taxonomy are abbreviated here as Types A, B, and C. According to Type A theories, all humans are polymorphously sexual, that is, capable of erotic and sexual interaction with either gender. External accidents, such as social pressure, legal sanctions, religious beliefs, historical or personal circumstances, determine the actual expression of each person's sexual feelings. Type B theories posit two or more sexual categories, usually but not always based on sexual object choice, to which all humans belong, though external pressures or circumstance may induce individuals in a given society to pretend (or even to believe) that they belong to a category other than their native one. The most common form of Type B taxonomy assumes that humans are heterosexual, homosexual, and bisexual but that not all societies allow expression of all varieties of erotic disposition. Subsets or other versions of Type B categorize on the basis of other characteristics, for example, a predilection for a particular role in intercourse. Type C theories consider one type of sexual response normal (or "natural" or "moral" or all three) and all other variants abnormal ("unnatural," "immoral").

It will be seen that Type A theories are nominalist to the extent that they regard categorizations like "homosexual" and "heterosexual" as arbitrary conventions applied to a sexual reality that is at bottom undifferentiated. Type B theories are conversely realist in predicating categories that underlie human sexual experience even when obscured by social constraints or particular circumstances. Type C theories are essentially normative rather than epistemological but borrow from both sides of the universals question in assuming, by and large, that people are born into the normal category but become members of a deviant grouping by an act of the will, although some Type C adherents regard "deviants" as inculpably belonging to an "abnormal" category through mental or physical illness or defect.

That no two social structures are identical should require no proof; and since sexual categories are inevitably conditioned by social structure, no two systems of sexual taxonomy should be expected to be identical. A slight chronological or geographical shift would render one Type A system quite different from another one. But to state this is not to demonstrate that there are no constraints in human sexual epistemology. The frequency with which these theories or variations on them appear in Western history is striking.

The apparent gender blindness of the ancient world has often been adduced as proof that Type B theories were unknown before comparatively recent times. In Plutarch's *Dialogue on Love,* it is asserted that

> the noble lover of beauty engages in love wherever he sees excellence and splendid natural endowment without regard for any difference in physiological detail. The lover of human beauty [will] be fairly and equitably disposed toward both sexes, instead of supposing that males and females are as different in the matter of love as they are in their clothes.[6]

Such statements are commonplaces of ancient lore about love and eroticism, to the extent that one is inclined to believe that much of the ancient world was completely unaware of differentiation among humans in sexual object choice, as I have myself pointed out at length elsewhere.[7] But my statements and the evidence on which they rest can easily be misapprehended. Their purport is that ancient *societies* did not distinguish heterosexuality from homosexuality, not that all, or even most, individuals failed to make such a distinction.

A distinction can be present and generally recognized in a society without forming any part of its social structure. In some cultures, skin color is a major determinant of social status; in others, it is irrelevant. But it would be fatuous to assume that societies that did not "discriminate on the basis of" (i.e., make invidious distinctions concerning) skin color could not "discriminate" (distinguish) such differences. This same paranomastic subtlety must be understood in regard to ancient views of sexuality: city-states of the ancient world did not, for the most part, discriminate on the basis of sexual orientation and, as societies, appear to have been blind to the issue of sexual object choice, but it is not clear that individuals were unaware of distinctions in the matter.

It should be obvious, for instance, that in the passage cited above, Plutarch is arguing against precisely that notion that Padgug claims had not existed in precapitalist societies, that is, Type B theories. Plutarch believes that a normal human being is susceptible to attraction to either gender, but his comments are manifestly directed against the contrary view. Which attitude was more common in his day is not apparent, but it is clearly inaccurate to use his comments as demonstration that there was only one view. The polemical tone of his remarks, in fact, seems good evidence that the position he opposes was of considerable importance. The whole genre of debates about the types of love of which this dialogue is a representative[8] cuts both ways on the issue: on the one hand, arguing about the matter and adducing reasons for preferring one gender to the other suggests a kind of polymorphous sexuality that is not predirected by heredity or experience toward one gender or the other. On the other, in each of the debates there are factions that are clearly on one side or the other of the dichotomy not supposed to have existed before modern times: some disputants argue for attraction to males only; some for attraction to females only. Each side derogates the preference of the other side as distasteful. Sometimes bisexuality is admitted, but as a third preference, not as the general nature of human sexuality:

> Zeus came as an eagle to god-like Ganymede, as a swan came he to the fair-haired mother of Helen.

> So there is no comparison between the two things: one person likes one, another likes the other; I like both.[9]

This formulation of the range of human sexuality is almost identical to popular modern conceptions of Type B: some people prefer their own gender; some the opposite; some both. Similar distinctions abound in ancient literature. The myth of Aristophanes in Plato's *Symposium* is perhaps the most familiar example: its manifest and stated purpose is to explain why humans are divided into groups of predominantly homosexual or heterosexual interest. It is strongly implied that these interests are both exclusive and innate; that is stated outright by Longus, who describes a character as "homosexual by nature [*physei*]."[10]*

It is true that there were no terms in common use in Greece or Rome to describe categories of sexual preference, but it does not follow that such terms were wholly unknown: Plato, Athenaeus, and other writers who dealt with the subject at length developed terms to describe predominant or exclusive interest in the apposite gender.[11] Many writers, moreover, found it possible to characterize homosexuality as a distinct mode of erotic expression without naming it. Plautus, for example, characterized homosexual activity as the "mores of Marseilles," suggesting that he considered it a variant on ordinary human sexuality.[12] Martial found it possible to describe an exclusively heterosexual male, even though he had no terminology available to do so and was himself apparently interested in both genders.[13]

One even finds expressions of solidarity among adherents of one preference or another in ancient literature, as when Clodius Albinus, noted for his exclusively heterosexual interest, persecutes those involved in homosex-

*Among many complex aspects of Aristophanes' speech in the *Symposium* as an indication of contemporary sexual constructs, two are especially notable. (1) Although it is the sole Attic reference to lesbianism as a concept, male homosexuality is of much greater concern as an erotic disposition in the discussion than either female homosexuality or heterosexuality. (2) It is this, in my view, that accounts for the additional subtlety of age distinctions in male-male relations, suggesting a general pattern of older *erastes* and younger *eromenos.* Age differential was unquestionably a part of the construct of sexuality among elements of the population in Athens, but it can easily be given more weight than it deserves. "Romantic love" of any sort was thought to be provoked by and directed toward the young, as is clearly demonstrated in Agathon's speech a little further on, where he uses the greater beauty of young males and females interchangeably to prove that Love is a young god. In fact, most Athenian males married women considerably younger than themselves, but since marriage was not imagined to follow upon romantic attachment, this discrepancy does not appear in dialogues on Eros.

David Halperin argues in "Sex before Sexuality" [chapter 16 in this volume] that the speech does not indicate a taxonomy comparable to modern ones, chiefly because of the age differential, although, in fact, the creatures described by Aristophanes must have been seeking a partner of the same age, since, joined at birth, they were coeval. What is clear is that Aristophanes does not imagine a populace undifferentiated in experience or desire, responding circumstantially to individuals of either gender, but persons with lifelong preferences arising from innate character (or a mythic prehistory).

ual behavior,[14] or when a character who has spoken on behalf of love between men in one of the debates bursts out, "We are like strangers cut off in a foreign land . . . ; nevertheless, we shall not be overcome by fear and betray the truth,"[15] or when Propertius writes, "Let him who would be our enemy love girls; he who would be our friend enjoy boys."[16] That there is a jocular tone to some of these statements, especially the last, is certainly attributable to the fact that the distinctions involved in no way affected the well-being, happiness, or social status of the individuals, owing to the extreme sexual tolerance of ancient societies; but it does not cast doubt on the existence of the distinctions. Even when preferences are attributed ironically, as is likely the case in Plato's placing the myth of sexual etiology in the mouth of Aristophanes, the joke depends on the familiarity of the distinction.

Subtler indications of Type B taxonomies can also be found. In the *Ephesiaca,* a Hellenistic love novel by Xenophon of Ephesus, sexual categories are never discussed and are clearly not absolute, but they do seem to be well understood and constitute an organizing principle of individual lives. Habrocomes is involved throughout only with women, and when, after his long separation from his true love, Anthia, she desires to know if he has been faithful to her, she inquires only if he has slept with other women, although she knows that men have been interested in him, and it is clear that sex with a man would also constitute infidelity (as with Corymbus). It seems clear that Habrocomes is, in fact, heterosexual, at least in Anthia's opinion. Another character, Hippothoos, had been married to an older woman and attracted to Anthia but is apparently mostly gay: the two great loves of his life are males (Hyperanthes and Habrocomes); he left all to follow each of these, and at the end of the story, he erects a statue to the former and establishes his residence near that of the latter. The author tidies up all the couples at the end by reuniting Anthia and Habrocomes and introducing a new male lover (Clisthenes) for Hippothoos. This entire scenario corresponds almost exactly to modern conceptualizations: some people are heterosexual, some homosexual, some bisexual; the categories are not absolute, but they are important and make a substantial difference in people's lives.

Almost the very same constellation of opinions can be found in many other preindustrial societies. In medieval Islam, one encounters an even more overwhelming emphasis on homosexual eroticism than in classical Greek or Roman writing. It is probably fair to say that most premodern Arabic poetry is ostensibly homosexual, and it is clear that this is more than a literary convention. When Saadia Gaon, a Jew living in Muslim society in the tenth century, discusses the desirability of "passionate love,"[17] he apparently refers only to homosexual passion. There is the sort of love men have for their wives, which is good but not passionate; and there is the sort of love men have for each other, which is passionate but not good. (And what of the wives' loves? We are not told.) That Saadia assumes the ubiquity of homosexual passion is the more striking because he is familiar with Plato's discussion of homosexual and heterosexual varieties of love in the *Symposium.*[18]

Does this mean that classical Islamic society uniformly entertained Type A theories of human sexuality and regarded eroticism as inherently pansexual? No. There is much evidence in Arabic literature for the very same Type B dichotomies known in other cultures. Saadia himself cites various theories about the determination of particular erotic interests (e.g., astrological lore),[19] and in the ninth century, Jahiz wrote a debate involving partisans of homosexual and heterosexual desire, in which each disputant, like his Hellenistic counterpart, expresses distaste for the preference of the other.[20] Three debates of this sort occur in the *Thousand and One Nights,* a classic of Arabic popular literature.[21] "Homosexuals" are frequently (and neutrally) mentioned in classical Arabic writings as a distinct type of human being. That the "type" referred to involves predominant or exclusive preference is often suggested: in tale 142 of the *Nights,* for example, it is mentioned as noteworthy that a male homosexual does not dislike women; in tale 419, a woman observes a man staring longingly at some boys and remarks to him, "I perceive that you are among those who prefer men to women."

A ninth-century text of human psychology by Qustā ibn Luqā treats twenty areas in which humans may be distinguished psychologically.[22] One area is sexual-object choice: some men, Qustā, explains, are "disposed toward" *(yamîlu ilā)* women, some toward other men, and some toward both.[23] Qustā has no terminology at hand for these categories; indeed, for the second category, he employs the euphemism that such men are disposed toward "sexual partners other than women":[24] obviously lack of terminology for the homosexual/heterosexual dichotomy should not be taken as a sign of ignorance of it. Qustā, in fact, believed that homosexuality was often inherited, as did ar-Razi and many other Muslim scientific writers.[25]

It has been claimed that "homosexuality" was viewed in medieval Europe "not as a particular attribute of a certain type of person but as a potential in all sinful creatures."[26] It is certainly true that some medieval writers evinced Type A attitudes of this sort: patristic authors often address to their audiences warnings concerning homosexual attraction predicated on the assumption that any male might be attracted to another.[27] The

Anglo-Saxon life of Saint Eufrasia[28] recounts the saint's efforts to live in a monastery disguised as a monk and the turmoil that ensued: the other monks were greatly attracted by Agapitus (the name she took as a monk), and reproached the abbot for bringing "so beautiful a man into their minister" ("forþam swa wlitigne man into heora mynstre gelædde," p. 344). Although it is in fact a woman to whom the monks are drawn, the account evinces no surprise on anyone's part that the monks should experience intense sexual attraction toward a person ostensibly of their own gender.

Some theologians clearly regarded homosexual activity as a vice open to all rather than as the peculiar sexual outlet of a portion of the population, but this attitude was not universal and was often ambiguously or inconsistently held even by those who did most to promulgate it. Albertus Magnus and Thomas Aquinas both wrote of homosexual acts as sins that presumably anyone might commit, but both also recognized that it was somewhat more complex than this: Aquinas, following Aristotle, believed that some men were "naturally inclined" to desire sexual relations with other men—clearly a theory of Type B—and Albertus Magnus considered homosexual desire to be a manifestation of a contagious disease, particularly common among the wealthy, and curable through the application of medicine.[29] This attitude is highly reminiscent of psychiatric opinion in late Victorian times and a far cry from categorizing homosexuality simply as a vice.

"Sodomy" was defined by many clerics as the improper emission of semen—the gender of the parties and their sexual appetites being irrelevant—but many others understood *sodomita* to apply specifically to men who preferred sexual contact with other men, generally or exclusively, and *sodomia* to apply only to the sexual acts performed in this context.[30]

Medieval literature abounds in suggestions that there is something special about homosexuality, that it is not simply an ordinary sin. Many writers view it as the special characteristic of certain peoples; others argue that it is completely unknown among their own kind. There are constant associations of homosexual preference with certain occupations or social positions, clearly indicating that it is linked in some way to personality or experience. The modern association of homosexuality with the arts had as its medieval counterpart a regular link with the religious life: when Bernard of Clairvaux was asked to restore life to the dead son of a marquess of Burgundy, he had the boy taken to a private room and lay down upon him. No cure transpired; the boy remained lifeless. The chronicler, who had been present, nonetheless found humor in the incident and remarked, "That was the unhappiest monk of all. For I've never heard of any monk who lay down upon a boy that did not straightaway rise up after him. The abbot blushed and they went out as many laughed."[31]

Chaucer's pardoner, also a cleric, appears to be innately sexually atypical, and his association with the hare has led many to suppose that it is homosexuality that distinguishes him.[32] Even non-Christians linked the Christian clergy with homosexuality.[33]

Much of the literature of the High Middle Ages that deals with sexual-object choice assumes distinct dispositions, most often exclusive. A long passage in the *Roman d'Énéas* characterizes homosexual males as devoid of interest in women and notable in regard to dress, habits, decorum, and behavior.[34] Debates of the period characterize homosexual preference as innate or God-given, and in the well-known poem "Ganymede and Helen," it is made pellucidly clear that Ganymede is exclusively gay (before the intervention of the gods): it is Helen's frustration at his inability to respond properly to her advances that prompts the debate.[35] In a similar poem, "Ganymede and Hebe," homosexual relations are characterized as "decreed by fate," suggesting something quite different from an occasional vice.[36] Indeed, the mere existence of debates of this sort suggests very strongly a general conceptualization of sexuality as bifurcated into two camps distinguished by sexual-object choice. Popular terminology of the period corroborates this: as opposed to words like "sodomita," which might designate indulgence in a specific activity by any human, writers of the High Middle Ages were inclined to use designations like "Ganymede," whose associations were exclusively homosexual, and to draw analogies with animals like the hare and the hyena, which were thought to be naturally inclined to sexual relations with their own gender.

Allain of Lille invokes precisely the taxonomy of sexual orientation used in the modern West in writing about sexuality among his twelfth-century contemporaries: "Of those men who employ the grammar of Venus there are some who embrace the masculine, others who embrace the feminine, and some who embrace both."[37]

Clearly, all three types of taxonomy were known in Western Europe and the Middle East before the advent of modern capitalist societies. It is, on the other hand, equally clear that in different times and places one type of theory has often predominated over the others, and for long periods in many areas one or two of the three may have been quite rare. Does the prevalence of one theory over another in given times and places reveal something about human sexuality? Possibly, but many factors other than sexuality itself may influence, deform, alter, or transform conceptualization of sexuality among peoples and individuals, and much attention must be devoted to analyzing such factors and their efforts before it will be possible to use them effectively in analyzing the bedrock of sexuality beneath them. . . .

Ancient "pederasty," for example, seems to many to constitute a form of sexual organization entirely unrelated to modern homosexuality. Possibly this is so, but the differences seem much less pronounced when one takes into account the sexual context in which "pederasty" occurs. The age differential idealized in descriptions of relations between the "lover" and the "beloved" is less than the disparity in age between heterosexual lovers as recommended, for example, by Aristotle (nineteen years). "Pederasty" may often represent no more than the homosexual side of a general pattern of cross-generation romance.[38] Issues of subordination and power likewise offer parallel structures that must be collated before any arguments about ancient "homosexuality" or heterosexuality" can be mounted. Artemidorus Daldianus aptly encapsulates the conflation of sexual and social roles of his contemporaries in the second century A.D. in his discussion of the significance of sexual dreams:

> For a man to be penetrated [in a dream] by a richer and older man is good: for it is customary to receive from such men. To be penetrated by a younger and poorer is bad: for it is the custom to give to such persons. It signifies the same [i.e., is bad] if the perpetrator is older and poor.[39]

Note that these comments do not presuppose either Type A or Type B theories: they might be applied to persons who regard either gender as sexually apposite, or to persons who feel a predisposition to one or the other. But they do suggest the social matrix of a system of sexual distinctions that might override, alter, or disguise other taxonomies.

The special position of passive homosexual behavior, involving the most common premodern form of Type C theory, deserves a separate study, but it might be noted briefly that its effect on sexual taxonomies is related not only to status considerations about penetration, as indicated above, but also to specific sexual taboos that may be highly culturally variable. Among Romans, for instance, two roles were decorous for a free adult male, expressed by the verbs *"irrumo,"* to offer the penis for sucking, and *"futuo,"* to penetrate a female, or *"pedico,"* to penetrate a male.[40] Indecorous roles for citizen males, permissible for anyone else, were expressed in particular by the verbs *"fello,"* to fellate, and *"ceveo,"* not translatable into English.[41] The distinction between roles approved for male citizens and others appears to center on the giving of seed (as opposed to the receiving of it) rather than on the more familiar modern active/passive division. (American prison slang expresses a similar dichotomy with the terms "catchers" and "pitchers.") It will be seen that this division obviates to a large degree both the active/passive split—since both the *irrumator* and the *fellator* are conceptually active[42]—and the homosexual/heterosexual one, since individuals are categorized not according to the gender to which they are drawn, but to the role they play in activities that could take place between persons of either gender. It is not clear that Romans had no interest in the gender of sexual partners, only that the division of labor, as it were, was a more pressing concern and attracted more analytical attention.

Artemidorus, on the other hand, considered both "active" and "passive" fellatio to be categorically distinct from other forms of sexuality. He divided his treatment of sexuality into three sections—the natural and legal, the illegal, and the unnatural—and he placed fellatio, in any form, among illegal activities, along with incest. In the ninth-century translation of his work by Hunain ibn Ishaq (the major transmitter of Aristotelian learning to the West), a further shift is evident: Hunain created a separate chapter for fellatio, which he called "that vileness of which it is not decent even to speak."[43]

In both the Greek and the Arabic versions of this work, the fellatio that is objurgated is both homosexual and heterosexual, and in both, anal intercourse between men is spoken of with indifference or approval. Yet in the Christian West, the most hostile legislation regarding sexual behavior has been directed specifically against homosexual anal intercourse: fellatio has generally received milder treatment. Is this because fellatio is more widely practiced among heterosexuals in the West and therefore seems less bizarre (i.e., less distinctly homosexual)? Or is it because passivity and the adoption of what seems a female role in anal intercourse is particularly objectionable in societies dominated by rigid ideals of "masculine" behavior? It may be revealing, in this context, that many modern languages, including English, have skewed the donor/recipient dichotomy by introducing a chiastic active/passive distinction: The recipient (i.e., of semen) in anal intercourse is "passive"; in oral intercourse, he is "active." Could the blurring of the active/passive division in the case of fellatio render it less obnoxious to legislative sensibilities?

Beliefs about sexual categories in the modern West vary widely, from the notion that sexual behavior is entirely a matter of conscious choice to the conviction that all sexual behavior is determined by heredity or environment. The same individual may, in fact, entertain with apparent equanimity contradictory ideas on the subject. It is striking that many ardent proponents of Type C etiological theories who regard homosexual behavior as pathological and/or depraved nonetheless imply in their statements about the necessity for legal repression of homosexual behavior that it is potentially ubiquitous in the human population and that if legal sanctions are not maintained, everyone may suddenly become homosexual.

Humans of previous ages were probably not, as a whole, more logical or consistent than their modern descendants. To pretend that a single system of sexual categorization obtained at any previous moment in Western history is to maintain the unlikely in the face of substantial evidence to the contrary. Most of the current spectrum of belief appears to have been represented in previous societies. What that spectrum reveals about the inner nature of human sexuality remains, for the time being, moot and susceptible of many divergent interpretations. But if the revolution in modern historical writing—and the recovery of whatever past the "gay community" may be said to have—is not to be stillborn, the problem of universals must be sidestepped or at least approached with fewer doctrinaire assumptions. Both realists and nominalists must lower their voices. Reconstructing the monuments of the past from the rubble of the present requires quiet concentration.

Postscript (1988)[44]

This essay was written in 1983, and several of the points it raises now require clarification or revision. I would no longer characterize the constructionist/essentialist controversy as a "debate" in any strict sense: one of its ironies is that no one involved in it actually identifies him- or herself as an "essentialist," although constructionists (of whom, in contrast, there are many)[45] sometimes so label other writers. Even when applied by its opponents, the label seems to fit extremely few contemporary scholars.[46] This fact is revealing and provides a basis for understanding the controversy more accurately not as a dialogue between two schools of thought, but as a revisionist (and largely one-sided) critique of assumptions believed to underlie traditional historiography. This understanding is not unrelated to my nominalist/realist analogy: one might describe constructionism (with some oversimplification) as a nominalist rejection of a tendency to "realism" in the traditional historiography of sexuality. The latter treated "homosexuality" as a diachronic, empirical entity (not quite a "universal," but "real" apart from social structures bearing on it); constructionists regard it as a culturally dependent phenomenon or, as some would have it, not a "real" phenomenon at all. It is not, nonetheless, a debate, since no current historians consciously defend an essentialist point of view.

Second, although it is probably still accurate to say that "most" constructionists are historians of the nineteenth and twentieth centuries, a number of classicists have now added their perspective to constructionist theory. This has broadened and deepened the discussion, although, strikingly, few if any historians of periods between Periclean Athens and the late nineteenth century articulate constructionist views.[47]

Third, my own position, perhaps never well understood, has changed. In my book *Christianity, Social Tolerance, and Homosexuality,* I defined "gay persons"[48] as those "conscious of erotic inclination toward their own gender as a distinguishing characteristic" (44). It was the supposition of the book that such persons have been widely and identifiably present in Western society at least since Greco-Roman times, and this prompted many constructionists to label the work "essentialist." I would now define "gay persons" more simply as those whose erotic interest is predominantly directed toward their own gender (i.e., regardless of how conscious they are of this as a distinguishing characteristic). This is the sense in which, I believe, it is used by most American speakers, and although experts in a field may well wish to employ specialized language, when communicating with the public it seems to me counterproductive to use common words in senses different from or opposed to their ordinary meanings.

In this sense, I would still argue that there have been "gay persons" in most Western societies. It is not clear to me that this is an "essentialist" position. Even if societies formulate or create "sexualities" that are highly particular in some ways, it might happen that different societies would construct similar ones, as they often construct political or class structures similar enough to be subsumed under the same rubric (democracy, oligarchy, proletariat, aristocracy, etc.—all of which are both particular and general).[49]

Most constructionist arguments assume that essential positions necessarily entail a further supposition: that society does not create erotic feelings, but only acts on them. Some other force—genes, psychological forces, and so forth—creates "sexuality," which is essentially independent of culture. This was not a working hypothesis of *Christianity, Social Tolerance, and Homosexuality.* I was and remain agnostic about the origins and etiology of human sexuality.

· CHAPTER SIXTEEN ·

Sex Before Sexuality

Pederasty, Politics, and Power in Classical Athens

DAVID M. HALPERIN

David M. Halperin, who teaches queer theory at the the University of New South Wales in Sydney, Australia, offers a constructionist perspective on the issues raised in the last two selections. Building on the work of the late French philosopher Michel Foucault, Halperin argues that "sexuality"—as a positive, distinct, and constitutive feature of human personalities—is a relatively modern invention. In contrast to Boswell, he argues that ancient texts like Aristophanes' speech illustrate the radical difference between the ancient Greek experience of sex and our own. More broadly, he argues for the historical or cultural character of sexuality.

I

In 1992, when the patriots among us celebrated the five hundredth anniversary of the discovery of America by Christopher Columbus, our cultural historians may have wished to mark the centenary of an intellectual landfall of almost equal importance for the conceptual geography of the human sciences: the invention of homosexuality by Charles Gilbert Chaddock. Though he may never rank with Columbus in the annals of individual achievement, Chaddock would hardly seem to merit the obscurity that has surrounded him throughout the past hundred years. An early translator of

This chapter is reprinted with minor editorial revisions from "Sex Before Sexuality: Pederasty, Politics, and Power in Classical Athens," *Hidden from History: Exploring the Gay and Lesbian Past* (New York: Penguin, 1990) pp. 37–53. It was originally published, in a different form, as "One Hundred Years of Homosexuality," in *The Mêtis of the Greeks*, ed. Milad Doueihi, *Diacritics*, 16, no. 2 (Summer 1986): 34–35. The most complete version of the essay is available in David M. Halperin, *One Hundred Years of Homosexuality and Other Essays on Greek Love* (New York: Routledge, 1989).

Krafft-Ebing's *Psychopathia sexualis,* Chaddock is credited by the *Oxford English Dictionary*[1] with having introduced "homo-sexuality" into the English language in 1892, in order to render a German cognate twenty years its senior.[2] Homosexuality, for better or for worse, has been with us ever since.

Before 1892, there was no homosexuality, only sexual inversion. But, as George Chauncey Jr. has demonstrated:

> Sexual inversion, the term used most commonly in the nineteenth century, did not denote the same conceptual phenomenon as homosexuality. "Sexual inversion" referred to a broad range of deviant gender behavior, of which homosexual desire was only a logical but indistinct aspect, while "homosexuality" focused on the narrower issue of sexual object choice. The differentiation of homosexual desire from "deviant" gender behavior at the turn of the century reflects a major reconceptualization of the nature of human sexuality, its relation to gender, and its role in one's social definition.[3]

Throughout the nineteenth century, in other words, sexual preference for a person of one's own sex was not clearly distinguished from other sorts of nonconformity to one's culturally defined sex role: deviant object choice was viewed as merely one of a number of pathological symptoms exhibited by those who reversed, or "inverted," their proper sex roles by adopting a masculine or a feminine style at variance with what was deemed natural and appropriate to their anatomical sex. Political aspirations in women and (at least according to one expert writing as late as 1920) a fondness for cats in men were manifestations of a pathological condition, a kind of psychological hermaphroditism tellingly but not essentially expressed by the preference for a "normal" member of one's own sex as a sexual partner.[4]

This outlook on the matter seems to have been shared by the scientists and by their unfortunate subjects alike: inversion was not merely a medical rubric, then, but a category of lived experience. Karl Heinrich Ulrichs, for example, an outspoken advocate for the freedom of sexual choice and the founder, as early as 1862, of the cult of Uranism (based on Pausanias's praise of Uranian, or "heavenly," pederasty in Plato's *Symposium*), described his own condition as that of an *anima muliebris virili corpore inclusa*—a woman's soul confined by a man's body. That sexual-object choice might be wholly independent of such "secondary" characteristics as masculinity or femininity never seems to have occurred to anyone until Havelock Ellis waged a campaign to isolate object choice from role-playing and, concurrently, Freud, in his classic analysis of a drive in the *Three Essays* (1905), clearly distinguished in the case of the libido between the sexual "object" and the sexual "aim."[5]

The conceptual isolation of sexuality per se from questions of masculinity and femininity made possible a new taxonomy of sexual behaviors and psychologies based entirely on the anatomical sex of the persons engaged in a sexual act (same sex versus different sex); it thereby obliterated a number of distinctions that had traditionally operated within earlier discourses pertaining to same-sex sexual contacts and that had radically differentiated active from passive sexual partners, normal from abnormal (or conventional from unconventional) sexual roles, masculine from feminine styles, and pederasty from lesbianism: all such behaviors were now to be classed alike and placed under the same heading.[6] Sexual identity was thus polarized around a central opposition defined by the binary play of sameness and difference in the sexes of the sexual partners; people belonged henceforward to one or the other of two exclusive categories, and much ingenuity was lavished on the multiplication of techniques for deciphering what a person's sexual orientation "really" was—independent, that is, of beguiling appearances. Founded on positive, ascertainable, and objective behavioral phenomena—on the facts of who had sex with whom—the new sexual taxonomy could lay claim to a descriptive, transhistorical validity. And so it crossed the "threshold of scientificity"[7] and was enshrined as a working concept in the social sciences.

A scientific advance of such magnitude naturally demanded to be crowned by the creation of a new technical vocabulary, but, unfortunately, no objective, value-free words readily lent themselves to the enterprise. In 1891, just one year before the inauguration of "homosexuality," John Addington Symonds could still complain that "[t]he accomplished languages of Europe in the nineteenth century supply no terms for this persistent feature of human psychology, without importing some implication of disgust, disgrace, vituperation."[8] A number of linguistic candidates were quickly put forward to make good this lack, and "homosexuality" (despite scattered protests over the years) gradually managed to fix its social-scientistic signature upon the new conceptual dispensation. The word itself, as Havelock Ellis noted, is a barbarous neologism sprung from a monstrous mingling of Greek and Latin stock;[9] as such, it belongs to a rapidly growing lexical breed most prominently represented by the hybrid names given to other recent inventions—names whose mere enumeration suffices to conjure up the precise historical era responsible for producing them: for example, "automobile," "television."

Unlike the language of technology, however, the new terminology for describing sexual behavior was slow to take root in the culture at large. In his posthumous autobiographical memoir, *My Father and Myself* (1968), J. R. Ackerley recalls how mystified he was when about 1918, a Swiss friend asked him, "Are you homo or hetero?": "I had never heard either term before," he writes. Similarly, T. C. Worsley observes in his own memoir, *Flannelled Fool* (1966), that in 1929 "[t]he word [homosexual], in any case, was not in general use, as it is now. Then it was still a technical term, the implications of which I was not entirely aware."[10] These two memoirists, moreover, were not intellectually deficient men: at the respective times of their recorded bewilderment, Ackerley was shortly about to be, and Worsley already had been, educated at Cambridge. Nor was such innocence limited—in this one instance, at least—to the holders of university degrees: the British sociologist John Marshall, whose survey presumably draws on more popular sources, testifies that "a number of the elderly men I interviewed had never heard the term 'homosexual' until the 1950s."[11] The *Oxford English Dictionary*, originally published in 1933, is also ignorant of (if not willfully blind to) "homosexuality"; the word appears for the first time in the *OED*'s 1976 three-volume supplement.[12]

It is not exactly my intention to argue that homosexuality, as we commonly understand it today, didn't exist before 1892. How, indeed, could it have failed to exist? The very word displays a most workmanlike and scientific indifference to cultural and environmental factors, looking only to the sexes of the persons engaged in the sexual act. Moreover, if homosexuality didn't exist before 1892, heterosexuality couldn't have existed either (it came into being, in fact, like Eve from Adam's rib, eight years later),[13] and without heterosexuality, where would all of us be right now?

The comparatively recent genesis of heterosexuality—strictly speaking, a twentieth-century affair—should provide a clue to the profundity of the cultural issues over which, hitherto, I have been so lightly skating. How is it possible that until the year 1900 there was not a precise, value-free, scientific term available to speakers of the English language for designating what we would now regard, in retrospect, as the mode of sexual behavior favored by the vast majority of people in our culture? Any answer to that question—which, in its broadest dimensions, I shall leave for the intellectual heirs of Michel Foucault to settle—must direct our attention to the inescapable historicity of even the most innocent, unassuming, and seemingly objective of cultural representations. Although a blandly descriptive, rigorously clinical term like "homosexuality" would appear to be unobjectionable as a taxonomic device, it carries with it a heavy complement of ideological baggage and has, in fact, proved a significant obstacle to understanding the distinctive features of sexual life in the ancient world. It may well be that homosexuality properly speaking has no history of its own much before the beginning of our century. For, as John Boswell remarks, "If the categories 'homosexual/heterosexual' and 'gay/straight' are the inventions of particular societies rather than real aspects of the human psyche, there is no gay history."[14]

II

Of course, if we are to believe Foucault, there are basic historical and cultural factors that prohibit the easy application of the concept of homosexuality to persons living in premodern societies. For homosexuality presupposes sexuality: it implies the existence of a separate, sexual domain within the larger field of man's psychophysical nature, and it requires the conceptual demarcation and isolation of that domain from other, more traditional, territories of personal and social life that cut across it, such as carnality, venery, libertinism, virility, passion, amorousness, eroticism, intimacy, love, affection, appetite, and desire—to name but a few. The invention of homosexuality therefore had to await, in the first place, the eighteenth-century discovery and definition of sexuality as the total ensemble of physiological and psychological mechanisms governing the individual's genital functions and the concomitant identification of that ensemble with a specially developed part of the brain and nervous system; it had also to await, in the second place, the early-nineteenth-century interpretation of sexuality as a singular "instinct" or "drive," a mute force that shapes our conscious life according to its own unassailable logic and thereby determines, at least in part, the character and personality of each one of us.

Before the scientific construction of "sexuality" as a positive, distinct, and constitutive feature of individual human beings—an autonomous system within the physiological and psychological economy of the human organism—a person's sexual *acts* could be individually evaluated and categorized, but there was no conceptual apparatus available for identifying a person's fixed and determinate sexual *orientation*, much less for assessing and classifying it.[15] That human beings differ, often markedly, from one another in their sexual tastes in a great variety of ways (of which the liking for a sexual partner of a specific sex is only one, and not necessarily the most significant one) is an unexceptionable and, indeed, an ancient observation; but it is not immediately evident that differences in sexual preference are by their very nature more revealing about the temperament of individual human beings, more significant determinants of personal identity, than, for example, differences in dietary preference.[16] And yet, it would never occur to us to refer a person's dietary object choice to some innate, characterological disposition or to see in his or her strongly expressed and even unvarying preference for the white meat of chicken the symptom of a profound psychophysical orientation, leading us to identify him or her in contexts quite removed from that of the eating of food as, say, a "pectoriphage" or a "stethovore" (to continue the practice of combining Greek and Latin roots); nor would we be likely to inquire further, making nicer discriminations according to whether an individual's predilection for chicken breasts expressed itself in a tendency to eat them quickly or slowly, seldom or often, alone or in company, under normal circumstances or only in periods of great stress, with a clear or a guilty conscience ("ego-dystonic pectoriphagia"), beginning in earliest childhood or originating with a gastronomic trauma suffered in adolescence. If such questions did occur to us, moreover, I very much doubt whether we would turn to the academic disciplines of anatomy, neurology, clinical psychology, or genetics in the hope of obtaining a clear causal solution to them. That is because (1) we regard the liking for certain foods as a matter of taste; (2) we currently lack a theory of taste; and (3) in the absence of a theory, we do not normally subject our behavior to intense scientific or etiological scrutiny.

In the same way, it never occurred to premodern cultures to ascribe a person's sexual tastes to some positive, structural, or constitutive feature of his or her personality. Just as we tend to assume that human beings are not individuated at the level of dietary preference and that we all, despite many pronounced and frankly acknowledged differences from one another in dietary habits, share the same fundamental set of alimentary appetites, and hence the same "dieticity" or "edility," so most premodern and non-Western cultures, despite an awareness of the range of possible variations in human sexual behavior, refuse to individuate human beings at the level of sexual preference and assume, instead, that we all share the same fundamental set of sexual appetites, the same "sexuality." For most of the world's inhabitants, in other words, "sexuality" is no more a fact of life than "dieticity." Far from being a necessary or intrinsic constituent of the eternal grammar of human subjectivity, "sexuality" seems to be a uniquely modern, Western, even bourgeois production—one of those cultural fictions that in every society give human beings access to themselves as meaningful actors in their world and that are thereby objectivated.

At any rate, positivism dies hard, and sexual essentialism (the belief in fixed sexual essences) dies even harder. Not everyone will welcome a neo-historicist critique of "sexuality." Boswell, for example, has argued reasonably enough that any debate over the existence of universals in human culture must distinguish among the respective modes of being proper to words, concepts, and experiences: according to this line of reasoning, the ancients experienced gravity even though they lacked both the term and the concept; similarly, Boswell claims that the "manifest and stated purpose" of Aristophanes' famous myth in Plato's *Symposium* "is to explain why humans are divided into groups of predominantly homosexual or heterosexual interest," and so this text, along with a number of others, vouches for the existence of homosexuality as an ancient (if not a universal) category of human experience—however newfangled the word for it may be.[17] Now, the speech of Plato's Aristophanes would seem indeed to be a locus classicus for the differentiation of homo- from heterosexuality, because Aristophanes' taxonomy of human beings features a distinction between those who desire a sexual partner of the same sex as themselves and those who desire a sexual partner of a different sex. The Platonic passage alone, then, would seem to offer sufficient warrant for positing an ancient concept, if not an ancient experience, of homosexuality. But closer examination reveals that Aristophanes stops short of deriving a distinction between homo- and heterosexuality from his own myth just when the logic of his analysis would seem to have driven him ineluctably to it. That omission is telling—and it is worth considering in greater detail.

According to Aristophanes, human beings were originally round, eight-limbed creatures, with two faces and two sets of genitals—both front and back—and three sexes (male, female, and androgyne). These ancestors of ours were powerful and ambitious; in order to put them in their place, Zeus had them cut in two, their skin stretched over the exposed flesh and tied at the navel, and their heads rotated so as to keep that physical reminder of their daring and its consequences constantly before their eyes. The severed halves of each former individual, once reunited, clung to one another so desperately and concerned themselves so little with their survival as separate entities that they began to perish for lack of sustenance; those who outlived their mates sought out persons belonging to the same sex as their lost complements and repeated their embraces in a foredoomed attempt to recover their original unity. Zeus at length took pity on them, moved their genitals to the side their bodies now faced, and invented sexual intercourse, so that the bereaved creatures might at least put a temporary terminus to their longing and devote their attention to other, more important (if less pressing) matters. Aristophanes extracts from this story a genetic explanation of observable differences among human beings with respect to sexual-object choice and preferred style of life: males who desire females are descended from an original androgyne (adulterers come from this species), whereas males descended from an original male "pursue their own kind, and would prefer to remain single and spend their entire lives with one another, since by nature they have no interest in marriage and procreation but are compelled to engage in them by social custom" (191e–192b, quoted selectively). Boswell, understandably, interprets this to mean that, according to Plato's Aristophanes, homosexual and heterosexual interests are "both exclusive and innate."[18]

But that, significantly, is not quite the way Aristophanes sees it. The conclusions that he draws from his own myth help to illustrate the lengths to which classical Athenians were willing to go in order to avoid conceptualizing sexual behaviors according to a binary opposition between different- and same-sex sexual contacts. First of all, Aristophanes' myth generates not two, but at least three distinct "sexualities" (males attracted to males, females attracted to females, and—consigned alike to a single classification, evidently—males attracted to females as well as females attracted to males). Moreover, there is not the slightest suggestion in anything Aristophanes says that the sexual acts or preferences of persons descended from an original female are in any way similar to, let alone congruent or isomorphic with, the sexual acts or preferences of those descended from an original male; hence, nothing in the text allows us to suspect the existence of even an implicit category to which males who desire males and females who desire females *both* belong in contradistinction to some *other* category containing males and females who desire one another.[19] On the contrary, one consequence of the myth is to make the sexual desire of every human being *formally identical* to that of every other: we are all looking for the same thing in a sexual partner, according to Plato's Aristophanes—namely, a symbolic substitute for an originary object once loved and subsequently lost in an archaic trauma. In that respect, we all share the same "sexuality"—which is to say that, despite the differences in our personal preferences or tastes, we are not individuated at the level of our sexual being.

Second, and equally important, Aristophanes' account features a crucial distinction *within* the category of males who are attracted to males, an infrastructural detail missing from his description of each of the other two categories: "while they are still boys [i.e., pubescent or preadult],[20] they are fond of men, and enjoy lying down together with them and twining their limbs about them, . . . but when they become men they are lovers of boys. . . . Such a man is a pederast and philerast [i.e., fond of or responsive to adult male lovers]" at *different stages of his life* (*Symposium* 191e–192b, quoted selectively). Contrary to the clear implications of the myth, in other words, and unlike the people comprehended by the first two categories, those descended from an original male are *not* attracted to one another *without qualification*; rather, they desire boys when they are men and they take a certain (nonsexual) pleasure in physical contact with men when they are boys.[21] Now, since—as the foregoing passage suggests—the classical Athenians sharply distinguished the roles of pederast and philerast, relegating them not only to different age classes, but virtually to different "sexualities,"[22] what Aristophanes is describing here is not a single, homogeneous sexual orientation common to all those who descend from an original male, but rather a set of distinct and incommensurable behaviors that such persons exhibit in different periods of their lives; although his genetic explanation of the diversity of sexual-object choice among human beings would seem to require that there be some adult males who are sexually attracted to other adult males, Aristophanes appears to be wholly unaware of such a possibility, and in any case, he has left no room for it in his taxonomic scheme.[23] That omission is all the more unexpected because, as Boswell himself has pointed out (in response to the present argument), the archetypal pairs of lovers from whom all homoerotically inclined males are supposed to descend must themselves have been the same age as one another, inasmuch as they were originally halves of the same being.[24] No age-matched couples figure among their latter-day offspring, however: the social reality described by Aristophanes features an erotic asymmetry absent from the mythical paradigm used to generate it. In the world of contemporary Athenian actuality—at least, as Aristophanes portrays it—reciprocal erotic desire among males is unknown.[25] Those who descend from an original male are not defined as male homosexuals, but as willing boys when they are young and as lovers of youths when they are old. Contrary to Boswell's reading of the passage, then, neither the concept nor the experience of "homosexuality" is known to Plato's Aristophanes.

A similar conclusion can be drawn from careful examination of the other document from antiquity that might seem to vouch for the existence both of homosexuality as an indigenous category and of homosexuals as a native species. Unlike the myth of Plato's Aristophanes, a famous and much-excerpted passage from a classic work of Greek prose, the document to which I refer is little known and almost entirely neglected by modern historians of "sexuality";[26] its date is late, its text is corrupt, and, far from being a self-conscious literary artifact, it forms part of a Roman technical treatise. But despite its distance from Plato in time, in style, in language, and in intent, it displays the same remarkable innocence of modern sexual categories, and I have chosen to discuss it here partly in order to show what can be learned about the ancient world from texts that lie outside the received canon of classical authors. Let us turn, then, to the ninth chapter in the fourth book of *De morbis chronicis*, a mid-fifth-century A.D. Latin translation and adaptation by the African writer Caelius Aurelianus of a now largely lost work on chronic diseases by the Greek physician Soranus, who practiced and taught in Rome during the early part of the second century A.D.

The topic of this chapter is *molles* (*malthakoi* in Greek)—that is, "soft" or unmasculine men who depart from the cultural norm of manliness insofar as they actively desire to be subjected by other men to a "feminine" (i.e., receptive) role in sexual intercourse. Caelius begins with an implicit defense of his own unimpeachable masculinity by noting how difficult it is to believe that such people actually exist;[27] he then goes on to observe that the cause of their affliction is not natural (that is, organic), but rather is their own excessive desire, which—in a desperate and foredoomed attempt to satisfy itself—drives out their sense of shame and forcibly converts parts of their bodies to sexual uses not intended by nature. These men willingly adopt the dress, gait, and other characteristics of women, thereby confirming that they suffer not from a bodily disease, but from a mental (or moral) defect. After some further arguments in support of that point, Caelius draws an interesting comparison:

> For just as the women called *tribades* [in Greek], because they practise both kinds of sex, are more eager to have sexual intercourse with women than with men and pursue women with an almost masculine jealousy . . . so they too [i.e., the *molles*] are afflicted by a mental disease. (132–133)

The mental disease in question, which strikes both men and women alike and is defined as a perversion of sexual desire, would certainly seem to be nothing other than homosexuality as it is often understood today.

Several considerations combine to prohibit that interpretation, however. First of all, what Caelius treats as a pathological phenomenon is not the desire on the part of either men or women for sexual contact with a person of the same sex; quite the contrary. Elsewhere, in discussing the treatment of satyriasis (a state of abnormally elevated sexual desire accompanied by itching or tension in the genitals), he issues the following advice to people who suffer from it (*De morbis acutis*, 3.18.180–181):[28]

> Do not admit visitors and particularly young women and boys. For the attractiveness of such visitors would again kindle the feeling of desire in the patient. Indeed, *even healthy persons*, seeing them, would in many cases seek sexual gratification, stimulated by the tension produced in the parts [i.e., in their own genitals].[29]

There is nothing medically problematical, then, about a desire on the part of males to obtain sexual pleasure from contact with males; what is of concern to Caelius,[30] as well as to other ancient moralists, is the male desire to be sexually penetrated by males, for such a desire represents the voluntary abandonment of a "masculine" identity in favor of a "feminine" one. It is sex-role reversal, or *gender deviance*, that is problematized here and that also furnishes part of the basis for Caelius's comparison of *molles* to *tribades*, who assume a "masculine" role in their relations with other women and actively "pursue women with an almost *masculine* jealousy." Indeed, the "soft"—that is, sexually submissive—man, possessed of a shocking and paradoxical desire to surrender his masculine autonomy and precedence, is monstrous precisely because he seems to have "a woman's soul confined by a man's body" and thus to violate the deeply felt and somewhat anxiously defended sense of congruence on the part of the ancients among gender, sexual practices, and social identity.[31]

Second, the ground of the similitude between Caelius's *molles* and *tribades* is not that they are both homosexual, but rather that they are both *bi*sexual (in our terms). The *tribades* "are *more* eager to have sexual intercourse with women *than with men*" and "practise both kinds of sex"—that is, they have sex with both men and women.[32] As for the *molles*, Caelius's earlier remarks about their extraordinarily intense sexual desire imply that they turn to receptive sex because, although they try, they are not able to satisfy themselves by means of more conventionally masculine sorts of sexual activity, including insertive sex with women;[33] far from having desires that are structured differently from those of normal folk, these gender deviants desire sexual pleasure just as most people do, but they have such strong and intense desires that they are driven to devise some unusual and disreputable (though ultimately futile) means of gratifying them. That diagnosis becomes explicit at the conclusion of the chapter when Caelius explains why the disease responsible for turning men into *molles* is the only chronic disease that becomes stronger as the body grows older (137).

> For in other years when the body is still strong and can perform the normal functions of love, the sexual desire [of these persons] assumes a dual aspect, in which the soul is excited sometimes while playing a passive and sometimes while playing an active role. But in the case of old men who have lost their virile powers, all their sexual desire is turned in the opposite direction and consequently exerts a stronger demand for the feminine role in love. In fact, many infer that this is the reason why boys too are victims of this affliction. For, like old men, they do not possess virile powers; that is, they have not yet attained those powers which have already deserted the aged.[34]

"Soft" or unmasculine men, far from being a fixed and determinate sexual species, are evidently either men who once experienced an orthodoxly masculine sexual desire in the past or who will eventually experience such a desire in the future. They may well be men with a constitutional tendency to gender deviance, according to Caelius, but they are not homosexuals. Moreover, all the other ancient texts known to me that place in the same category both males who enjoy sexual contact with males and females who enjoy sexual contact with females display one or the other of the two taxonomic strategies employed by Caelius Aurelianus: if such men and women are classified alike, it is either because they are both held to *reverse* their proper sex roles and to adopt the sexual styles, postures, and modes of copulation conventionally associated with the opposite sex or because they are both held to *alternate* between the personal characteristics and sexual practices proper, respectively, to men and to women.[35] No category of homosexuality, defined in such a way as to contain men and women alike, is indigenous to the ancient world.

No scruple need prevent *us,* to be sure, from qualifying as "homosexual" any person who seeks sexual contact with another person of the same sex, whether male of female. But the issue before us isn't whether or not we can accurately apply our concept of homosexuality to the ancients—whether or not, that is, we can discover in the historical record of classical antiquity evidence of behaviors or psychologies that are amenable to classification in our own terms (obviously, we can, given the supposedly descriptive and transhistorical nature of those terms); the issue isn't even whether or not the ancients were able to express within the terms provided by their own conceptual schemes an experience of something approximating to homosexuality as we understand it today.[36] The real issue confronting any cultural historian of antiquity, and any critic of contemporary culture, is, first of all, how to recover the terms in which the experiences of individuals belonging to past societies were actually constituted and, second, how to measure and assess the differences between those terms and the ones we currently employ. For, as this very controversy over the scope and applicability of sexual categories illustrates, concepts in the human sciences—unlike in this respect, perhaps, concepts in the natural sciences (such as gravity)—do not merely describe reality, but, at least partly, constitute it. What this implies about the issue before us may sound paradoxical, but it is, I believe, profound—or, at least, worth pondering: although there have been, in many different times and places (including classical Athens), persons who sought sexual contact with other persons of the same sex as themselves, it is only within the last hundred years or so that such persons (or some portion of them) have been homosexuals.

Instead of attempting to trace the history of "homosexuality" as if it were a *thing*, therefore, we might more profitably analyze how the significance of same-sex sexual contacts has been variously constructed over time by members of human living groups. Such an analysis will probably lead us into a plurality of only partly overlapping social and conceptual territories, a series of cultural formations that vary as their constituents change, combine in different sequences, or compose new patterns. In the following paragraphs, I shall attempt to draw a very crude outline of the cultural formation underlying the classical Athenian institution of pederasty, an outline whose details will have to be filled in at some later point if this aspect of ancient Greek social relations is ever to be understood historically.

III

The attitudes and behaviors publicly displayed by the citizens of Athens (to whom the surviving evidence for the classical period effectively restricts our power to generalize) tend to portray sex not as a collective enterprise in which two or more persons jointly engage, but rather as an action performed by one person upon another. The foregoing statement does not purport to describe positively what the experience of sex was "really" like for all members of Athenian society, but to indicate how sex is *represented* by those utterances and actions of free adult males that were intended to be overheard and witnessed by other free adult males. Sex, as it is constituted by this public, masculine discourse, is either act or impact: it is not knit up in a web of mutuality, not something one invariably has *with* someone. Even the verb "*aphrodisiazein*," meaning "to have sex" or "to take active sexual pleasure," is carefully differentiated into an active and a passive form; the active form occurs, tellingly, in a late antique list (that we nonetheless have good reason to consider representative for ancient Mediterranean culture, rather than eccentric to it) of acts that "do not regard one's neighbors but only the subjects themselves and are not done in regard to or through others: namely, speaking, singing, dancing, fist-fighting, competing, hanging oneself, dying, being crucified, diving, finding a treasure, having sex, vomiting, moving one's bowels, sleeping, laughing, crying, talking to the gods, and the like."[37] As John J. Winkler, in a commentary on this passage, observes, "It is not that second parties are not present at some of these events (speaking, boxing, competing, having sex, being crucified, flattering one's favorite divinity), but that their successful achievement does not depend on the cooperation, much less the benefit, of a second party."[38]

Not only is sex in classical Athens not intrinsically relational or collaborative in character; it is, further, a deeply polarizing experience: it serves to divide, to classify, and to distribute its participants into distinct and radically dissimilar categories. Sex possesses this valence, apparently, because it is conceived to center essentially on, and to define itself around, an asymmetrical gesture, that of the penetration of the body of one person by the body—and, specifically, by the phallus[39]—of another. Phallic penetration, moreover, is construed as sexual "activity"; even if a sexual act does not involve physical penetration, it still remains polarized by the distribution of phallic pleasure: the partner whose pleasure is promoted is considered "active," while the partner who puts his or her body *at the service* of another's pleasure is deemed "passive"—read "penetrated," in the culture's unself-conscious ideological shorthand. Sexual penetration and sexual "activity" in general are, in other words, thematized as domination: the relation between the "active" and the "passive" sexual partner is thought of as the same kind of relation as that obtaining between social superior and social inferior, between master and servant.[40] "Active" and "passive" sexual roles are therefore necessarily isomorphic with superordinate and subordinate social status; hence, an adult, male citizen of Athens can have legitimate sexual relations only with statutory minors (his inferiors not in age, but in social and political status): the proper targets of his sexual desire include, specifically, women, boys, foreigners, and slaves—all of them persons who do not enjoy the same legal and political rights and privileges that he does.[41] Furthermore, what a citizen does in bed reflects the differential in status that distinguishes him from his sexual partner: the citizen's superior prestige and authority express themselves by his sexual precedence—by his power to initiate a sexual act, his right to obtain pleasure from it, and his assumption of an "active" sexual role. What Paul Veyne has said about the Romans can apply equally well to the classical Athenians: they were indeed puritans when it came to sex, but (unlike modern bourgeois Westerners) they were not puritans about conjugality and reproduction; rather, like many Mediterranean peoples, they were puritans about virility.[42]

The very enterprise of inquiring into ancient Greek "sexuality," then, necessarily obscures the nature of the phenomenon it is designed to elucidate because it effectively isolates sexual norms from social practices and thereby conceals the strict sociological correspondences between them. In classical Athens, sex, as we have seen, was not simply a private quest for mutual pleasure that absorbed, if only temporarily, the social identities of its participants. Sex was a manifestation of public status, a declaration of social identity; it did not so much express an individual's unique "sexuality" as it served to position social actors in the places assigned to them (by virtue of their political standing) in the hierarchical structure of the Athenian polity. Instead of reflecting the peculiar sexual orientation of individual Athenians, the sexual protocols of classical Athens reflected a marked division in the social organization of the city-state between a superordinate group, composed of citizens, and a subordinate group, composed of noncitizens; sex between members of the first group was practically inconceivable, whereas sex between a member of the first group and a member of the second group mirrored in the minute details of its hierarchical arrangement the relation of structured inequality that governed their wider social interaction. Far from being interpreted as an expression of commonality, as a sign of some shared sexual status or orientation, sex between social superordinate and subordinate served, at least in part, to articulate the social distance between them. To assimilate both the senior and the junior partner in a pederastic relationship to the same "sexuality," for example, would therefore have struck a classical Athenian as no less bizarre than to classify a burglar as an "active criminal," his victim as a "passive criminal," and the two of them alike as partners in crime[43] (burglary—like sex, as the Greeks understood it—is, after all, a "nonrelational" act). The sexual identities of the ancient Greeks—their experiences of themselves as sexual actors and as desiring human beings—were hardly autonomous; quite the contrary. They were inseparable from, if not determined by, their social identities, their outward, public standing. Indeed, the classical Greek record strongly supports the conclusion drawn (from a quite different body of evidence) by the French anthropologist Maurice Godelier: "[i]t is not sexuality which haunts society, but society which haunts the body's sexuality."[44]

In classical Athens, then, sexual partners came in two different kinds—not male and female, but active and passive, dominant and submissive. The relevant features of a sexual object were not so much determined by a physical typology of genders as by the social articulation of power. That is why the currently fashionable distinction between homosexuality and heterosexuality had no meaning for the classical Athenians: there were not, so far as they knew, two different kinds of "sexuality," two differently structured psychosexual states or modes of affective orientation, but a single form of sexual experience, which all free adult males shared—making due allowance for variations in individual tastes, as one might make for individual palates. Thus, in the Third Dithyramb by the classical poet Bacchylides, the Athenian hero Theseus, voyaging to Crete among the seven youths and seven maidens destined for the Minotaur and defending one of the maidens from the sexual advances of the libidinous Cretan commander, warns him vehemently against molesting *any one* of the Athenian youths (*tin' êïtheôn:* 43)—that is, any girl *or boy*. Conversely, the antiquarian *littérateur* Athenaeus, writing six or seven hundred years later, is amazed that Polycrates, the tyrant of Samos in the sixth century B.C., did not send any boys *or women* along with the other luxury articles he imported to Samos for his personal use during his reign, "despite his passion for relations with males" (12.540c–e). Now, *both* the notion that an act of heterosexual aggression in itself makes the aggressor suspect of homosexual tendencies *and* the mirror-opposite notion that a person with marked homosexual tendencies is bound to hanker after heterosexual contacts are nonsensical to us, associating as we do sexual-object choice with a determinate kind of "sexuality," a fixed sexual nature, but it would be a monumental task indeed to enumerate all the ancient documents in which the alternative "boy or woman" occurs with perfect nonchalance in an erotic context, as if the two were functionally interchangeable. Scholars sometimes describe this cultural formation as a bisexuality of penetration[45] or as a heterosexuality indifferent to its object, but I think it would be more accurate to describe it as a single, undifferentiated phallic "sexuality" of penetration and determination, a sociosexual discourse whose basic terms are phallus and nonphallus.[46]

If there is a lesson that historians should draw from this picture of ancient sexual attitudes and behaviors, it is that we need to de-center *sexuality* from the focus of the interpretation of sexual experience. Just because modern bourgeois Westerners are so obsessed with sexuality, so convinced that it holds the key to the hermeneutics of the self (and, hence, to social psychology as an object of historical study), we ought not therefore to conclude that everyone has always considered sexuality a basic and irreducible element in, or a central feature of, human life. On the contrary, if the sketch I have offered is accurate, it seems that many ancients conceived of "sexuality" in nonsexual terms: what was fundamental to their experience of sex was not anything *we* would regard as essentially sexual; rather, it was something essentially social—namely, the modality of power relations that informed and structured the sexual act. Instead of viewing public and political life as a dramatization of individual sexual psychology, as we often tend to do, they saw sexual behavior as an expression of the dominant themes in contemporary social relations. When Artemidorus, a master dream analyst who lived and wrote in the second century A.D., came to address the meaning of sexual dreams, for example, he almost never presumed that such dreams were *really* about sex: they were about the rise and fall of the dreamer's public fortunes, the vicissitudes of his domestic economy.[47] If a man dreams of having sex with his mother, according to Artemidorus, his dream signifies nothing in particular about his own sexual psychology, his fantasy life, or the history of his relations with his parents; it may signify—depending on the family's circumstances at the time, the sexual postures of the partners in the dream, and the mode of penetration—that the dreamer will be successful in politics, that he will go into exile or return from exile, that he will win his lawsuit, obtain a rich harvest from his lands, or change professions, among many other things (1.79). Artemidorus's system of dream interpretation begs to be compared to the indigenous dream lore of certain Amazonian tribes, equally innocent of "sexuality," who (despite their quite different sociosexual systems) also believe in the predictive value of dreams and similarly reverse what modern bourgeois Westerners take to be the natural flow of signification in dreams (i.e., from what is public and social to what is private and sexual): in both Kagwahiv and Mehinaku culture, for example, dreaming about the female genitalia portends a wound; dreamt wounds do not symbolize the female genitalia.

To discover and to write the history of sexuality has long seemed to many a sufficiently radical undertaking in itself, inasmuch as its effect (if not the intention behind it) is to call into question the very naturalness of what we currently take to be essential to our individual natures. But in the course of implementing that ostensibly radical project, many historians of sexuality seem to have reversed—perhaps unwittingly—its radical design: by preserving "sexuality" as a stable category of historical analysis not only have they not denaturalized it, but, on the contrary, they have newly idealized it. To the extent, in fact, that histories of "sexuality" succeed in concerning themselves with *sexuality*, to just that extent are they doomed to fail as *histories* (Foucault himself taught us that much), unless they also include as an integral part of their proper enterprise the task of demonstrating the historicity, conditions of emergence, modes of construction, and ideological contingencies of the very categories of analysis that undergird their own practice. Instead of concentrating our attention specifically on the history of sexuality, then, we need to define and refine a new, and radical, historical sociology of psychology, an intellectual discipline designed to analyze the cultural poetics of desire, by which I mean the processes whereby sexual desires are constructed, mass-produced, and distributed among the various members of human living groups. We must train ourselves to recognize conventions of feeling as well as conventions of behavior and to interpret the intricate texture of personal life as an artifact, as the determinate outcome, of a complex and arbitrary constellation of cultural processes. We must, in short, be willing to admit that what seem to be our most inward, authentic, and private experiences are actually, in Adrienne Rich's admirable phrase, "shared, unnecessary/and political."[48]

· CHAPTER SEVENTEEN ·

The Reproduction of Butch-Fem Roles

A Social Constructionist Approach

ELIZABETH LAPOVSKY KENNEDY

AND MADELINE DAVIS

Elizabeth Lapovsky Kennedy and Madeline Davis, co-authors of the Lambda Literary Award–winning Boots of Leather, Slippers of Gold: The History of a Lesbian Community, *share their research on butch-fem roles in Buffalo, New York, from 1930–1965. Taking a constructionist approach and drawing on numerous interviews, Kennedy and Davis argue that although these roles seem constant and fixed, they in fact change in response to social conditions and have different meanings for different people.*

. . . . .

All commentators on twentieth-century lesbian life have noted the prominence of butch-fem roles.[1] Their presence was unmistakable in prefeminist communities where the butch projected the male image of her particular time period—at least in dress and mannerism—and the fem, the female image; and all members were usually one or the other. The tenacity of butch-fem roles underlines the appeal of an essentialist theory, which assumes that sexuality and gender transcend time and culture and reflect biological or psychological givens. However, our study of the Buffalo lesbian community's culture, social organization, and consciousness reveals

This chapter is reprinted with revisions from "The Reproduction of Butch-Fem Roles: A Social Constructionist Approach," Kathy Peiss and Christina Simmons, eds., *Passion and Power: Sexuality in History* (Philadelphia: Temple University Press, 1989), pp. 241–256.

significant changes within this seeming continuity. Our approach views sexuality as socially constructed, that is, created by human actors in culturally and historically conditioned ways. In this essay, we argue that social constructionism provides a necessary dimension for understanding how butch-fem roles have operated in the community and in the development of individual identity.[2]

Essentialist approaches to butch-fem roles, as well as to homosexuality in general, have a long tradition.[3] The nineteenth-century medical literature considered the "invert," the man or woman whose character and mannerisms appeared to imitate those of the "opposite sex," as congenitally flawed. These researchers had little commentary on cases of more "normal" appearing behavior—passivity in women, aggressiveness in men—in which the desired object was nevertheless of the same sex. By the early 1990s, psychologists and sexologists, led by Sigmund Freud, began to explore homosexuality in terms of childhood trauma and parental insufficiency.[4] This approach never fully supplanted theories of congenital causation but nevertheless was extremely powerful as a new kind of essentialism, which viewed homosexuality as a psychological disorder caused by abnormal personality development.[5] Over the years, essentialism has at times been adopted by the lesbian and gay community and used as a basis from which to argue for tolerance and acceptance. Radclyffe Hall's *The Well of Loneliness* is an apt example; the novel pleads for the acceptance of Stephen, an unmistakably masculine lesbian, who cannot help being who she is.[6] The essentialist tradition still has a powerful influence on contemporary thinking about sexuality. For instance, the dominant ideology of our society considers the distinction between men and women as fixed and ultimately based in biology. Similarly, it categorizes lesbians and gay men as distinct kinds of people.[7] Such ideas unquestionably lurk in the background of popular thinking about butch-fem roles as well.

The relatively new social constructionist approach aims to reveal the temporal and cultural dimensions of the continuities that essentialists take for granted. Jonathan Katz explains this eloquently in his pioneering *Gay American History:*

> I will be pleased if this book helps to revolutionize the traditional concept of homosexuality. This concept is so profoundly ahistorical that the very existence of Gay history may be met with disbelief. The common image of the homosexual has been a figure divorced from any temporal-social context. The concept of homosexuality must be historicized. Ancient Greek pederasty, contemporary homosexual

> "marriages" and lesbian-feminist partnerships all differ radically. Beyond the most obvious fact that homosexual relations involve persons of the same gender, and include feelings as well as acts, there is no such thing as homosexuality in general, only particular historical forms of homosexuality. There is no evidence for the assumption that certain traits have universally characterized homosexual (or heterosexual) relations throughout history. The problem of the historical researcher is thus to study and establish the character and meaning of each varied manifestation of same-sex relations within a specific time and society.[8]

In this essay, we want to further the scope of social constructionist research by addressing ourselves to the subject of butch-fem roles: Are they indeed constant in community culture and individual identity, and therefore subject to a fixed biological or psychological interpretation, or do they need to be seen in the total social context of a developing lesbian community? After providing some background information for our research, we will document the meaning of roles for this community and show how the specific content of roles has changed over time. We will then look at how our narrators came to their role identities and consider their understanding of lesbianism as inborn or a product of social forces.

Lesbian communities began to develop in the large industrial centers of Europe and America at the turn of the century; Buffalo was no exception.[9] Our research has positively identified an upper-class community in Buffalo during the 1920s and black and white working-class communities during the 1930s, and it suggests that these communities existed even earlier. (This difference in dates is more a reflection of the sources available for learning about each community than of age. Our data on the upper-class women come from articles about them in local newspapers, while our information on the working-class women comes primarily from their own testimonies and therefore can go only as far back as their ages and memories permit.)[10] Our research has focused on working-class lesbians from 1930 to 1965, because we wanted to check our hunch that their consciousness, culture, and social life were formative in the emergence of the gay liberation movement of the 1960s.[11] In this chapter, we will treat the working-class lesbian community as a unified whole, even though it consisted of separate black and white communities that overlapped only to a limited degree, and we will use material from both black and white women. Over nine years we have collected oral histories from forty-five narrators, including nine women of color, all of whom were participants in this community at some time and some of whom were leaders. Our narrators' stories were much richer than we had ever imagined and confirmed our suspicions about their role in shaping lesbian history and politics.

Our primary concern has been to document the political and social evolution of this working-class lesbian community, looking at both its internal dynamics and its response to the changing nature of oppression. During this period, the community existed predominantly in bars, since these were the only places where people could gather publicly, break the isolation of lesbian life, and develop both friendships and lover relationships. The oppressive tenor of the times is captured in a narrator's memory of what her older sister, who was already a lesbian, said to her upon learning that she was going to join the life in the early 1950s. They had gone to an after-hours club together in New York City, and a friend of her sister asked our narrator to dance. After two or three dances, our narrator returned to the table and noticed that her sister was crying. When she asked why, her sister said:

> "I don't like the way you're looking around here. This isn't the life for you." I said, "If it's good enough for you why isn't it good enough for me?" My sister replied, "Look around at all these people that are laughing, joking, they're having a ball—you think they are. Inside they're being ripped apart. Do you know what it's like to live this kind of life? Every day when you get out of bed, before your feet hit the floor, you've gotta say to yourself, come on, get up, you may get smacked right in the face again today, some way, somehow. . . . If you can get up everyday not knowing what this day's gonna bring, whether your heart's gonna be ripped out, whether you're gonna be ridiculed, or whether people are gonna be nice to you or spit in your face, if you can face living that way, day in and day out, then you belong here; if you can't . . . get the hell out."[12]

Although the risks involved in coming together were great, lesbians persevered and began to forge a community with a rich culture and a strong sense of solidarity and pride.[13]

Despite the fact that butch-fem roles were prominent in our narrators' memories, we at first viewed them as peripheral to the growth and development of the community. Only after several years of study did we come to understand that we could not even conceive of the transformation of the community without analyzing them. They were a complex phenomenon that pervaded all aspects of community life.[14] These roles had two dimensions. First, they constituted a code of personal behavior, particularly in the areas of image and sexuality. Butches affected a masculine style, while fems appeared characteristically female. Butch and fem also complemented each other in an erotic system in which the butch was expected to be both the doer and the giver; the fem's passion was the butch's fulfillment.[15] Second, butch-fem roles were what we call a "social imperative." They were the organizing principle for this community's relation to the outside world and for its members' relationships with one another. The presence of the butch with her distinctive dress and mannerisms, or the butch-fem couple, announced lesbianism to the public. The butch, in her willingness to affirm who she was and take the consequences, was the primary indicator of lesbianism to the heterosexual world. Her aggressive style set the tone of resistance to lesbian oppression. In addition, butch-fem roles established the guidelines for forming love relationships and friendships. Two butches could be friends but never lovers; the same was true for two fems. Given this social dimension of butch-fem roles, whether her identity felt like a natural expression of self or something falsely imposed, a lesbian needed to adopt a role to participate comfortably in the community and receive its benefits.

This social dimension of roles helps to explain their tenacity. But why should the opposition of masculine and feminine be woven into lesbian culture and become a fundamental organizing principle? Modern lesbian culture developed in the context of the late nineteenth and early twentieth century when elaborate hierarchical dimensions were made between the sexes and gender was a fundamental organizing principle of cultural life. Given the nineteenth-century polarization of masculinity and femininity, Katz argues, one of the few ways for women to achieve independence in work and travel and to escape passivity was to "pass" as men.[16] In a similar vein, Jeffrey Weeks holds that the adoption of male images by lesbians at the turn of the century broke through women's and lesbians' invisibility, a necessity if lesbians were to become part of public life.[17] Expanding this approach, Esther Newton situates the adoption of male imagery in the context of the New Woman's search for an independent life and delineates how male imagery helped to break through nineteenth-century assumptions about the sexless nature of women and to introduce overt sexuality into women's relationships with one another.[18]

We agree with these interpretations and modify them for the conditions of the 1930s, 1940s, and 1950s. During this period, an effective way for the lesbian community to express the challenge presented by its affirmation of women's sexual love of women was to manipulate the basic ingredient of patriarchy—the hierarchical distinction between male and female. Butch-fem couples flew in the face of convention and outraged society by usurping male privilege in appearance and sexuality. At a time when the community was developing solidarity and consciousness, but had not yet formed lesbian political groups, butch-fem roles were the only structure for organizing against heterosexual dominance.[19] In a sense, they were a prepolitical form of resistance.[20]

The social imperative of butch-fem roles is most apparent in the evolution of lesbian bar culture even in the short period from 1930 to 1965. During the forties, lesbian bar life began to flourish in Buffalo, developing a rich culture and consciousness of kind. World War II established an atmosphere where women could easily go out alone, thereby creating more space for the lesbian community. This growth in community culture and social life, in conjunction with the repression of the McCarthy era, some of which was directed specifically against homosexuals and lesbians, created a new element of defiance. Bar lesbians in the fifties went even further in asserting their identities than those in the forties and aggressively fought for the right to be themselves. Their bold rebelliousness generated the kind of consciousness that made gay liberation possible.

Butch-fem roles were the key element in this transformation of the community's stance toward the straight world. In the forties, butches and butch-fem couples endured the harassment they received from being obvious lesbians with a strategy of passive resistance similar to that of "turning the other cheek." But in the fifties, one segment of the community, the street dykes, aggressively fought back when provoked, defending their relationships and community standards.

> Even right now it's very easy for the kids coming out now, but back then it wasn't, and I've been beaten up, I've been hit by guys. And I've fought back; sometimes I won; sometimes I lost. But I wasn't fighting to prove that I was big and bad and tough and wanted to be a man. I was fighting to survive. And I just can't see it. Things back then were horrible and I think that because I fought like a man to survive I made it somehow easier for the kids coming out today. I did all their fighting for them. I'm not a rich person. I don't have a lot of money; I don't even have a little money. I would have nothing to leave anybody in this world, but I have that that I can leave to the kids who are coming out now, who will come out into the future. That I left them a better place to come out into. And that's all I have to offer, to leave them. But I wouldn't deny it. Even though I was getting my brains beaten up I would never stand up and say, "No don't hit me. I'm not gay; I'm not gay." I wouldn't do that. I was maybe stupid and proud, but they'd come up and say, "Are you gay?" And I'd say,

> "Yes I am." Pow, they'd hit you. For no reason at all. It was silly and it was ridiculous, and I took my beatings and I survived it.

(By acknowledging the different responses to maltreatment in the 1940s and 1950s, we do not mean to imply that the fifties butch was braver or more courageous than her predecessors. Rather, we argue that each kind of butch behavior was appropriate for the general situation in the society at large and for internal developments in the community itself. All stages of lesbian history required courage, initiative, and persistence.)

Our narrators' memories of their first impression of the bars capture vividly the differences between the butch roles in the 1940s and the 1950s. One narrator who went to Ralph Martin's, a popular lesbian and gay bar of the forties, remembers the butches she met there with affection:

> And the butches were very butchie, but they were gentle, they were a gentle group. I was only fifteen when I met a lot of these real real machos, but they were gentle. Of course, I had hair down to my rear end when I really went to my first club, and they accepted me, there was nothing where they . . . "Hey, you got long hair, you don't belong in our group," something like that you know. They just had respect for me and I did for them.

In the fifties, this mode of behavior was completely replaced by a tough image. One narrator remembers an influential conversation with two new friends shortly after entering the bars:

> They were two of the, I guess, the star dykes around town, and I remember one time the three of us were together, we must have been standing at the bar, because I remember when [one] pounded her fist on the bar or table, we were talking about being gay, and she said, "If you want to be butch you gotta be rough, tough, and ready," boom! She pounded her fist on the bar. And well, it scared me, I didn't know if I could measure up to all of that but I figured I would have to try 'cause I knew I was a butch, I knew that's what I was.

Other changes occurred in butch-fem roles that correlated with the move toward public defiance. As suggested by the quotations, the forties community adamantly refused to instruct newcomers, while the fifties community reached out to them and helped them learn their butch role. One narrator remembers a younger butch who in the early forties kept asking her questions. She always told her, "I will not tell you anything. Anything you find out will be on your own. Do what you have to do." In contrast, all of our narrators who entered the bars in the fifties remember either reaching out to someone or someone reaching out to them: "[W]ith new butches you [tried] to befriend them. It ain't easy bein' alone. . . . Today it's a little more difficult. Someone walks into a bar and they're totally ignored. Before . . . you wanted to take them in for their own protection."

At the same time that the fifties community accepted the responsibility of instructing newcomers, it became less tolerant of deviance in butch-fem roles, another change from the 1940s. In the forties, lesbians belonged to a role-identified community that tolerated the small number who didn't conform to roles and allowed much latitude in the way people expressed their role identity. One of our narrators said of the forties, "At that time almost everyone was in roles. For at least ninety-five percent there was no mistaking." Then she wondered out loud, "Did we do it to them, push people into roles?" She answered herself, "No, they preferred it that way, we didn't do it." By the fifties, those who did not conform could not be in the community. As one narrator, a well-respected butch of the late fifties, remembers:

> Well, you had to be [into roles]. If you weren't, people wouldn't associate with you. . . . You had to be one or the other or you just couldn't hang around. There was no being versatile or saying, "Well, I'm neither one. I'm just homosexual or lesbian." You know, they didn't even talk about that. It was basically a man-woman relationship. . . . You had to play your role.

Although this rigidification paralleled what was happening in the larger society, it cannot be interpreted simply as imitative. The increasingly defiant stand of the community in relation to the heterosexual world increased the pressure and strain associated with butch-fem roles and hence produced a greater concern with rules and appropriate behavior. Butches had to know how to be tough and how to handle themselves in a fight. If they didn't, they could be in great danger.

Our analysis that the powerful continuity of butch-fem roles derives from their contribution to lesbian social organization, not the inherent biological or psychological makeup of every lesbian, is also supported by our narrators' varied experiences in developing their role identities. Although some narrators knew their identity from an early age, many had to develop an identity as part of the community. Two of our butch narrators who found the bars in the thirties remember being sure of their roles as butches before finding a gay community. One remembers that she was always more masculine. She looked that way and had that air about her. The other gives many examples of her tendencies toward being butch in early life. She remembers reveling in the boyish shoes her father made her wear because she was so hard on her shoes and related a humorous tale of getting her first short haircut in the thirties:

> Then the boy's bob came out. My father took me to a barber he knew, and he got carried away and was telling the guy how to cut it up around the ears. My mother screamed, "What happened to your hair?" [Then] I used to take scissors into the bathroom and cut my hair, and my mother would say, "How come your hair doesn't grow?" I would say, "Gee, I don't know!"

The same narrator couldn't remember a time when she wasn't "after the girls. . . . A father caught me rubbing against his daughter, standing on the running board of the car. I was sent home and forbidden to play with the girl again." When we asked if she was consciously initiating sexual contact, even though she was young at the time, she responded, "Definitely." These two women did not have to learn a role identity when they entered the bars but simply learned appropriate ways to develop and express their already established identity.

Our third narrator who came out in the thirties, however, does not emphasize her early butch identity but, rather, the quest involved in finding a role. "If you're in gay life, you're in gay life, whichever—if you want to play the fem or be the butch, you certainly have to go out and find it, one way or the other, what part you are going to play." This captures the experience of those who came to the lesbian community without knowing their role identity. Since butch-fem was built on the opposition of masculine and feminine characteristics, it was harder for a fem to realize a distinctive identity while growing up in the context of customary expectations of feminine behavior. In addition, a significant portion of butch narrators also were not conscious of a role identity before entering the community. One narrator recalls that she went to her first bar with her boyfriend in the 1940s, not knowing what to expect and certainly with no preconceived idea of a butch identity. She learned from the community itself that she was butch, as is evident in her description of her first dance:

> I never danced, never, not even at proms. I danced, let's face it, but I didn't follow good; so I got out and it was just a natural thing. I grabbed her and I led. She was tiny and cute, and she says, "You're gay." I says, "Oh yeah, I'm happy," and I meant it. It was sincere. She

> thought I was pulling her leg. And of course you're always going to try to act older because of where you are. And she said, "No," she said, "I knew you were a butch when you walked in the door. I don't care if you've got long hair or what." And I said, "Oh, I'm engaged to be married." She said, "I don't care if you're engaged, got long hair, I know you're a gay butch." I says, "Oh, no. I'm going, Oh God." Well, we finished our dance and I joined her group.

We have much more information on the complex process of creating role identity for women who entered the bars in the fifties, because we have been able to interview many more. Like their predecessors, some of our narrators knew they were butch from an early age and simply had to learn appropriate butch behavior upon entering the community:

> Nine years old, I knew [I was a stud]. I used to beat up boys; girls—I would just treat them like little doll babies. But I never cared for a doll. . . . I had two brothers and a sister and my younger brother used to get cap pistols, trucks and things, I got dolls. . . . I used to beat him up and take his trucks and cap pistols and give him my dolls.

Another common memory of butch narrators who spent their childhoods in the forties is feeling comfortable in boys' clothes at an early age. One narrator remembers, "I was under ten when I was wearing [my brother's] clothes when nobody was around. I always felt that I was in drag in women's clothing even as a child." This same narrator had powerful fantasies of being a cowboy:

> I was a little chubby . . . so when I was in fifth grade . . . I used to have this fantasy that I was a cowboy. This excess weight I had was just sort of like props that I had on my body, and when I would leave the classroom I'd take off this excess weight and put on my cowboy suit and get on my horse and ride away.

Cowboy fantasies were common for young lesbians of this period. Another narrator who was called "Tom" for Tomboy, from about age six or seven, always envisioned herself as the heroic Roy Rogers. After school, she would race home, take off her girl's clothes, and don her cowboy outfit. "I was Roy Rogers."

The clarity and forcefulness of these women's perceptions of their butch identities from an early age are striking, but their experiences were not those of all butch lesbians. Other narrators did not know their identities until they entered the community, and still others had difficulty finding the appropriate role for themselves. In some cases, people came out one way and then changed their identification. One narrator remembers with humor that her mother had more insight into her developing role identity than she herself did:

> She (my second relationship) was on the masculine side but I was very attracted to her, and so I naturally took the feminine approach. We started to see each other and then we started to go together and we really loved each other but we weren't making it, we were constantly hassling and fighting and arguing. And I talked to my mother and said, "Gee, I don't know what it is. I really like her." . . . And my mother said, "Maybe you're not happy in the way you're living your life with her." I said, "What do you mean?" She said—my mother would get embarrassed when she tried to explain things in daylight—and she said, "Before you met [Joan] you used to dress a little different, you wore slacks and that. Now you're in dresses all the time and you put makeup on. You don't seem like you're happy. Maybe you should go back to what you were and let her be a little more feminine." I kind of thought about that and I talked it over with this girl, and do you know that that relationship lasted for six years?

Although lesbians only rarely switched roles during a relationship, it was common for people to change their roles after their first relationships. Such a change was associated with coming out and finding your place in the community and your sexual preferences. Coming out fem and then becoming butch was the most usual direction of this early change. There was a common saying among butches in the lesbian community, "Today's love affair is tomorrow's competition." One butch narrator remembers the pain that fems could cause by switching roles, "especially when they come back and take the girl you are with away. The only way she can get at you is that way, and it works; and then you're alone." Another narrator explains this switching as due not only to inexperience, but to the kind of vulnerability required of fems:

> Some would start out real fem and the minute they got hurt by a butch . . . the next time you'd see them they'd be real butchie. . . . They'd be dressed up really butchie. . . . Usually the butches broke up with them. They'd start getting really butchie too. I don't know if they think butch is better.

Changing of roles even occurred after a person had been out a long time:

> I've seen a lot of girls come out and be fem and wind up butch. I've seen a lot of girls that were butch turn fem . . . a lot, a whole lot. Sometimes it shocks me. Me, I could never do that. To say, well I'm gonna turn a fem, and go out with a man, or I'm gonna turn a fem and just be that. No, I couldn't do that. I've been livin' the way I am too long. But I've seen a lot do it. I've seen a lot of girls who I wouldn't even believe they could switch, turn from one side to the other.

This phenomenon of switching indicates both the power and social nature of roles. A lesbian who was not sure of her role could not simply explore. She had to take a role, and if she was not comfortable in one, then she could take the other. For many lesbians, roles had to be learned and involved an element of conscious choice. One fem who was—and still is—very famous for her beauty and attractiveness, emphasizes this element of conscious choice when explaining what she feels determines a person's role: "I don't know how they get their role because I think it's a matter of choice, what they feel like they want to do. I suppose. It's hard to say. Because sometimes, I feel like I might want to turn stud. Really!"

In addition to those who switched roles, this community also had members who were never completely comfortable in roles, even though they appeared to adapt.

> I think on the surface I identified . . . when I was involved in the gay community, on the surface, you know, you either had to be butch or fem. And I was always the, I guess you'd say, the butch appearing one—back to the days when DA haircuts were popular.[21]

But this woman did a lot of joking about roles even at a time when rules were strict and serious:

> Thinking back I can remember one of the things I used to say, people would say, "Are you butch or are you fem?" And I used to say, "Well, the only difference to me between the butch or a fem is when you get up on the dance floor so you don't have to argue who's going to lead." And I have another saying since then: "My biggest decision when I get up every morning is whether to be an aggressive fem or a nelly butch."

Although the women we interviewed who were uncomfortable in roles were not the majority of this community, a surprising number expressed some degree of discomfort. The fact that they adapted just enough to get by is yet another confirmation that roles are not an intrinsic part of lesbians' biological or psychological makeup, but are a fundamental organizing principle of participation in the community.

In keeping with our narrators' varied experiences in finding their role identities, the community has not had, nor does it now have, a hegemonic view about what constitutes a true lesbian. Many narrators see the butch lesbian as the true lesbian. Other narrators consider anyone who stays with women and is part of the community a lesbian. Two of our butch narrators who came out in the thirties disagree with each other on the subject, and their argument, which they said was quite common among members of the community in the past, eloquently explores the central issues.

During the interview, Leslie took the position that only butches are lesbians. She is a lesbian [butch] and is never attracted to another like herself. Rather, she is always attracted to a more feminine type of person. Arden, on the other hand, thought that all women who stay with women are lesbians, butch or fem, as long as they don't flip back and forth between women and men. Each tried to convince the other of the rightness of her position, but neither was successful. Leslie asked Arden about two women who had been Arden's instructors in sex. These women had been married; didn't Arden consider them bisexual? Arden: "No, they didn't go back and forth. Once they were in the crowd they stayed. It was good fun and they liked it." The friends then discussed the women who had started seeing lesbians during the war while their husbands were away. Some of these women went back and forth while others did not. Leslie again did not agree with Arden that those who stayed with women were lesbians. A final argument revolved around the identity of Ramona, a past lover of Leslie's, who was very feminine and had never been with a man. Arden saw her as a lesbian while Leslie did not. Leslie believed that her own involvement with sixteen-year-old Ramona had indelibly influenced the impressionable young woman, who might not otherwise have pursued relationships with women. It was impossible for the two friends to come to an agreement.

At another interview, Leslie and Arden continued their disagreement on a different level. Leslie emphasized how the pressures of heterosexual life might influence a nonlesbian: "[w]omen of all kinds get involved in the fun of gay life. They like the fun and freedom of gay life, and it has nothing to do with sexual preference." Arden countered, underlining the forces that encouraged lesbians to pursue heterosexual marriage: "[b]ut also there is another side. I think that there were many women who liked being with women, who preferred women, but who get the Mrs. because they wanted that status."

The similarity of Leslie's position to that of the Kinsey reports, which were published after she came of age, is quite striking.[22] Leslie is using a continuum model in which there are "true lesbians," who only have sex with women, and fems whom she considers bisexuals, who can have sex with either men or women. In fact, she believes that the majority of the world is bisexual. In addition, her idea that only butches are true lesbians bears a striking similarity to early medical theories.[23] Arden, on the other hand, has the incipient analysis of a social constructionist. In her view, if women spend time in the lesbian community and consider themselves lesbians, they are lesbians, whether they are butch or fem. Furthermore, even though they hold these differing views about the nature of lesbianism, both women are cognizant of the social forces that influence a woman to participate in either the lesbian or heterosexual world.

In the fifties community, similar disagreements existed. "There was always that . . . jealousy. If you'd see [a fem] looking at a man, you'd think, 'What are you looking at him for?' You couldn't think of them as a lesbian—a lesbian wouldn't do that." When pressed further, this narrator said, "They're not as true as we are. I bet mostly all of the old [butches] feel that way." And to our surprise, some fems of that period concurred with this opinion. In their view, because they weren't the initiators, or because they didn't frequently make love to another woman, they weren't true lesbians. However, some fems disagreed. One fem who came out in the fifties, and left the life for sixteen years of marriage beginning in the early sixties, felt that she was a lesbian during the fifties when she moved with the crowd and is a lesbian again today.

Disagreements about what created a true lesbian went beyond this one issue of whether butches and fems were both lesbians. Women in the community also disagreed about the role of biology. Those who came to their butch identity at an early age tend to attribute it to physiological causes. Others claim that they don't know what ultimately caused their lesbianism. One respected butch humorously relates her opinion of how she became a lesbian:

> I don't know. You know people ask me . . . when I tell them I've been gay all my life . . . "How did you get to be gay all your life?" And I tell them the story. I say, "Well you see, the way it was with me is when I was born the doctor was so busy with my mother, it was a hard birth for her, . . . that it was the nurse that slapped my ass to bring that first

breath of life into me. And I liked the touch of that feminine hand so much that I've been gay ever since."

In conclusion, our research suggests that the reproduction of butch-fem roles involves complex issues of psychosocial identity, as well as community instruction and pressure, and that the power and continuity of roles derive in part from their centrality in organizing lesbian relations with the straight world. We argue that an analysis of butch-fem roles that is located in the context of the growth and development of a specific community has more explanatory power than essentialism. In Buffalo, as lesbians moved from a situation of relative isolation toward the political stance of the homophile and gay liberation movements, the content and meaning of butch-fem roles changed from that of building culture and community to confronting heterosexual society and fighting for dignity and respect. Some lesbians knew their role identity before entering the community, while others had to learn it, and all had to learn the content of butch-fem roles for the Buffalo community at the particular time they entered. Many members of the community adhered to essentialist explanations of their situation. This echoed essentialism in the dominant culture and provided for many a supportive sense of inescapable identity. However, others did not find essentialism a good description of their own experiences or of the variety of ways women participated in the community. They generated, from the social relations of their lives, alternative explanations that approached those of present-day social constructionists.

· CHAPTER EIGHTEEN ·

Christian Brotherhood or Sexual Perversion?

Homosexual Identities and the Construction of Sexual Boundaries in the World War I Era

GEORGE CHAUNCEY

George Chauncey, professor of history at the University of Chicago, describes sexual relations between men at a naval training station in Newport, Rhode Island, around 1920. Chauncey explains how many sailors considered themselves to be "normal" men despite their having sex with men identifed as "queers." He also recounts a fascinating court case involving the U.S. Navy and the Episcopal Church, a case that raises questions about the relationship between sexual behavior and sexual identity.[1]

· · · · ·

In the spring of 1919, officers at the Newport (Rhode Island) Naval Training Station dispatched a squad of young enlisted men into the community to investigate the "immoral conditions" obtaining there. The decoys sought out and associated with suspected "sexual perverts," had sex with them, and learned all they could about homosexual activity in Newport. On the basis of the evidence they gathered, naval and municipal authorities arrested more than twenty sailors in April and sixteen civilians in July, and the decoys testified against them at a naval court of inquiry and several civilian trials. The entire investigation received little attention before the navy accused a prominent Episcopal clergyman who worked at the YMCA of soliciting homosexual contacts there. But when civilian and then naval

This chapter is reprinted with minor editorial revisions from "Christian Brotherhood or Sexual Perversion: Homosexual Identities in the Construction of Sexual Boundaries in the World War I Era," *Journal of Social History* 19 (1985) pp. 189–212.

officials took the minister to trial on charges of being a "lewd and wanton person," a major controversy developed. Protests by the Newport Ministerial Union and the Episcopal bishop of Rhode Island and a vigorous editorial campaign by the *Providence Journal* forced the navy to conduct a second inquiry in 1920 into the methods used in the first investigation. When that inquiry criticized the methods but essentially exonerated the senior naval officials who had instituted them, the ministers asked the Republican-controlled Senate Naval Affairs Committee to conduct its own investigation. The committee agreed and issued a report in 1921 that vindicated the ministers' original charges and condemned the conduct of the highest naval officials involved, including Franklin D. Roosevelt, President Wilson's assistant secretary of the navy, and the 1920 Democratic vice-presidential candidate.[2]

The legacy of this controversy is a rich collection of evidence about the organization and phenomenology of homosexual relations among white working-class and middle-class men and about the changing nature of sexual discourse in the World War I era.[3] On the basis of the 3,500 pages of testimony produced by the investigations, it is possible to reconstruct the organization of a homosexual subculture during this period, how its participants understood their behavior, and how they were viewed by the larger community, thus providing a benchmark for generalizations about the historical development of homosexual identities and communities. The evidence also enables us to reassess current hypotheses concerning the relative significance of medical discourse, religious doctrine, and folk tradition in the shaping of popular understandings of sexual behavior and character. Most important, analysis of the testimony of the government's witnesses and the accused churchmen and sailors offers new insights into the relationship between homosexual behavior and identity in the cultural construction of sexuality. Even when witnesses agreed that two men had engaged in homosexual relations with each other, they disagreed about whether both men or only the one playing the "woman's part" should be labeled as "queer." More profoundly, they disagreed about how to distinguish between a "sexual" and a "nonsexual" relationship; the navy defined certain relationships as homosexual and perverted that the ministers claimed were merely brotherly and Christian. Because disagreement over the boundary between homosexuality and homosociality lay at the heart of the Newport controversy, its records allow us to explore the cultural construction of sexual categories in unusual depth.

The Social Organization of Homosexual Relations

The investigation found evidence of a highly developed and varied gay subculture in this small seaport community and a strong sense of collective identity on the part of many of its participants. Cruising areas, where gay men and "straight" sailors[4] alike knew that sexual encounters were to be had, included the beach during the summer and the fashionable Bellevue Avenue close to it, the area along Cliff Walk, a cemetery, and a bridge. Many men's homosexual experiences consisted entirely (and irregularly) of visits to such areas for anonymous sexual encounters, but some men organized a group life with others who shared their inclinations. The navy's witnesses mentioned groups of servants who worked in the exclusive "cottages" on Bellevue Avenue and of civilians who met at places such as Jim's Restaurant on Long Wharf.[5] But they focused on a tightly knit group of sailors who referred to themselves as "the gang,"[6] and it is this group whose social organization the first section of this paper will analyze.

The best-known rendezvous of gang members and of other gay sailors was neither dark nor secret: "[T]he Army and Navy YMCA was the headquarters of all cocksuckers [in] the early part of the evening," commented one investigator, and, added another, "everybody who sat around there in the evening . . . knew it."[7] The YMCA was one of the central institutions of gay male life; some gay sailors lived there, others occasionally rented its rooms for the evening so that they would have a place to entertain men, and the black elevator operators were said to direct interested sailors to the gay men's rooms.[8] Moreover, the YMCA was a social center, where gay men often had dinner together before moving to the lobby to continue conversation and meet the sailors visiting the YMCA in the evening.[9] The ties that they maintained through such daily interactions were reinforced by a dizzying array of parties; within the space of three weeks, investigators were invited to four "fagott part[ies]" and heard of others.[10]

Moreover, the men who had developed a collective life in Newport recognized themselves as part of a subculture extending beyond a single town; they knew of places in New York and other cities "where the 'queens' hung out," made frequent visits to New York, Providence, and Fall River, and were visited by gay men from those cities. An apprentice machinist working in Providence, for instance, spent "week-ends in Newport for the purpose of associating with his 'dear friends,' the 'girls,' " and a third of the civilians arrested during the raids conducted in the summer were New York City residents working as servants in the grand houses of Newport. Only two of the arrested civilians were local residents.[11]

Within and sustained by this community, a complex system of personal identities and structured relationships took shape, in which homosexual behavior per se did not play a determining part. Relatively few of the men who engaged in homosexual activity, whether as casual participants in anonymous encounters or as partners in ongoing relationships, identified themselves or were labeled by others as sexually different from other men on that basis alone. The determining criterion in labeling a man as "straight" (their term) or "queer" was not the extent of his homosexual activity, but the gender role he assumed. The only men who sharply differentiated themselves from other men, labeling themselves as "queer," were those who assumed the sexual and other cultural roles ascribed to women; they might have been termed "inverts" in the early twentieth-century medical literature, because they not only expressed homosexual desire, but "inverted" (or reversed) their gender role.[12]

The most prominent queers in Newport were effeminate men who sometimes donned women's clothes—when not in uniform—including some who became locally famous female impersonators. Sometimes referred to as "queens," these men dominated the social activities of the gang and frequently organized parties at their off-base apartments to which gay and "straight" sailors alike were invited. At these "drags," gang members could relax, be openly gay, and entertain straight sailors from the base with their theatrics and their sexual favors. One gay man described a party held in honor of some men from the USS *Baltimore* in the following terms:

> I went in and they were singing and playing. Some were coked up that wasn't drunk. And there was two of the fellows, "Beckie" Goldstein and Richard that was in drags, they call it, in costume. They had on some kind of ball gowns, dancing costumes. They had on some ladies' underwear and ladies' drawers and everything and wigs. . . . I saw them playing and singing and dancing and somebody was playing the piano. . . . Every once in a while "Beckie" would go out of the room with a fellow and . . . some would come back buttoning up their pants.[13]

Female impersonation was an unexceptional part of navy culture during the World War I years, sufficiently legitimate—if curious—for the *Providence Journal* and the navy's own magazine, *Newport Recruit,* to run lengthy stories and photo-essays about the many theatrical productions at the navy base in which men took the female roles.[14] The ubiquity of such drag shows and the fact that numerous "straight"-identified men took part in them sometimes served to protect gay female impersonators from suspicion. The landlord of one of the gay men arrested by the navy cited the sailor's stage roles in order to explain why he hadn't regarded the man's wearing women's clothes as "peculiar," and presumably the wife of the training station's commandant, who loaned the man "corsets, stockings, shirt waists, [and] women's pumps" for his use in *H.M.S. Pinafore,* did not realize that he also wore them at private parties.[15]

But if in some circles the men's stage roles served to legitimate their wearing drag, for most sailors such roles only confirmed the impersonators' identities as queer. Many sailors, after all, had seen or heard of the queens' appearing in drag at parties where its homosexual significance was inescapable. According to the navy's investigators, for instance, numerous sailors in uniform and "three prize fighters in civilian clothes" attended one "fagott party" given in honor of a female impersonator visiting Newport to perform at the Opera House. Not only were some of the men at the party—and presumably the guest of honor—in drag, but two men made out on a bed in full view of the others, who "remarked about their affection for each other."[16] Moreover, while sailors commonly gave each other nicknames indicating ethnic origin (e.g., "Wop" Bianchia and "Frenchman" La Favor) or other personal characteristics (e.g., "Lucky" and "Pick-axe"), many of them knew the most prominent queers *only* by their "ladies' names," camp nicknames they had adopted from the opera and cinema such as "Salome," "Theda Bara," and "Galli Curci."[17]

Several of the navy's witnesses described other signs of effeminacy one might look for in a queer. A straight investigator explained that "it was common knowledge that if a man was walking along the street in an effeminate manner, with his lips rouged, his face powdered, and his eye-brows pencilled, that in the majority of cases you could form a pretty good opinion of what kind of a man he was . . . a 'fairy.' "[18] One gay man, when pressed by the court to explain how he identified someone as "queer," pointed to more subtle indicators: "[h]e acted sort of peculiar; walking around with his hands on his hips. . . . [H]is manner was not masculine. . . . The expression with the eyes and the gestures. . . . If a man was walking around and did not act real masculine, I would think he was a cocksucker."[19] A sailor, who later agreed to be a decoy, recalled that upon noticing "a number of fellows . . . of effeminate character" shortly after his arrival at Newport, he decided to look "into the crowd to see what kind of fellows they were and found they were perverts."[20] Effeminacy had been the first sign of a deeper perversion.

The inverts grouped themselves together as "queers" on the basis of their effeminate gender behavior,[21] and they all played roles culturally defined as feminine in sexual contacts. But they distinguished among themselves on the basis of the feminine sexual behavior they preferred, categorizing themselves as "fairies" (also called "cocksuckers"), "pogues" (men who liked to be "browned," or anally penetrated), and "two-way artists" (who enjoyed both). The ubiquity of these distinctions and their importance to personal self-identification cannot be overemphasized. Witnesses at the naval inquiries explicitly drew the distinctions as a matter of course and incorporated them into their descriptions of the gay subculture. One "pogue" who cooperated with the investigation, for instance, used such categories to label his friends in the gang with no prompting from the court: "Hughes said he was a pogue; Richard said he was a cocksucker; Fred Hoage said he was a two-way artist." While there were some men about whom he "had to draw my own conclusions; they never said directly what they was or wasn't," his remarks made it clear that he was sure they fit into one category or another.[22]

A second group of sailors who engaged in homosexual relations and participated in the group life of the gang occupied a more ambiguous sexual category because they, unlike the queers, conformed to masculine gender norms. Some of them were heterosexually married. None of them behaved effeminately or took the "woman's part" in sexual relations, they took no feminine nicknames, and they did not label themselves—nor were they labeled by others—as queer. Instead, gang members, who reproduced the highly gendered sexual relations of their culture, described the second group of men as playing the "husbands" to the "ladies" of the "inverted set." Some husbands entered into steady, loving relationships with individual men known as queer; witnesses spoke of couples who took trips together and maintained monogamous relationships.[23] The husbands' sexual—and sometimes explicitly romantic—interest in men distinguished them from other men: one gay man explained to the court that he believed the rumor about one man being the husband of another must have "some truth in it because [the first man] seems to be very fond of him, more so than the average man would be for a boy."[24] But the ambiguity of the sexual category such men occupied was reflected in the difficulty observers found in labeling them. The navy, which sometimes grouped such men with the queers as "perverts," found it could only satisfactorily identify them by describing what they *did,* rather than naming what they *were.* One investigator, for instance, provided the navy with a list of suspects in which he carefully labeled some men as "pogues" and others as "fairies," but he could only identify one man by noting that he "went out with all the above named men at various times and had himself sucked off or screwed them through the rectum."[25] Even the queers' terms for such men—"friends" and "husbands"—identified the men only *in relation to* the queers, rather than according them an autonomous sexual identity. Despite the uncertain definition of their sexual identity, however, most observers recognized these men as regular—if relatively marginal—members of the gang.

The social organization of the gang was deeply embedded in that of the larger culture; as we have seen, its members reproduced many of the social forms of gendered heterosexuality, with some men playing "the woman's part" in relationships with conventionally masculine "husbands." But the gang also helped men depart from the social roles ascribed to them as biological males by that larger culture. Many of the "queers" interrogated by the navy recalled having felt effeminate or otherwise "different" most of their lives. But it was the existence of sexual subcultures—of which the gang was one—that provided them a means of structuring their vague feelings of sexual and gender difference into distinctive personal identities. Such groups facilitated people's exploration and organization of their homosexuality by offering them support in the face of social opprobrium and providing them with guidelines for how to organize their feelings of difference into a particular social form of homosexuality, a coherent identity and way of life. The gang offered men a means of assuming social roles that they perceived to be more congruent with their inner natures than those prescribed by the dominant culture and sometimes gave them remarkable strength to publicly defy social convention.

At the same time, the weight of social disapprobation led people within the gang to insist on a form of solidarity that required conformity to its own standards. To be accepted by the gang, for instance, one had to assume the role of pogue, fairy, two-way artist, or husband and present oneself publicly in a manner consistent with that labeling. But some men appear to have maintained a critical perspective on the significance of the role for their personal identities. Even while assuming one role for the purpose of interaction in the gang, at least some continued to explore their sexual interests when the full range of those interests was not expressed in the norms for that role. Frederick Hoage, for instance, was known as a "brilliant woman" and a "French artist" (or "fairy"), but he was also reported surreptitiously to have tried to "brown" another member of the gang—behavior inappropriate to a "queer" as defined by the gang.[26]

Gang members, who believed they could identify men as pogues or fairies even if the men themselves had not yet recognized their true natures, sometimes intervened to accelerate the process of self-discovery. The gang scrutinized newly arrived recruits at the YMCA for likely sexual partners and queers, and at least one case is recorded of their approaching an effeminate but straight-identified man named Rogers in order to bring him out as a pogue. While he recalled always having been somewhat effeminate, after he joined the gang Rogers began using makeup "because the others did," assumed the name "Kitty Gordon," and developed a steady relationship with another man (his "husband").[27] What is striking to the contemporary reader is not only that gang members were so confident of their ability to detect Rogers's homosexual interests that they were willing to intervene in the normal pattern of his life, but that they believed they could identify him so precisely as a "latent" (not their word) pogue.

Many witnesses indicated that they had at least heard of "fairies" before joining the service, but military mobilization, by removing men like Rogers from family and neighborhood supervision and placing them in a single-sex environment, increased the chances that they would encounter gay-identified men and be able to explore new sexual possibilities. Both the opportunities offered by military mobilization and the constraints of hometown family supervision were poignantly reflected in Rogers's plea to the court of inquiry after his arrest. After claiming that he had met gay men and had homosexual experiences only after joining the navy, he added:

> I got in their company. I don't know why; but I used to go out with them. I would like to say here that these people were doing this all their lives. I never met one until I came in the Navy. . . . I would like to add that I would not care for my folks to learn anything about this; that I would suffer everything, because I want them to know me as they think I am. This is something that I never did until I came in the Navy.[28]

Straight witnesses at the naval inquiry demonstrated remarkable familiarity with homosexual activity in Newport; like gay men, they believed that queers constituted a distinct group of people, "a certain class of people called 'fairies.' "[29] Almost all of them agreed that one could identify certain men as queer by their mannerisms and carriage. At the second court of inquiry, a naval official ridiculed the bishop of Rhode Island's assertions that it was impossible to recognize "fairies" and that he had never even heard of the term, as if claiming such naiveté were preposterous:

> Then you don't know whether or not it is common to hear in any hotel lobby the remark, when a certain man will go by, and somebody will say, "There goes a fairy?" You have *never* heard that expression used in that way?[30]

Most people also knew that such men had organized a collective life, even if they were unfamiliar with its details. As we have seen, many sailors at the naval training station knew that the YMCA was a "headquarters" for such people, and Newport's mayor recalled that "it was information that was common . . . in times gone by, summer after summer," that men called "floaters" who appeared in town "had followed the fleet up from Norfolk."[31] In a comment that reveals more about straight perceptions than gay realities, a navy officer described gay men to the Newport chief of police as "a gang who were stronger than the Masons . . . [and who] had signals and a lot of other stuff . . . [T]hey were perverts and well organized."[32]

Straight people's familiarity with the homosexual subculture resulted from the openness with which some gay men rejected the cultural norms of heterosexuality. Several servicemen, for instance, mentioned having encountered openly homosexual men at the naval hospital, where they saw patients and staff wear makeup and publicly discuss their romances and homosexual experiences.[33] The story of two gang members assigned to the Melville coaling station near Newport indicates the extent to which individual queers, with the support of the gang, were willing to make their presence known by defying social convention, even at the cost of hostile reactions. "From the time they arrived at the station they were both the topic of conversation because of their effeminate habits," testified several sailors stationed at Melville. They suffered constant harassment; many sailors refused to associate with them or abused them physically and verbally, while their officers assigned them especially heavy workloads and ordered their subordinates to "try to get [one of them] with the goods."[34] Straight sailors reacted with such vigor because the gay men flaunted their difference rather than trying to conceal it, addressing each other with "feminine names," witnesses complained, and "publish[ing] the fact that they were prostitutes and such stuff as that."[35] At times they were deliberately provocative; one astounded sailor reported that he had "seen Richard lying in his bunk take one leg and, putting it up in the air, ask everyone within range of his voice and within range of this place how they would like to take it in this position."[36]

Even before the naval inquiry began, Newport's servicemen and civilians alike were well aware of the queers in their midst. They tolerated them in many settings and brutalized them in others, but they thought they knew what they were dealing with: perverts were men who behaved like women. But as the inquiry progressed, it inadvertently brought the neat boundaries separating queers from the rest of the men into question.

Disputing the Boundaries of the "Sexual"

The testimony generated by the navy investigation provided unusually detailed information about the social organization of men who identified themselves as "queer." But it also revealed that many more men than the queers were regularly engaging in some form of homosexual activity. Initially, the navy expressed little concern about such men's behavior, for it did not believe that straight sailors' occasional liaisons with queers raised any questions about their sexual character. But the authorities' decision to prosecute men not normally labeled as queer ignited a controversy that ultimately forced the navy and its opponents to define more precisely what they believed constituted a homosexual act and to defend the basis upon which they categorized people participating in such acts. Because the controversy brought so many groups of people—working- and middle-class gay- and straight-identified enlisted men, middle-class naval officers, ministers, and town officials—into conflict, it revealed how differently those groups interpreted sexuality. A multiplicity of sexual discourses coexisted at a single moment in the civilian and naval seaport communities.

The gang itself loosely described the male population beyond its borders as "straight," but its members further divided the straight population into two different groups: those who would reject their sexual advances, and those who would accept them. A man was "trade," according to one fairy, if he "would stand to have 'queer' persons fool around [with] him in any way, shape or manner."[37] Even among "trade," gay men realized that some men would participate more actively than others in sexual encounters. Most gay men were said to prefer men who were strictly "straight and [would] not reciprocate in any way," but at least one fairy, as a decoy recorded, "wanted to kiss me and love me [and] . . . insisted and begged for it."[38] Whatever its origins, the term "trade" accurately described a common pattern of interaction between gay men and their straight sexual partners. In Newport, a gay man might take a sailor to a show or to dinner, offer him small gifts, or provide him with a place to stay when he was on overnight leave; in exchange, the sailor allowed his host to have sex with him that night, within whatever limits the sailor cared to set. The exchange was not always so elaborate: the navy's detectives reported several instances of gay men meeting and sexually servicing numerous sailors at the YMCA in a single evening. Men who were "trade" normally did not expect or demand direct payment for their services, although gay men did sometimes lend their partners small amounts of money without expecting it to be returned, and they used "trade" to refer to some civilians who, in contrast to the sailors, paid *them* for sexual services. "Trade" normally referred to straight-identified men who played the "masculine" role in sexual encounters solicited by queers.[39]

The boundary separating trade from the rest of men was easy to cross. There were locations in Newport where straight men knew they could present themselves in order to be solicited. One decoy testified that, to infiltrate the gang, he merely sat with its members in the YMCA lobby one evening. As the decoy had already been in Newport for some time, presumably without expressing any interest in the gang, a gang member named Kreisberg said

> he was surprised to see me in such company. I finally told him that I belonged to the gang and very soon after that Kreisberg . . . said "So we can consider you trade?" I replied that he could. Very soon Kreisberg requested that I remove my gloves as he, Kreisberg, wanted to hold my hands. Kreisberg acknowledged that he was abnormal and wanted to spend the night with me.[40]

Almost all straight sailors agreed that the effeminate members of the gang should be labeled "queer," but they disagreed about the sexual character of a straight man who accepted the sexual advances of a queer. Many straight men assumed that young recruits would accept the sexual solicitations of the perverts. "It was a shame to let these kids come in and run into that kind of stuff," remarked one decoy; but his remarks indicate he did not think a boy was "queer" just because he let a queer have sex with him.[41] Most pogues defined themselves as "men who like to be browned," but straight men casually defined pogues as "[people] *that you can 'brown'*" and as men who "offered themselves in the same manner which women do."[42] Both remarks imply that "normal" men could take advantage of the pogues' availability without questioning their own identities as "straight"; the fact that the sailors made such potentially incriminating statements before the naval court indicates that this was an assumption they fully expected the court to share (as, in fact, it did). That lonesome men could unreservedly take advantage of a fairy's availability is perhaps also the implication, no matter how veiled in humor, of the remark made by a sailor stationed at the Melville coaling station: "It was common talk around that the Navy Department was getting good. They were sending a couple of 'fairies' up there for the 'sailors in Siberia.' As we used to call ourselves . . . meaning that we were all alone."[43] The strongest evidence of the social acceptability of trade was that the enlisted men who served as decoys volunteered to take on the role of trade for the purpose of infiltrating the gang but were never even asked to consider assuming the role of queer. Becoming trade, unlike becoming a queer, posed no threat to the decoys' self-image of social status.

While many straight men took the sexual advances of gay men in stride, most engaged in certain ritual behavior designed to reinforce the distinction between themselves and the queers. Most important, they played only the "masculine" sex role in their encounters with gay men—or at least claimed that they did—and observed the norms of masculinity in their own demeanor. They also ridiculed gay men and sometimes beat them up after sexual encounters. Other men, who feared it brought their manhood into question simply to be approached by a "pervert," were even more likely to attack gay men. Gang members recognized that they had to be careful about whom they approached. They all knew friends who had received severe beatings upon approaching the wrong man.[44] The more militant of the queers even played on straight men's fears. One of the queers at the Melville coaling station "made a remark that 'half the world is queer and the other half trade,' " recalled a straight sailor, who then described the harassment the queer suffered in retribution.[45]

It is now impossible to determine how many straight sailors had such sexual experiences with the queers, although Alfred Kinsey's research suggests the number might have been large. Kinsey found that 37 percent of the men he interviewed in the 1930s and 1940s had engaged in some homosexual activity and that a quarter of them had had "more than incidental homosexual experience or reactions" for at least three years between the ages sixteen and fifty-five, even though only 4 percent were exclusively homosexual throughout their lives.[46] Whatever the precise figures at Newport, naval officials and queers alike believed that very many men were involved. Members of the court of inquiry never challenged the veracity of the numerous reports given them of straight sailors having sex with the queers; their chief investigator informed them on the first day of testimony that one suspected pervert had fellated "something like fifteen or twenty young recruits from the Naval Training Station" in a single night. As the investigation progressed, however, even the court of inquiry became concerned about the extent of homosexual activity uncovered. The chief investigator later claimed that the chairman of the first court had ordered him to curtail the investigation because " '[i]f your men [the decoys] do not knock off, they will hang the whole state of Rhode Island.' "[47]

Naval officials never considered prosecuting the many sailors who they fully realized were being serviced by the fairies each year, because they did not believe that the sailors' willingness to allow such acts "to be performed upon them" in any way implicated their sexual character as homosexual. Instead, they chose to prosecute only those men who were intimately involved in the gang, or otherwise demonstrated (as the navy tried to prove in court) that homosexual desire was a persistent, constituent element of their personalities, whether or not it manifested itself in effeminate behavior. The fact that naval and civilian authorities could prosecute men only for the commission of specific acts of sodomy should not be construed to mean that they viewed homosexuality simply as an act rather than as a condition characteristic of certain individuals; the whole organization of their investigation suggests otherwise. At the January 1920 trial of Reverend Samuel Kent, the prosecution contended that

> we may offer evidence of other occurrences similar to the ones the indictment is based on for the purpose of proving the disposition on the part of this man. I submit that it is a well known principle of evidence that in a crime of this nature where disposition, inclination, is an element, that we are not confined to the specific conduct which we have complained of in the indictment, that the other incidents are gone into for their corroborative value as to intent, as to disposition, inclination.[48]

As the investigation and trials proceeded, however, the men prosecuted by the navy made it increasingly difficult for the navy to maintain standards that categorized certain men as "straight" even though they had engaged in homosexual acts with the defendants. This was doubtless particularly troubling to the navy because, while its opponents focused their questions on the character of the decoys in particular, by doing so they implicitly questioned the character of *any* man who had sex with a "pervert." The decoys testified that they had submitted to the queers' sexual advances only in order to rid the navy of their presence, and the navy, initially at least, guaranteed their legal immunity. But the defendants readily charged that the decoys themselves were tainted by homosexual interest and had taken abnormal pleasure in their work. Reverend Kent's lawyers were particularly forceful in questioning the character of any man who would volunteer to work as a decoy. As one decoy after another helplessly answered each question with a quiescent "Yes, sir," the lawyers pressed them:

> Q. You volunteered for this work?
> A: Yes sir.
> Q. You knew what kind of work it was before you volunteered, didn't you?
> A. Yes, sir.
> Q. You knew it involved sucking and that sort of thing, didn't you?
> A. I knew that we had to deal with that, yes, sir.
> Q. You knew it included sodomy and that sort of thing, didn't you?
> A. Yes, sir.
> Q. And you were quite willing to get into that sort of work?
> A. I was willing to do it, yes, sir.
> Q. And so willing that you volunteered for it, is that right?

A. Yes, sir. I volunteered for it, yes, sir.
Q. You knew it included buggering fellows, didn't you?[49]

Such questions about the decoys' character were reinforced when members of the gang claimed that the decoys had sometimes taken the initiative in sexual encounters.

The defendants thus raised questions about the character of any man capable of responding to the advances of a pervert, forcing the navy to reexamine its standards for distinguishing "straight" from "perverted" sexuality. At the second naval court of inquiry, even the navy's judge advocate asked the men about how much sexual pleasure they had experienced during their contacts with the suspects. As the boundaries distinguishing acceptable from perverted sexual response began to crumble, the decoys recognized their vulnerability and tried to protect themselves. Some simply refused to answer any further questions about the sexual encounters they had described in graphic detail to the first court. One decoy protested that he had never responded to a pervert's advances: "I am a man. . . . The thing was so horrible in my sight that naturally I could not become passionate and there was no erection," but was immediately asked, "Weren't [the other decoys] men, too?" Another, less fortunate decoy had to plead:

> Of course, a great deal of that was involuntary inasmuch as a man placing his hand on my penis would cause an erection and subsequent emission. That was uncontrollable on my part. . . . Probably I would have had it [the emission] when I got back in bed anyway. . . . It is a physiological fact.[50]

But if a decoy could be suspected of perversion simply because he had a certain physiological response to a pervert's sexual advances, then the character of countless other sailors came under question. Many more men than the inner circle of queers and husbands would have to be investigated. In 1920, the navy was unprepared to take that step. The decision of the Dunn Inquiry to condemn the original investigation and the navy's decision to offer clemency to some of the men imprisoned as a result of it may be interpreted, in part, as a quiet retreat from that prospect.

Christian Brotherhood under Suspicion

The navy investigation raised fundamental questions concerning the definition of a "sexual relationship" itself when it reached beyond the largely working-class milieu of the military to label a prominent local Episcopal clergyman, Samuel Kent, and a YMCA volunteer and churchman, Arthur Leslie Green, as homosexual. When Kent fled the city, the navy tracked him down and brought him to trial on sodomy charges. Two courts acquitted him despite the fact that five decoys claimed to have had sex with him, because the denials of the respected minister and of the numerous clergymen and educators who defended him seemed more credible. Soon after Kent's second acquittal in early 1920, the bishop of Rhode Island and the Newport Ministerial Union went on the offensive against the navy. The clergymen charged that the navy had used immoral methods in its investigation, by instructing young enlisted men "in details of a nameless vice" and sending them into the community to entrap innocent citizens. They wrote letters of protest to the secretary of the navy and the president, condemned the investigation in the press, and forced the navy to convene a second court of inquiry into the methods used in the first inquiry. When it exculpated senior naval officials and failed to endorse all of the ministers' criticisms, the ministers persuaded the Republican-controlled Senate Naval Affairs Committee to undertake its own investigation, which eventually endorsed all of the ministers' charges.[51]

The simple fact that one of their own had been attacked did not provoke the fervor of the ministers' response to the navy investigation, nor did they oppose the investigation simply because of its "immoral" methods. Close examination of the navy's allegations and of the ministers' countercharges suggests that the ministers feared that the navy's charges against the two churchmen threatened to implicate them all. Both Green and Kent were highly regarded local churchmen; Kent had been asked to preach weekly during Lent, had received praise for his work at the naval hospital during an influenza epidemic, and, at the time of the investigation, was expected to be named superintendent of a planned Seaman's Church Institute.[52] Their behavior had not differed markedly from that of the many other men who ministered to the needs of the thousands of boys brought to Newport by the war. When the navy charged that Kent's and Green's behavior and motives were perverted, many ministers feared that they could also be accused of perversion and, more broadly, that the inquiry had questioned the ideology of nonsexual Christian brotherhood that had heretofore explained their devotion to other men. The confrontation between the two groups fundamentally represented a dispute over the norms for masculine gender behavior and over the boundaries between homosociality and homosexuality in the relations of men.

The investigation threatened Newport's ministers precisely because it repudiated those conventions that had justified and institutionalized a mode of behavior for men of the cloth or of the upper class that would have been perceived as effeminate in other men. The ministers' perception of this threat is reflected in their repeated criticism of the navy operatives' claim that they could detect perverts by their "looks and actions."[53] Almost all sailors and townspeople, as we have seen, endorsed this claim, but it put the ministers as a group in an extremely awkward position, for the major sign of a man's perversion, according to most sailors, was his being effeminate. As the ministers' consternation indicated, there was no single norm for masculine behavior at Newport; many forms of behavior considered effeminate on the part of working-class men were regarded as appropriate to the status of upper-class men or to the ministerial duties of the clergy. Perhaps if the navy had accused only working-class sailors, among whom effeminacy was more clearly deviant from group norms, of perversion, the ministers might have been content to let this claim stand. But when the naval inquiry also identified churchmen associated with such an upper-class institution as the Episcopal Church of Newport as perverted because of their perceived effeminacy, it challenged the norms that had heretofore shielded men of their background from such suspicions.

One witness tried to defend Kent's "peculiar" behavior on the basis of the conventional norms when he contended that "I don't know whether you would call it abnormal. He was a minister."[54] But the navy refused to accept this as a defense, and witnesses repeatedly described Kent and Green to the court as "peculiar," "sissyfied," and "effeminate." During his daily visits to patients at the hospital, according to a witness named Brunelle, Green held the patients' hands and "didn't talk like a man—he talk[ed] like a woman to me."[55] Since there is no evidence that Green had a high-pitched or otherwise "effeminate" *voice*, Brunelle probably meant Green addressed men with greater affection than he expected of a man. But all ministers visited with patients and spoke quiet, healing words to them; their position as ministers had permitted them to engage in such conventionally "feminine" behavior. When the navy and ordinary sailors labeled this behavior "effeminate" in the case of Green and Kent, and further claimed that such effeminacy was a sign of sexual perversion, they challenged the legitimacy of many Christian social workers' behavior.

During the war, Newport's clergymen had done all they could to minister to the needs of the thousands of boys brought to the naval training station. They believed they had acted in the spirit of Christian brotherhood, but the naval inquiry seemed to suggest that less lofty motives were at work. Ministers had loaned sailors money, but during the inquiry, they heard Green accused of buying sex. They had visited boys in the hospital and now heard witnesses insinuate that this was abnormal: "I don't know what [Kent's] duties were, but he was always talking to some boys. It seems though he would have special boys to talk to. He would go to certain fellows [patients] and probably spend the afternoon with them."[56] They had given boys drives and taken them out to dinner and to the theater, and now heard Kent accused of lavishing such favors on young men in order to further his salacious purposes. They had opened their homes to the young enlisted men, but now heard Kent accused of inviting boys home in order to seduce them.[57] When one witness at the first court of inquiry tried to argue that Green's work at the YMCA was inspired by purely "charitable" motives, the court repudiated his interpretation and questioned the motives of *any* man who engaged in such work:

> Do you think a normal active man would peddle stamps and paper around a Hospital and at the Y.M.C.A.? . . . Do you think that a man who had no interest in young boys would voluntarily offer his services and work in the Y.M.C.A. where he is constantly associated with young boys?[58]

The ministers sought to defend Kent—and themselves—from the navy's insinuations by reaffirming the cultural interpretation of ministerial behavior as Christian and praiseworthy. While they denied the navy's charge that Kent had had genital contact with sailors, they did not deny his devotion to young men, for to have done so would have implicitly conceded the navy's interpretation of such behavior as salacious—and thus have left all ministers who had demonstrated similar devotion open to suspicion. Reverend John H. Deming of the Ministerial Union reported that numerous ministers shared the fear of one man who was "frantic after all he had done for the Navy":

> When this thing [the investigation] occurred, it threw some of my personal friends into a panic. For they knew that in the course of their work they had had relations with boys in various ways; they had been alone with them in some cases. As one boy [a friend] said, frequently boys had slept in the room with him. But he had never thought of the impropriety of sleeping alone with a navy boy. He thought probably he would be accused.[59]

Rather than deny the government's claim that Kent had sought intimate relationships with sailors and devoted unusual attention to them, therefore, Kent and his supporters depicted such behavior as an honorable part of the man's ministry. Indeed, demonstrating just how much attention

Kent had lavished on boys became as central to the strategy of the ministers as it was to that of the government, but the ministers offered a radically different interpretation of it. Their preoccupation with validating ministerial behavior turned Kent's trial and the second naval inquiry into an implicit public debate over the cultural definition of the boundaries between homosociality and homosexuality in the relations of men. The navy had defined Kent's behavior as sexual and perverted; the ministers sought to reaffirm that it was brotherly and Christian.

Kent himself interpreted his relations with sailors as "[t]rying to be friends with them, urging them to come to my quarters and see me if they wanted to, telling them—I think, perhaps, I can best express it by saying 'Big Brotherhood.' " He quoted a letter from another minister commending his "brotherly assistance" during the influenza epidemic, and he pointed out that the Episcopal War Commission provided him with funds with which to take servicemen to the theater "at least once a week" and to maintain his automobile in order to give boys drives "and get acquainted with them."[60] He described in detail his efforts to minister to the men who had testified against him, explaining that he had offered them counsel, a place to sleep, and other services just as he had to hundreds of other enlisted men. But he denied that any genital contact had taken place and, in some cases, claimed he had broken off the relationships when he realized that the *decoys* wanted sexual contact.

Kent's lawyers produced a succession of defense witnesses—respected clergymen, educators, and businesspeople who had known Kent at every stage of his career—to testify to his obvious affection for boys, even though, by emphasizing this aspect of his character, they risked substantiating the navy's case. The main point of their testimony was that Kent was devoted to boys and young men and had demonstrated such talent in working with them that they had encouraged him to focus his ministry on them. Kent's lawyers prompted a former employer from Kent's hometown of Lynn, Massachusetts, to recall that Kent, a "friend of [his] family, and especially [his] sons and sons' associates," had "[taken] charge of twelve or fourteen boys [from Lynn] and [taken] them down to Sebago Lake," where they camped for several weeks "under his charge." The bishop of Pennsylvania recalled that, as Kent's teacher at the Episcopal Theological School in Cambridge in 1908, he had asked Kent to help him develop a ministry to Harvard men, "because [Kent] seemed peculiarly fitted for it in temperament and in experience, and in general knowledge of how to approach young men and influence them for good." The sentiments of Kent's character witnesses were perhaps best summarized by a judge who sat on the Episcopal War

Commission that employed Kent. The judge assured the court that Kent's reputation was "excellent; I think he was looked upon as an earnest Christian man [who] was much interested in young men."[61]

The extent to which Kent's supporters were willing to interpret his intimacy with young men as brotherly rather than sexual is perhaps best illustrated by the effort of Kent's defense lawyer to show how Kent's inviting a decoy named Charles Zipf to sleep with him was only another aspect of his ministering to the boy's needs. Hadn't the decoy told Kent he was "lonesome" and had no place to sleep that night, the defense attorney pressed Zipf in cross-examination, before Kent invited him to spend the night in his parish house? And after Kent had set up a cot for Zipf in the living room, hadn't Zipf told Kent that he was "cold" before Kent pulled back the covers and invited him to join him in his bed?[62] The attorney counted on the presumption of Christian brotherhood to protect the minister's behavior from the suspicion of homosexual perversion, even though the same evidence would have seemed irrefutably incriminating in the case of another man.

Kent's defense strategy worked. Arguments based on assumptions about ministerial conduct persuaded the jury to acquit Kent of the government's charges. But Newport's ministers launched their campaign against the navy probe as soon as Kent was acquitted because they recognized that it had succeeded in putting their devotion to men under suspicion. It had raised questions about the cultural boundaries distinguishing homosexuality from homosociality that the ministers were determined to lay to rest.

But while it is evident that Newport's ministers feared the consequences of the investigation for their public reputations, two of their charges against the navy suggest that they may also have feared that its allegations contained some element of truth. The charges reflect the difference between the ministers' and the navy's understanding of sexuality and human sinfulness, but the very difference may have made the navy's accusations seem plausible in a way that the navy could not have foreseen. First, the ministers condemned the navy for having instructed young enlisted men—the decoys—"in the details of a nameless vice" and having ordered them to use that knowledge. The naval authorities had been willing to let their agents engage in sexual acts with the "queers" because they were primarily concerned about people manifesting a homosexual disposition rather than those engaging occasionally in homosexual acts. The navy asserted that the decoys' investigative purpose rendered them immune from criminal prosecution even though they had committed illegal sexual acts. But the ministers viewed the decoys' culpability as "a moral question . . . not a technical question at all"; when the decoys had sex with other men, they had "scars placed on their souls," because, inescapably, "having immoral relations with men is an immoral act."[63] The sin was in the act, not the motive or the disposition. In addition, the ministers charged that the navy had directed the decoys to entrap designated individuals and that no one, no matter how innocent, could avoid entrapment by a skillful decoy. According to Bishop Perry, the decoys operated by putting men "into compromising positions, where they might be suspected of guilt, [even though they were] guiltless persons." Anyone could be entrapped because an "innocent advance might be made by the person operated upon and he might be ensnared against his will."[64] Implicitly, any clergyman could have done what Kent was accused of doing. Anyone's defenses could fall.

The ministers' preoccupation with the moral significance of genital sexual activity and their fear that anyone could be entrapped may reflect the continued saliency for them of the Christian precept that *all* people, including the clergy, were sinners subject to a variety of sexual temptations, including those of homosexual desire.[65] According to this tradition, Christians had to resist homosexual temptations, as they resisted others, but simply to desire a homosexual liaison was neither a singular failing nor an indication of perverted character. The fact that the ministers never clearly elucidated this perspective and were forced increasingly to use the navy's own terms while contesting the navy's conclusions may reflect both the ministers' uncertainty and their recognition that such a perspective was no longer shared by the public.

In any case, making the commission of specified physical acts the distinguishing characteristic of a moral pervert made it definitionally impossible to interpret the ministers' relationships with sailors—no matter how intimate and emotionally moving—as having a "sexual" element, so long as they involved no such acts. Defining the sexual element in men's relationships in this narrow manner enabled the ministers to develop a bipartite defense of Kent that simultaneously denied he had had sexual relationships with other men and yet celebrated his profound emotional devotion to them. It legitimized (nonphysical) intimacy between men by precluding the possibility that such intimacy could be defined as sexual. Reaffirming the boundaries between Christian brotherhood and perverted sexuality was a central objective of the ministers' very public debate with the navy. But it may also have been a private significance to churchmen forced by the navy investigation to reflect on the nature of their brotherhood with other men.

Conclusion

The richly textured evidence provided by the Newport controversy makes it possible to reexamine certain tenets of recent work in the history of sexuality, especially the history of homosexuality. Much of that work, drawing on sociological models of symbolic interactionism and the labeling theory of deviance, has argued that the end of the nineteenth century witnessed a major reconceptualization of homosexuality. Before the last century, according to this thesis, North American and European cultures had no concept of the homosexual-as-person; they regarded homosexuality as simply another form of sinful behavior in which anyone might choose to engage. The turn of the century witnessed the "invention of the homosexual," that is, the new determination that homosexual desire was limited to certain identifiable individuals for whom it was an involuntary sexual orientation of some biological or psychological origin. The most prominent advocates of this thesis have argued that the medical discourse on homosexuality that emerged in the late nineteenth century played a determining role in this process, by creating and popularizing this new model of homosexual behavior (which they have termed the "medical model" of homosexuality). It was on the basis of the new medical models, they argue, that homosexually active individuals came to be labeled in popular culture—and to assume an identity—as sexual deviants different in nature from other people, rather than as sinners whose sinful nature was the common lot of humanity.[66] . . .

The Newport evidence helps put the significance of the medical discourse in perspective; it also offers new insights into the relationship between homosexual behavior and identity. Recent studies that have established the need to distinguish between homosexual behavior (presumably a transhistorically evident phenomenon) and the historically specific concept of homosexual identity have tended to focus on the evolution of people whose *primary* personal and political "ethnic" identification is as gay and who have organized a multidimensional way of life on the basis of their homosexuality. The high visibility of such people in contemporary Western societies and their growing political significance make analysis of the historical development of their community of particular scholarly interest and importance.[67] But the Newport evidence indicates that we need to begin paying more attention to *other* social forms of homosexuality—other ways in which homosexual relations have been organized and understood, differentiated, named, and left deliberately unnamed. We need to specify the *particularity* of various modes of homosexual behavior and the relationships between those modes and particular configurations of sexual identity.

For even when we find evidence that a culture has labeled people who were homosexually active as sexually deviant, we should not assume a priori that their homosexual activity was the determinative criterion in the labeling process. As in Newport, where many men engaged in certain kinds of homosexual behavior yet continued to be regarded as "normal," the assumption of particular sexual rules and deviance from gender norms may have been more important than the coincidence of male or female sexual partners in the classification of sexual character. "Fairies," "pogues," "husbands," and "trade" might all be labeled "homosexuals" in our own time, but they were labeled—and understood themselves—as fundamentally different kinds of people in World War I–era Newport. They all engaged in what we would define as homosexual behavior, but they and the people who observed them were more careful than we to draw distinctions between different modes of such behavior. To classify their behavior and character using the simple polarities of "homosexual" and "heterosexual" would be to misunderstand the complexity of their sexual system. Indeed, the very terms "homosexual behavior" and "identity," because of their tendency to conflate phenomena that other cultures may have regarded as quite distinct, appear to be insufficiently precise to denote the variety of social forms of sexuality we wish to analyze.[68]

The problems that arise when different forms of homosexual activity and identity are conflated are evidenced in the current debate over the consequences of the development of a medical model of homosexuality. Recent studies, especially in lesbian history, have argued that the creation and stigmatization of the public image of the homosexual at the turn of the century served to restrict the possibilities for intimacy between all women and all men, by making it possible to associate such intimacy with the despised social category of the homosexual. This thesis rightly observes that the definition of "deviance" serves to establish behavioral norms for everyone, not just for the deviant. But it overlooks the corollary of this observation, that the definition of "deviance" serves to legitimize some social relations even as it stigmatizes others; and it assumes that the turn-of-the-century definition of "sexual inversion" codified the same configuration of sexual and gender phenomena that "homosexuality" does today. But many early-twentieth-century romantic friendships between women, for instance, appear to have been unaffected by the development of a public lesbian persona, in part because that image characterized the lesbian primarily as a "mannish woman," which had the effect of excluding from its stigmatizing purview all conventionally feminine women, no matter how intimate their friendships.[69]

The stigmatized image of the queer also helped to legitimate the behavior of men in Newport. Most observers did not label as "queer" either the ministers who were intimate with their Christian brothers or the sailors who had sex with effeminate men, because neither group conformed to the dominant image of what a queer should be like. Significantly, though, in their own minds, the two groups of men legitimized their behavior in radically different ways: the ministers' conception of the boundary between acceptable and unacceptable male behavior was almost precisely the opposite of that obtaining among the sailors. The ministers made it impossible to define their relationships with sailors as "sexual" by making the commission of specified physical acts the distinguishing characteristic of a moral pervert. But even as the ministers argued that their relatively feminine character and deep emotional intimacy with other men were acceptable so long as they engaged in no physical contact with them, the sailors believed that their physical sexual contact with the queers remained acceptable so long as they avoided effeminate behavior and developed no emotional ties with their sexual partners.

At the heart of the controversy provoked and revealed by the Newport investigation was a confrontation among several such definitional systems, a series of disputes over the boundaries between homosociality and homosexuality in the relations of men and over the standards by which their masculinity would be judged. The investigation became controversial when it verged on suggesting that the homosocial world of the navy and the relationships between sailors and their Christian brothers in the Newport ministry were permeated by homosexual desire. Newport's ministers and leading citizens, the Senate Naval Affairs Committee, and, to some extent, even the navy itself repudiated the Newport inquiry because they found such a suggestion intolerable. Although numerous cultural interpretations of sexuality were allowed to confront one another at the inquiry, ultimately certain cultural boundaries had to be reaffirmed in order to protect certain relations as "nonsexual," even as the sexual nature of others was declared and condemned. The Newport evidence reveals much about the social organization and self-understanding of men who identified themselves as "queer." But it also provides a remarkable illustration of the extent to which the boundaries established between "sexual" and "nonsexual" relations are culturally determined, and it reminds us that struggles over the demarcation of those boundaries are a central aspect of the history of sexuality.

· CHAPTER NINETEEN ·

Strangers at Home

Bisexuals in the Queer Movement

CAROL QUEEN

Carol Queen, a cultural sexologist, writer, and bisexual activist, discusses the challenges of being bisexual in the contemporary gay and lesbian rights movement. Queen dispels some common myths about bisexuality and argues that bisexuals are an integral part of the "queer" community whose presence can be instructive to both homosexuals and heterosexuals alike.

· · · · ·

As a bisexually identified adolescent, I was alone with my difference. My lot was no different from that of all the lesbian, gay, bisexual, gender-bent, and otherwise queer youths whose hearts and hormones send different messages than those heard by our straight "peers."

I went off to college vowing to find others, and did, at the Gay People's Alliance. They were warm and welcoming until I said I was bi. Then their eyes rolled, and I know in retrospect what they were thinking: "another poor closet case influenced by Elton John." Patiently it was explained to me that almost every young gay person eases into her or his rightful homosexual identity by leaning on a "safer" and "more socially acceptable" bisexual identification, which provides the person just coming out with a cushion of "heterosexual privilege" until s/he acquires enough gay pride to drop the charade.

In short, I'd grow out of it.

Not much had been written about bisexuality—it was 1974. I found only a couple of bi-positive pieces written from what I now might call a "queer

---

This chapter is reprinted with minor editorial revisions from *Out/Look* No. 16 (Spring 1992) pp. 23, 29–33.

Utopian" perspective: "in a nonsexist and nonhomophobic world, we might all be bisexual." There was a queer movement in the 1970s, too, embracing a wider rainbow of nonhetero, alternative sexualities than the already-becoming-staid gay movement found acceptable; but before long, the radical discourse about queerdom fell out of favor as the gay movement worked its way toward the political mainstream.

I was barely seventeen. I had just kissed my first woman. Maybe my new friends in the gay community were right about, as they termed it, this "phase."

I saw that the polite distance between my new gay friends and me would be an obstacle to establishing relationships with women. My few forays into erotic desire for straight women bore the same fruit they usually do for "gold-star" lesbians—frustration and emotional pain. There was no community of bisexual women with whom to explore my attractions. I did what many other bisexual people have done—I stopped insisting I be acknowledged and accepted as bisexual. I lived and loved, passing, in the gay community, and for many years, only a few people realized that I still harbored erotic desires for men and that, occasionally, I acted on them.

Please understand that identifying as heterosexual—relying on that elusive "privilege"—never once occurred to me. I was not and am not heterosexual. Discourse was binary, with only two possible sexual orientations from which to choose, and identifying as heterosexual was not an option. Closeting myself about my bisexuality gave me access to a community where I desperately wanted to belong, and for the next ten years *did* belong, as an activist, an advocate, and a lover of women—a lesbian.

Perhaps only a queer who has had the narrowness of the closet work at her/his sense of self will understand how this felt to me and to the many other lesbian and gay community members who hide the truths of their sexual lives. I was an out lesbian with a dirty secret, at odds with the expressed ethics of a queer community that said "out" was good—but hadn't accepted me warmly when, naively, I had taken them at their word.

The bones of this story are not just mine. Many other bisexuals have carved out lives (hidden or not) among lesbians and gays. The lesbian and gay movement must come to terms with the position of bisexual people within it because we're already here. It won't help to vote whether or not bisexuals should be let in: we *are* in. Nor can there be a vote to exclude us; bisexual people whose longtime and cherished home is the lesbian and gay community will do what we've always done to stay affiliated with it—we will fight, or lie and deny that our opposite-sex relationships have any meaning. Many of us come out of our closet only when we get so sick of it that staying in threatens our sanity or our sense of authenticity. Some of us come out when sexual behavior with an other-sex partner leads to love and we can't bring ourselves to deny it. And, increasingly these days, bisexuals are coming out because they realize they can—that a growing bisexual community exists to welcome them.

Why Are We Arguing?

Why are we, even for a minute, searching for the experiences and attitudes that divide bisexuals from lesbians and gay men? Why aren't we searching for what we hold in common? As bisexual theorist Amanda Udis Kessler notes, we "share the same issues, and not just 'half the time.' We don't get half-gaybashed when we walk down the street with our same-sex lovers. . . . We don't get half-fired from our jobs, or lose only half of our children in court battles. . . . Lesbian/gay issues are our issues, and we want to work on them with lesbians and gay men."

Working in concert with lesbians and gay men, though, can be emotionally difficult; we're forced to contend with the feeling that many of our queer sisters and brothers see us as strangers in the house. These and other factors have led bisexual women and men to look to each other for community.

The question of bisexual participation in the lesbian and gay movement is not new, in spite of the attention the recent resurgence of the bisexual movement has received. Bisexuals have generated debate at least as far back as Stonewall. The lesbian and gay movement grapples with issues of sexual diversity—bi and otherwise—because it's fully diverse itself, a microcosm of the larger society in which homosexuality is only the biggest of many secrets that refuse to stay silenced.

I assume that what is healthy for us in our workplaces and families of origin—to own our experience and insist it be honored—is equally right in our queer families of choice and our political organizations. When I finally came out again as bisexual, ten years after my first attempt, I was struck by how many people in my small-city gay community found excuses to chat with me privately so they could confide their feelings of concern about their own opposite-sex desires or to confess that they'd even gone so far as to secretly act on them. These whispered confidences show me that Alfred Kinsey, who did so much to help us all out of the closet earlier in this century, was right to sketch us on a continuum, not in fixed categories. But Kinsey had nothing to say about our community affiliations, and it is clear to me that one reason these secrets are not usually aired is because they threaten our sense of who we are and where we are at home.

Many bisexuals and gay men seem to have bought the line that bisexuals, "confused" about their sexual identities, make unstable mates and community members. Absent from the discourse has been the revelation that many bisexuals are in fact not confused—that the confusion lies, if anywhere, in the reactions of monosexuals to us. Nothing in either our homophobic culture or our homosexual counterculture helps us with the shock that our desires and affections are not always labeled "either/or." Sometimes a bisexual "phase" may be an indicator of confusion generated by a person's internalized homophobia, but I think a more common confusion comes from a monosexual's realization that the walls of her/his box are beginning to crumble.

Many bisexuals do not seek refuge in a homophobic closet that contains both pleasure and privilege. Those who do are the people many bisexuals and gays think of as representative of bi-ness. That "honor" has gone to those who mirror the gay community's own antipathy. Heterosexuals are not the only people who fall prey to stereotyped thinking: thus the bisexual role models my gay community of the seventies recognized were mostly rock stars who were said to be closeted about their homosexuality. This is a gay cultural version of our parents' assumptions that homosexual Boy Scouts would grow up to be Liberace—other models of being gay aren't envisioned because they're not seen. When our role models are circumscribed or removed, how are we to be guided in our development?

The bisexual and gay community knows the effects of this silencing, but it has ironically adopted as forebears some historical figures who were probably bisexual. Some bisexuals want to take back the Virginia Woolfs and Oscar Wildes, but I think we ought to share them—the sexually divergent, and often gender-bent, people of yesterday can be heroes to all of us. Besides, it can be argued that none of us has any business labeling people who are no longer around to speak for themselves; it displays a distressingly ahistorical perspective to use late-twentieth-century constructs to describe the lives lived in a social context we can never fully understand. Lesbians and gay men might argue that in the presence of the kind of supportive community we now rely on, people having same- as well as other-sex relationships in other times might have elected to be what we now define as gay. We'll never know. Many people in other eras have exhibited exclusively same-sex erotic behavior. Denying that both homo- and heterosexual activity might naturally occur in one person's lifetime (either then or now) is an academic version of some monosexuals' favorite game: Make Them Choose.

Some gays and bisexuals wonder at many bisexuals' angry emphasis on biphobia in the gay community: Don't we know who our real enemies are? The answer is yes, and the dismal truth is that we *expect* homophobia—who in this culture hasn't been subtly or overtly warned against crossing that line? Bisexual anger has a simple genesis: we expected more of others who have faced homophobia.

Seeds of Anger

Representatives of bisexual-feminist separatism may feel singled out as special targets of our anger and distress. To the extent that this is true, the seeds of anger lie in bisexual separatism as a politic: in this reading of feminism, specific sex acts take on politicized meaning. These are said to have consequences for the consciousness of the person performing them. Lesbian feminism is arguably the most proscriptive gay or lesbian politic, generating in its adherents the greatest tendency to judge others' (especially sexual) behavior. Gay men, for example, seem more likely to cite personal antipathy or simple stereotypes about bisexuals as a source of their chagrin. A great many bisexual women, particularly those who are feminist and lesbian-identified, have felt both personally and politically rejected and judged by the separatist sisters. Even those with no such experience may feel wary having heard other bisexual women's stories. No one likes to feel attacked, even politically.

In today's climate of attack against sexual minorities, we have little to gain from separatism. Much as we need to honor our differences, we must understand that the strategic risks we run as fractionalized peoples are greater than any risks to individuals' identities. Struggling toward a more inclusive community does not mean we have to put an end to difference—it means we have to deal with it.

I understand the antipathy some gays and lesbians feel about bisexuals; I felt it myself when I was trying to live within a normative lesbian community. I sometimes feel it today in the presence of bisexual people who are not queer-identified: once a faggot-bi boyfriend and I were at a bi Thanksgiving celebration at which all the men were visibly nervous about Boyfriend's fey mannerisms. The two of us left shaking our heads, having felt not home, but homophobia. The difference between a gay-identified and a heterosexually identified bisexuality challenges us when we come together to build bisexual identity. But I have to ask: How will any of those (mostly newly out) bisexuals ever come to be queer-identified if they have no access to the queer community? How will they learn the folkways of the lesbian/gay world if that world does not welcome them as bisexuals?

Ironically, there is a strong feminist bent to the organized bisexual movement today. Activists push to include political issues that have seen more play in the lesbian-feminist community than elsewhere in the lesbian and gay world. Issues of access and inclusion around race, economic status, and dis/abilities have been high priorities at nationally and regionally organized conferences. Bisexual women are no more comfortable with sexism than lesbians, in spite of the fact that some lesbians code some bi women's sexual practices as inherently sexist.

With the rise of the queer movement, we still define ourselves in relation—nay, opposition—to a culturally conservative heterosexual norm, but we are increasingly aware that gold-star lesbians and gay men are not the only people who lead dissident lives and that, in fact, heterosexual behavior does not always equal "straight." When I strap on a dildo and fuck my male partner, we are engaging in "heterosexual" behavior, but I can tell you that it feels altogether *queer,* and I'm sure my grandmother and Jesse Helms would say the same. Reifying other-sex behavior and making its absence the basis of gay politics doesn't strike me as very careful analysis. Sexual variation brought out of the closet is seen as dangerous and dissident by the status quo—please remember that homosexuality is not the only sexual behavior for which people have been arrested, institutionalized, or persecuted.

· PART FOUR ·

Public Policy

· CHAPTER TWENTY ·

Make War, Not Love

The Pentagon's Gay Ban Is Wise and Just

JOHN LUDDY

John Luddy, a defense policy analyst at the Heritage Foundation and a former Marine infantry officer, argues that homosexuality is incompatible with military service. After rejecting the current "Don't Ask, Don't Tell" compromise (see introduction to this volume), Luddy argues that banning gays and lesbians from the military is neither judgmental nor ideological: it is simply a necessary condition for maintaining unit cohesion and thus maximizing combat effectiveness. Luddy rejects the race analogy (cf. Paul Siegel in the following essay) and argues that lifting the ban would have disastrous—even life-threatening—results.

. . . . .

The intensity of the 1993 debate over President Clinton's plan to end the ban on open homosexuals serving in the military should have surprised no one, for few things get Americans so riled up as thinking about sex and talking about rights. It was unfortunate, however, that the controversy focused more on the presumed rights of homosexuals than on the principles that are fundamental to a strong military.

Those who opposed the ban tried to dismiss the ensuing public outcry as a moral crusade orchestrated by the religious Right. But this dismissal underestimated the public's genuine concern. Senator Sam Nunn and Joint Chiefs of Staff Chairman Colin Powell, both of whom supported the ban, are hardly right-wing fanatics. Nor are most other Americans, who view this as more than a matter of prejudice: they may not condone hatred

This chapter is reprinted with minor editorial revisions from *Policy Review* (Spring 1993):68-71.

of or intolerance toward homosexuals, but they innately understand how sexuality in the ranks could endanger men in uniform.

The uproar subsided when the Pentagon established its current policy, commonly known as "Don't Ask, Don't Tell." Beyond its apparent legal vulnerability—having been routinely challenged in the courts by both sides, and recently ruled unconstitutional by U.S. District Court Judge Eugene Nickerson in Brooklyn—"Don't Ask, Don't Tell" is based on a misguided premise: that homosexual military personnel who are allowed to serve clandestinely under the policy will abstain from homosexual behavior, which the policy deems "incompatible with military service."

In trying to please both sides, the new policy implies that it matters not whether someone is homosexual, but simply whether that person engages in homosexual activity. But is it reasonable public policy to assume that homosexuals will abstain from sexual activity for the duration of their enlistment? Would anyone make this assumption about heterosexuals?

If homosexuality is incompatible with military service, it should be prohibited outright. Other behavior "incompatible with military service," such as drug abuse and sexual harassment, is not tolerated in private; there is simply no reason why homosexuality should be dealt with differently. Looking the other way when homosexuals seek to join the armed forces sends the message that they are welcome so long as they remain celibate or do not get caught. Such a policy is disingenuous and unrealistic. Even worse, by encouraging deception by homosexuals and self-deception by their commanders, it directly undermines the personal integrity so vital to sustaining the moral authority of command.

Banning homosexuals from the military is both wise and just. It is wise because it accounts for real people functioning in the real world and recognizes that despite their best intentions, heterosexuals and homosexuals are above all human. It is just because it can be defended without recourse to any criticism of homosexuality on moral grounds; indeed, the only moral basis for the ban is the assertion that preventing unnecessary loss of life is more important than sexuality of any variety. Thus, a ban against homosexuals in the military is neither judgmental or ideological. It is based on the recognition that military life cannot provide for different individual lifestyles and that distractions in combat, sexual or otherwise, get people killed.

The Marine Corps Is Not Burger King

The primary objective of the armed forces is to win battles with as few casualties as possible. For the president or any other leader to permit anything that detracts from this objective to influence military policy and training constitutes gross negligence and is truly immoral. While the military has been better at providing equal opportunity to women and minorities than any other part of society, this has until now been a fortuitous side benefit, not an objective or an obligation.

Combat is a team endeavor. To win in combat, individuals must be trained to subjugate their individual instinct for self-preservation to the needs of their unit. Since most people are not naturally inclined to do this, military training must break down an individual and recast him as part of a team. This is why recruits give up their first names and why they look, act, dress, and train alike. To paraphrase an old drill instructor, the Marine Corps is not Burger King—you can't have it your way.

The purpose of this training, which is continually reinforced throughout the military culture, is to build unit cohesion. Unit cohesion—on an athletic team, in a family, in a marriage, and on the battlefield—hinges on trust. Military leaders gain the trust of their subordinates by demonstrating such attributes as character, courage, sound judgment, respect, and loyalty. Soldiers trust each other because of their shared values, objectives, training, and other experiences. To risk one's life willingly demands a degree of trust in one's comrades and one's commanders not found in any other environment on earth. Although such demands occasionally may be made of firefighters or police, soldiers fight in wars, where such demands are routine.

It is difficult to foresee a time when homosexuals and heterosexuals no longer see each other as different in a fundamental way. With the slightest introspection, the reasonable person quickly realizes that bonds of trust will be difficult to create within a group of men if there is sexuality beneath the surface. The thought that your comrade might have sexual feelings for you—*even if he is suppressing those feelings*—will make such trust impossible. The slightest inkling that a commander is influenced by his sexuality—even to the extent that he must resist that influence—will destroy his effectiveness as a leader. Soldiers must trust each other, and their commanders, if they are to risk their lives in causes our nation deems appropriate. When trust is absent among civilians, society, although demeaned, still survives. But breaking trust within the military will cause our soldiers to die, our battles to be lost, and our interests to be threatened.

No Right to Serve

Access to the military is not a right enjoyed by all Americans. It is not guaranteed in the Constitution or anywhere else. Indeed, to build effective units, the armed forces routinely deny the privilege of military service to patriotic Americans who are too tall, too short, too fat, color-blind, flat-footed, and mentally or physically handicapped in any way. Single parents are not allowed to enlist, nor are chronic bed wetters. This is not a judgment of the inherent worth of these people as human beings; indeed, each of these individuals properly enjoys numerous civil rights. It is simply a determination that they are not suited for military service.

In a 1993 decision in California, U.S. District Court Judge Terry Hatter ordered the Navy to reinstate an openly gay petty officer because, in his opinion, the Pentagon's policy on homosexuals was based merely on "cultural myths and false stereotypes." This language attempts to join the gay rights movement to the civil rights movement and strikes a responsive chord among Americans who believe in civil rights and have yet to shake the burden of collective guilt over past injustices visited upon various racial and ethnic minorities. But logically, neither this language nor the linkage behind it make sense.

Skin color and sexual orientation are different. It is no irony that black Americans have strongly rejected attempts by homosexuals to cloak themselves in the civil rights movement. No clearer statement of this view can be found than General Colin Powell's response to a letter from Representative Pat Schroeder of Colorado. To Ms. Schroeder's patronizing assertion that "I am sure you are aware that your reasoning would have kept you from the mess hall a few decades ago, all in the name of good order and discipline and regardless of your dedication and conduct," General Powell responded:

> I am well aware of the attempts to draw parallels between this position and positions used years ago to deny opportunities to African-Americans. . . . I can assure you I need no reminders concerning the history of African-Americans in the defense of their nation and the tribulations they faced. I am part of that history.
>
> Skin color is a benign, non-behavioral characteristic. Sexual orientation is perhaps the most profound of human behavioral characteristics. Comparison of the two is a convenient but invalid argument. I believe the privacy rights of all Americans in uniform have to be considered, especially since those rights are often infringed upon by the conditions of military service.
>
> As Chairman of the Joint Chiefs of Staff, as well as an African-American fully conversant with history, I believe the policy we have adopted is consistent with the necessary standards of good order and discipline required in the armed forces.

A lot of interesting things occur in bedrooms all across America. If minorities begin to be defined based on sexual behavior, there will soon be some fascinating civil rights cases. If the concept of "civil rights" is to continue to mean anything, it cannot be extended to various groups of people based on how they seek sexual pleasure. As for the president's assertion that in the absence of untoward behavior it is wrong to discriminate based on status alone, one notes that society discriminates on precisely this basis all the time. My behavior in a women's locker room might be above reproach, but I am still not allowed to enter one, simply because of my status as a male. Perhaps—to apply General Powell's standards to a civilian situation—my mere status might be a threat to good order and discipline.

Consider Judge Hatter's reference to "cultural myths and false stereotypes." It is true that to accept racial integration of the armed forces, whites had to overcome what were truly false stereotypes and cultural myths. In the case of homosexuals, heterosexuals may likewise learn that homosexuals are not compulsive perverts, weaker or less masculine, or a physical threat of any kind. These are myths and stereotypes. But it is neither a myth nor a stereotype that homosexual men have sex with other men. It is this specific behavior to which people react.

Attraction, Jealousy, Hurt, Shame

What would be the effect of mixing homosexuals and heterosexuals in combat? Begin by making two assumptions: first, that homosexuality is viewed as entirely normal, natural, and otherwise acceptable throughout the population; and second, that the order has been given to admit open homosexuals and that every military person attempts to execute it in good faith. Even under these highly unlikely conditions, the presence of homosexuals in a military unit would still be an invitation for disaster.

Military leaders are responsible for the training, morale, and physical well-being of each member of their unit. They must first mold a group of individuals into a cohesive team and then lead them into battle. To their men, they must appear capable, physically and mentally tough, brave, and, above all, fair. Their typical responsibilities include, but are not limited to: planning a mission; navigating and otherwise controlling the movement of their troops; maintaining communication with their commander; directing aircraft and artillery fire to support their attack; arranging for resupply of food and ammunition; coordinating with other ground units; and seeing that casualties are treated and evacuated if necessary. They often do all of this in darkness, miserable weather, or both, and always with an enemy trying to kill them. They must continually make decisions that may cost one man's life and spare another's, such as choosing who is assigned a dangerous mission and which of the wounded is treated and evacuated first. Should they be asked to contend with human sexual emotions as well?

Most people hope that most people have enough common sense and experience to know that human sexuality is enormously complex. Even in the most civilized society, sexuality is never far from the surface. It can inspire attraction or revulsion, intimacy or objectification, trust or fear, jealousy, hurt, or shame. Any of these emotions can be enormously distracting and disruptive. Civilian employers recognize this and enact various policies that proscribe fraternization in the workplace. Still, as any woman—and some men—will attest, these rules are broken every day. Yet while the highest price a civilian will pay for sexual distractions will be some form of degradation, or the loss of a job, reputation, or career, distractions in the military cause people to suffer physical mutilation and often death. If this sounds extreme, consider the following.

A heterosexual lieutenant must order one of his squads to attack a machine gun position that has taken his platoon under fire. Two squads are in position to attack: one is led by a homosexual sergeant. The lieutenant must decide: if he sends the homosexual sergeant, and the sergeant is killed, will the platoon's other homosexual troops think that the lieutenant sent the sergeant because he dislikes homosexuals? Will they trust him with their lives in the future? If the lieutenant were homosexual, and found himself attracted to the sergeant—he is, of course, only human—would he spare that sergeant from dangerous missions and send the other squad instead? What would be the effect on the platoon's morale if he were even perceived as doing so? Above all, would weighing these issues cause him to hesitate while the lives of his men hang in the balance?

If every decision is made, and reacted to, with even the slightest chance that sexual attraction or revulsion played a part in it, how could those decisions be trusted? If a man does not trust his leaders or those around him, will he willingly put his life in their hands?

The Stakes Are Life and Death

In this scenario, no heterosexual is an irrational bigot, no homosexual is either compulsive or perverse, and no sexual advance or contact takes place: in short, no stereotypes are present. Indeed, society's view as to which type of sexual activity is or is not acceptable is irrelevant: were the proportion of homosexuals and heterosexuals in society reversed, this argument rightly would continue to be used to ban homosexuals from the armed forces. The clearest and strongest reason for the ban is to remove the influence of sexuality—not heterosexuality, not homosexuality, just sexuality, period—from an environment where the stakes are literally life and death.

Dry-Cleaning the Troops and Other Matters

A Critique of "Don't Ask, Don't Tell"

PAUL SIEGEL

Paul Siegel, professor of communication arts at Gallaudet University, criticizes the U.S. military's "Don't Ask, Don't Tell" policy (see introductory essay). In part I of his essay, Siegel argues that those who oppose gays in the military, like those who once opposed blacks in the military, exhibit "secondhand prejudice": they claim not to be prejudiced themselves, but argue that the ban is justified by the prejudice of the majority of young recruits, whose cohesiveness would be undermined by the introduction of the disfavored group. In part II, Siegel examines and dismisses the argument that introducing openly gay servicemembers to a military setting would violate the privacy of heterosexual servicemembers. Finally, in part III, he revisits the analogy between racial prejudice and antigay prejudice.

I. Secondhand Prejudice and the Heckler's Veto

Although it is arguable that the military's new "don't ask, don't tell" policy is barely an advance over the previous outright ban on homosexual recruits, the testimony offered in Senator Nunn's hearings on the ban revealed a perversely comforting pattern of dissociation from homophobic attitudes. Among senators and witnesses alike, even those most vociferously arguing in support of the ban felt the need to indicate that it was not they who would have difficulty working in close quarters with openly gay comrades. Rather, they pointed to the raw recruits, many barely out of their teens, often from the lower end of the socioeconomic continuum, who would presumably be unable to deal with the issue. Certainly the most dramatic example of this phenomenon was Marine Colonel Fred Peck's admission that he would strongly advise his gay son never to enlist in the Marines, for fear that the young man's life would be in danger at the hands of his own comrades.

Those who support the military's gay ban on the basis of *others'* presumed antigay bias manifest a form of secondhand prejudice that is inimical to basic constitutional principles. The Supreme Court has held on a number of occasions that even the most seemingly benign and reluctantly imposed discriminatory practices cannot be justified by pointing to the fears of a community's more prejudiced members. Thus, for example, in 1984, the Supreme Court ruled that a divorced mother could not be denied custody of her children for having embarked upon a romantic relationship with a man of another race, even while Chief Justice Burger's majority opinion admitted that it would "ignore reality" to suggest that children in such circumstances will not be "subject to a variety of pressures and stresses." The Constitution may not be able to control individuals' bigoted attitudes, Burger wrote, "but neither can it tolerate them."[1] The very next year, the Court held that a Texas town could not selectively require petitioners to obtain the permission of all nearby homeowners before being permitted to set up a group home for retarded adults. In this latter case, Justice White concluded for the Court that "an irrational prejudice against the mentally retarded" was involved.[2]

The constitutional proscription against secondhand prejudice is given voice in the "heckler's veto" doctrine from First Amendment jurisprudence. In its most pristine form, the doctrine stands for the principle that we cannot silence a speaker because she may upset the sensibilities of others. Thus was Dick Gregory permitted to march in Mayor Daley's neighborhood,[3] and Gregory Johnson's conviction for burning the American flag in the presence of many who were extremely upset by his conduct was overturned.[4] The heckler's veto doctrine has appeared on a number of occasions to safeguard the interests of gay litigants, perhaps the most notable example being young Aaron Fricke, who won the right to bring a same-sex date to his high school prom despite the likelihood that this action would cause some of his classmates much distress.[5]

The military leadership offers two main reasons for refusing to enlist open gays, both of which rely upon a prediction of negative reaction from heterosexual soldiers. The first argument is the privacy rationale, usually presented in a context that includes reference to the cramped quarters and shared shower and toilet facilities forced upon some soldiers. We separate men and women, so the reasoning goes, so won't we also have to separate gays and straights?

The second reason is the more global claim that the presence of open gays will jeopardize "unit cohesion," that it will lower the morale of the vast majority of the troops. Proponents of this line of argument recognize the need to distinguish antigay prejudice from racial prejudice, in that the military has done a remarkable job of creating a highly racially integrated environment, even though the majority of white soldiers favored continued segregation when President Truman's directive was issued back in 1948. The remainder of this chapter seeks to demonstrate that the military's advocacy of its antigay policies, whether phrased as an issue of sexual modesty or as one of morale, is a textbook example of secondhand prejudice.

II. Sexual Modesty and the Military

Arguments for keeping the gay ban in deference to the privacy needs of the majority of (presumably heterosexual) soldiers have been based on an analogy to the armed forces' relatively recent experience of more fully integrating women into military roles. Such arguments depend in large part upon the assertion that many privacy issues accruing to the military are unique to that setting. Thus, for example, Professor David Schlueter of the St. Mary's School of Law reminded members of Senator Nunn's committee that a soldier's living space "is often a small two-person tent, a cramped berth in a submarine, or an open-bay barracks where a large number of individuals share not only a common sleeping area but a common shower and restroom facilities as well."[6] It is precisely because of the close quarters in which some categories of military personnel must serve that our policy has been to separate living and bathing facilities for men and women. Several participants in the gay military debate argued that the same reasoning would mandate separating gays from straights. Congressman Henry Hyde (Rep.-Illinois) asserted that just as it would seem "unconscionable" to force our daughters in the military to dress and shower in close proximity to men, so too would be requiring heterosexuals to disrobe in the company of "people whose sexual orientation and arousal level is exactly the same and maybe more."

Congressman Hyde's reference to sexual arousal levels carries with it the presumption—one echoed in the questioning by senators of several witnesses in the Nunn hearing room—that the main reason we segregate males and females in military settings is to avoid sexual conduct.

Sexual modesty, however, is not simply the opposite of sexual lasciviousness. The genders shield their bodies from each other for reasons far more complex than to avoid signaling a desire for sexual comingling. Sexual modesty, especially women's in reference to men, is often a very physical manifestation of a much larger phenomenon. Our society's long history of complementary sex roles assigns males and females into separate spheres.[7] Our genders define which doors we are permitted to enter and which are closed to us, which conversations we will be privy to, and which will be denied us. Meetings between men and women are "explorations and adventures into the unknown."[8] The ramifications of this deceptively complex truth—that men and women function in quite different worlds—can be as playful as the frequent jokes in the *Cathy* comic strip about how men and women manifest fundamentally different life coping styles, or as serious as the Supreme Court's ruling that sexual harassment claims must sometimes be judged using the perspective of a reasonable *woman*.[9] In any event, so widespread are the effects of gender segregation in our society that some linguists even treat communication between the sexes as a form of intercultural communication.

Consider the controversy in some locales surrounding public breast-feeding. While some of the resistance to public breast-feeding stems from men's "inability to make a distinction between what is female and what is sexual, . . . the truth is that there's nothing sexy about nursing in public, a process that usually includes a deft disarrangement of garments and . . . is quite like hiding a soccer ball beneath your shirt."[10] Again, the impetus to segregate the sexes often has nothing to do with the fear of sexual behavior.

The societal norm against exposure of the naked body to the opposite sex is applied asymmetrically. We are far more concerned with protecting women from having to reveal their naked bodies to men than vice versa. We do this out of a recognition of the difference in power between men and women.[11] Thus, while many police departments have established policies dictating that strip searches of suspects will be conducted only by officers of the same gender, the rules are seen as a means of protecting female suspects. When hospitals debate whether or not to employ mixed-sex wards as a cost-cutting move, it is the privacy of their female patients that weighs more heavily on the side of sex segregation. Similarly, the California Fair Employment and Housing Commission recently held that a hospital that forbade male nurses to attend pregnant women during labor and delivery was not in violation of that state's employment discrimination statutes.[12]

Men and women experience nakedness differently. We seek to protect our daughters, and women in general, because of their perceived powerlessness. We should feel no corollary need to protect heterosexual servicemen and women from their lesbian and gay counterparts, in that it is the latter groups who wield the lesser power.

The analogy between gender segregation and the posited need for segregation based on sexual orientation thus is at best an imperfect one. There is no history of segregating lesbians from heterosexual females, or gay males from heterosexual ones, that would correspond to the long history of segregating the sexes themselves. As openly gay Massachusetts Congressman Barney Frank explained in a debate with Senator Dan Coats on a *Face the Nation* broadcast, "gay men and straight men have been sharing showers for a very long time. . . . We don't have ourselves dry-cleaned."

III. Maybe It *Is* the Same: Premature Rejection of the Race Analogy

Consider again the words of former Chairman of the Joint Chiefs of Staff Colin Powell, as quoted by John Luddy in the previous essay. Powell contrasted racial prejudice and antigay prejudice by suggesting that the former is a reaction to a "benign, *non*behavioral characteristic" (emphasis added). This is a sadly ironic oversimplification of racism and of prejudice generally. Prejudices may be *triggered* by nonbehavioral characteristics such as skin color, but the prejudice itself is an attribution of behaviors and attitudes to members of the group manifesting the characteristic. When racists say negative things about African Americans, such statements generally do not focus on skin color or Negroid physical characteristics. In our own society, the two most fundamental threads of antiblack racism are attributions of dangerousness and of unproductiveness (the latter being sometimes manifested in the belief that blacks are not as intelligent as whites, sometimes in the belief that they are lazy).

"There is nothing more painful to me at this stage in my life than to walk down the street and hear footsteps and start thinking about robbery. Then look around and see somebody white *and feel relieved*." These words, spoken by none other than the Reverend Jesse Jackson at a meeting of the PUSH organization on Chicago's south side in 1993, encapsulate the first of the two threads of antiblack racism in our society: the attribution of violent criminal intent to African Americans, especially to young male African Americans. It is the same attribution that created a *cause célèbre* at the offices of the *Washington Post* several years earlier, when Richard Cohen's magazine column expressed sympathy with white jewelry shop owners who used an electric buzzer entry system to exclude young black males from their shops. These shopkeepers were not acting out of unadorned racism,

Cohen claimed. Rather they were reacting to a fear of the combination of race, age and gender. Such a reaction is not entirely unfounded, in that "young black males commit an inordinate amount of urban crime."[13]

The assumption of black dangerousness forces upon African Americans a coping style that makes it "folly to compete for a taxi on a street corner with whites. It means realizing that prudence dictates dressing up whenever you are likely to encounter strangers (including clerks, cops, and doormen) who can make your life miserable by mistaking you for a tramp, a slut, or a crook."[14] The crucial point again is that these strangers are reacting not to "benign" racial features, but rather to behavioral attributions based upon those features.

There is a second thread of racist attributions borne by African Americans in this society. Whereas young black males are feared as potentially violent, almost all blacks are presumed less competent than whites. In a *Times-Picayune* poll in New Orleans, for example, white respondents reported their belief that blacks are not only more violent, but also less intelligent and more lazy than themselves. The majority of white respondents attributed blacks' relatively low socioeconomic standing to a "lack of motivation or willpower."

Even those African Americans who have seemingly "made it" in the corporate world are not spared the presumption of relative incompetence. Author and journalist Ellis Cose tells of a visit to his office by an African American colleague, an assistant managing editor for the *New York Times*. The conversation turned to a mutual friend at the *Times*, also an African American male, who would likely be passed over for an important promotion because of the paper's fear of "having a *black* journalist fail in such a visible position." Cose's visitor mused that "failure at the highest levels . . . was a privilege apparently reserved for whites."[15]

Even this cursory analysis of racial discrimination reveals precisely what General Powell contends does not exist. The dynamics of discrimination, almost by definition, require behavioral attributions. The specific behavioral attributions may be ludicrous, or they may be factually based. The crucial point is that General Powell's posited distinction between attributions based upon skin color and attributions based upon declared sexual orientation is unpersuasive.

IV. Conclusion

"Don't ask, don't tell" amounts to granting a government imprimatur to secondhand prejudice. Although the Supreme Court has as of the time of this writing not agreed to hear any of the cases that directly challenge the policy,[16] such governmental acquiescence to others' personal animus against recognizable minority groups has been rejected by the Court in numerous circumstances, especially when such animus takes the form of a "heckler's veto" aimed at squelching acts of speech (such as coming out as openly gay).

While General Powell's attempt to contrast the nature of antigay and antiblack prejudice was unconvincing, a silver lining emerges from looking back to the military's long struggle with racial integration begun in the 1940s. A mere three years after President Truman's 1948 order, the proportion of white soldiers opposing racial integration had dropped from 80 percent to 44 percent. The military's model for sensitivity training on racial and other diversity issues has been lauded and unabashedly copied in the civilian world. Moreover, there are striking similarities between the obstacles faced by the military in enforcing President Truman's directive and that which will be faced by the military should the Supreme Court find the current homosexual ban unconstitutional. As then NAACP President William Gibson told the Nunn committee, the very same arguments seen now for keeping the homosexual ban had been used two generations ago: "They said whites would not shower with blacks, they would not sleep in the same barracks, they would not take orders from black superiors."

There is thus no reason to conclude that the military is incapable of devising sensitivity training that, together with leadership by example, would serve to smooth the transition to a more liberal policy. Much research in the civilian sector indicates that such training can be highly effective. These data are very consistent with the often reported finding that persons who are knowingly acquainted with at least one gay person are much less likely to report antigay animus than are those who do not believe they have any gay friends or acquaintances.

The upside of being part of an invisible minority may thus be that to know us is to love us.

· CHAPTER TWENTY-TWO ·

The Case for Outing

RICHARD D. MOHR

Richard D. Mohr, professor of philosophy at the University of Illinois, Urbana, defends "outing"—the revealing of a closeted person's homosexuality—by appeal to the concept of dignity. He argues that gay people must not be forced to play along with, and thus enhance, social conventions that degrade gay existence. According to Mohr, the social convention of the closet, with its demand that each gay person keep every other gay person's secret secret, is just such a degrading convention. Mohr maintains, however, that outing is not justified as a punitive mechanism.

. . . . .

The disclosure on the Internet in July 1996 that Arizona Republican Congressman Jim Kolbe is gay and his public acknowledgment of this fact the next month—just as the national gay news magazine *The Advocate* was going to press with the story—catapulted the issue of outing back into national headlines. Gays outed Kolbe in response to his voting for the insidiously anti-gay Defense of Marriage Act. Gays deemed that the socially liberal Republican was not liberal enough. But two can play that game. In 1994, far-right Congressman Robert Dornan outed fellow-Republican Congressman Steve Gunderson on the floor of the House. Dornan deemed Gunderson too liberal. In both cases, the outing was vindictive—aimed at punishing and incapacitating its target.

Such outings are of dubious political worth. In the November 1996 elections, Kolbe was reelected, Dornan was not. More important, such outings are morally reprehensible. In order for vindictive outing to be effective, the outer counts upon the amassed anti-gay forces in society to strike out against the person outed. Such outing legitimates the use of anti-gay forces as a political tool and, in that very use, strengthens them.

Vindictive outings are not limited to the political realm. In January 1996, gay novelist and wit Armistead Maupin outed comedienne Lily Tomlin in the *Village Voice* for her failure to come out in her role as the narrator for the movie *The Celluloid Closet,* a history of gay cinema. And a number of gay military court cases have resulted from vindictive outings, as when a disgruntled "roommate" outed her Air Force major "girlfriend" to the military police. But such illegitimate, vindictive outings are not the only form of outing. Not all outing points fingers. Not all outing recriminates. Not all outing shouts from soapboxes to stir up the homophobic crowds.

Some outing is simply news—the letting come to light of a person's sexual orientation in relevant contexts. Take 1995's biggest outing story. After twenty-six years of marriage, *Rolling Stone* founder Jann Wenner left his wife and three sons to move into a Manhattan hotel with a former male model who now works as a designer for Calvin Klein. Despite Wenner's and his wife's efforts to have the story suppressed, it ran anyway—not in the tabloids and tattlers, but in *Newsweek, New York* magazine, *Advertising Age,* the *Boston Herald,* and the *Wall Street Journal.* What made the story particularly newsworthy was that in 1993 Wenner had jumped on the "family values" bandwagon and had begun publishing a yuppie magazine, *Family Life,* to portray the glories of the heterosexual nuclear family. What was missing from this portrait? The editor himself.

The American press is no longer creating "beards" nor assuring silences for would-be closet cases in order to deflect attention away from gay issues and gay lives as though gayness were just too embarrassing to mention. To its credit, the press is gradually abandoning both its past policy of "don't ask, don't tell" when it comes to gayness and its phony belief that to discuss unasked someone's sexual *orientation* (as opposed to his or her sexual acts) is to violate that person's privacy. It is time that gays carry over these trends into their daily lives as well.

People need to let the gayness of individuals come up when it is relevant, rather than going along with the shaming social convention of the closet, the demand that every gay person is bound to keep every other gay person's secret secret. For the closet is the site where anti-gay loathing and gay self-loathing mutually reinforce each other. Even people who are out of the closet demean themselves when they maintain other people's closets. For the closet's secret is a dirty little secret that degrades all gay people.

To put the point systematically, living by the convention of the closet—whether one is closeted oneself or not—is a commitment to viewing gayness as disgusting, horrible, unspeakably gross, in short, as abjection. Core cases of abjection are excrement, vomit, pus, and the smells associated with these. It is exactly around just these (only ever half-acknowledged) abject matters that society sets up rituals requiring that one may neither inquire nor report about them—rituals of the form "don't ask, don't tell." Take, for example, the case of flatulence in a crowded elevator: no one tells; no one asks; everyone acts as though nothing is amiss, and so this behavior reinforces the abject thing's status as loathsome. This daunting effort to repress knowing and acknowledgment requires a blanket of silence to be cast over the abject thing. To tell of the abject is to break a taboo, for names, like scents, are enough to bring the abject back to full consciousness. And to ask about the abject is to be reminded of its constantly recurring, lurking, louring presence just beyond oneself.

The chief problem of the closet as a social institution, then, is not that it promotes hypocrisy, requires lies, sets snares, blames the victim when snared, and causes unhappiness—though it does have all these results. No, the chief problem with the closet is that it treats gays as less than human, less than animal, less even than vegetable—it treats gays as reeking scum, the breath of death.

Therefore, each time a gay person finds the closet morally acceptable for himself or others, he degrades himself as gay and sinks to the level of abjection dictated for gays by the dominant culture. No gay person with sufficient self-respect and dignity can be required to view himself or other gays in this way. In consequence, the openly gay person, in order to live morally, must not play along with the convention of the closet, lest he degrade himself. He must allow gayness to come up in conversations when it is relevant.

Moral outing is simply living in the truth and withdrawing from the social conventions that degrade gay existence.

· CHAPTER TWENTY-THREE ·

Outing, Ethics, and Politics

A Reply to Mohr

JAMES S. STRAMEL

James S. Stramel, who teaches philosophy at Santa Monica College, argues that outing is a presumptive violation of the right to privacy, which protects individual identity, dignity, and autonomy from intrusive and damaging physical and informational access. He also directly responds to the argument for "dignity-based outing" offered by Richard D. Mohr in the previous chapter. According to Stramel, although moral virtue requires that gays work toward openness, one's dignity as a gay person is not inevitably damaged by refraining from outing. Stramel concedes, however, that sometimes justice and civic virtue will support outing.

. . . . .

Outing is publicizing a closeted person's homosexuality against his or her wishes. I take for granted that gratuitous, malicious, and vindictive outings are wrong. Utilitarian outings—those done for the good of the gay community or society generally—are on firmer footing, but there are, in the end, many reasons to doubt the overall utility of the practice. My main objection, however, is that utility-based outing (whether it approximates blackmail or not) is coercive other-definition. Activists who publicly define others as gay in the name of progress for "the gay community" objectionably use the outee as a means to their own ends—ends, moreover, that the outee may not regard as also being his own.

Does Outing Violate the Right to Privacy?

Outing has often been condemned as a violation of the right to privacy. However, Richard Mohr and others following him have ridiculed this claim as "a lot of hot air" and a "phony belief."[1] Since an adequate defense of the privacy argument would require many more pages than I have here, I can only briefly summarize the main reasons why the privacy objection to outing cannot be summarily dismissed.[2]

Sex and sexuality have long been regarded as paradigmatically private matters, both morally and legally. Defenders of outing often emphasize, however, that to reveal a person's sexual orientation is not to say anything at all about his or her sexual behavior, which is private. Employing Sissela Bok's distinction between privacy and secrecy, Mohr claims that privacy protects against the unwanted access of others to one's person, whereas concealment of the information that one is gay is a secret. This wrongly suggests that privacy protects only against certain forms of physical or causal access to persons. But even Mohr admits that some information is privacy protected, for example, one's medical records. Moreover, a firm distinction between privacy and secrecy runs counter to long-standing traditions in ethics and law and cannot be maintained.

The right to privacy protects individual identity, autonomy, and dignity by shielding the individual (in body and mind) from various forms of unwanted access—both informational and physical—whether by the state or by other individuals. One of the basic and most important functions of this right is to maximize our opportunities to be self-determining, especially with respect to matters of fundamental importance to individual personality (including one's body, sexuality, home, and marital, reproductive, and family decisions). This includes a large measure of individual control over the division between publicity and privacy, rather than having this determined by others. Given the intimate and volatile character of sexual identity and its importance in our lives, gay people have a strong prima facie interest in being free from unwanted public disclosures. Unwanted and untimely exposure jeopardizes all the benefits of self-disclosure and can do real damage to one's identity interests—not to mention the significant consequential harms an outee may suffer at the hands of intolerant others.

It is sometimes argued that a person's heterosexual orientation is clearly not private; so, by parity, neither is homosexual orientation. But this obviously overlooks radical differences in the meaning and value attached to different sexual orientations. Whether—and the extent to which—sexual orientation is appropriately public is a contingent matter, depending on the personal and social meanings and values of sexual orientation in a given social context. Homosexual orientation is normatively private not because it is an inherently private fact, but because privacy protects against the material and spiritual damage that unwarranted access to or distribution of sensitive personal information can do to individual identity, dignity, and autonomy.

Does appealing to privacy commit one to the repugnant and false view that gayness is bad and shameful, something to be kept hidden? Not at all: the right to privacy protects the individual against unwarranted public portrayals, not just the shameful ones. The right to privacy immunizes against the wrongful transformation of a private life into a public life open to scrutiny and judgment. To say that a public disclosure of homosexuality is offensive is not to say that homosexuality is offensive or shameful. Compare outing with the publication of a rape victim's identity: that a particular woman has been raped, while deplorable, is not a shaming fact about her, yet it is routinely and rightly regarded as privacy-protected information. In both cases, it is the disclosure itself—and not necessarily the fact disclosed—that is offensive and damaging.

While I have been arguing for a prima facie privacy right against outing, I do not mean to suggest that outing is never justified. A number of competing interests may be sufficiently important to override a person's privacy interests. One such case is that of elected officials who pursue antigay policies and legislation as a cover for their own homosexuality. The voting public has a strong democratic interest in knowing what motivates an official's actions; hypocritical behavior, lying, and deception also bear on the person's character and fitness for office. Note, however, that such outings are not justified by hypocrisy alone, nor as vindictive punishment for voting "improperly." Nor is this a utilitarian defense of the practice: political outing fosters voters' abilities to make informed and autonomous choices, while it may or may not produce better overall outcomes.

Mohr's Dignity-Based Outing

In place of more common utilitarian defenses of outing, Mohr claims that by not outing others one knows to be gay, the openly gay person is participating in "the secret of the closet." He thereby degrades himself by "commit[ting] his life to the very values that keep him oppressed" and trades his own dignity for the happiness of the closet case. So, in defense of their dignity and the dignity of all gays, out gays living in the truth may—are even expected to—"out nearly everyone he or she knows to be gay."

If there is a prima facie privacy right against outing, then (as Mohr admits) even dignity-based outing would not be justified; but I also find Mohr's position troubling on its own terms. Outing may diminish gay dignity, both individual and collective, because the public regards homosexuality as bad or immoral and sees outing as punishment. Rather than serving to dismantle antigay attitudes, outing utilizes and reinforces the notion that homosexuality is shameful. Even when conscientiously motivated, the practice can look petty and vindictive.

Perhaps the most repugnant feature of all outing is that it steals from the outee a major opportunity to take control of and assume responsibility for his identity, integrity and dignity—to come out on his own principles. Mohr complains that this argument—"dressed up in the finery of liberal cant"—misunderstands the scope and possible materials of dignity and the complexity of coming out. Shifting attention to the outee, Mohr says the relevant questions are: (1) Can a person, though outed, still have access to enough dignity to be highly dignified? (2) Are conditions such that individuals can achieve a rich life of their own making given the cussedness of their social and material circumstances? (3) Can the outee still have a positive, robust, dignifying relation to his sexual orientation? I agree that the answer to each question is yes. But none of this refutes the claim that outing wrongly diminishes the dignity of the outee.

It is certainly possible to imagine situations in which a failure to identify a person as gay would involve the loss of one's own dignity. But it is simply not plausible to claim that a person who decides not to out another out of respect for her autonomy and dignity necessarily regards homosexuality as shameful or has committed her life to the oppression of gays. Except in unusual circumstances, the threat to my dignity of your closetude—and my leaving you there—is negligible. As Mohr observes, dignity has many sources, and I can still be highly dignified despite forgoing the opportunity to out you. To see this, we can stand Mohr's questions on their heads to inquire whether a gay person can have access to enough dignity to be highly dignified, a rich life of his own making, and a robust dignifying relation to his sexual orientation—all without engaging in outing. Here too, the answer is yes.

Like many other groups, gay people are faced with a situation in which society unfairly and severely stigmatizes them for having a particular characteristic. One's dignity as a given type of person does not require outing every person one knows to share the relevant characteristic. Compare again the situation of gays to that of women who have been raped. Through no fault of their own rape victims are saddled with a status that is not inherently disrespectable, but that often prompts disrespectful treatment. Suppose that Anne was a victim of rape but has been able to rid herself of the shame and stigma rape victims often internalize; she now works actively in rape-prevention programs, counseling women and giving public talks in which she "comes out" as herself a victim of rape. If Anne knows that

Brenda was also raped but remains "closeted," how does Anne's failure to out her cause a loss of Anne's dignity?

Mohr grants that outing can diminish the outee's dignity, but he holds that this will rarely outweigh the dignity gained for all gays by outing because the indignity bred by the secret of the closet is so great and pervasive. I think Mohr too readily trades concrete and significant individual harms and indignities for a hypothetical and incremental increase in the abstract quantity of overall dignity.

It is important to realize that objecting to outing does not require defending the closet. Lesbians and gays should certainly be encouraged to come out as a matter of moral virtue. But as long as homosexuality is stigmatized in ways that heterosexuality is not, being publicly gay will be personally dangerous and politically volatile. Except in unusual circumstances, individuals should have the freedom to decide for themselves whether to join the sociopolitical fray, rather than being made political footballs by others professing to know better the proper course for their lives.

There is no one way—certainly no correct way—to be gay, although some gays speak as if there were. What being gay means to a person and whether, when, and to what extent one shall be publicly identified as gay are decisions properly left to the individual. Tyranny takes many forms—wherever a person is victimized by coercive power. Outers, who know well that information is power, commit a tyranny of the few. In doing so, they betray one of gay activism's fundamental values: the right to pursue one's life free from domination and interference by others.

· CHAPTER TWENTY-FOUR ·

How Domestic Partnerships and "Gay Marriage" Threaten the Family

ROBERT H. KNIGHT

Robert H. Knight, director of cultural studies at the Family Research Council (FRC), presents a case against same-sex marriage and domestic partnership. After providing a history of the recent push in favor of these measures, Knight argues that same-sex "marriage" is impossible by definition and that legalizing same-sex unions would threaten families, children, and ultimately, civilization. FRC research assistant Dan Garcia and Lambda Report *editor Peter L. La Barbera contributed to this chapter.*

· · · · ·

For several years, homosexual activists have promoted the extension of marital benefits to same-sex couples (and, in some cases, unmarried heterosexual couples) in corporations and in the law. This practice, called "domestic partnerships" is billed as an extension of tolerance and civil rights, but it would actually undermine the institutions of marriage and family. So, too, would the drive to confer actual marital status on same-sex relationships through the legalization of so-called gay marriage.

Policies and laws that confer partner benefits or marital status on same-sex couples should be opposed because they:

1. send a clear signal that companies or cities no longer consider marriage a priority worth encouraging above other kinds of relationships;
2. deny the procreative imperative that underlies society's traditional protection of marriage and family as the best environment in which to raise children;

This chapter is reprinted with revisions from *Insight*, a bulletin of the Family Research Council.

3. seek to legitimize same-sex activity and homosexuals' claim that they should be able to adopt children, despite the clear danger this poses to children's development of healthy sexual identities;
4. injure the crucial kinship structure, which is derived from marriage and family and imparts continuity, community, and stability to societies;
5. violate freedom of religion, as more and more devout Christian, Jewish and Muslim employees and citizens are told that they must accept as "moral" what their faiths teach is immoral;
6. mock the idea of commitment, since most domestic partner laws allow for easy dissolution of the relationship and the registry of several partners (consecutively) a year;
7. and breed cynicism, because they defy common understanding about the relative worth of particular relationships. Societies must have intact families to survive; societies do not need any homosexual relationships in order to flourish. To equate them is to lie about them.

Furthermore, the drive for homosexual status is undergirded by faulty assertions of scientifically based findings, such as the now-discredited, Kinsey-derived 10 percent estimate of homosexuality in the population; the media-touted, but unproven, "genetic link" to homosexual behavior; and the deliberate misinterpretation of key psychological studies about homosexuality. A burgeoning "ex-gay movement" is leading thousands out of homosexual behavior, and many former homosexuals are getting married and having children.[1]

A Growing Campaign

Across America, cities, corporations and universities are being lobbied or intimidated into confering marital benefits on same-sex couples. Many major cities, including Atlanta, Baltimore, Boston, Chicago, Hartford, New York, Rochester, Seattle, and the California cities of Los Angeles, San Francisco, Sacramento, Oakland, Berkeley, Laguna Beach, Santa Cruz, and West Hollywood, have extended employee family benefits to same-sex partners. In the District of Columbia, the city council voted in 1992 to add domestic partners to the city's health insurance policy, but the policy was deleted by Congress in an appropriations bill. Proponents plan to try again to enact the extension.[2]

In 1990, Stanford University adopted rules granting unmarried couples, including homosexuals, access to dormitories and other campus facilities. Later, "family housing," which had been set aside primarily for married couples with children, was officially opened to homosexuals. Many other campuses have extended benefits such as campus housing to same-sex couples, including the University of Chicago, Harvard, Columbia, Dartmouth, Iowa, Iowa State, the University of Wisconsin, Minnesota, Northwestern, Illinois, Indiana, Iowa, Tufts, and the Massachusetts Institute of Technology.[3]

An estimated 2 percent of the nation's corporations have extended family benefits to same-sex partners.[4] Many others have added the term "sexual orientation" to their nondiscrimination policies. The co-chair of the National Gay and Lesbian Task Force, Elizabeth Birch, is also senior litigation counsel at Apple Computer. She says, "No area has more potency than the advancement of gay rights in the workplace."[5] Companies and institutions with same-sex benefits include Walt Disney Company, Kodak, IBM, BankAmerica, Time Warner, Levi-Strauss, Apple, Lotus, Intel, Microsoft, MCA, Viacom, Oracle Systems Corp., Coors, Digital, Ben & Jerry's, Minnesota Public Radio, Montefiore Hospital in New York, the *Village Voice* newspaper, Borland International, the Federal National Mortgage Association, and Xerox.[6] Institutions that promote homosexuality through diversity training and officially sanctioned homosexual employees' groups include many major universities, AT&T (with a 1,000-member homosexual employees group), U.S. West, Xerox, and such federal agencies as the departments of Agriculture, Commerce, Education, Energy, Housing and Urban Development, Interior, State, and Veterans Affairs as well as the U.S. Postal Inspection Service.[7]

In Hawaii, Circuit Court Judge Kevin Chang ruled in December 1996 that the state failed to show a "compelling interest" in denying marital status to homosexual couples. He ordered the state to issue marriage licenses to same-sex couples, but he stayed his own order pending an appeal to the Hawaii Supreme Court by the state. A constitutional conflict looms should the Hawaii courts legalize "gay marriage," because under the U.S. Constitution's full faith and credit clause, states must accord reciprocity to other states in such matters as marriage and drivers' licenses. So, theoretically, a homosexual couple could marry in Honolulu, move to California, and demand that the Golden State recognize their "marriage." To forestall this, Congress passed the Defense of Marriage Act in September 1996, which was signed into law by President Clinton. The law defines marriage for federal purposes solely as the union of a man and a woman, and it allows states to refuse to recognize same-sex "marriages" from other states. By February 1997, eighteen states had passed their own marriage protection laws, with efforts under way in another twenty.

The Homosexual Agenda

Why is all this happening right now? It seems like only yesterday that homosexual activists wanted only "tolerance," demanding no special rights to compete with the prevailing moral order. But now, activists are on the verge of actually changing the definitions of marriage and family.

Homosexual activist Michelangelo Signorile speaks with a candor not found in most media portrayals of the issue. Discussing ways to advance homosexuality, he urges activists:

> to fight for same-sex marriage and its benefits and then, once granted, redefine the institution of marriage completely, to demand the right to marry not as a way of adhering to society's moral codes but rather to debunk a myth and radically alter an archaic institution that as it now stands keeps us down. The most subversive action lesbians and gay men can undertake—and one that would perhaps benefit all of society—is to transform the notion of "family" entirely.[8]

Signorile is right about the subversive nature of the goal of "gay marriage," but homosexuals would not have to go to any lengths to "redefine" marriage once granted that status. The very act of obtaining recognition for same-sex relationships on a par with marriage would transform the notion of "family" entirely.

While Signorile might be dismissed as just one voice, his views are in keeping with those of other high-profile homosexual activists. Franklin Kameny, a Washington, D.C.-based leader of the homosexual rights movement for three decades, has this to say about families:

> the "traditional" family has been placed upon such a lofty pedestal of unquestioning and almost mindless, ritualistic worship and endlessly declared but quite unproven importance that rational discussion of it is often well-nigh impossible . . . there is no legitimate basis for limiting the freedom of the individual to structure his family in nontraditional ways that he finds satisfying.[9]

Thomas Stoddard, leader of the drive to lift the military's ban on homosexuals and former president of the Lambda Legal Defense Fund—now known as the Lambda Legal Defense and Education Fund, a homosexual legal foundation—sees marriage as the prime vehicle to advance societal acceptance of homosexuality:

> I must confess at the outset that I am no fan of the "institution" of marriage as currently constructed and practiced . . . Why give it such prominence? Why devote resources to such a distant goal? Because marriage is, I believe, the political issue that most fully tests the dedication of people who are not gay to full equality for gay people, and also the issue most likely to lead ultimately to a world free from discrimination against lesbians and gay men. Marriage is much more than a relationship sanctioned by law. It is the centerpiece of our entire social structure, the core of the traditional notion of "family."[10] 

Lesbian activist Paula Ettelbrick, former legal director of the Lambda Legal Defense and Education Fund and now policy director for the National Center for Lesbian Rights, supports the "right" of homosexuals to marry, but opposes marriage as oppressive in and of itself. She says homosexual marriage does not go far enough to transform society:

> Being queer is more than setting up house, sleeping with a person of the same gender, and seeking state approval for doing so . . . Being queer means pushing the parameters of sex, sexuality, and family, and in the process, transforming the very fabric of society . . . As a lesbian, I am fundamentally different from non-lesbian women . . . In arguing for the right to legal marriage, lesbians and gay men would be forced to claim that we are just like heterosexual couples, have the same goals and purposes, and vow to structure our lives similarly . . . We must keep our eyes on the goals of providing true alternatives to marriage and of radically reordering society's views of reality.[11]

Marriage, Domestic Partnerships, and the Law

No jurisdictional unit in the United States—town, city, or state—recognizes same-sex couples as "married." Protections favoring marriage are built into the law and the culture because of the central importance of the family unit as the building block of civilization. In 1888, the U.S. Supreme Court described marriage "as creating the most important relation in life, as having more to do with the morals and civilization of a people than any other institution."[12]

However, some jurisdictions—notably, San Francisco—are moving toward redefining the family to include same-sex relationships, and there is a movement within the legal community to overhaul the definitions of "marriage" and "family." A note in the *Harvard Law Review* in 1991 advocated replacing the formal definition of "family" with an elastic standard based "mainly on the strength or duration of emotional bonds," regardless of sexual orientation. The note recommends redefining the family through "domestic-partner" or family "registration" statutes that go beyond the limited benefits now conferred by existing domestic partnership laws so as to "achieve parity" between marriage and other relationships.[13]

In November 1996, San Francisco passed a law requiring companies doing business with the city to offer domestic-partner benefits to employees. Subsequently, the city threatened United Airlines with the loss of facilities at San Francisco International Airport if it did not comply. The city also reached an agreement with Catholic Charities, which receives annually more than $5 million for its programs to feed and house the homeless. The groundwork for these actions was laid in 1990, when San Francisco mayor Art Agnos appointed lesbian activist Roberta Achtenberg (later named by President Clinton to be assistant secretary of the U.S. Department of Housing and Urban Development) to chair the Mayor's Task Force on Family Policy. The final report of the task force defines the family this way:

> a unit of interdependent and interacting persons, related together over time by strong social and emotional bonds and/or by ties of marriage, birth, and adoption, whose central purpose is to create, maintain, and promote the social, mental, physical and emotional development and well being of each of its members.[14]

In this definition, which could reasonably be described as a formulation by homosexual activists, marriage is no longer the foundation for families but secondary to "strong social and emotional bonds." This definition is so vague that multiple-partner unions are not excluded, nor any imaginable combination of persons, including a fishing boat crew. The whole point is to demote marriage to the level of any other conceivable relationship.

The task force's definition of "domestic partners" is almost as vague, but it limits the relationship to two partners: "two people who have chosen to share all aspects of each other's lives in an intimate and committed relationship of mutual caring and love." The District of Columbia City Council legislation defines "domestic partner" as "a person with whom an individual maintains a committed relationship," which is defined as "a familial relationship between two individuals characterized by mutual caring and the sharing of a mutual residence." One of the partners must be a city employee "at least eighteen years old and . . . competent to contract";

"not be related by blood closer than would prohibit marriage in the District"; and "be the sole domestic partner of the other person"; both must "not be married."[15] Applicants would qualify by signing a "declaration of domestic partnership" to be filed with the mayor; the declaration could be terminated by filing a termination statement with the mayor, which takes effect six months after filing. After that, another partner could be registered. Benefits include granting of sick leave, health insurance, and funeral leave.[16]

Domestic-partnership laws have been imposed or enacted by governmental agencies without much say from the public. When citizens do get a chance to give their views, they reject the notion. In May 1994, the city of Austin, Texas became the first U.S. jurisdiction to overturn an existing domestic partners law when the citizenry voted 62 percent to 38 percent to undo what the city council had enacted. In other jurisdictions, notably Cincinnati, Tampa, and Lewiston, Maine, voters overwhelmingly voted to roll back homosexual rights laws, which are the foundation of the claim for the "right" of domestic-partnership status. Even in liberal San Francisco, voters rejected domestic partnerships in 1991, although the policy was later approved.

In the courts, the issue has returned repeatedly since 1976, when the famous "palimony" case of *Marvin v. Marvin* held that a property agreement between two unmarried adults who live together and engage in sex is enforceable in a court of law.[17] In most cases, judges, with some notable exceptions, have rejected claims made by homosexual partners to marital-type recognition concerning property allocation and custody of children. In September 1993, a Virginia judge awarded custody of a boy to his grandmother, removing him from his mother's lesbian household.[18] An appeals court overturned that ruling but was itself overruled by a higher court. In California, a lesbian lost her bid to enforce a "co-parenting" agreement with a biological mother after the couple terminated their relationship.[19] In July 1993, the West Virginia Supreme Court in July 1993 granted a lesbian mother a stay of an order to remand custody of her children to their father. A circuit court had issued the order, citing as cause that the mother had moved in with her lesbian companion.[20]

Hawaii

In May 1993, the Hawaii Supreme Court ruled, in a 3-to-2 vote, that the state's exclusion of same-sex couples from marital status may be unconstitutional because it amounts to sex discrimination. Marriage is a civil right, the court said, and when the state says who may marry (and by implication, who may not), it violates the guarantee of equal protection under the law. The court invited the state to offer compelling reasons why marriage should be limited to opposite-sex couples.

In April 1994, the state legislature overwhelmingly passed a bill defining "marriage" in the traditional sense and defending it as the time-honored foundation for procreating and raising children. In 1996, Judge Chang struck down the law as violative of Hawaii's equal rights amendment prohibiting discrimination because of sex. Many observers expect the liberal Hawaii Supreme Court to mandate "gay marriage." Also pending in Hawaii is a domestic-partnership bill, which Senator Ann Kobayashi, a homosexual rights supporter, once praised as "a foot in the door" toward legalization of same-sex "marriage." Meanwhile, voters in 1996 approved a state constitutional convention to be held in 1998 in order to amend the constitution to protect marriage. And in 1997, both houses of the Hawaiian legislature approved a constitutional amendment limiting marriage to one-man, one-woman couples. If it clears legal hurdles, the amendment will go before the voters in November 1998. Polls show that 70–75 percent of Hawaiians oppose legalizing same-sex marriages.[21]

Homosexual activists, including those in Hawaii, often compare their quest for marital status with an interracial couple's legal victory in *Loving v. Virginia.* In that 1967 case, the Supreme Court struck down laws preventing marriage between people of different races as violating the equal protection and due process clauses of the Fourteenth Amendment to the Constitution.

But the court never came close to redefining the institution of marriage itself, which is what would have to occur for same-sex relationships to be accorded marital status. The false equation of a benign, nonbehavioral characteristic such as skin color with an orientation based precisely on behavior finds no support within the law.

In the 1970s, homosexuals unsuccessfully challenged marriage laws in the states of Minnesota, Kentucky, and Washington. In the Minnesota case, the state supreme court noted, "The institution of marriage as a union of man and woman, uniquely involving the procreating and rearing of children within a family, is as old as the book of Genesis . . . This historic institution is more deeply founded than the asserted contemporary concept of marriage and societal interests for which petitioners contend."[22]

Other relationships have not been accorded the same status as marriage because they do not contribute in the same way to a community. To put it bluntly, societies can get along quite well without homosexual relationships, but no society can survive without heterosexual marriages and families. In fact, because the term "heterosexual marriage" is redundant, the term "marriage" will mean in this paper what it has always meant: the social, legal, and spiritual union of a man and a woman. "Gay marriage" is an oxymoron, an ideological invention designed to appropriate the moral capital of marriage and family toward the goal of government-enforced acceptance of homosexuality.

The Importance of Definition

> Marriage a: the state of being united to a person of the opposite sex as husband or wife b: the mutual relation of husband and wife: wedlock c: the institution whereby men and women are joined in a special kind of social and legal dependence for the purpose of founding and maintaining a family.
>
> —*Webster's Third New International Dictionary*

To place domestic-partner relationships on a par with marriage denigrates the marital imperative. But to describe such relationships as "marriage" destroys the definition of marriage altogether. When the meaning of a word becomes more inclusive, the exclusivity that it previously defined is lost. For instance, if the state of Hawaii decided to extend the famous—and exclusive—"Maui onion" appellation to all onions grown in Hawaii, the term "Maui onion" would lose its original meaning as a specific thing. Consumers would lack confidence in buying a bag of "Maui onions" if all onions could be labeled as such. The same goes for any brand name or for wine from Bordeaux as opposed to wine from California. Likewise, if "marriage" in Hawaii ceases to be the term used solely for the social, legal, and spiritual bonding of a man and a woman, the term "marriage" becomes useless. Other states rightly could challenge Hawaii's marriage licenses as meaning something entirely different from what is meant in Pennsylvania or California.

Homosexual activist Tom Stoddard acknowledges that

> enlarging the concept to embrace same-sex couples would necessarily transform it into something new . . . Extending the right to marry to gay people—that is, abolishing the traditional gender requirements of marriage—can be one of the means, perhaps the principal one, through which the institution divests itself of the sexist trappings of the past.[23]

In other words, while many homosexual spokespeople say they want only to be left alone to enjoy the benefits of marriage, Stoddard rightly sees the expanded definition as a way of attacking the institution itself.

Let's return to the Maui onion example: Hawaii's garlic growers could demand that the exclusive use of the term "Maui onions" gives onion farmers an advantage and is therefore "discriminatory." Of course, garlic growers could qualify for the "Maui onion" label by growing onions in Maui under the Maui requirements. Likewise, homosexuals are not denied the right to marry. Like anybody else, they can qualify for the appellation of marriage by fulfilling its requirements. But they cannot call same-sex relationships "marriage" since they are lacking a basic requirement; they are missing an entire sex. The joining of the two sexes in permanence is the very essence of marriage. Once the "one man, one woman" definition is abandoned, there is no logical reason for limiting "marriage" to two people or even to people. Why not have three partners? Or why not a man and his daughter? Or a man and his dog? The logical reason to extend "marriage" to homosexual couples has nothing to do with marital integrity, but only reflects the fact that homosexuals want the same status regardless of its real meaning. Anything less, they say, is a denial of human rights. If so, then a threesome or a foursome seeking marital status can similarly claim that their sexual proclivities must be recognized by society and the law as the equal of marriage and that, if they are not, they are facing discrimination.

The point is that destroying definitions does enormous damage not only to marriage, but to the idea of truth. Calling the union of two lesbians a "marriage" is telling a lie, and official recognition of this lie breeds the sort of cynicism found in totalitarian societies, where lies are common currency.

The Myth of Homosexual Monogamy

In 1992, organizers of the homosexuals' 1993 March on Washington met in Texas to draft a platform of demands. Known as "the Texas platform," it was later toned down to make it more palatable to a mass audience. The original section on family, however, is revealing as to the intentions of the movement. In addition to Demand No. 40, "the recognition and legal protection of all forms of family structures," the writers called for Demand No. 45, "legalization of same-sex marriages," and Demand No. 46, "legalization of multiple partner unions."[24]

An enormous body of research indicates that monogamy is not the norm for the average homosexual.[25] But even when it is, the result is not necessarily healthier behavior. A study published in the journal *AIDS* found that men in steady relationships practiced more anal intercourse and oral-anal intercourse than those without a steady partner.[26] In other words, the exclusivity of the relationship did not diminish the incidence of unhealthy behavior that is the essence of homosexual sexual activity. Curbing promiscuity would help curb the spread of AIDS and the many other sexually transmitted diseases that are found disproportionately among homosexuals, but there is little evidence that "monogamous" homosexual relationships function that way. A British study also published in the journal *AIDS* found that most "unsafe" sex acts occur in steady relationships.[27]

In April 1994, the homosexual-oriented magazine *Genre* examined current practices among male homosexuals who live with partners. The author concluded that the most successful relationships are possible largely because the partners have "outside affairs."

> "I think we are seeing a new phenomenon in the gay community," announces Guy Baldwin, an L.A.-based psychologist whose practice is mostly comprised [*sic*] of gay men. "It is the appearance of the well-adjusted open gay marriage." Historically, Baldwin argues, gay men have always engaged in erotic experiences outside a primary relationship, "but they have done so with a great deal of trepidation, soul-searching and lots of beating up on themselves." For Baldwin's part, what's new is that gay men are no longer holding themselves up to the rigorous standards offered by mainstream society, which equates emotional fidelity with erotic exclusivity . . . "With all the talk about legalizing marriage for gays, there's an assumption in the minds of most people I talk to that only rarely does that legalization include monogamy." [28]

According to the *Genre* article, in 1993, David P. McWhirter and Andrew M. Mattison, authors of *The Male Couple,*

> reported that in a study of 156 males in loving relationships lasting from one to 37 years, only seven couples considered themselves to have been consistently monogamous. Most understood outside sex, and even outside love, as the norm. "It should be recognized that what has survival values in a heterosexual context may be destructive in a homosexual context," argues a couple in the McWhirter and Mattison study." They add, "Life-enhancing mechanisms used by heterosexual men and women should not necessarily be used as a stan-

> dard by which to judge the degree of a homosexual's adjustment." In other words, to adapt heterosexual models to homosexual relations is more than just foolhardy; it's an act of oppression.[29]

Former homosexual William Aaron explains why "monogamy" has a different meaning among homosexuals:

> In the gay life, fidelity is almost impossible. Since part of the compulsion of homosexuality seems to be a need on the part of the homophile to "absorb" masculinity from his sexual partners, he must be constantly on the lookout for [new partners]. Consequently the most successful homophile "marriages" are those where there is an arrangement between the two to have affairs on the side while maintaining the semblance of permanence in their living arrangement.[30]

Sexual Revolution: Leveler of Civility

As the research of the late Harvard sociologist Pitirim Sorokin reveals, no society has loosened sexual morality outside of marriage and survived. Analyzing studies of cultures spanning several thousand years on several continents, Sorokin found that virtually all political revolutions that brought about societal collapse were preceded by sexual revolutions in which marriage and family were no longer accorded premier status.[31] To put it another way, as marriage and family ties disintegrate, the social restraints learned in families also disintegrate. Chaos results, and chaos ushers in tyrants who promise to restore order by any means, as Sorokin notes.

Self-governing people require a robust culture founded on marriage and family, which nurture the qualities that permit self-rule: deferred gratification, self-sacrifice, respect for kinship and law, and property rights. These qualities are founded upon sexual restraint, which permits people to pursue long-term interests, such as procreating, raising the next generation, and securing benefits for one's children.

According sex outside marriage the same protections and status as the marital bond would destroy traditional sexual morality, not merely expand it. One can no more "expand" a definition or moral principle than one can continually expand a yardstick and still use it as a reliable measure.

The drive to de-legitimize marriage by hijacking its status for other relationships, including unmarried opposite-sex couples, is being funded and directed by the homosexual rights movement. Lawsuits filed against landlords unwilling to rent to unmarried couples out of religious conviction are largely the work of the Lambda Legal Defense and Education Fund, the American Civil Liberties Union's homosexual legal project, and other homosexual activist organizations intent on using government power to force acceptance of their agenda. If the rights of landlords to refuse to aid and abet what they consider sinful behavior are abridged, it is a small legal step to force landlords, even in households with children, to rent to anyone regardless of sexual orientation. In this way, freedom for homosexuals would be expanded, but at the expense of the freedom of those who find homosexuality destructive, immoral, and unhealthy.

So far, the courts generally have rejected the claims of homosexuals and unmarried couples in this regard. In a series of recent cases, the courts have ruled that landlords cannot be compelled by law to betray their religious objections to fornication. But in 1996, the California Supreme Court overturned a 1994 ruling by an appeals court that the California Fair Employment and Housing Commission erred in fining a sixty-one-year-old landlady, Evelyn Smith, $954 for refusing to rent a duplex to an unmarried couple. The agency had also required Smith to post a sign saying she would not discriminate against unmarried people.[32] The three-judge panel found that the order "penalizes [Smith] for her religious belief that fornication and its knowing facilitation are sinful." The state supreme court, however, brushed aside Smith's religious claims, saying that she was free to sell the property and give up being a landlord.

The Boston-based Gay and Lesbian Advocates and Defenders had filed an amicus brief in the case, and Lambda Legal Defense Fund senior staff attorney Evan Wolfson denounced the earlier verdict in Smith's favor. He said that religious beliefs should retreat "when it comes to public good, such as public housing and access to public housing."[33] Wolfson apparently ignored the distinction between government-run "public housing" and private property, as owned by Smith.

In other cases, courts have upheld the rights of landlords in Massachusetts, Minnesota, Illinois, and in several California jurisdictions.[34]

The Importance of Family Ties

For thousands of years, in all successful cultures, homosexuality has been discouraged through social norms and legal prohibition. Cultures have always found it necessary to encourage new marriages and protect existent marriages by extending rewards and privileges for this productive behavior and by extending sanctions and stigmas to unproductive behavior, such as promiscuous sex and homosexual sex. Research and common sense show that the health of any given society depends largely on the number of intact, mom-and-dad families. People living in other arrangements benefit from the social order derived from the marital order.

Marriage-based kinship is essential to stability and continuity. A man is more apt to sacrifice himself to help a son-in-law than some unrelated man (or woman) living with his daughter. Kinship entails mutual obligations and a commitment to the future of the community. Homosexual relationships are a negation of the ties that bind—the continuation of kinship through procreation of children. To accord same-sex relationships the same status as a marriage is to accord them a value that they cannot possibly have. Marriages benefit more than the two people involved, or even the children that are created. Their influence reaches children living nearby, as young minds seek out role models. The stability they bring to a community benefits all. And the best chance for having a successful, strong marriage is to grow up in a family with a strong marriage as its foundation. This does not mean that people in divorced families or single-parent homes are unable to achieve their own strong family, just that it is more difficult since their role models did not reflect the mom-and-dad family on a daily, long-term basis. A homosexual household compounds the problem not only by lacking one entire sex in the household's foundational relationship, but also by presenting an aberrant form of sexuality as something "normal."

Protecting Children

A major reason for discouraging societal recognition of homosexual relationships on the partnership level or as "marriages" is the boost such arrangements give to the concept of homosexual adoption of children. Currently, only two states, Florida and New Hampshire, have laws preventing homosexuals from adopting children.[35] This low number is based on the fact that the issue has been considered unthinkable and thus unnecessary, not based on people's favoring the practice of adoption by homosexuals. Recent polls indicate strong societal disapproval of homosexual adoptions. But approval of same-sex relationships undermines much of the moral argument against same-sex couples adopting children. If two same-sex people are seen as the equivalent of husband and wife, it becomes easier for homosexuals to argue, falsely, that a same-sex couple provides the same environment for raising children.

Breaking More Windows

The purpose of marriage is to stabilize sexuality and to provide the best environment in which to procreate and raise children. Sex outside marriage traditionally has been discouraged not only because of the dangers of sexually transmitted diseases and out-of-wedlock births but also because of the dangers it poses to stable families. Crime scholar James Q. Wilson describes "the broken window effect," in which failure to curb breaches in civil order leads to more breaches. He noticed that a building in a tough part of a city had all its windows intact, unlike others around it. After one window was broken, however, all the other windows soon met the same fate. Likewise, if a culture does not discourage extramarital sexuality, the stable marriages are threatened because of the erosion of cultural, social, and finally, legal, support. Plagued by a high rate of divorce, teen pregnancies, and STD epidemics, America can only unravel the social fabric further by legitimizing homosexuality.

Conclusion

"Domestic partnerships" and "gay marriages" are being advocated as an extension of tolerance and as a matter of civil rights, but these are really wedges designed to overturn traditional sexual morality, as is acknowledged by many homosexual activists themselves. There is little or no support within the law for such formulations, and there is no U.S. jurisdiction that recognizes homosexual "marriage." Voters and corporations should resist the demands made upon them to equate family life with behavior that has been deemed unhealthy, immoral, and destructive to individuals and societies in cultures the world over.

Who Needs Marriage?

JONATHAN RAUCH

Journalist Jonathan Rauch argues that there are good reasons for society to recognize lesbian and gay marriage. In asking "What is marriage for?" Rauch is concerned not with why people get married, but with why society recognizes marriages. After considering several possible justifications—including love, tradition, and children—he argues in favor of two of the reasons he considers most important: marriage settles males, and it provides reliable caregivers in times of crisis. According to Rauch, society has just as much of an interest in promoting these aims in the case of homosexuals as it does in the case of heterosexuals.

· · · · ·

Whatever else marriage may or may not be, it is certainly falling apart. Half of today's new marriages will end in divorce, and far more costly still (from a social point of view) are the marriages that never happen at all, leaving mothers poor, children fatherless, and neighborhoods chaotic. With a sense of timing worthy of Neville Chamberlain, at just this moment, homosexuals are pressing to be able to marry, and Hawaii's courts are moving toward letting them do so. I'll believe in gay marriage in America when I see it, but if it gets as far as being even temporarily legalized in Hawaii, then the uproar about this final insult to a besieged institution will be deafening.

Whether gay marriage makes sense—and, for that matter, whether straight marriages makes sense—depends on what marriage is actually for. Oddly enough, at the moment, secular thinking on this question is shockingly sketchy. Gay activists say: marriage is for love, and we love each other, therefore we should be able to marry. Traditionalists say: marriage is for children, and homosexuals do not (or should not) have children, there-

---

This chapter is reprinted with minor editorial revisions from Bruce Bawer, ed., *Beyond Queer: Challenging Gay Left Orthodoxy* (New York: Free Press, 1996), pp. 296–313. Copyright 1996 by Jonathan Rauch.

fore you should not be able to marry. That, unfortunately, pretty well covers the spectrum. I say "unfortunately" because both views are wrong. They misunderstand and impoverish the social meaning of marriage.

I admit to being an interested party: I am a homosexual, and I want the right to marry. In fact, I want more than the right; I want the actual marriage (when Mr. Wonderful comes along, God willing). Nevertheless, I do not want to destroy the most basic of all social institutions, backbone of the family, and bedrock of civilization. It is not enough for gay marriage to make sense for gay people; if they ask society to recognize and bless it, it should also make sense from society's broader point of view.

So what is marriage for?

Against Love

In its religious dress, marriage has a straightforward justification. It is as it is because that is how God wants it. Depending on the religion, God has various things to say about who may marry and what should go on within a marriage. Modern marriage is, of course, based upon traditions that religion helped to codify and enforce. But religious doctrine has no special standing in the world of secular law and policy, with all due apologies to the "Christian nation" crowd. If we want to know what and whom marriage is for in modern America, we need a sensible secular doctrine.

At one point, marriage in secular society was largely a matter of business: cementing family ties, providing social status for men and economic support for women, conferring dowries, and so on. Marriages were typically arranged, and "love" in the modern sense was no prerequisite. In Japan today, there are remnants of this system, and it works surprisingly well. Couples stay together because they view their marriage as a partnership: an investment in social stability for themselves and their children. Because Japanese couples don't expect as much emotional fulfillment as Americans do, they are less inclined to break up. They also take a somewhat more relaxed attitude toward adultery. What's a little extracurricular love, provided that each partner is fulfilling his or her many other marital duties?

In the West, of course, love is a defining element. The notion of lifelong love is charming, if ambitious, and certainly love is a desirable element of marriage. It cannot, however, be the defining element in society's eyes. You may or may not love your husband, but the two of you are just as married either way. You may love your mistress, but that certainly does not make her your spouse. Love helps make sense of marriage from an emotional point of view, but it is not terribly important, I think, in making sense of marriage from the point of view of social policy.

If blessing love does not define the purpose of secular marriage, what does? Neither the law nor secular thinking provides a very clear answer to this question. Today, marriage is almost entirely a voluntary arrangement whose contents are up to the people making the deal. There are few if any behaviors that automatically end a marriage. If a man beats his wife—which is about the worst thing he can do to her—he may be convicted of assault, but his marriage is not automatically dissolved. Couples can be adulterous (or "open") yet still be married, so long as that is what they choose to be. They can be celibate, too; consummation is not required. All in all, it is an impressive and also rather astonishing victory for modern individualism that so important an institution should be so bereft of formal social instruction as to what should go on inside of it.

Secular society tells us only a few things about marriage. Among them are the following. First, marriage happens only with the consent of the parties. Second, the parties are not children. Third, a number of parties is two. Fourth, one is a man and the other a woman. Within those rules, a marriage is whatever anyone says it is. So the standard rules say almost nothing about what marriage is for.

Against Tradition

Perhaps it doesn't matter what marriage is for. Perhaps it is enough simply to say that marriage is as it is and should not be tampered with. This sounds like a crudely reactionary position. In fact, however, of all the arguments against reforming marriage, it is probably the most powerful.

I'll call it a Hayekian argument, after the great libertarian economist F. A. Hayek, who developed this line of thinking in his book *The Fatal Conceit.* In a market system, the prices generated by impersonal forces may not make sense from any one person's point of view, but they encode far more information than even the cleverest person could ever gather. In a similar fashion, human societies evolve rich and complicated webs of nonlegal rules in the forms of customs, traditions, and institutions. Like prices, the customs generated by societies may often seem irrational or arbitrary. But the very fact that they are the customs that have evolved implies that there is a kind of practical logic embedded in them that may not be apparent from even a sophisticated analysis. And the web of custom cannot be torn apart and reordered at will, because once its internal logic is violated, it falls apart. Intellectuals, like Marxists or feminists, who seek to deconstruct and rationally rebuild social traditions will produce not better order, but merely chaos. Thus hallowed social tradition should not be tampered with except in the very last extremity.

For secular intellectuals who are unhappy with the evolved framework for marriage and who are excluded from it—in other words, for people like me—this Hayekian argument is very troubling. It is also very powerful. Age-old stigmas on illegitimacy and out-of-wedlock pregnancy were crude and unfair to women and children. On the male side, shotgun marriages were, in an informal way, coercive and intrusive. But when modern societies began playing around with the age-old stigmas on illegitimacy and divorce and all the rest, whole portions of the social structure just caved in.

So the Hayekian view argues strongly against gay marriage. It says that the current rules for marriage may not be the best ones, and they may even be unfair. But they are all we have, and once you say that marriage need not be male-female, soon marriage will stop being anything at all. You can't mess with the formula without causing unforeseen consequences, possibly including the implosion of the institution of marriage itself.

But I demur. There are problems with the Hayekian position. The biggest is that it is untenable in its extreme form and unhelpful in its milder version. In its extreme form, it implies that no social reforms should ever be undertaken. Indeed, no social laws should be passed, because they will interfere with the natural evolution of social mores. One would thus have to say that because in the past slavery was customary in almost all human societies, it should not have been forcibly abolished. Obviously, neither Hayek nor his sympathizers would actually say this. They would point out that slavery violated fundamental moral principles and was scaldingly inhumane. But in doing so, they do what must be done if we are to be human: they establish a moral platform from which to judge social rules. They thus acknowledge that abstracting social debate from moral concerns is not possible.

If the ban on gay marriage were only mildly unfair and if the social costs of changing it were certain to be enormous, then the ban could stand on Hayekian grounds. However, if there is any social policy today that has a fair claim to being scaldingly inhumane, it is the ban on gay marriage. As conservatives tirelessly and rightly point out, marriage is the most fundamental institution of society. To bar any class of people from marrying as they choose is an extraordinary deprivation. When, not so long ago, it was illegal in parts of America for blacks to marry whites, no one could claim this was a trivial disenfranchisement. Granted, gay marriage raises issues that interracial marriage does not; but no one can argue that the deprivation itself is a minor one.

To outweigh such a serious claim and rule out homosexual marriage purely on Hayekian grounds, saying that bad things might happen is not enough. Bad things might always happen. Bad things happened as a result of legalizing contraception, but that did not make it the wrong thing to do, and in any case, good things happened also. It is not at all clear, on the merits, that heterosexual marriage would be eroded by legalizing homosexual marriage. On the contrary, marriage might be strengthened if it were held out as the norm for everybody, including homosexuals.

Besides, it seems doubtful that extending marriage to, say, another 3 or 5 percent of the population would have anything like the effects that no-fault divorce has had, to say nothing of contraception and the sexual revolution. By now, the "traditional" understanding of marriage has been tampered with by practically everybody in all kinds of ways. It is hard to think of a bigger affront to tradition, for instance, than allowing married women to own property independently of their husbands or allowing them to charge their husbands with rape. Surely it is a bit unfair to say that marriage may be reformed for the sake of anyone and everyone except homosexuals, who must respect the dictates of tradition.

Faced with these problems, the milder version of the Hayekian argument says, not that social traditions shouldn't be tampered with at all, but that they shouldn't be tampered with lightly. Fine, and thank you. In this case, no one is talking about casual messing around or about some lobby's desire to score political points; the issue is about allowing people to live as grown-ups and full citizens. One could write pages on this point, but I won't. I'll set human rights claims to one side and in return ask the Hayekians to recognize that appeals to blind tradition and to the risks inherent in social change do not, a priori, settle anything in this instance. They merely warn against frivolous change. If the issue at hand is whether gay marriage is good or bad for society as well as for gay people, there is no avoiding a discussion about the *purpose* of marriage.

Against Children

So we turn to what has become the standard view of marriage's purpose. Its proponents would probably like to call it a child-centered view, but a more accurate description would call it an antigay view, as will become clear. Whatever you call it, it is certainly the view that is heard most often, and in the context of the debate over gay marriage, it is heard almost exclusively. In its most straightforward form, it goes as follows (I quote from James Q. Wilson's fine book *The Moral Sense*):

> A family is not an association of independent people; it is a human commitment designed to make possible the rearing of moral and healthy children. Governments care—or ought to care—about families for this reason, and scarcely for any other.

Wilson speaks about "family" rather than "marriage" as such, but one may, I think, read him as speaking of marriage without doing any injustice to his meaning. The resulting proposition—government ought to care about marriage almost entirely because of children and scarcely for any other reason—seems reasonable. It certainly accords with our common-sense feeling that marriage and children go together. But there are problems. The first, obviously, is that gay couples may have children, either through adoption or (for lesbians) by using artificial insemination. I will leave for some other essay the contentious issue of gay adoption. For now, the obvious point is that if the mere presence of children is the test, then homosexual relationships can certainly pass it.

You might note, correctly, that heterosexual marriages are more likely to wind up with children in the mix than homosexual ones. When granting marriage licenses to heterosexuals, however, we do not ask how likely the couple is to have children. We assume that they are entitled to get married whether they end up with children or not. Understanding this, conservatives often then make an interesting further move. In seeking to justify the state's interest in marriage, they shift from the actual presence of children to the anatomical possibility of making them. Hadley Arkes, a law professor and prominent opponent of homosexual marriage, makes the case this way:

> The traditional understanding of marriage is grounded in the "natural teleology of the body"—in the inescapable fact that only a man and a woman, and only two people, not three, can generate a child. Once marriage is detached from that natural teleology of the body, what ground of principle would thereafter confine marriage to two people rather than some larger grouping? That is, on what ground of principle would the law reject the claim of a gay couple that their love is not confined to a coupling of two, but that they are woven into a larger ensemble with yet another person or two?

What he seems to be saying is that where the possibility of natural children is nil, the meaning of marriage is nil. If marriage is allowed between members of the same sex, then the concept of marriage has been emptied of content except to ask whether the parties love each other. Then anything goes, including polygamy. This reasoning presumably is what antigay activists have in mind when they claim that once gay marriage is legal, marriage to pets will follow close behind.

Arkes and his sympathizers have here made two mistakes, both of them instructive. To see them, break down the Arkes-type claim into two components:

1. Two-person marriage derives its special status from the anatomical possibility that the partners can create natural children.
2. Apart from 1, two-person marriage has no purpose sufficiently strong to justify its special status. That is, absent justification 1, anything goes.

The first proposition is peculiar, because it is wholly at odds with the way society actually views marriage. Leave aside the insistence that natural, as opposed to adoptive, children define the importance of marriage. The deeper problem, apparent right away, is the issue of sterile heterosexual couples. Here the "anatomical possibility" crowd has a problem, for a homosexual union is, anatomically speaking, nothing but one variety of sterile union and no different even in principle: a woman without a uterus has no more potential for giving birth than a man without a vagina.

It may sound like carping to stress the case of barren heterosexual marriage; the vast majority of newlywed heterosexual couples, after all, can have children and probably will. But the point here is fundamental. There are far more sterile heterosexual unions in America than homosexual ones. The "anatomical possibility" crowd cannot have it both ways. If the possibility of children is what gives meaning to marriage, then a postmenopausal woman who tries to take out a marriage license should be turned away at the courthouse door. What's more, she should be hooted at and condemned for stretching the meaning of marriage beyond its natural basis and so reducing the institution to frivolity. People at the Family Research Council or Concerned Women for America should point at her and say, "If she can marry, why not polygamy? Why not marriage to pets?"

Obviously, the "anatomical" conservatives do not say this, because they are sane. They instead flail around, saying that sterile men and women were at least born with the right-shaped parts for making children, and so on. As they struggle to include sterile heterosexual marriages while excluding homosexual ones, their position is soon revealed to be a nonposition. It says that the "natural children" rationale defines marriage when homosexuals are involved but not when heterosexuals are involved. When the parties to union are sterile heterosexuals, the justification for marriage must be something else. But what?

Now arises the oddest part of the "anatomical" argument. Look at proposition 2 above. It says that, absent the anatomical justification for marriage, anything goes. In other words, it dismisses the idea that there might be some other compelling reasons for society to sanctify marriage above other kinds of relationships. Why would anybody want to make this move? I'll just hazard a guess: to exclude homosexuals. Any rationale that justifies sterile heterosexual marriages can also apply to homosexual ones. For instance, marriage makes women more financially secure. Very nice, say the conservatives. But that rationale could be applied to lesbians, so it's definitely out.

The end result of this stratagem is perverse to the point of being funny. The attempt to ground marriage in children (or the anatomical possibility thereof) falls flat. But having lost that reason for marriage, the antigay people can offer no other. In their fixation on excluding homosexuals, they leave themselves no consistent justification for the privileged status of *heterosexual* marriage. They thus tear away any coherent foundation that secular marriage might have, which is precisely the opposite of what they claim they want to do. If they have to undercut marriage to save it from homosexuals, so be it!

If you feel my argument here has a slightly Thomist ring, the reason, of course, is that the "child-centered" people themselves do not really believe that natural children are the only, or even the overriding, reason society blesses marriage. In the real world, it's obvious that sterile people have every right to get married and that society benefits by allowing and, indeed, encouraging them to do so. No one seriously imagines that denying marriage to a sterile heterosexual couple would strengthen the institution of marriage, or that barring sterile marriages would even be a decent thing to do. The "natural children" people know this perfectly well, and they admit it implicitly when they cheerfully bless sterile unions. In truth, their real posture has nothing at all to do with children, or even with the "anatomical possibility" of children. It is merely antigay. All it really says is this: the defining purpose of marriage is to exclude homosexuals.

This is not an answer to the question of what marriage is for. Rather, it makes of marriage, as Richard Mohr aptly puts it, "nothing but an empty space, delimited only by what it excludes—gay couples." By putting a nonrationale at the center of modern marriage, these conservatives leave the institution worse off than if they had never opened their mouths. This is not at all helpful.

If one is to set hypocrisy aside, one must admit that there are compelling reasons for marriage other than children—reasons that may or may not apply to homosexual unions. What might those reasons be?

Rogue Males and Ailing Mates

For the record, I would be the last to deny that children are one central reason for the privileged status of marriage. Rather, I gladly proclaim it. When men and women get together, children are a likely outcome; and, as we are learning in ever more unpleasant ways, when children appear without two parents, all kinds of trouble ensues. Without belaboring the point, I hope I won't be accused of saying that children are a trivial reason for marriage. They just cannot be the only reason.

And what are the others? I can think of several possibilities, such as the point cited above about economic security for women (or men). There is a lot of intellectual work to be done trying to sort out which are the essential reasons and which incidental. It seems to me that the two strongest candidates are these: settling males and providing reliable caregivers. Both purposes are critical to the functioning of a humane and stable society, and both are much better served by marriage—that is, by one-to-one lifelong commitment—than by any other institution.

Wilson writes, in *The Moral Sense,* of the human male's need to hunt, defend, and attack. "Much of the history of civilization can be thought of as an effort to adapt these male dispositions to contemporary needs by restricting aggression or channeling it into appropriate channels," he says. I think it is probably fair to say that civilizing young males is one of any society's two or three biggest problems. Wherever unattached males gather in packs, you see no end of trouble: wildings in Central Park, gangs in Los Angeles, football hooligans in Britain, skinheads in Germany, fraternity hazings in universities, grope lines in the military, and (in a different but ultimately no less tragic way) the bathhouses and wanton sex of gay San Francisco or New York in the 1970s.

For taming males, marriage is unmatched. "Of all the institutions through which men may pass—schools, factories, the military—marriage has the largest effect," Wilson writes. A token of the casualness of current thinking about marriage is that the man who wrote those words could, later in the very same book, say that government should care about fostering families for "scarcely any other" reason than children. If marriage—that is, the binding of men into couples—did nothing else, its power to settle men, to keep them at home and out of trouble, would be ample justification for its special status.

Of course, women and older men don't generally travel in marauding or orgiastic packs. But in their case, the second rationale comes strongly into play. A second enormous problem for society is what to do when someone is beset by some sort of burdensome contingency. It could be cancer, a broken back, unemployment, or depression; it could be exhaustion from work or stress under pressure. If marriage has any meaning at all, it is that when you collapse from a stroke, there will be at least one other person whose "job" is to drop everything and come to your aid; or that when you come home after being fired by the postal service, there will be someone to persuade you not to commit a massacre.

All by itself, marriage is society's first and, often, second and third line of support for the troubled individual. Absent a spouse, the burdens of contingency fall immediately and sometimes crushingly upon people who have more immediate problems of their own (relatives, friends, neighbors), then upon charities and welfare programs that are expensive and often not very good. From the broader society's point of view, the unattached person is an accident waiting to happen. Married people are happier, healthier, and live longer; married men have lower rates of homicide, suicide, accidents, and mental illness. In large part, the reason is simply that married people have someone to look after them, and know it.

Obviously, both of these rationales—the need to settle males, the need to have people looked after—apply to sterile people as well as to fertile ones, and apply to childless couples as well as to ones with children. The first explains why everybody feels relieved when the town delinquent gets married, and the second explains why everybody feels happy when an aging widow takes a second husband. From a social point of view, it seems to me, both rationales are far more compelling as justification of marriage's special status than, say, love. And both of them apply to homosexuals as well as to heterosexuals.

Take the matter of settling men. It is probably true that women and children, more than just the fact of marriage, help civilize men. But that hardly means that the settling effect of marriage on homosexual men is negligible. To the contrary, being tied into a committed relationship plainly helps stabilize gay men. Even without marriage, coupled gay men have steady sex partners and relationships that they value, so they tend to be less wanton. Add marriage, and you bring to bear a further array of stabilizing influences. One of the main benefits of publicly recognized marriage is that it binds couples together not only in their own eyes, but also in the eyes of society at large. Around the partners is weaved a web of expectations that they will spend nights together, go to parties together, take out mortgages together, buy furniture at Ikea together, and so on—all of which helps tie them together and keep them off the streets and at home. ("It's 1:00 A.M.; do you know where your husband is?" Chances are you do.) Surely that is a very good thing, especially as compared to the closet-gay culture of furtive sex with innumerable partners in parks and bathhouses.

The other benefit of marriage—caretaking—clearly applies to homosexuals, with no reservations at all. One of the first things many people worry about when coming to terms with their homosexuality is, "Who will take care of me when I'm old?" Society needs to care about this, too, as the AIDS crisis has made horribly clear. If that crisis showed anything, it is that homosexuals can and will take care of each other, sometimes with breathtaking devotion—and that no institution can begin to match the care of a devoted partner. Legally speaking, marriage creates kin. Surely, society's interest in kin creation is strongest of all for people who are unlikely to be supported by children in old age and who may well be rejected by their own parents in youth.

Gay marriage, then, is far from being a mere exercise in political point making or rights mongering. On the contrary, it serves two of the three social purposes that make marriage so indispensable and irreplaceable for heterosexuals. Two out of three may not be the whole ball of wax, but it is more than enough to give society a compelling interest in marrying off homosexuals.

Moreover, marriage is the *only* institution that adequately serves these purposes. People who are uncomfortable with gay marriage—including some gay people—argue that the benefits can just as well be had through private legal arrangements and domestic-partnership laws. But only the fiduciary and statutory benefits of marriage can be arranged that way, and therein lies a world of difference. The promise of one-to-one lifetime commitment is very hard to keep. The magic of marriage is that it wraps a dense ribbon of social approval around each partnership, then reinforces commitment with a hundred informal mechanisms from everyday greetings ("How's the wife?") to gossipy sneers ("Why does she put up with that cheating bastard Bill?"). The power of marriage is not just legal, but social. It seals its promise with the smiles and tears of family, friends, and neighbors. It shrewdly exploits ceremony (big, public weddings) and money (expensive gifts, dowries) to deter casual commitment and to make bailing out embarrassing. Stag parties and bridal showers signal that what is beginning is not just a legal arrangement, but a whole new stage of life. "Domestic-partner" laws do none of these things. Me, I can't quite imagine my mother sobbing with relief as she says, "Thank heaven, Jonathan has finally found a domestic partner."

I'll go further: far from being a substitute for the real thing, "lite" marriage more likely undermines it. Marriage is a deal between a couple and society, not just between two people: society recognizes the sanctity and autonomy of the pair-bond, and in exchange, each spouse commits to being the other's caregiver, social worker, and police officer of first resort. Each marriage is its own little society within society. Any step that weakens this deal by granting the legal benefits of marriage without also requiring the public commitment is begging for trouble.

From gay couples' point of view, pseudomarriage is second best to the real thing; but from society's point of view, it may be the worst policy of all. From both points of view, gay marriage—real social recognition, real personal commitment, real social pressure to shore up personal commitment—makes the most sense. That is why government should be wary of offering "alternatives" to marriage. And, one might add, that is also why the full social benefits of gay marriage will come only when churches as well as governments customarily bless it: when women marry women in big church weddings as mothers weep and priests, solemnly smiling, intone the vows.

Against Gay Divorce

So gay marriage makes sense for several of the same reasons that straight marriage makes sense; fine. That would seem a natural place to stop. But the logic of the argument compels one to go a twist further. If I am right, then there are implications for heterosexuals and homosexuals alike—not entirely comfortable ones.

If society has a strong interest in seeing people married off, then it must also have some interest in seeing them stay together. For many years, that interest was assumed and embodied in laws and informal stigmas that made divorce a painful experience. My guess is that this was often bad for adults but quite good for children, though you could argue that point all day. In any event, things have radically changed. Today, more and more people believe that a divorce should be at least a bit harder to get.

I'm not going to wade into the debate about toughening the divorce laws. Anyway, in a liberal society, there is not much you can do to keep people together without trampling their rights. The point that's relevant here is that, if I'm right, the standard way of thinking about this issue is incomplete, even misleading. The usual argument is that divorce is bad for children, which is why we should worry about it. I wouldn't deny this for a moment. Some people advocate special counseling or cooling-off periods for divorcing couples with children. That may well be a good idea. But it should not be assumed that society has no interest in helping childless couples stay together, also—for just the reason I've outlined. Childless couples, of course, include gay couples. In my opinion, if one wants to shore up the institution of marriage, then one had better complicate divorce (if that's what you're going to do) for all couples, including gay ones and childless heterosexual ones. Otherwise, you send the message that marriage can be a casual affair if you don't happen to have children. Gay spouses should understand that once they are together, they are *really* together. The upshot is that gay divorce should be every bit as hard to get as straight divorce—and both should probably be harder to get than is now the case.

Another implication follows, too. If it is good for society to have people attached, then it is not enough just to make marriage available. Marriage should also be *expected.* This, too, is just as true for homosexuals as for heterosexuals. So if homosexuals are justified in expecting access to marriage, society is equally justified in expecting them to use it. I'm not saying that out-of-wedlock sex should be scandalous or that people should be coerced into marriage or anything like that. The mechanisms of expectation are more subtle. When Grandma cluck-clucks over a still-unmarried young man, or when Mom says she wishes her little girl would settle down, she is expressing a strong and well-justified preference—one that is quietly echoed in a thousand ways throughout society and that produces subtle but important pressure to form and sustain unions. This is a good and necessary thing, and it will be as necessary for homosexuals as for heterosexuals. If gay marriage is recognized, single gay people over a certain age should not be surprised when they are subtly disapproved of or pitied. That is a vital part of what makes marriage work.

Moreover, if marriage is to work, it cannot be merely a "lifestyle option." It must be privileged. That is, it must be understood to be better, on average, than other ways of living. Not mandatory, not good where everything else is bad, but better: a general norm, rather than a personal taste. The biggest worry about gay marriage, I think, is that homosexuals might get it but then mostly not use it. Unlike a conservative friend of mine, I don't think that gay neglect of marriage would greatly erode what remains of the bonding power of heterosexual marriage (remember, homosexuals are only a tiny fraction of the population). But it would certainly not help, and in any case, it would denude the benefits and cheapen the meaning of homosexual marriage. And heterosexual society would rightly feel betrayed if, after legalization, homosexuals treated marriage as a minority taste rather than as a core institution of life. It is not enough, I think, for gay people to say we want the right to marry. If we do not use it, shame on us.

· CHAPTER TWENTY-SIX ·

Against Marriage

CLAUDIA CARD

Claudia Card, professor of philosophy at the University of Wisconsin, Madison, discusses gay marriage from a lesbian-feminist persective. Card opposes legal marriage (both heterosexual and homosexual) not because she believes that committed partnerships are a bad thing, but because she believes that state involvement in such partnerships has serious moral costs. Although Card does not support measures like the Defense of Marriage Act, which permits states not to recognize same-sex marriages performed in other states, she does argue that lesbians and gays (as well as heterosexuals) would be better off, all things considered, without the option of legal marriage.

· · · · ·

The title of this chapter is deliberately provocative, because I fear that radical feminist perspectives on marriage are in danger of being lost in the quest for equal rights. My concern, however, is specific. I am skeptical of legal marriage as a way to gain a better life for lesbian and gay lovers or as a way to provide a supportive environment for lesbian and gay parents and their children. Of course, some are happy with marriage as it now exists. My concern is with the price of that joy borne by those trapped by marriage and deeply unlucky in the company they find there. Nevertheless, nothing that I say is intended to disparage the characters of many magnificent women who have struggled in and around this institution to make the best of a trying set of options.

Backgrounds

My perspective on marriage is influenced not only by others' written reports and analyses, but also by my own history of being raised in a lower-

---

This chapter is reprinted with revisions from "Against Marriage and Motherhood," *Hypatia* Vol. 11 No. 3 (Summer 1996).

middle-class white village family by parents married (to each other) for more than three decades, by my firsthand experiences of urban same-sex domestic partnerships lasting from two and one-half to nearly seven years (good ones and bad, some racially mixed, some white, generally mixed in class and religious backgrounds), and by my more recent experience as a lesbian feminist whose partner of the past decade is not a domestic partner.

Because it appears unlikely that the legal rights of marriage in the European-American model of this institution currently at issue in our courts will disappear or even be seriously eroded during my lifetime, my opposition to them here takes the form of skepticism primarily in the two areas mentioned above: ethical theorizing and lesbian/gay activism. I believe that lesbians or gays should be reluctant to put our activist energy into attaining legal equity with heterosexuals in marriage—not because the existing discrimination against us is in any way justifiable, but because this institution is so deeply flawed that it seems to me unworthy of emulation and reproduction.

When confronted with my negative attitudes toward marriage, some recoil as though I were proposing that we learn to do without water and oxygen on the ground that both are polluted (even killing us). Often, I believe, this reaction comes from certain assumptions that the reader or hearer may be inclined to make, which I here note in order to set aside at the outset.

My opposition to marriage is not an opposition to intimacy, nor to long-term relationships of intimacy, nor to durable partnerships of many sorts.[1] I understand marriage as a relationship to which the state is an essential third party. Also, like the practices of footbinding and suttee, which, according to the researches of Mary Daly, [2] originated among the powerful classes, marriage in Europe was once available only to those with substantial social power. Previously available only to members of propertied classes, the marriage relation has come to be available in modern northern democracies to any adult heterosexual couple neither of whom is already married to someone else. This is what lesbian and gay agitation for the legal right to marry is about. This is what I find calls for extreme caution.

Marriage in the history of modern patriarchies has been mandatory for and oppressive to women, and it has been criticized by feminists on those grounds. My concerns, however, are as much for the children as for the women that some of these children become and for the goal of avoiding

Thanks to Harry Brighouse, Vicky Davion, Virginia Held, Sara Ruddick, anonymous reviewers for *Hypatia,* and especially to Lynne Tirrell for helpful comments and suggestions and to audiences who heard ancestors of this essay at the Pacific and Central Divisions of the American Philosophical Association in 1995.

the reproduction of patriarchy. Virginia Held, one optimist about the potentialities of marriage, conceives families as being constructed of noncontractual relationships.[3] She notes that although Marxists and recent communitarians might agree with her focus on noncontractual relationships, their views remain uninformed by feminist critiques of patriarchal families. The family from which she would have society and ethical theorists learn, ultimately, is a postpatriarchal family. But what is a "postpatriarchal family"? Is it a coherent concept?

"Family" is itself a family resemblance concept. Many contemporary lesbian and gay partnerships, households, and friendship networks fit no patriarchal stereotypes and are not sanctified by legal marriage, although their members still regard themselves as "family."[4] But should they? Many social institutions, such as insurance companies, do not honor such conceptions of "family." Family, as understood in contexts where material benefits tend to be at stake, is not constituted totally by noncontractual relationships. At its core is to be found one or more marriage contracts. For those who would work to enlarge the concept of family to include groupings that are currently totally noncontractual, in retaining patriarchal vocabulary there is a danger of importing patriarchal ideals and of inviting treatment as deviant or "second class" at best.

"Family," our students learn in Women's Studies 101, comes from the Latin *familia,* meaning "household," which in turn came from *famulus,* which, according to the *OED,* meant "servant." The ancient Roman *paterfamilias* was the head of a household of servants and slaves, including his wife or wives, concubines, and children. He had the power of life and death over them. The ability of contemporary male heads of households to get away with battering, incest, and murder suggests to many feminists that the family has not evolved into anything acceptable yet. Would a household of persons whose relationships with one another transcend (as those of families do) sojourns under one roof continue to be rightly called "family" if no members had significant social support for treating other members abusively? Perhaps the postpatriarchal relationships envisioned by Held and by so many lesbians and gay men should be called something else, to mark that radical departure from family history. But it is not just a matter of a word. It is difficult to imagine what such relationships would be.

Lesbian (or Gay) Marriage?

A special vantage point is offered by the experience of lesbians and gay men, among whom there is currently no consensus (although much strong feeling on both sides) on whether to pursue the legal right to marry a same-sex lover.[5] When heterosexual partners think about marriage, they usually consider the more limited questions of whether they (as individuals) should marry (each other) and, if they did not marry, what the consequences would be for children they might have or raise. They consider these questions in the context of a state that gives them the legal option of marriage. Lesbians and gay men are currently in the position of having to consider the larger question of whether the legal option of marriage is a good idea, as we do not presently have it in relation to our lovers. We have it, of course, in relation to the other sex, and many have exercised it as a cover, as insurance, for resident alien status, and so forth. If it is because we already have rights to marry heterosexually that right-wing attackers of lesbian or gay rights complain of our wanting "special rights," we should reply that, of course, any legalization of same-sex marriage should extend that "privilege" to heterosexuals as well.

The question whether lesbians and gay men should pursue the right to marry is not the same as the question whether the law is wrong in its refusal to honor same-sex marriages. Richard Mohr defends gay marriage from that point of view as well as I have seen it done.[6] Evan Wolfson develops powerfully an analogy between the denial of marriage to same-sex couples and the antimiscegenation laws that were overturned in the United States just little more than a quarter century ago.[7] What I have to say should apply to relationships between lovers (or parents) of different races as well as to those of same-sex lovers (or parents). The ways we have been treated are abominable. But it does not follow that we should seek legal marriage.

It is one thing to argue that others are wrong to deny us something and another to argue that what they would deny us is something we should fight for the right to have. I do not deny that others are wrong to exclude same-sex lovers and lovers of different races from the rights of marriage. I question only whether we should fight for those rights, even if we do not intend to exercise them. Suppose that slave owning in some mythical society were denied to otherwise free women, on the ground that such women as slave owners would pervert the institution of slavery. Women (both free and unfree) could (unfortunately) document empirically the falsity of beliefs underlying such grounds. It would not follow that women should fight for the right to own slaves, or even for the rights of other women to own slaves. Likewise, if marriage is a deeply flawed institution, even though it is a special injustice to exclude lesbians and gay men arbitrarily from participating in it, it would not necessarily advance the cause of justice on the whole to remove the special injustice of discrimination.

About same-sex marriage, I feel something like the way I feel about prostitution. Let us, by all means, *decriminalize* sodomy and so forth. Although marriage rights would be *sufficient* to enable lovers to have sex legally, such rights should not be *necessary* for that purpose. Where they *are* legally necessary and also available for protection against the social oppression of same-sex lovers, as for lovers of different races, there will be enormous pressure to marry. Let us not pretend that marriage is basically a good thing on the ground that durable intimate relationships are. Let us not be eager to have the state regulate our unions. Let us work to remove barriers to our enjoying of some of the privileges presently available only to heterosexual married couples. But in doing so, we should also be careful not to support discrimination against those who choose not to marry and not to support continued state definition of the legitimacy of intimate relationships. I would rather see the state *de*regulate heterosexual marriage than see it begin to regulate same-sex marriage.

As the child of parents married to each other for thirty-two years, I once thought I knew what marriage meant, even though laws vary from one jurisdiction to another and the dictionary, as Mohr notes, sends us around in a circle, referring us to "husband" and "wife," in turn defined by "marriage." Mohr argues convincingly that "marriage" need not presuppose the gendered concepts of "husband" and "wife."[8] I will not rehearse that ground here. History seems to support him. After reading cover to cover and with great interest John Boswell's *Same-Sex Unions in Premodern Europe*,[9] however, I no longer feel so confident that I know when a "union" counts as a "marriage." Boswell, who discusses many kinds of unions, refrains from using the term "marriage" to describe the same-sex unions he researched, even though they were sanctified by religious ceremonies. Some understandings of such unions, apparently, did not presuppose that the partners were not at the same time married to someone of the other sex.

Mohr, in his suggestions for improving marriage law by attending to the experience of gay men, proposes that sexual fidelity not be a requirement.[10] What would remain without such a requirement, from a legal point of view, sounds to me like mutual *adoption*, or guardianship. Adoption, like marriage, is a way to become next-of-kin. This could have substantial economic consequences. But is there any good reason to restrict mutual adoption to two parties at a time? If mutual adoption is what we want, perhaps the law of adoption is what we should use, or suitably amend. And yet the law of adoption is not without its problematic aspects, some similar to those of the law of marriage. For it does not specify precisely a guardian's rights and responsibilities. Perhaps those who want legal contracts with each other would do better to enter into contracts the contents and duration of which they specifically define.

As noted above, my partner of the past decade is not a domestic partner. She and I form some kind of fairly common social unit that, so far as I know, remains nameless. Along with such namelessness goes a certain invisibility, a mixed blessing to which I will return. We do not share a domicile (she has her house; I have mine). Nor do we form an economic unit (she pays her bills; I pay mine). Although we certainly have fun together, our relationship is not based simply on fun. We share the sorts of mundane details of daily living that Mohr finds constitutive of marriage (often in her house; often in mine). We know a whole lot about each other's lives that the neighbors and our other friends will never know. In times of trouble, we are each other's first line of defense, and in times of need, we are each other's main support. Still, we are not married. Nor do we yearn to marry. Yet if marrying became an option that would legitimate behavior otherwise illegitimate and make available to us social securities that will no doubt become even more important to us as we age, we and many others like us might be pushed into marriage. Marrying under such conditions is not a totally free choice.

Because of this unfreedom, I find at least four interconnected kinds of problems with marriage. Three may be somewhat remediable in principle, although if they were remedied, many might no longer have strong motives to marry. I doubt that the fourth problem, which I also find most important, is fixable.

The first problem, perhaps easiest to remedy in principle (if not in practice) is that employers and others (such as units of government) often make available only to legally married couples benefits that anyone could be presumed to want, married or not, such as affordable health and dental insurance, the right to live in attractive residential areas, visitation rights in relation to significant others, and so forth. Spousal benefits for employees are a significant portion of many workers' compensation. Thus married workers are often, in effect, paid more for the same labor than unmarried workers.[11] This is one way in which people who do not have independent access to an income often find themselves economically pressured into marrying. Historically, women have been in this position oftener than men, including, of course, most pretwentieth-century lesbians, many of whom married men for economic security.

The second problem is that even though divorce by mutual consent is now generally permitted in the United States, the consequences of divorce can be so difficult that many who should divorce do not. This to some extent is a continuation of the benefits problem. But also, if one partner can sue the other for support or receive a share of the other's assets to which they would not otherwise have been legally entitled, there are new economic motives to preserve emotionally disastrous unions.

The third issue, which would be seriously troublesome for many lesbians, is that legal marriage as currently understood in northern democracies is monogamous in the sense of one *spouse* at a time, even though the law in many states no longer treats "adultery" (literally "pollution") as criminal. Yet many of us have more than one long-term intimate relationship during the same time period. Any attempt to change the current understanding of marriage so as to allow plural marriage partners (with plural contracts) would have economic implications that I have yet to see anyone explore.

Finally, the fourth problem, the one that I doubt is fixable (depending on what "marriage" means), is that the legal rights of access that married partners have to each other's persons, property, and lives make it all but impossible for a spouse to defend herself (or himself), or to be protected against torture, rape, battery, stalking, mayhem, or murder by the other spouse. Spousal murder accounts for a substantial number of murders each year. This factor is made worse by the presence of the second problem mentioned above (difficulties of divorce that lead many to remain married when they should not), which provides motives to violence within marriages. Legal marriage thus enlists state support for conditions conducive to murder and mayhem.

The point is not that all marriages are violent. It is not about the frequency of violence, although the frequency appears high. The points are, rather, that the institution places obstacles in the way of protecting spouses (however many) who need it and is conducive to violence in relationships that go bad. Battery is, of course, not confined to spouses. Lesbian and gay battery is real.[12] But the law does not protect unmarried batterers or tend to preserve the relationships of unmarried lovers in the way that it protects husbands and tends to preserve marriages.

Why, then, would anyone marry? Because it is a tradition, glorified and romanticized. It grants status. It is a significant (social) mark of adulthood for women in patriarchy. It is a way to avoid certain hassles from one's family of origin and from society at large—hassles to oneself, to one's lover (if there is only one), and to children with whom one may live or whom one may bring into being. We need better traditions. And women have long needed other social marks of adulthood and ways to escape families of origin.

Under our present exclusion from the glories of legal matrimony, the usual reason why lesbians or gay men form partnerships and stay together is because we care for each other. We may break up for other kinds of reasons (such as one of us being assigned by an employer to another part of the country and neither of us being able to afford to give up our jobs). But when we stay together, that is usually because of how we feel about each other and about our life together. Consider how this basic taken-for-granted fact might change if we could marry with the state's blessings. There are many material benefits to tempt those who can into marrying, not to mention the improvement in one's social reputation as a reliable citizen (and for those of us who are not reliable citizens, the protection against having a spouse forced to testify against us in court).

Let us consider each of these four problems further. The first was that of economic and other benefits, such as insurance that employers often make available only to marrieds, the right of successorship to an apartment, inheritance rights, and the right to purchase a home in whatever residential neighborhood one can afford. The attachment of such benefits to marital status is a problem in two respects. First, because the benefits are substantial, not trivial, they offer an ulterior motive for turning a lover relationship into a marriage—even for pretending to care for someone, deceiving oneself as well as others. As Emma Goldman argued in the early twentieth century, when marriage becomes an insurance policy, it may no longer be compatible with love.[13] Second, the practice of making such benefits available only to marrieds discriminates against those who, for whatever reason, do not marry. Because of the first factor, many heterosexuals who do not fundamentally approve of legal marriage give in and marry anyhow. Because of the second factor, many heterosexual feminists, however, refuse legal marriage (although the state may regard their relationships as common-law marriages).

Now add to the spousal benefits problem the second difficulty, that of the consequences of getting a divorce (for example, consequences pertaining to shared property, alimony, or child-support payments and difficulties in terms of access to children), especially if the divorce is not friendly. Intimate partnerships beginning from sexual or erotic attraction tend to be of limited viability, even under favorable circumstances. About half of all married couples in the United States at present get divorced, and probably most of the other half should. But the foreseeable consequences of divorce provide motives to stay married for many spouses who no longer love each other (if they ever did) and have even grown to hate each other. Staying married ordinarily hampers one's ability to develop a satisfying lover relationship with someone new. As long as marriage is monogamous in the sense of one *spouse* at a time, it interferes with one's ability to obtain spousal benefits for a new lover. When spouses grow to hate each other, the acccss that was a joy as lovers turns into something highly dangerous. I will return to this.

Third, the fact of multiple relationships is a problem even for relatively good marriages. Mohr, as noted, argues in favor of reforming marriage so as not to require sexual exclusiveness rather than officially permitting only monogamy. Yet he was thinking not of multiple spouses, but of a monogamous marriage in which neither partner expects sexual exclusiveness of the other. Yet one spouse per person is monogamy, however promiscuous the spouses may be. The advantages that Mohr enumerates as among the perks of marriage apply only to spouses, not to relationships with additional significant others who are not one's spouses. Yet the same reasons that lead one to want those benefits for a spouse can lead one to want them for additional significant others. If lesbian and gay marriages were acknowledged in northern democracies today, they would be legally as monogamous as heterosexual marriages, regardless of the number of one's actual sexual partners. This does not reflect the relationships that many lesbians and gay men have or want.

Boswell wrote about same-sex unions that did not preclude simultaneous heterosexual marriages.[14] The parties were not permitted to formalize unions with more than one person of the same sex at a time, however. Nor were they permitted to have children with a person of the other sex to whom they were not married. Thus, in a certain restricted sense, each formal union was monogamous, even though one could have both kinds at once.

Christine Pierce argues, in support of the option to legalize lesbian and gay marriages, that lesbian and gay images have been cast too much in terms of individuals—she mentions *The Well of Loneliness*,[15] for example—and not enough in terms of relationships, especially serious relationships involving long-term commitments.[16] Marriage gives visibility to people "as couples, partners, family, and kin," a visibility that lesbians and gay men have lacked and that could be important to dispelling negative stereotypes and assumptions that our relationships do not embody many of the same ideals as those of many heterosexual couples, partners, family, and kin.[17] This is both true and important.

It is not clear, however, that legal marriage would offer visibility to our relationships as they presently exist. It might well change our relationships so that they became more like heterosexual marriages, loveless after the first few years but hopelessly bogged down with financial entanglements or children (adopted or products of turkey-baster insemination or previous marriages), making separation or divorce (at least in the near future) too difficult to contemplate, giving rise to new motives for mayhem and murder. Those who never previously felt pressure to marry a lover might confront not just new options, but new pressures and traps.

My views on marriage may surprise those familiar with my work on the military ban.[18] For I have argued against the ban and in favor of lesbian and gay access to military service, and I argued that even those who disapprove of the military should object to wrongful exclusions of lesbians and gay men. In the world in which we live, military institutions may well be less dispensable than marriage, however in need of restraint military institutions are. But for those who find legal marriage objectionable, should I be moved here by what moved me there—namely, that it is one thing not to exercise an option and another to be denied the option, that denying us the option for no good reason conveys that there is something wrong with us, thereby contributing to our public disfigurement and defamation, and that these considerations give us good reasons to protest being denied the option even if we never intend to exercise it? I am somewhat, but not greatly moved by such arguments in this case. The case of marriage seems to me more like the case of slavery than like that of the military.

Marriage and military service are in many ways relevantly different. Ordinarily, marriage (like slavery) is much worse, if only because its impact on our lives is usually greater. Marriage is supposed to be a lifetime commitment. It is at least open-ended. When available, it is not simply an option, but tends to be coercive, especially for women in a misogynist society. For those who choose it, it threatens to be a dangerous trap. Military service is ordinarily neither a lifetime nor an open-ended commitment; one signs up for a certain number of years. During war, one may be drafted (also for a limited time) and, of course, even killed, but the issue has not been whether to draft lesbians and gay men. Past experience shows that gay men will be drafted in war, even if barred from enlistment in peace. When enlistment is an option, it does not threaten to trap one in a relationship from which it will be extremely difficult to extricate oneself in the future. There is some analogy with the economically coercive aspect of the marriage "option." Because those who have never served are ineligible for substantial educational and health benefits, many from low- (or no-) income families enlist to obtain such things as college education and even health and dental insurance. However, the service one has to give for such benefits as an enlistee is limited compared to spousal service. Being killed is a risk in either case.

In such a context, pointing out that many marriages are very loving, not at all violent, and proclaim to the world two people's honorable commitment to each other seems to me analogous to pointing out, as many slave owners did, that many slave owners were truly emotionally bonded with their slaves, that they did not whip them, and that even the slaves were proud and honored to be the slaves of such masters.

Some of the most moving stories I hear in discussions of gay marriage point out that the care rendered the ill by families is a great service to society and that the chosen families of gay AIDS patients deserve to be honored in the same way as any family based on a heterosexual union. The same, of course, applies to those who care for any lesbian or gay cancer patients or for those with severe disabilities or other illnesses. But is this a service to society? Or to the state? The state has a history of depending on families to provide care that no human being should be without in infancy, illness, and old age. Lesbians and gay men certainly have demonstrated our ability to serve the state in this capacity as well as heterosexuals. But where does this practice leave those who are not members of families? Or those who object on principle to being members of these unions as sanctified by the state?

To remedy the injustices of discrimination against lesbians, gay men, and unmarried heterosexual couples, many municipalities are experimenting with domestic-partnership legislation. This may be a step in the right direction, insofar as it is a much more voluntary relationship, more specific, more easily dissolved. Yet, partners who are legally married need not share a domicile unless one of them so chooses; in this respect, eligibility for the benefits of domestic partnership may be more restrictive than that for marriage. And the only domestic-partnership legislation that I have seen requires that one claim only one domestic partner at a time, which does not distinguish it from monogamous marriage.[19]

Whatever social unions the state may sanction, it is important to realize that they become state-defined, however they may have originated. One's rights and privileges as a spouse can change dramatically with one's residence, as Betty Mahmoody discovered when she went with her husband to Iran for what he had promised would be a temporary visit.[20] She found after arriving in Iran that she had no legal right to leave without her husband's consent, which he then denied her, leaving as her only option for returning to the United States to escape illegally (which she did). Even if a couple would not be legally recognized as married in a particular jurisdiction, if they move from another jurisdiction in which they *were* legally recognized as married, they are generally legally recognized as married in the new jurisdiction, and they are held to whatever responsibilities the new jurisdiction enforces. The case of Betty Mahmoody is especially interesting because it involves her husband's right of access. Spousal rights of access do not have the same sort of contingency in relation to marriage as, say, a right to family rates for airline tickets.

Marriage is a legal institution the obligations of which tend to be highly informal—that is, loosely defined, unspecific, and inexplicit about exactly what one is to do and about the consequences of failing. In this regard, a marriage contract differs from the contract of a bank loan. In a legal loan contract, the parties' reciprocal obligations become highly formalized. In discharging the obligations of a loan, one dissolves the obligation. In living up to marriage obligations, however, one does not dissolve the marriage or its obligations; if anything, one strengthens them. As I have argued elsewhere, the obligations of marriage and those of loan contracts exhibit different paradigms.[21] The debtor paradigm is highly formal, whereas the obligations of spouses tend to be relatively informal and fit better a paradigm that I have called the "trustee paradigm." The obligations of a trustee, or guardian, are relatively abstractly defined. A trustee or guardian is expected to exercise judgment and discretion in carrying out the obligations to care, protect, or maintain. The trustee *status* may be relatively formal—precisely defined regarding dates on which it takes effect, compensation for continuing in good standing, and the consequences of losing the status. But consequences of failing to do this or that specific thing may not be specified or specifiable, because what is required to fulfill duties of caring, safekeeping, protection, or maintenance can be expected to vary with circumstances, changes in which may not be readily foreseeable. A large element of discretion seems ineliminable. This makes it difficult *to hold a trustee accountable for abuses* while the status of trustee is retained, and it also means that it is difficult to prove that the status should be terminated. Yet the only significant sanction against a trustee may be withdrawal of that status. Spousal status and parental status fit the trustee model, rather than the debtor model, of obligation. This means that it is difficult to hold a spouse or a parent accountable for abuse.

Central to the idea of marriage, historically, has been intimate access to the persons, belongings, activities, even histories of each other. More important than sexual access, marriage gives spouses physical access to each other's residences and belongings, and it gives access to information about each other, including financial statuses, that other friends and certainly the neighbors do not ordinarily have. For all that has been said about the privacy that marriage protects, what astonishes me is how much privacy one gives up in marrying.

This mutual access appears to be a central point of marrying. Is it wise to abdicate legally one's privacy to that extent? What interests does it serve? Anyone who in fact cohabits with another may seem to give up similar privacy. Yet, without marriage, it is possible to take one's life back without encountering the law as an obstacle. One may even be able to enlist legal help in getting it back. In this regard, uncloseted lesbians and gay men presently have a certain advantage—which, by the way, "palimony" suits threaten to undermine by applying the idea of common-law marriage to same-sex couples.[22]

Boswell argued that, historically, what has been important to marriage is consent, not sexual relations. But consent to what? What is the point of marrying? Historically, for the propertied classes, he notes, the point of heterosexual marriage was either dynastic or property concerns or both. Dynastic concerns do not usually figure in arguments for lesbian or gay marriage. Although property concerns do, they are among the kinds of concerns often better detached from marriage. That leaves as a central point of marriage the legal right of cohabitation and the access to each other's lives that this entails.

It might still be marriage if sexual exclusivity, or even sex, were not part of it, but would it still be marriage if rights of cohabitation were not part of it? Even marrieds who voluntarily live apart retain the *right* of cohabitation. Many rights and privileges available to marrieds today might exist in a legal relationship that did not involve cohabitation rights (for example, insurance rights, access to loved ones in hospitals, rights to inherit, and many other rights presently possessed by kin who do not live with one another). If the right of cohabitation is central to the concept of legal marriage, it deserves more critical attention than philosophers have given it.

Among the trappings of marriage that have received attention and become controversial, ceremonies and rituals are much discussed. I have no firm opinions about ceremonies or rituals. A far more important issue seems to me to be the marriage *license*, which receives hardly any attention at all. Ceremonies affirming a relationship can take place at any point in the relationship. But a license is what one needs to initiate a legal marriage. To marry legally, one applies to the state for a license, and marriage, once entered into, licenses spouses to certain kinds of access to each other's persons and lives. It is a mistake to think of a license as simply enhancing everyone's freedom. One person's license, in this case, can be another's prison. Prerequisites for marriage licenses are astonishingly lax. Anyone of a certain age, not presently married to someone else, and free of certain communicable diseases automatically qualifies. A criminal record for violent crimes is, to my knowledge, no bar. Compare this with other licenses, such as a driver's license. In Wisconsin, to retain a driver's license, we submit periodically to eye exams. Some states have more stringent requirements. To obtain a driver's license, all drivers have to pass a written and a behind-the-wheel test to demonstrate knowledge and skill. In Madison, Wisconsin, even to adopt a cat from the humane society, we have to fill out a form demonstrating knowledge of relevant ordinances for pet guardians. Yet to marry, applicants need demonstrate no knowledge of the laws pertaining to marriage, nor any relationship skills nor even the modicum of self-control required to respect another human being. And once the marriage exists, the burden of proof is always on those who would dissolve it, never on those who would continue it in perpetuity.

Further disanalogies between drivers' and marriage licenses confirm that in our society there is greater concern for victims of bad driving than for those of bad marriages. You cannot legally drive without a license, whereas it is now in many jurisdictions not illegal for unmarried adults of whatever sex to cohabit. One can acquire the status of spousehood simply by cohabiting heterosexually for several years, whereas one does not acquire a driver's license simply by driving for years without one. Driving without the requisite skills and scruples is recognized as a great danger to others and treated accordingly. No comparable recognition is given the dangers of legally sanctioning the access of one person to the person and life of another without evidence of the relevant knowledge and scruples of those so licensed. The consequence is that married victims of partner battering and rape have less protection than anyone except children. What is at stake are permanently disabling and life-threatening injuries, for those who survive. I do not, at present, see how this vulnerability can be acceptably removed from the institution of legal marriage. Measures could be taken to render its disastrous consequences less likely than they are presently but at the cost of considerable state instrusion into our lives.

The right of cohabitation seems to me central to the question of whether legal marriage can be made an acceptable institution, especially to the question of whether marriage can be envisaged in such a way that its partners could protect themselves, or be protected, adequately against spousal rape and battery. Although many states now recognize on paper the crimes of marital rape and stalking and are better educated than before about marital battering, the progress has been mostly on paper. Wives continue to die daily at a dizzying rate.

Thus I conclude that legalizing lesbian and gay marriage, turning a personal commitment into a license regulable and enforceable by the state, is probably a very bad idea and that lesbians and gay men are probably better off, all things considered, without the "option" (and its consequent pressures) to obtain and act on such a license, despite some of the immediate material and spiritual gains to some of being able to do so. Had we any chance of success, we might do better to agitate for the abolition of legal marriage altogether.

· CHAPTER TWENTY-SEVEN ·

A Gay and Straight Agenda

RICHARD D. MOHR

Richard D. Mohr, professor of philosophy at the University of Illinois, Urbana, and a noted gay intellectual, offers his perspective on the cultural changes currently underway regarding homosexuality. After examining and rejecting the claim that gay rights are somehow "special rights," he goes on to suggest that gayness should be viewed as an important property, rather than as an irrelevant property, of people who are gay. Mohr concludes by emphasizing the ongoing need for gay politics to focus on cultural transformation.

• • • • •

Pat Buchanan is right when he says that America is in the midst of a cultural war, a war for the hearts, minds, and soul of the nation, a war over America's understanding of itself. By "culture," I mean the system of ideas and values by which a society defines itself to itself and whose maintenance constitutes the life of that society.

The nation's current struggle with lesbian and gay issues is a central battle, possibly *the* central battle in this war over culture. For lesbians and gay men now constitute for the culture's mind its paradigm of deviance, its exemplar of degeneracy. For instance, it used to be that you could tell who the bad guy was in a movie because he wore a black hat. Now he is simply coded as gay—as in *Braveheart*, *J.F.K.*, and *The Silence of the Lambs.* Sexual queerness has become the culture's sign of the disreputable pure and simple. For some time now, gayness has been the culture's distilled essence of what not to be—and so too by contraposition, gayness determines what one should be. In the culture's mind, gayness has served as evil made concrete and given life.

It is chiefly, then, in its engagement with lesbian and gay issues that the nation will decide whether it is fundamentally committed to the general values of liberty and equality, which enable individuals to lead their lives by their own lights and with equal dignity, or whether the nation is committed to some specific vision of what constitutes proper living—be it leftist or rightist, populist or elitist, secular or religious—but that, in any case, the nation is willing to demand of and impose upon everyone.

A Taboo's Ending

So the stakes are high, and the proximate political scene after the 1996 elections does not seem promising—if it ever was. Still, I suggest that America is at a turning point on gay issues and is undergoing an important structural change that bodes well for the long haul. It is now at least acceptable to inquire about these issues in public discussion. The taboo blanketing talk of lesbians and gay men is dissolving.

The clearest indicator of this shift can be found in the mass media. As recently as the mid-1980s, the *New York Times* refused to print the word "gay"; now it carries more gay news than the national gay newsmagazine *The Advocate.* On April 30, 1997, forty-two million watched the episode of ABC's comedy *Ellen* in which, for the first time, a lead character announced herself to be gay. Except for the Academy Awards, the episode was the highest-rated show on ABC all year. Only one ABC affiliate—that in Birmingham, Alabama—refused to carry the program. A week earlier, the actress who plays Ellen came out of the closet on the cover of *Time* magazine. According to the *New York Times,* the same television season that saw Ellen come out featured twenty-two other openly gay characters in recurring roles.

And little barriers to talk are falling as well. Along with the usual hateful remarks and telephone numbers, truckstop graffiti now include elaborate commentaries on homophobia and gay life in America. Children can now read a nationally syndicated comic strip with a gay male character. And for the first time, New York City's elected community school boards have been joined by open lesbians, who will raise gay issues affecting the education and the moral training of the young.

The importance of lifting the taboo on gay speech and gay issues should not be underestimated. First, it will have—is having—a significant effect on the public lives of many nongay people, and there are slews of them. Studies have shown that, on gay issues, people are greatly affected in their opinions by how they think other people will perceive them. Taboos encourage, indeed enforce, the aping of opinions from one person to the next, causing them to circulate independently of both critical assessment and authentic feeling. The result is that many nongay people feel socially required to be gay-fearing or gay-hating, even when they are not homophobic by personal inclination. Many people do not on their own feel hostile to gays but feel compelled to go along with the rituals that degrade and silence gay life, lest they themselves be viewed as morally suspect. As the taboos over talking about gay men and lesbians break down, so too will the echoes and apings that have maintained so many of the social forces directed against gays. Nongay people will be able to express in public contexts their own real feelings. Gay Congressman Barney Frank has perceptively noted that people are now less homophobic than they think they should be. This fortuitous and surprising gap provides great opportunity to those working for gays' justice.

Further, with the ending of the taboo, anti-gay forces can no longer automatically count on visceral responses of revulsion to carry the day. This change, in turn, has several corollary consequences. First, with the collapse of the taboo, it is increasingly difficult for society to maintain the rituals that demonize gays and lesbians. Rituals of taboo create an eerie supernatural realm unspeakably beyond the pale and then populate it with ghouls and monsters. With the taboo's collapse, gays, in society's eye, are becoming less like monsters and demons and more like hippies and Mormons—or in Newt Gingrich's favored analogy, like alcoholics. Maybe not something nice, maybe something odd, something one might not chose for oneself, but gays are no longer something monstrous, repulsive, unthinkably abject. Though not an ideal attainment, this state does mark major cultural change.

Second, note that it is okay to know and be around alcoholics and Mormons—and now, even around gay folk. Without demonization, it is hard, perhaps impossible, to conceptualize homosexuality as a vampire-like corruptive contagion, a disease that spreads itself to the pure and innocent by mere proximity. This change of conceptualization will eventually abate the stereotype of the gay man as child molester and, more generally, as sex-crazed predator. And this change has already markedly lessened for straight folk both fear *of* association and guilt *by* association. For really the first time, it is now possible for gays to have straight allies, people who cannot instantly and effectively be tarred and dismissed with the slur "queer lover."

Finally, the collapse of the taboo and its visceral effects means that anti-gay forces now have to argue for and give rational accounts of their positions. And the good news here is that the arguments are all on the side of gays. Moreover, the very ground rules of reasoned discourse—

commitments to honesty, consistency, and fair play—make it inherently a force for liberalism.

The Right senses and fears the cultural shift underway. It seems tacitly to recognize that to win the cultural wars, it must shore up the deeply fractured taboo. Just look where Christian supremacists and other rightists are investing their energies. They are *not* trying to "punish the sin" by restoring sodomy laws to states without them. Rather, they want to get "the sinner" to shut up. Thus, they chiefly focus on representations of gay life. They target museum exhibitions, the funding of the arts, school curricula, public television, gay books, and the presence of gays in parades. Their referendum drives, which swept the country in the late 1970s and again in the early 1990s, should also be seen as part of this pattern. Usually cast as constitutional amendments to state or city charters, the referenda attempt preemptively to sweep the whole "gay thing" off the political agenda, out of the arena of public discussion. But however successful as politics, the Right's referendum strategies necessarily tripped over themselves as a cultural project, even before the Supreme Court declared them unconstitutional in its May 1996 case *Romer v. Evans.* For the more the Right has to talk about things gay, the more the taboo collapses. Pat Buchanan's, Pat Robertson's, and Newt Gingrich's yammering on about the gay thing, however mindless and wrongheaded, undoes them.

The new opportunity for reasoned discourse raises the question, though, "Now that we can talk, what should we be saying?" Especially for nongay people, the long night of socially enforced silence on gay issues has largely left a void in social thinking. Media channels are open, but little of substance is being conveyed. This is true even of your "higher class" of mass media, like the *New York Times.* During 1993, the *Times* ran six op-eds on gays in the military, but not one of them reached the sexual politics on which the issue pivoted.

I want to do three things here of a general programmatic nature. First, I want to offer a response to the currently most common anti-gay canard, the charge that somehow gay rights are special rights and that gays are not a "legitimate" minority. To date, that two-word sound bite—"special rights"—has managed to paralyze gays and our straight allies. Second, I want to sketch a positive (dare I say) agenda, suggesting that we need to begin thinking more about gayness as a relational property, as a form of human bonding that is important to, rather than irrelevant to, how people lead their lives. Finally, I will suggest that, for the foreseeable future, those committed to realizing justice for gays should adopt a broad-gauged politics directed toward changing the general culture, rather than a narrow politics focused on specific legislative reform.

Special Rights?

In the nation's current political discourse, everyone presumes that if a right can be framed as special, it is somehow illegitimate. So not surprisingly, rhetorical flourishes of both liberals and conservatives make proprietary claims upon equality. For instance, in Cincinnati's famous 1993 anti-gay referendum initiative, the group launching the referendum baptized its organization Equal Rights, Not Special Rights, while the gay side called its organization Equality Cincinnati. Both sides claimed equality as their principle. Clearly, America is confused about the nature of equality.

The "no special rights" side seems to take equality to mean equal opportunity or identical access to whatever government is offering by way of privileges or possessions. In consequence, these people suppose that any legislation that gives something to a specified group violates equality. And, indeed, equality understood as equal opportunity is quite entrenched in America's folk rhetoric of justice. For example, the chief federal agency for the enforcement of the 1964 Civil Rights Act is called the Equal Employment Opportunity Commission.

Still, this sense of equality does not capture all, or even the core, of what equality is. Equality is at heart a principle of nondegradation. It asserts that people are not to be held in lesser regard—as morally lesser beings—independently of their actions. Consider laws that bar interracial marriage. In form, they treat blacks and whites the same, for they deny them identical access—to each other. Blacks can't marry whites; whites can't marry blacks. What, then, is the inequality in antimiscegenation laws? They are inequitable not because they denied equality of opportunity to blacks, but because they were part of a system that holds blacks in morally lesser regard independently of what they individually do. Such laws view blacks as dirty, loathsome, and abject.

Or again, consider the nation's paradigmatically racist joke: "What do you call a black millionaire physicist who's just won the Nobel Prize?" The answer, usually shouted, is the N-word. Notice that the person in the joke has availed himself of and realized opportunity as fully as anyone could. The joke's butt could not launch a suit against the joke's teller claiming that he has been denied access to some right, some freedom, some opportunity, for he has it all. Rather, the joke's belittling fun presumes that the physicist's disesteem is entirely a matter of a perceived status having nothing to do with his actions. In the joke's moral system, which is to say America's popular morality, this person never could be equal no matter what he did. Equality, then, in the first instance, is a principle of nondegradation, and only derivatively, if at all, it is a principle about similar access.

The "no special rights" people, then, are understandably but profoundly confused about equality. It is true that equality is a right that everyone has, for everyone has a right not to be treated as a morally lesser being because of some status he or she has, some group membership independent of any action that puts the person in the group. Yet, given this understanding of equality, both assertions and violations of it will always need to make reference to the specific treatment of some group, will turn on whether some group has been degraded. Here, justice requires looking to the specifics of history and social custom, not to generic human nature, in order to determine whether some law or treatment promotes or violates equality.

Have gays as a group historically been treated as less than fully human, as loathsome and abject beings? The answer from the social record of jokes, slang, symbolic legislation (like military policy and unenforced sodomy laws), family policy, religious teachings, and medical history is a clear yes. The courts, then, should grant gays constitutional equal protections against degrading treatments by governments. And legislatures should pass civil rights legislation for gays that militates against the humiliation, degradation, and insult caused by discrimination in housing, employment, and public accommodations. Such laws are not special treatments in any way that is morally objectionable. To the contrary, they are treatments that equality as a general principle of nondegradation requires.

Please note that this understanding of what groups deserve mention in civil rights legislation and constitutional law—what the political and religious Right likes to call "legitimate minorities"—should not be and indeed is not limited to groups whose defining feature is tethered to an immutable characteristic such as skin color or biological sex. Rather, this understanding of equality easily assigns minority status to religious groups and the disabled, even when the disability in question results from an action for which the disabled person is responsible, such as a botched suicide or a negligently caused accident. In other words, it is okay for the gay rights movement to give up its dogged adherence to the belief that gayness is an immutable characteristic caused by chromosomes, hormones, irreversibly congested Oedipal complexes, or whatever. We don't need that commitment in order to deserve not being degraded. And it is worth reminding evangelicals that they are protected by civil rights legislation and constitutional law that treats them as a legitimate minority even though their religion, by their own accounting, is something they chose. The relevant moral and political question is whether the members of the group are socially held in lesser regard *independently* of their actions.

Though now chiefly targeted at gays, the rhetoric of "no special rights" is covertly an attack on all civil rights legislation, since all civil rights legislation warrantably specifies which groups fall within its protections. This rhetoric of "no special rights," which currently is also being recycled through the affirmative action debates, is particularly insidious, for it uses the "good vibes" associated with assertions of equality to advance what is really a mentality of division and divisiveness, of "us versus them." Therefore, other legally protected minorities—blacks, Hispanics, women, Mormons, Jews, the disabled—all need to be particularly mindful that gay rights do not steal anything from them, but rather help solidify the very principle of equality in virtue of which they have such rights in the first place. It is perhaps no accident that in June 1995, six months after Newt Gingrich's second-in-command, Dick Armey, got away with calling Barney Frank a "fag," Armey called the NAACP "a misguided special interest organization."[1]

Gayness as Connection

This argument against the charge "special rights" provides gays a defensive shield. But what should be the positive aims of the fight for gay rights? Too often, I suggest, gays and our allies have argued that gayness does not matter, that gayness is irrelevant, that, after all, gays are just humans, too. These rhetorical moves are inadvertent, even well-intentioned, erasures of gayness. They suppose that gayness is a property, like having an eye color or wearing an earring, that a person could have in isolation from all other people and without significant effect on others. And it is perfectly understandable that gays and others have taken up this strategy.

First, the gay rights movement for the longest part of its duration was singularly focused on civil rights legislation. Indeed, in the 1970s and early 1980s, if one used the expression "gay rights," one was presumed to mean legislated civil rights for gays. And in this context, if gayness is irrelevant in general, then presumptively it is irrelevant to flying a plane, serving a meal, teaching a class, or being a cop. And so it would be unjust for society to discriminate on the basis of sexual orientation, since sexual orientation is not the basis for anything—or so it goes. Second, if gayness is an irrelevant property, then it is easier to make analogies between gayness and race, especially if (as per one of the Right's main fantasies) race is viewed simply as a matter of skin color and not as a system of cultural expectations and subcultural inventions. Finally, the view that gayness doesn't matter had a strategic pull. If a person's being gay was an irrelevant (or, even better, an immutable) characteristic, then other people would not have to be so afraid of it, afraid that they might be it or get it. As a tactic against persecution and a plea for tolerance, it wasn't a bad strategy. But if we stick with it now, we will be stuck indeed.

In our social projects, we need to be thinking of gayness not as something that a person can have in splendid isolation from others; it takes two to be queer. Instead, we need to conceptualize gayness as a relational property, a connection between persons, a human bonding, one in need of attendance and social concern. Gayness places or situates the gay person in social and interpersonal contexts. It is both an outflow and a reception of perception, desire, affection, and knowing—both biblical and cognitive. We need to stop claiming that gayness is an irrelevant property and begin recognizing that it is crucially important to people's lives and identities, to social history, and, as the gay studies crowd is showing, to understanding central components of many of society's most important concepts and cherished institutions.

Following this line of thought into the realm of public policy, we need to take more seriously that fundamental form of connectedness that is sex and cease treating the sexual law reform movement as an awkward political and educational stepchild. Sodomy law reform has never been a central part of the gay rights movement—apparently because sex is just too embarrassing to deal with. Indeed, sodomy law reform started before the gay rights movement got off the ground, when in 1961 Illinois became the first state to have "consenting adult laws." And the reform movement had ground nearly to a halt by the time the gay rights movement got up a head of steam. Nearly half the states still have sodomy laws; in five of these, the laws apply only to gay sex. Though the Nevada legislature dropped its sodomy law in 1993, it was the first state to do so in a decade. None has done so since. And court challenges have not had much success since 1986, when in *Bowers v. Hardwick,* the U.S. Supreme Court upheld what it dubbed "homosexual sodomy" laws against privacy claims based on the federal Constitution.

Now, admittedly, sodomy laws are not frequently enforced, but even unenforced, they have many collateral effects, for example, in employment and custody cases. The courts use them to justify other forms of discrimination against gays, to deny gays equal protection rights, and to destroy gay families. More than this, unenforced sodomy laws tell gays and lesbians, "You are scum." And, on the plane of the nation's ideals, their denying gays and lesbians sex tells gays and lesbians,"You are alone. Your being is not a form of connection."

Add to this the sexual gloom emanating from the AIDS crisis, and it is time now not only to defend sex against this tide, but to valorize it, indeed to acknowledge that it is one of the central values of human life: as the chief portal to ecstasy, as the satisfaction of a recurrent natural need, and as the near occasion of, undergirding for, and necessary prompt to love.

Strategically, nothing is to be gained and potentially much is to be lost by avoiding these issues, especially as it seems that the nation is again, as in the early 1930s, heading into an intensely antisexual period, even into sexual hysteria. Signs of this hysteria include Clinton's December 1994 firing of his surgeon general, Joycelyn Elders, for suggesting that masturbation might be a legitimate subject to raise in sex education classes; the 1995 flap over Calvin Klein jeans ads as kiddie porn; and Congress's imposition of so-called decency censorship on the Internet, purportedly to "save our children."

Strategies of appeasement certainly do not work here. In 1994, under pressure from the United States instigated by Jesse Helms, the United Nations threw out the International Lesbian and Gay Association (ILGA) from its UN advisory position even after ILGA acquiesced to U.S. and UN demands that it throw out of its group membership the North American Man-Boy Love Association. This tawdry series of events shows that strategies of appeasement, avoidance, and silence simply strengthen the Right's hand. At both federal and state levels, the country is currently passing Soviet-style sex-offender laws. Some require the registration and publicizing of released sex offenders; others provide for lifetime custodial incarceration. Given that gay men are the culture's sign for the sexual predator and child molester, these frankly fascistic laws should be seen as having anti-gay forces as their engine and gays themselves as their cultural targets, even if they are crafted in orientation-neutral language. Gays, especially gay conservatives, are sticking their heads dangerously in the sand when they systematically refuse to discuss sex. And straight folk, too, may have to overcome some personal uneasiness if they are to be of help here.

Sex as connectedness is woven into other important dimensions of our lives. It is a necessary part and positive contribution to marital relations; it supports and shapes the whole as a foundation does a house. And this is why friendships, whatever their emotional and spiritual intensity, lack the warmth and depth of love relationships. There is a kernel of truth in the Catholic doctrine that a marriage unconsummated is not a marriage at all. In understanding gayness as connectedness, we need to begin paying more attention to issues of gay marriage, domestic partnership, and child rearing. We cannot simply cede the "family values" agenda to the Right.

Caught up in the old defensive gayness-doesn't-matter mode, the national gay lobbying and litigative groups have been slow to take up these issues. The Lambda Legal Defense Fund, for instance, though now a champion for gay marriage, was a Johnny-come-lately in challenges to laws barring same-sex marriage; indeed, it positively discouraged such suits. Here, "the people" far outstripped their "leaders" in recognizing social needs and setting political agendas.

Again, that's because gayness matters. For gays, sexuality affects—is a foreground presence in—everyday existence, whereas for straights, sexuality, especially what might be called "heterosexual presumption," is an unacknowledged background phenomenon. For straights, sexuality is like the air at room temperature: pervasive and dominant, yet entirely unnoticed. This socially induced asymmetry, which parallels a similar asymmetry between racial whiteness and blackness, unjustifiably permits straights to accuse gays of being obsessed with sex should gays make any mention of sex at all, even while straights' lives themselves are pervasively structured by sexuality. The reason that gay marriage has become such a major issue for gays is that both gayness and marriage have their roots in everyday existence. Marriage becomes a way of incorporating gayness as connectedness into the everyday. To put it somewhat poetically, marriage is intimacy given substance through the medium of day-to-day living. Marriage is the fused intersection of love's sanctity and necessity's demand.

Currently, society and its discriminatory impulse make gay coupling very difficult. Still, even against oppressive odds, gays and lesbians have shown an amazing tendency to nest. The portraits of gay and lesbian committed relationships that emerge from ethnographic studies, like Kath Weston's *Families We Choose*, suggest that in the ways lesbian and gay couples arrange their lives, they fulfill the definition of marriage in an exemplary manner. Both the development of intimacy through choice and the proper valuing of love are interwoven in the day-to-day activities of gay couples. Choice improves intimacy. It makes sacrifices meaningful. It gives love its proper weight. Those lesbian and gay couples who have survived the odds show that the structure of more usual couplings is not a matter of destiny, but one of personal responsibility. The so-called basic unit of society turns out not to be a unique atom, but one that can adopt different parts and be adapted to different needs.

The required blending of intimacy and the everyday explains much of the legal content of marriage. Marital law promotes the patient attendance that such life requires (by providing for privacy, nurture, support, and persistence), and it protects against the occasions when necessity is cussed rather than opportune, especially when life is marked by changed circumstance—crisis, illness, or destruction. It should not be surprising, then, that gays and lesbians—as a matter of pride and need—are shifting issues of family life to the top of their political agenda. Gay sex, gay love, gay life, and gay presence all matter.

Progress Report

Paradoxically, across this range of issues, the law is, in general, moving backward even as society is moving forward. As a backlash to the Hawaii Supreme Court's broad hints that it will soon require the legal acknowledgment of gay marriages, sixteen state legislatures in 1996 wrote specific requirements of heterosexuality into their former neutrally worded marriage laws. And immediately prior to the 1996 federal elections, Congress passed and the president signed into law the so-called Defense of Marriage Act, which bars any federal acknowledgment of same-sex marriages and spares the states from having to recognize out-of-state same-sex marriages. In response to a smattering of bench-level cases granting second-parent adoptions to gay couples, a number of states have begun barring gay adoptions.

By contrast to such government retrenchments, cultural and social forms are cutting a different, if difficult, path. Take religion. Mainline Protestant denominations are now gripped in titanic struggles over issues of gay connectedness. This should not come as a surprise given the Christian commitment to an ethics of love, an ethics that says you are not alone. And despite the spate of heresy trials, excommunications, disfellowships, and the like in the 1990s, I expect that by the end of the new millennium's first decade, most mainline denominations will come around on gay issues, acknowledging that, yes, gay love is love, and recognizing in turn that gay love calls for social husbandry and institutional reform. The Unitarian-Universalist Association, the United Church of Christ, and Reform Judaism have already come around to this position.

In increasing numbers, large and even conservative corporations, like Walt Disney Studios and Coors Brewing, are offering their gay employees domestic-partnership benefits. But the most amazing and sudden progress on this range of issues has come from the most surprising of quarters: the insurance industry. Surprising, because insurance companies are inherently conservative institutions. Their well-being and very existence depend upon the usual, the normal, the average, the steady, the predictable. Only cats hate change more. Yet the February 6, 1995, issue of *National Underwriter* quotes experts claiming that "[n]ow most carriers . . . offer domestic partner benefits under group coverage." It used to be that companies and towns wishing to offer domestic-partnership benefits to gay employees were unable to find any insurer at all willing to carry their health policies. Now, they have the luxury of competitive bids. Barriers to gay couples directly getting joint insurance are dropping, too. In January 1995, the Allstate Insurance Company began writing homeowner policies for same-sex couples that are identical to those of heterosexually married couples.[2] Another sign of private-sector progress afoot is the new practice of some newspapers to run announcements of holy union ceremonies among their wedding notices. Especially in contrast to what state governments have been doing, such private-sector progress is the sort of thing that might inspire one to become a libertarian.

Change the Culture

And this private-sector progress is occurring because the culture of the United States itself is changing. Especially in light of the 1994 and 1996 federal elections, the gay movement now and for the foreseeable future needs to advance as a general cultural project rather than a narrowly political one. While not shunning such standard political forms as electing officials and passing bills, gays should not be focusing on them either. Consistent political progress will be made only when we change the general cognitive atmosphere and the effective feelings of the "common man," constituted and driven as they are by stereotypes, bogeys, and vestiges of taboo. The needed change will occur not by accommodating these feelings or pandering to populist dogmas, but by changing the culture that bears and nurtures them. Change the culture, and political forms will, in general and in the long run, follow suit. And don't underestimate the strength of cultural forces. Remember that it was blue jeans and videocassettes that won the Cold War for the West, not hydrogen bombs and uranium-clad tanks.

Now, the good news is that gays and their allies have or are rapidly coming to have, creative access to the machinery of cultural change: the media, even media empires, the arts, books, magazines, editorial pages, educational forums, talk shows, movies, plays, computer networks, and religious study groups. To a large degree, hope for a better gay future lies along these vectors of transformation, rather than in posterpaint and cardboard.

When gays do choose to invest in politics narrowly understood, strategies should be chosen with an eye to their effect in transforming culture, rather than specifically as means of garnering votes. Political participation itself is a cultural form that, if played out correctly, can have positive cultural consequences even in the face of electorial failure. Note that a placard that says "No on 2: Stop Discrimination" does no educating, changes

Compare: if *X* is president, then *X* lives in the White House; Chelsea Clinton is not president, therefore Chelsea Clinton does not live in the White House.

21. Actually, Williams makes the point with regard to celibacy, while making an analogy between celibacy and homosexuality. See chapter 6 of this volume.

22. All biblical quotations are from the New Revised Standard Version.

23. See also Deut. 23:19, Lev. 25:35–37, Neh. 5:7–10, Jer. 15:10, Ezek. 22:12, and Luke 6:35. For a fuller explication of the analogy between homosexuality and usury, see John Corvino, "The Bible Condemned Usurers, Too," *Harvard Gay and Lesbian Review* 3, no. 4 (Fall 1996): 11–12.

24. See Richard P. McBrien, *Catholicism,* study ed. (San Francisco: Harper & Row, 1981), 1020.

25. *Loving v. Virginia,* 388 U.S. 1967.

26. One might object here that I am equivocating on the term "relationship," since throughout the paper I have been discussing acts, not relationships. But I maintain that Tommy and Jim's sexual act is *relational* in a way that Tommy and Fido's simply could not be. Even apart from their love for each other, Tommy and Jim have capacities for mutual communication and respect that Tommy and Fido simply do not have. Thus, one can approve of Tommy and Jim's sexual act without implying anything about Tommy and Fido's (possible) sexual acts: the two are fundamentally different.

Chapter 2: Bradshaw, "A Reply to Corvino"

1. Many of the contributors to this volume do so. See also Jeffrey Satinover, *Homosexuality and the Politics of Truth* (Grand Rapids, MI: Baker Books, 1996). Much of this work could be read as a point-by-point rebuttal of the section of Corvino's essay dealing with harm. To take only a single example, Corvino cites the University of Chicago study as evidence that promiscuity among homosexuals is not as great as widely believed (note 11). But, as Satinover observes, this study was meant to be a representative sampling of the entire population and therefore included only a relatively small number of homosexuals. Other studies involving larger numbers of homosexuals have continued to show high rates of promiscuity.

2. I ignore an argument popular in antiquity to the effect that homosexual acts both manifest and intensify a sort of character defect. See chapter 3 by John Finnis in this volume; cf. Ramsay MacMullen, "Greek Attitudes to Roman Love," *Historia* 27 (1982): 484–502.

3. See A. Swidler, ed., *Homosexuality and World Religions* (Valley Forge, PA: Trinity Press, 1993).

4. See the exchange between Daniel A. Helminiak and Thomas E. Schmidt in chapters 7 and 8 of this volume.

5. I am aware, of course, that revisionists claim that the sin of the Sodomites was inhospitality. See Thomas Schmidt, *Straight and Narrow? Compassion and Clarity in the Homosexuality Debate* (Downers Grove, IL: InterVarsity Press, 1995), 86–89 for a decisive refutation.

6. See Schmidt, *Straight and Narrow?,* chapter 3.

7. Michael Grant, *The Twelve Caesars* (New York: Charles Scribner's Sons, 1975), 244.

8. C. S. Lewis, *Perelandra* (New York: Macmillan, 1965)

9. Lewis, *Perelandra,* 108–109.

10. Lewis, *Perelandra,* 110.

11. Diogenes Laertius, *Lives of the Eminent Philosophers,* ed. R. D. Hicks (Cambridge, MA: Harvard University Press, 1925) vii.123.

12. Cf. Eph. 4:25, "we are members [*mele,* literally 'limbs'] one of another."

13. William Shakespeare, *The Tempest*, v.1.183.

14. For a brilliant fictional exploration of the fragmentation of the person through the abuse of sex, see Walker Percy's novel *Love in the Ruins* (New York: Farrar, Straus & Giroux, 1971). See also John Wauck, "Fables of Alienation," *Human Life Review* (Spring 1991): 73–94.

Chapter 3: Finnis, "Sexual Orientation"

1. For Socrates, see for example Kenneth Dover, *Greek Homosexuality* (Cambridge, MA: Harvard University Press, 1978), 154–159; letter from Sir Kenneth Dover to John Finnis, dated 23 January 1994, in Finnis, "Law, Morality, and 'Sexual Orientation,'" *Notre Dame Journal of Law, Ethics & Public Policy* 9 (1995) 19, note 16; R. E. Allen, *The Dialogues of Plato* vol. 2 *The Symposium* (New Haven, CT: Yale University Press, 1991), 18; Gregory Vlastos, *Socrates, Ironist and Moral Philosopher* (Ithaca, NY: Cornell University Press, 1991), 38–39. For Plato, see for example Dover, *Greek Homosexuality*, 159; Allen, *Dialogues*, 18–19; Vlastos, *Platonic Studies* (Princeton, NJ: Princeton University Press, 1973/1981) 25; Anthony W. Price, *Love and Friendship in Plato and Aristotle* (Oxford University Press, 1990), 89, 224–5, 229–35. For Aristotle, see for example. Allen, *Dialogues*, 18; Price, *Love*, 225. See also Allen, *Dialogues*, 99–102 for a critique of Martha Nussbaum, whose attempts to show that Socrates, Plato, and Aristotle approved of homosexual conduct are dissected in Finnis, "Law," 17–25, and Finnis, "'Shameless Acts' in Colorado: Abuse of Scholarship in Constitutional Cases," *Academic Questions* 7 (1994) 19–41, note 10.

2. See Plato, *Gorgias* 494–495, especially 494e1–5, 495b3.

3. Aristotle, *Ethics* VIII,12: 1162a16–30; see also the probably pseudo-Aristotle, *Oeconomica* I,3–4: 1343b12–1344a22; III.

4. Plutarch, *Life of Solon* 20, 4; *Erotikos* 769.

5. See *Erotikos* 768d–770a

6. Stephen Macedo, "The New Natural Lawyers," *Harvard Crimson*, October 28, 1993, writes: "In effect, gays can have sex in a way that is open to procreation, and to new life. They can be, and many are, prepared to engage in the kind of loving relations that would result in procreation—were conditions different. Like sterile married couples, many would like nothing better." Here fantasy has taken leave of reality. Anal or oral intercourse, whether between spouses or between males, is no more a biological union "open to procreation" than is intercourse with a goat by a shepherd who fantasizes about breeding a faun; each "would" yield the desired mutant "were conditions different." Biological union between humans is the *inseminatory* union of male genital organ with female genital organ; in most circumstances it does not result in generation, but it is the behavior that unites biologically because it is the behavior which, as behavior, is suitable for generation. (See also note 11 below.)

7. For the whole argument, see Germain Grisez, *The Way of the Lord Jesus*, vol. 2, *Living a Christian Life* (Quincy, IL: Franciscan Press, 1993), 634–9, 648–54, 662–4.

8. Plato, *Gorgias* 494–5, esp. 494e1–5, 495b3.

9. Plutarch, *Life of Solon* 20, 3.

10. Or deliberately contracepted, which I omit from the list in the text only because it would no doubt not now be accepted by secular civil law as preventing consummation— a failure of understanding.

11. "All we can say is that conditions would have to be more radically different in the case of gay and lesbian couples than sterile married couples for new life to result from sex . . . but what is the moral force of that? The new natural law theory does not make moral judgments based on natural facts." Macedo, "New Natural Lawyers." Macedo's phrase "based on" equivocates between the first premises of normative arguments (which must be normative) and the

other premise(s) (which can and normally should be factual and where appropriate can refer to natural facts such as that the human mouth is not a reproductive organ).

12. The criminal law upheld in *Bowers v. Hardwick* seems to me unsound in principle. But it is proper, in principle, to prohibit the advertising or marketing of homosexual services, the maintenance of places of resort for homosexual activity, and the promotion of homosexualist "lifestyles" via education and public media of communication, and to withhold recognition from homosexual "marriages" and forbid the adoption of children by homosexually active people, and so forth.

13. John Finnis, "Law, Morality, and 'Sexual Orientation,'" *Notre Dame Law Review* 69 (1994) 1049; reprinted with additions, *Notre Dame Journal of Law, Ethics & Public Policy* 9 (1995) 11.

14. See Aquinas, IV *Sent.* q. 26 q. 1 a. 4c (= *Summa Theologiae* Supp. q. 41 a. 4c); d. 31 q. 2 a. 2 (= Supp. q. 41 a. 5) ad 2 & ad 4; q. 2 a. 3c (= Supp. q. 49 a. 6c) & tit. & obj. 1; *Commentary on I Corinthians,* c.7 ad v. 6 [329]; *Summa Theologiae* II-II q. 154 a. 8 ad 2; *De Malo* q. 15 a. 1c. For a much fuller treatment of Aquinas' sex ethics, see John Finnis, *Aquinas* (Oxford: Oxford University Press, 1998), chapter V.4.

15. All extra-marital sex (and even conditional assent {consensus} to it) is contrary to nature *inasmuch as (and because)* it is contrary to reason's requirements: see Aquinas, *De Malo,* q. 15 a. 1 ad 7.

16. See Aquinas, *Summa Theologiae* I-II q. 94 a. 2c. In his treatment of sex ethics, Aquinas usually refers to the good of marriage, insofar as it is always at stake in the spouses' sexual activity, as the good of *fides,* i.e. of *mutual commitment in marriage.* The literal translation of *fides* would be faith(fullness), but in English this suggests merely absence of infidelity (i.e. of sexual relations with other persons), whereas Aquinas explains (IV *Sent.* d. 31 q. 1 a. 2c & ad 3 (= Supp. q. 49 a. 2c & ad 3); *Commentary on I Cor.* c. 7.1 ad v. 2 [318]) that marital *fides* involves also, and primarily, a positive willingness to be maritally, including sexually, united (on a basis of mutuality and absolute equality in initiating or requesting intercourse).

17. Thoroughly misrepresented in John T. Noonan, *Contraception* (Cambridge, MA: Harvard U.P., 1965, 1986); John Boswell, *Christianity, Social Tolerance, and Homosexuality* (Chicago: University of Chicago Press, 1980). Koppelman's view of Aquinas (and so of the whole tradition) has (not perhaps unreasonably, but certainly unfortunately) been reliant upon these writers: see the longer version of his present essay: Koppelman, "Is Marriage Inherently Heterosexual?," *American Journal of Jurisprudence* 42 (1997); and for a discussion of Noonan's and Boswell's misreadings, see Finnis, "The Good of Marriage and the Morality of Sexual Relations," *American Journal of Jurisprudence* 42 (1997).

18. The marriage of a couple who have reason to believe that they are incapable of generating children is considered, once the basic lines of the argument are in place, below.

19. Marriage is a complex but unified good inasmuch as its unitive goodness is inseparable from its procreative significance (even where procreation is *per accidens* impossible). Aquinas' train of thought sets out one way of understanding and acknowledging this inseparability.

20. See Aquinas, *De Malo* q. 15 a. 2 ad 4; IV *Sent.* d. 33 q. 1 a. 3 sol. 2 (= Supp. q. 65 a. 4c).

21. In grading the gravity of *types* of sexual vice, Aquinas does not try to estimate the culpability of particular acts of particular persons, culpability which may sometimes be much diminished by passion that fetters freedom and/or by confusion of mind (e.g. ideology, fantasy) that obscures rational deliberation towards choice.

22. So John Corvino is mistaken in asserting that the tradition represented by Aquinas is inconsistent (see chapter 1 in this volume); it is perfectly consistent to judge both that all non-marital sex acts are wrong and that "intimacy and pleasure" are (as Aquinas vigorously teaches) acceptable motives for spouses to engage in marital intercourse of a kind which

actualizes and expresses both sides of the two-sided good of marriage: their marital commitment to each other and marriage's orientation towards procreation (even if procreation cannot actually follow from this or even any act of intercourse of this couple in their circumstances).

23. Koppelman sometimes, inconsistently, speaks as if they are not reproductive if and only if they belong to people who are completely sterile, e.g., "a woman whose diseased uterus has been removed."

24. See also the response to Macedo on this point by Robert P. George and Gerard V. Bradley, "Marriage and the Liberal Imagination," *Georgetown Law Journal* 84 (1995) 301 at 311 n. 32.

25. The organic unity which is instantiated in an act of the reproductive kind is not, as Macedo and Koppelman reductively imagine, the unity of penis and vagina. It is that unity of the man and the woman which is consummated in their intentional, consensual *act* of seminal emission/reception in the woman's reproductive tract.

26. See further George and Bradley, "Marriage."

27. Not yet disentangled from the Catholic teaching on marriage she is "changing her mind" away from, Callahan just takes for granted that there will only be one partner. The assumption, as we shall see, is groundless.

28. See the surveys and discussions by homosexual sociologists and writers cited in Germain Grisez, *The Way of the Lord Jesus* vol. 3 *Difficult Moral Problems* (Quincy, IL: Franciscan Press, 1997) 108, 110; also John F. Harvey, *The Truth about Homosexuality* (Ignatius Press, 1996).

29. Koppelman (like Leo Strauss) has not fully, or at all, come to grips with the radically teleological character of contemporary "Darwinian" biology's account of the molecular-biological genetic primordia, fundaments, or engine of evolution. But that, like the half-truth of the "disenchantment" of the universe, is an issue with no bearing on the present argument.

30. Those, however, who search out infertile spouses, choosing them *precisely for their infertility*, may well be manifesting the kind of contempt for the marital good which Philo Judaeus condemned in the rather confused passage from which Koppelman and Boswell quote some overheated fragments.

Chapter 4: Koppelman, "Homosexual Conduct"

1. Germain Grisez, *The Way of the Lord Jesus, Vol. 2: Living a Christian Life* (Quincy, IL: Franciscan Press, 1993), 570; Grisez is quoting Genesis 2:24.

2. Ibid., 653.

3. Ibid.

4. Robert P. George, "Recent Criticism of Natural Law Theory," *University of Chicago Law Review* 55 (1988): 1371, 1392.

5. Sidney Callahan, "Why I Changed My Mind: Thinking about Gay Marriage," *Commonweal* (April 22, 1994): 7.

6. Grisez, *The Way*, 634.

7. Ibid., 570.

8. Ibid., 618; emphasis added.

9. John Finnis, chapter 3 in this volume.

10. See John Boswell, *Christianity, Social Tolerance, and Homosexuality: Gay People in Western Europe from the Beginning of the Christian Era to the Fourteenth Century* (Chicago: University of Chicago Press, 1980), 148.

11. Philo, *De specialibus legibus,* 3.36, translated and quoted in Boswell, *Christianity,* 155.

12. Grisez, *The Way,* 572.

13. Ibid., 572–73.

14. Ibid., 637.

15. Ibid., 689.

16. See Charlotte J. Patterson, "Children of Lesbian and Gay Parents," *Child Development* 63 (1992): 1025 .

17. Finnis, chapter 3 in this volume.

18. Ibid.

19. Stephen Macedo, "The New Natural Lawyers," *Harvard Crimson* (October 28, 1993).

20. Finnis, chapter 3 in this volume.

21. Stephen Macedo, "Homosexuality and the Conservative Mind," *Georgetown Law Journal* 84, no. 2 (1995): 280.

22. Grisez, *The Way,* 634.

23. Germain Grisez, *The Way of the Lord Jesus,* vol. 1 (Quincy, IL: Franciscan Press, 1993), 68; emphasis added.

24. Leo Strauss, *Natural Right and History* (Chicago: University of Chicago Press, 1953), 8.

25. With apologies to Robert Nozick, whose famous comparison of doctoring, the essential goal of which is healing the sick, and "schmoctoring," the essential goal of which is earning money for the practitioner, I have borrowed here. See Robert Nozick, *Anarchy, State, and Utopia* (New York: Basic Books, 1974), 235.

26. The question thus phrased, with its implicit allusion to Nozick, was put to me by Michael Bratman.

27. John Finnis, *Fundamentals of Ethics* (Oxford: Clarendon Press, 1983), 44; emphases in original.

28. Nozick, *Anarchy,* 42–45.

29. Ibid., 43.

30. Finnis, *Fundamentals,* 37–42.

31. Grisez, *The Way,* vol. 1, 208.

32. See Finnis, *Fundamentals,* 48.

33. Grisez, *The Way,* vol. 2, 650.

34. John M. Finnis, "Personal Integrity, Sexual Morality and Responsible Parenthood," *Anthropos: Rivistadi di Studi Sulla Persona e la Famiglia* 1 (1985): 43, 47.

35. Grisez, *The Way,* vol. 2, 650.

36. Ibid., vol. 1, 124.

37. Ibid., vol. 2, 664.

38. Ibid., 654.

39. Thus Macedo observes (in "Homosexuality and the Conservative Mind" [273n53]) that, while it would plainly be bad to plug into the experience machine for life, it is unclear why it would be bad to plug into it for short periods occasionally. Finnis has addressed this objection in *Fundamentals of Ethics* (48):

> [W]e should warn anyone contemplating a limited period on the machine that he had better arrange *in advance* for someone else to unplug him. For anyone plugged into the machine is unlikely to be capable, *de facto,* of understanding the desirability of

> those goods of activity, authenticity and reality which give reason for unplugging; or, if he can in some sense understand those goods while submerged in his world of mere experience, he is unlikely to be motivated by them. Both our powers of intelligent discernment and our intelligent desire to act intelligently (i.e., for the sake of understood goods) are likely to be overwhelmed by the massively possessive experience of feelings, satisfactions, etc. Some such submerging of reason by passions is well-known to us in our own daily life, is it not?

But this simply shows that plugging into the experience machine is *dangerous*, not that it is *bad in itself*. While pleasure has an addictive quality that a prudent person will recognize, it does not follow that one should never act for the sake of pleasure alone.

40. Grisez, *The Way*, vol. 1, 105.

41. Ibid., vol. 2, 650.

42. Ibid.

43. Ibid., vol. 1, 139.

44. Germain Grisez, Joseph Boyle, and John Finnis, "Practical Principles, Moral Truth, and Ultimate Ends," *American Journal of Jurisprudence* 32 (1987): 99, 141.

45. Grisez, *The Way*, vol. 2, 650–651.

46. Ibid., 537.

47. Ibid., 536–537.

48. Robert P. George and Gerard V. Bradley, "Marriage and the Liberal Imagination," *Georgetown Law Journal* 84, no. 2 (1995): 317.

49. Stephen Macedo, "Reply to Critics," *Georgetown Law Journal* 84, no. 2 (1995): 330, 332.

50. Paul Baumann, "An Incarnational Ethic: Listening to One Another," *Commonweal* (January 28, 1994): 19. I am grateful to Paul Sigmund for calling my attention to this article.

51. Ibid., 19.

Chapter 7: Helminiak, "The Bible on Sexuality"

1. George Peabody Gooch, *History and Historians in the Nineteenth Century* (New York: Longmans, Green & Co., 1913).

2. Daniel A. Helminiak, *What the Bible Really Says about Homosexuality* (San Francisco: Alamo Square Press, 1994). Unless otherwise indicated, the New Revised Standard Version is quoted throughout.

3. Robin Scroggs, *Homosexuality in the New Testament: Contextual Background for Contemporary Debate* (Philadelphia: Fortress Press, 1983).

4. L. William Countryman, *Dirt, Greek, and Sex: Sexual Ethics in the New Testament and Their Implications for Today* (Philadelphia: Fortress Press, 1988).

5. John Boswell, *Christianity, Social Tolerance, and Homosexuality: Gay People in Western Europe from the Beginning of the Christian Era to the Fourteenth Century* (Chicago: University of Chicago Press, 1980).

6. Richard B. Hays, "Relations Natural and Unnatural: A Response to John Boswell's Exegesis of Romans 1," *Journal of Religious Ethics* 14, (1986): 184–215. Thomas E. Schmidt, *Straight and Narrow? Compassion and Clarity in the Homosexuality Debate* (Downers Grove, IL: InterVarsity Press, 1955).

7. Victor Paul Furnish, "Homosexuality," in *The Moral Teaching of Paul* (Nashville, TN: Abingdon Press, 1979), 52–83. See also Victor Paul Furnish, "The Bible and Homosexuality:

Reading the Texts in Context," in Jeffrey S. Siker, ed., *Homosexuality in the Church: Both Sides of the Debate,* (Louisville, KY and Westminster: John Knox Press, 1994), 18–35.

8. Bernadette J. Brooten, *Love between Women: Early Christian Responses to Female Homoeroticism.* (Chicago: University of Chicago Press, 1996).

Chapter 8: Schmidt, "Romans 1:26–27 and Biblical Sexuality"

1. I attempt to keep references to a minimum in this essay. Readers who seek more detailed arguments and thorough documentation should consult chapters 2–5 of my book, *Straight and Narrow? Compassion and Clarity in the Homosexuality Debate* (Downers Grove, IL: InterVarsity Press, 1995). For a comparison of modern revisionist views to those of ancient Gnostics, see my article "Sex, Heresies, and Half-Forgotten Manuscripts," *Regeneration Quarterly* 1, no. 3 (Summer 1995): 23–25.

2. L. William Countryman, *Dirt, Greed, and Sex* (Philadelphia: Fortress Press, 1988). This argument was first advanced by John Boswell, *Christianity, Social Tolerance, and Homosexuality* (New Haven, CT: Yale University Press, 1980), 112–113n72. Countryman extends the thesis with a much more integrative, comprehensive, and detailed account of the terminology of the passage (see esp. 98–123 for the material I refer to below). Daniel A. Helminiak provides a useful summary of these and other revisionists in *What the Bible Really Says about Homosexuality* (San Francisco: Alamo Square Press, 1994).

3. Countryman, *Dirt, Greed, and Sex,* 123.

4. Ibid., 86.

5. Ibid., 104–109.

6. Helminiak, *What the Bible Really Says,* 65.

7. Boswell, *Christianity,* 109–113.

Chapter 9: Byne and Lasco, "Origins of Sexual Orientations"

1. Fernando Nottebohm, "The Origins of Vocal Learning," *American Naturalist* 105 (1972): 116–140.

2. Graeme Hanson and Lawrence Hartmann,"Latency Development in Prehomosexual Boys," in Robert Cabaj and Terry Stein, eds., *The Textbook of Homosexuality* (Washington, D.C.: American Psychiatric Press, 1996), 253–266.

3. Sandor Rado, *Adaptional Psychodynamics: Motivation and Control,* Jean Jameson and Henriette Klein, eds. (New York: Science House, 1969).

4. John Money, Mark Schwartz, and Viola G. Lewis, "Adult Erotosexual Status and Hormonal Masculinization and Demasculinization: 46,XX Congenital Virilizing Adrenal Hyperplasia and 46,XY Androgen-Insensitivity Syndrome Compared," *Psychoneuroendocrinology* 9 (1984) 405–414.

5. Richard C. Freidman and Jennifer Downy, "Neurobiology and Sexual Orientation: Current Relationships," *Journal of Neuropsychiatry and Clinical Neuroscience* 5 (1993): 131–153.

6. J. Michael Bailey and K. J. Zucker, "Childhood Sex-typed Behavior and Sexual Orientation: A Conceptual Analysis and Quantitative Review," *Developmental Psychology* 31, no. 1 (1995): 43–55.

7. Hanson and Hartmann, "Latency Development," 253–266.

8. Richard Isay, *Being Homosexual: Gay Men and Their Development* (New York: Avon, 1989).

9. Daryl J. Bem, chapter 10 of this volume.

10. For a more detailed review of the neuroendocrine literature, see William Byne and Bruce Parsons, "Human Sexual Orientation: The Biologic Theories Reappraised," *Archives of General Psychiatry* 50 (March 1993): 228–239.

11. Dörner, 1976, quoted in H. F. L. Meyer-Bahlburg, "Psychoendocrine Research on Sexual Orientation: Current Status and Future Options," *Progress in Brain Research* 61 (1982): 375–398.

12. Robert J. Stoller and Gilbert H. Herdt "Theories of Origins of Male Homosexuality: A Cross-Cultural Look," *Archives of General Psychiatry* 42, no. 4 (April 1985): 399–404.

13. Robert W. Goy and Bruce S. McEwen, *Sexual Differentiation of the Brain* (Cambridge, MA: MIT Press, 1980).

14. Diana Miller, "Why Discussions of Sexual Orientation Make My Head Spin," Presentation at symposium no. 55, "Psychiatric Attempts to Change Sexual Orientation," 148th annual meeting of the American Psychiatric Association, Miami, FL, 1995.

15. Goy and McEwen, *Sexual Differentiation.*

16. Meyer-Bahlburg, "Psychoendocrine Research."

17. Simon LeVay, "A Difference in the Hypothalamic Structure between Heterosexual and Homosexual Men," *Science* 253 (1993): 1034–1037.

18. William Byne, "Science and Belief: Psychobiological Research on Sexual Orientation," *Journal of Homosexuality* 28 (1995): 303–344.

19. Brian A. Gladue, Richard Green, and Ronald E. Hellman, "Neuroendocrine Response to Estrogen and Sexual Orientation," *Science* 225 (1984): 1496–1499; Gunter Dörner, Wolfgang Rhode, Fritz Stahl, Lothar Krell, and Wolf-Gunther Masius, "A Neuroendocrine Predisposition for Homosexuality in Men," *Archives of Sexual Behavior* 4 (1975): 1–8.

20. Byne and Parsons, "Human Sexual Orientation," 228–239.

21. Roger A. Gorski, J. H. Gordon, James E. Shryne, A.M. Southam, "Evidence for a Morphological Sex Difference within the Medial Preoptic Area of the Rat Brain," *Brain Research* 148 (1978): 336–346.

22. Simon LeVay and Dean Hamer, "Evidence for a Biological Influence in Male Homosexuality," *Scientific American* 270 (1994): 44–49.

23. Byne, "Science and Belief," 303–344.

24. LeVay, "A Difference,"1034–1037.

25. Byne and Parsons, "Human Sexual Orientation," 228–239; also discussed in William Byne and Edward Stein, "Ethical Implications of Scientific Research on the Causes of Sexual Orientation," *Health Care Analysis* (in press).

26. William Byne, "Biology and Homosexuality: Implications of Neuroendocrinological and Neuroanatomical Studies," in *Textbook of Homosexuality,* Cabaj and Stein, eds., 129–146.

27. Dick F. Swaab and Michel A. Hoffman, "An Enlarged Suprachiasmatic Nucleus in Homosexual Men," *Brain Research* 537 (1990): 141–148.

28. Byne, "Science and Belief," 303–344.

29. Katherine M. Bishop and Douglas Walston, "Sex Differences in the Human Corpus Callosum: Myth or Reality?" *Neuroscience and Biobehavioral Reviews* (in press).

30. John Money and Anke A. Ehrhardt, *Man and Woman, Boy and Girl* (Baltimore, MD: Johns Hopkins University Press, 1972).

31. Jennifer P. Macke et al., "Sequence Variation in the Androgen Receptor Gene Is Not a Common Determination of Male Sexual Orientation," *American Journal of Human Genetics* 53 (1993): 844–852.

32. Richard C. Pillard and James D. Weinrich, "Evidence of Familial Nature of Male Ho-

mosexuality," *Archives of General Psychiatry* 43 (1986): 808–812; J. Michael Bailey and Richard C. Pillard, "A Genetic Study of Male Sexual Orientation," *Archives of General Psychiatry* 48 (Dec. 1991): 1089–1096.

33. Bailey and Pillard, "Genetic Study."

34. Byne and Parsons, "Human Sexual Orientation"; Terry R. McGuire, "Is Homosexuality Genetic? A Critical Review and Some Suggestions," in John P. DeCecco and David Allen Parker, eds., *Sex, Cells, and Same-Sex Desire: The Biology of Sexual Preference,* (New York: Harrington Park Press, 1995), 115–146.

35. Dean H. Hamer, Stella Hu, Victoria L. Magnuson, Nan Hu, and Angela M. L. Pattatucci, "A Linkage between DNA Markers on the X Chromosome and Male Sexual Orientation," *Science* 261 (July 16, 1993): 321–327.

36. Discussed in Byne and Stein, "Ethical Implications."

37. McGuire, "Is Homosexuality Genetic?" 142.

Chapter 10: Bem, "The EBE Theory"

1. Alan P. Bell, Martin S. Weinberg, and Sue Kiefer Hammersmith, *Sexual Preference: Its Development in Men and Women* (Bloomington: Indiana University Press, 1981). The percentages in Table 10.1 have been calculated from the data given in the separately published appendix: Alan P. Bell, Martin S. Weinberg, and Sue Kiefer Hammersmith, *Sexual Preference: Its Development in Men and Women: Statistical Appendix* (Bloomington: Indiana University Press, 1981), 74–75, 77.

2. A summary review of retrospective studies appears in J. Michael Bailey, and Kenneth J. Zucker, "Childhood Sex-Typed Behavior and Sexual Orientation: A Conceptual Analysis and Quantitative Review," *Developmental Psychology,* 31 (1995) 43–55. Seven prospective studies are summarized in Kenneth J. Zucker, and Richard Green, "Psychological and Familial Aspects of Gender Identity Disorder," *Child and Adolescent Psychiatric Clinics of North America,* 2(1993): 513–542. The largest of these is fully reported in Richard Green, *The 'Sissy Boy Syndrome' and the Development of Homosexuality* (New Haven: Yale University Press, 1987).

3. Edward. A. Westermarck, *The History of Human Marriage,* (London: Macmillan, 1891). Observations on children of the kibbutzim will be found in Bruno Bettelheim, *The Children of the Dream* (New York: Macmillan, 1969); Albert Israel Rabin, *Growing Up in a Kibbutz* (New York: Springer, 1965); Joseph Shepher, "Mate Selection among Second Generation Kibbutz Adolescents and Adults: Incest Avoidance and Negative Imprinting," *Archives of Sexual Behavior* (1971): 1, 293–307; Melford E. Spiro, *Children of the Kibbutz* (Cambridge, MA: Harvard University Press, 1958); and Y. Talmon, "Mate Selection in Collective Settlements," *American Sociological Review* (1964,): 29, 481–508.

4. Gilbert Herdt, *Sambia: Ritual and Gender in New Guinea* (New York: Holt, Rinehart and Winston, 1987).

5. Horwicz, quoted in Henry Theophilus Finck, *Romantic Love and Personal Beauty: Their Development, Causal Relations, Historic and National Peculiarities* (London: Macmillan, 1887).

6. Elaine Walster, "Passionate Love," in Bernard I. Murstein, ed., *Theories of Attraction and Love* (New York: Springer, 1971): 85–99. Stanley Schachter and Jerome E. Singer, "Cognitive, Social, and Physiological Determinants of Emotional State," *Psychological Review* (1962): 69, 379–399.

7. Gregory L. White and Thomas D. Kight, "Misattribution of Arousal and Attraction: Effects of Salience of Explanations for Arousal," *Journal of Experimental Social Psychology,* (1984): 20, 55–64.

8. Peter W. Hoon, John P. Wincze, and Emily Franck Hoon, "A Test of Reciprocal Inhibi-

tion: Are Anxiety and Sexual Arousal in Women Mutually Inhibitory?" *Journal of Abnormal Psychology,* 86 (1977): 65–74; Sharlene A. Wolchik, Vicki E. Beggs, John P. Wincze, David K. Sakheim, David H., Barlow, and Matig Mavissakalian, "The Effect of Emotional Arousal on Subsequent Sexual Arousal in Men," *Journal of Abnormal Psychology,* 89 (1980): 595–598.

9. Two additional mechanisms for transforming exotic into erotic, the opponent process and imprinting, are discussed in the original version of this essay(see footnote on chapter–opening page), 326–327.

10. The twin studies are J. Michael Bailey and Richard C. Pillard, "A Genetic Study of Male Sexual Orientation," *Archives of General Psychiatry,* 48 (1991): 1089–1096; J. Michael Bailey, Richard C. Pillard, Michael C. Neale, and Yvonne Agyei, "Heritable Factors Influence Sexual Orientation in Women," *Archives of General Psychiatry,* 50 (1993): 217–223; and J. Michael Bailey and N. G. Martin, "A Twin Registry Study of Sexual Orientation," Paper presented at the annual meeting of the International Academy of Sex Research, Provincetown, MA, September, 1995.

11. For citations to the supporting evidence on these points, see the original version of this essay (see footnote on chapter-opening page), 328.

12. Several hypothetical scenarios have been offered. For a discussion of these and their shortcomings, see ibid., 328–329.

13. The evidence purporting to show a link between sexual orientation and prenatal hormones and brain neuroanatomy is discussed in the longer version of this essay (ibid., 329–330).

14. Ronald C. Fox, "Bisexual Identities," in Anthony R. D'Augelli and Charlotte J. Patterson, eds., *Lesbian, Gay and Bisexual Identities Over the Lifespan* (New York: Oxford University Press, 1995), 48–86.

15. Martin S. Weinberg, Colin J. Williams, and Douglas W. Pryor, *Dual Attraction: Understanding Bisexuality* (New York: Oxford University Press, 1994).

16. Edward I. Laumann, John H. Gagnon, Robert T. Michael, and Stuart Michaels, *The Social Organization of Sexuality: Sexual Practices in the United States* (Chicago: University of Chicago Press, 1994).

17. Sandra Lipsitz Bem, "The Lenses of Gender: Transforming the Debate on Sexual Inequality" (New Haven, CT: Yale University Press, 1993), vii.

18. This section has been prepared for this volume and does not appear in the original article.

19. "*Advocate* Poll results," *The Advocate* February 6, 1996, 8.

20. Green, "Psychological and Familial Aspects," 318.

Chapter 11: Stein, "Relevance of Scientific Research"

1. As quoted by John D'Emilio, *Sexual Politics, Sexual Communities: The Making of a Homosexual Minority in the United States, 1940–1970* (Chicago: University of Chicago Press, 1983), 153.

2. The most prominent studies are reviewed in Simon LeVay, *Queer Science: The Use and Abuse of Research on Homosexuality* (Cambridge, MA: MIT Press, 1996). For criticism of these theories, see William Byne and Bruce Parsons, "Sexual Orientation: The Biological Theories Reappraised," *Archives of General Psychiatry* 50 (1993); 228–239; Edward Stein, review of Simon LeVay's, *Queer Science: The Use and Abuse of Research on Homosexuality, Journal of Homosexuality,* (1997); and Edward Stein, *Sexual Desires: Science, Theory and Ethics* (Oxford, NY: Oxford University Press, 1997).

3. For discussion of the ethical issues, see Aaron Greenberg and J. Michael Bailey; "Do Biological Explanations of Homosexuality Have More Legal or Political Implications?" *Journal of Sex Research* 30 (1993), 245–251; Janet Halley, "Sexual Orientation and the Politics of Biology: A Critique of the New Argument from Immutability," *Stanford Law Review* 46 (1994), 503–568; and William Byne and Edward Stein, "Ethical Implications of Medical and Biological Research on the Causes of Sexual Orientation," *Health Care Analysis* 4 (1997).

4. Here, "biological" is meant to include hormonal, genetic, neurophysiological, and other such bases. It is not meant to include the sense of "biological" in which everything psychological is biologically based. Humans are the sort of entities that can have sexual orientations, while computers and one-celled organisms are not. Why? Because of our biological and psychological structure.

5. I do not here mean to be engaging in constitutional analysis of the equal protection clause of the Fourteenth Amendment or legal analysis of federal civil rights legislation. At issue here is the more abstract ethical and political question of whether a biological basis for homosexuality entails that lesbians and gay men deserve special protection against discrimination. For discussion of the legal issues, see Richard Mohr, *Gays/Justice* (New York: Columbia University Press, 1990), esp. chaps. 5–7; Morris Kaplan, "Autonomy, Equality, Community: The Question of Lesbian and Gay Rights," *Praxis International* 11 (1991), 195–213; and Cass Sunstein, "Sexual Orientation and the Constitution: A Note on the Relation between Due Process and Equal Protection," *University of Chicago Law Review* 55 (Fall 1988), 1161–1179.

6. For good critiques of the idea that homosexuality is "unnatural," see Mohr, *Gays/Justice*, 34–38; and Michael Ruse, *Homosexuality: A Philosophical Inquiry* (Oxford: Blackwell, 1988), 188–192. Both Mohr and Ruse conclude that biology will not tell us what is "natural" in any morally interesting sense.

7. See Edward O. Wilson, *On Human Nature* (Cambridge, MA: Harvard University Press, 1978), 142–147. For a summary and a sympathetic discussion of sociobiology's attempts to deal with homosexuality, see Michael Ruse, *Homosexuality*, esp. Chap. 6. For a careful (and damning) critique of the general program of sociobiology, see Philip Kitcher, *Vaulting Ambition: Sociobiology and the Quest for Human Nature* (Cambridge, MA: MIT Press, 1985). For critiques of sociobiological theories of homosexuality, see Douglas Futuyma and Stephen Risch, "Sexual Orientation, Sociobiology, and Evolution," *Journal of Homosexuality* 9 (1983–1984), 157–168; and Paul Bloom and Edward Stein, "Reasoning Why," *American Scholar* 60 (1990), 315–320.

8. Something like this premise is defended by Michael Levin, "Why Homosexuality Is Abnormal," *Monist* 67 (1984), 251–283. For a response, see Timothy Murphy, "Homosexuality and Nature: Happiness and the Law at Stake," *Journal of Applied Philosophy* 4 (1987), 195–204.

9. See Elliott Sober, *The Nature of Selection* (Cambridge, MA: MIT Press, 1984), esp. 97–102, for his discussion of the selection of/selection for distinction.

10. A philosophical cottage industry has developed around coming up with an account of the distinction between natural and unnatural (or perverted) sex. The founding essay is Thomas Nagel, "Sexual Perversion," *Journal of Philosophy* 66 (1969), 5–17. Important subsequent essays on this topic include Robert Solomon, "Sexual Paradigms," *Journal of Philosophy* 71 (1974), 336–345; and Alan Goldman, "Plain Sex," *Philosophy and Public Affairs* 6 (1977), 267–287. None of these three accounts appeal to biological evidence to ground the notion of natural sex. On all three of these accounts, homosexual sex is *not* unnatural sex—although see Sara Ruddick, "Better Sex," in Robert Baker and Frederick Elliston, eds., *Philosophy and Sex*, 2nd ed. (Buffalo, NY: Prometheus, 1984), 280–299. This is not to say that I agree with any of these accounts of what natural sex is. Insofar as I think there is a coherent sense of "natural" here, I agree with Nagel that it will be a *psychological* notion.

11. CBS News/*New York Times* Poll, February 9–11, 1993, showed that people who think that homosexuality is biologically based are more likely to favor lesbian and gay rights than those who do not.

12. For a suggestive early discussion of this question, see Lawrence Crocker, "Meddling with the Sexual Orientation of Children," in Onora O'Neill and William Ruddick, eds., *Having Children* (Oxford, NY: Oxford University Press, 1979), 145–154. For a more recent discussion, see Timothy Murphy, "Reproductive Controls and Sexual Destiny," *Bioethics* 4 (1990), 121–142. See also Edward Stein, "Choosing the Sexual Orientation of Children," unpublished manuscript.

13. Such moral arguments can be found, for example, in Mohr, *Gays/Justice*, and in Kaplan, "Autonomy, Equality, Community."

Chapter 12: Golden, "Women's Sexual Identities"

1. Adrienne Rich, "Compulsory Heterosexuality and Lesbian Existence," *Signs* 5 (Summer 1980): 631–660.

2. "Radicalesbians, Woman-Identified Women," in Ann Koedt, Ellen Levine, and Anita Rapone, eds., *Radical Feminism* (New York: Quadrangle Books, 1973).

3. Blanche Wiesen Cook, "Female Support Networks and Political Activism," *Chrysalis* 3 (1977): 43–61.

4. Ann Ferguson, "Compulsory Heterosexuality and Lesbian Existence: Defining the Issues," *Signs* 7 (Autumn 1981): 158–172.

5. Ibid., 166.

6. Jacquelyn Zita, "Compulsory Heterosexuality and Lesbian Existence: Defining the Issues," *Signs* 7 (Autumn 1981): 172–187.

7. Barbara Ponse, *Identities in the Lesbian World* (Westport, CT: Greenwood Press, 1978).

8. Lisa Orlando, "Loving Whom We Choose: Bisexuality and the Lesbian/Gay Community," *Gay Community News*, February 25, 1984.

9. Leon Festinger, *A Theory of Cognitive Dissonance* (Evanston, IL: Row, Peterson, 1957).

10. Vivienne Cass, "Homosexual Identity Formation: A Theoretical Model," *Journal of Homosexuality* 4 (Fall 1979): 219–235.

11. Susan Yarborough, "Lesbian Celibacy," *Sinister Wisdom* 11 (Fall 1979): 24–29.

12. Dorothy Dinnerstein, *The Mermaid and the Minotaur: Sexual Arrangements and Human Malaise* (New York: Harper & Row, 1976).

13. Nancy Chodorow, *The Reproduction of Mothering: Psychoanalysis and the Sociology of Gender* (Berkeley: University of California Press, 1978).

14. Beth Firestein, *Bisexuality: The Psychology and Politics of an Invisible Minority* (Thousand Oaks, CA: Sage, 1996).

15. Carla Golden, "What's in a Name? Sexual Self-Identification among Women," in R. Savin-Williams and K. Cohen, eds., *The Lives of Lesbians, Gays, and Bisexuals* (Fort Worth, TX: Harcourt Brace & Co., 1996), 229–249.

16. Simon LeVay, "A Difference in Hypothalamus Structure between Heterosexual and Homosexual Men," *Science* 253 (1991): 1034–1037.

17. J. Michael Bailey and Richard Pillard, "A Genetic Study of Male Sexual Orientation," *Archives of General Psychiatry* 48 (1991): 1089–1096.

18. Dean Hamer, Stella Hu, Victoria Magnuson, Nan Hu, and Angela Pattatucci, "A Linkage Between DNA Markers on the X Chromosome and Male Sexual Orientation," *Science* 261 (1993): 321–327.

19. J. Michael Bailey, Richard Pillard, Michael Neale, and Yvonne Agyei, "Heritable Factors Influence Sexual Orientation in Women," *Archives of General Psychiatry*, 50 (1993): 217–223.

20. Stella Hu, Angela Pattatucci, C. Patterson, L. Li, D. Fulker, S. Cherny, L. Kuglyak, and Dean Hamer, "Linkage between Sexual Orientation and Chromosome Xq28 in Males But Not Females," *Nature Genetics* 11 (1995): 248–256.

21. Angela Pattatucci, and Dean Hamer, "Development and Familiality of Sexual Orientation in Females," *Behavior Genetics* 25 (1995): 407–420.

22. See, for example: Laura Brown, "Lesbian Identities: Concepts and Issues," in A. D'Augelli and C. Patterson, eds., *Lesbian, Gay, and Bisexual Idenitites over the Lifespan* (Oxford, New York: Oxford University Press, 1995), 3–23; Kristin Esterberg, "Being a Lesbian and Being in Love: Constructing Identities through Relationships," *Journal of Gay and Lesbian Social Services* 1(1994): 57–84; Carla Golden, "What's in a Name?"; Paula Rust, " 'Coming Out' in the Age of Social Constructionism: Sexual Identity Formation among Lesbian and Bisexual Women," *Gender and Society* 7 (1993): 50–77; Vera Whisman, *Queer by Choice: Lesbians, Gay Men, and the Politics of Identity* (New York: Routledge, 1996).

Chapter 13: Suppe, "Explaining Sexuality"

1. D. Lester provides a helpful summary of the main etiological research from the late 1930s to the mid-1970s: *Unusual Sexual Behavior: The Standard Deviations* (Springfield, IL: Charles C. Thomas, 1975). Martin S. Weinberg and Alan P. Bell also give a comprehensive selection of abstracts of research up through about 1970: *Homosexuality: An Annotated Bibliography* (New York: Harper & Row, 1972). Michael Ruse critically evaluates much of the more recent research, as well as some earlier studies: *Homosexuality: A Philosophical Inquiry* (Oxford: Blackwell, 1988).

2. Suppe, "Explaining Homosexuality"; see footnote on chapter-opening page for full citation information.

3. Lynda I. A. Birke, "Is Homosexuality Hormonally Determined?" *Journal of Homosexuality* 6, no. 4 (1981): 35–49, reprinted in Noretta Koertge, ed., *Nature and Causes of Homosexuality: A Philosophic and Scientific Inquiry* (New York: Haworth Press, 1981); N. R. Gartrell, "Hormones and Homosexuality," in W. Paul, J. Weinrich, J. C. Gonsiorek, and M. E. Hotvedt, eds., *Homosexuality: Social, Psychological, and Biological Issues* (Beverly Hills, CA: Sage, 1982), 169–182; J. C. Gonsiorek, "Psychological Adjustment and Homosexuality," *Catalog of Selected Documents in Psychology* 7, no. 2 (1977): 45, and microfiche MS 1478 (available through the American Psychological Association); Lester, *Unusual Sexual Behavior*; W. Ricketts, "Biological Research on Homosexuality: Ansell's Cow or Occam's Razor?" *Journal of Homosexuality* 9, no. 4 (1984): 65–93, reprinted in J. DeCecco, ed., *Bisexual and Homosexual Identities: Critical Clinical Issues* (New York: Haworth Press, 1984); M. Ruse, "Are There Gay Genes? Sociobiology and Homosexuality," *Journal of Homosexuality* 6, no. 4 (1981): 5–34, reprinted in Koertge, ed., *Nature and Causes*; Ruse, *Homosexuality*; Edward Stein, "Evidence for Queer Genes: An Interview with Richard Pillard," *GLQ* 1 (1993).

4. Alan P. Bell, Martin S. Weinberg, and S. K. Hammersmith, *Sexual Preference: Its Development in Men and Women* (Bloomington: Indiana University Press, 1981); and Alan P. Bell, Martin S. Weinberg, and S. K. Hammersmith, *Sexual Preference: Its Development in Men and Women: Statistical Abstract* (Bloomington: Indiana University Press, 1981). For an evaluation of the adequacy of their sample, see my "The Bell and Weinberg Study: Future Priorities for Research on Homosexuality," *Journal of Homosexuality* 6, no. 4 (1981): 69–97; reprinted in Koertge, ed., *Nature and Causes.*

5. For summaries, see M. Shively and J. DeCecco, "Components of Sexual Identity,"

Journal of Homosexuality 2 (1976): 9–27; Frederick Suppe, "Curing Homosexuality," in R. Baker and F Elliston, eds., *Philosophy and Sex,* rev. ed. (Buffalo, NY: Prometheus, 1984), 391–420; Frederick Suppe, "In Defense of a Multidimensional Approach to Sexuality," *Journal of Homosexuality* 10, nos. 3–4 (1984): 7–14; and various papers in J. DeCecco and M. Shively, eds., *Bisexual and Homosexual Identities: Critical Theoretical Issues* (New York: Haworth Press, 1984), and in Kenneth Plummer, ed., *The Making of the Modern Homosexual* (Totowa, NJ: Barnes & Noble, 1981).

6. See, for example, Alan Bell, "Research on Homosexuality: Back to the Drawing Board," *Archives of Sexual Behavior* 4 (1975): 421–431.

7. D. Crane, *Invisible Colleges: Diffusion of Knowledge in Scientific Communities* (Chicago: University of Chicago Press, 1972).

8. See Frederick Suppe, "Credentialing Scientific Claims," *Perspectives on Science* 1 (1973): 153–203.

9. D. Shapere, *Reason and the Search for Knowledge* (Dordrecht, Netherlands: Reidel, 1984).

10. L. Laudan, *Progress and Its Problems: Towards a Theory of Scientific Growth* (Berkeley: University of California Press, 1977), and *Science and Values: The Aims of Science and Their Role in Scientific Debate* (Berkeley: University of California Press, 1984).

11. I. Lakatos, "Falsification and the Methodology of Scientific Research Programmes," in Lakatos and A. Musgrave, eds., *Criticism and the Growth of Scientific Knowledge* (Cambridge: Cambridge University Press, 1974), 91–196.

12. T. Kuhn, *Structure of Scientific Revolutions,* enlarged ed. (Chicago: University of Chicago Press, 1970).

13. S. Toulmin, *Human Understanding,* vol. 1 (Princeton, NJ: Princeton University Press, 1972).

14. The foregoing extracts themes common to Shapere, Toulmin, Lakatos, Laudan, and Kuhn but ignores many of the idiosyncratic differences that distinguish their positions. Thus my use of "progressive" and "degenerating" research is more inclusive than Lakatos's and divorced from his specific characterization of a research program.

15. J. Michael Bailey and Richard C. Pillard, "A Genetic Study of Male Sexual Orientation," *Archives of General Psychiatry* 48 (1991): 1090.

16. G. Dörner, W. Rohde, F. Stahl, LS. Krell, W. G. Masius, "A Neuroendocrine Predisposition from Homosexuality in Men," *Archives of Sexual Behavior* 4 (1975): 1–8; and G Dörner, T. Greier, L. Ahrens, L. Krell, G. Münx, H. Sieler, E. Kittner, and H. Müller, "Prenatal Stress as a Possible Aetiogenetic Factor of Homosexuality in Human Males," *Endokrinologie* 75, no. 3 (1980): 365–368.

17. Simon LeVay, "A Difference in Hypothalamic Structure between Heterosexual and Homosexual Men," *Science* 253 (1991): 1034–1037.

18. M. Baringa, "News and Comment: Is Homosexuality Biological?" *Science* 253 (1991): 956–957.

19. American Psychiatric Association, *Diagnostic and Statistical Manual of Mental Disorders,* 3rd ed. (Washington, DC: American Psychiatric Association, 1980).

20. Frederick Suppe, "Classifying Sexual Disorders: The Diagnostic and Statistical Manual of the American Psychiatric Association," *Journal of Homosexuality* 9, no. 4 (1984): 9–28, reprinted in DeCecco, ed., *Bisexual and Homosexual Identities*; and "The Diagnostic and Statistical Manual of the American Psychiatric Association: Classifying Sexual Disorders," in Earl E. Shelp, ed., *Sexuality and Medicine,* vol. 2 (Dordrecht, Netherlands: Reidel, 1987), 111–136.

21. Frederick Suppe, "Medical and Psychiatric Perspectives on Human Sexuality," in Shelp, ed., *Sexuality and Medicine*, vol. 1, 17–37.

22. Jonathan Katz, *Gay/Lesbian Almanac: A New Documentary* (New York: Harper Colophon Books, 1983).

23. One of my main themes in this essay is that even the current classifications are grossly underdifferentiated, thus they constitute pseudocategories of little scientific merit and are nonspecific categories unlikely to have common etiologies.

24. For example, Dörner et al., "Neuroendocrine Predisposition"; Dörner et al., "Prenatal Stress"; and LeVay, "Difference in Hypothalamic Structure."

25. E. Lewin and T. A. Lyons, "Everything in Its Place: The Coexistence of Lesbianism and Motherhood," in Paul et al., eds., *Homosexuality*, 249–274; M. Hotvedt and J. B. Mandel, "Children of Lesbian Mothers," in Paul et al., eds., *Homosexuality*, 275–286.

Chapter 14: Plato, "Aristophanes' Speech"

1. Pausanias gave a speech about what he believes to be the two kinds of Eros: the base sort, which focuses solely upon the needs of the flesh, and the noble sort, which spurs lovers on to acts of virtue. Since Eryximachus is a doctor, he gave a speech explaining Eros from the medical perspective, as the healthy balance of opposites in the body. Aristophanes is a comic playwright, and so his speech will exemplify his chosen profession.

2. Eros is often translated as "love," which I believe blanches the sense of the Greek. In the Greek, Eros means "desire," or "magnetic attraction"—a force ranging from overwhelming lust to an adolescent crush, depending upon its context. In Hesiod's *Theogony*, Eros is the second divine power to arise from Chaos, coming only after Earth (Gaia), whose birth can be considered both the most basic differentiation of matter from void, and the necessary precondition for later acts of Eros-inspired creation. The universe could not exist without Eros.

3. At risk of attributing modern notions and terminology to classical Athenians, I believe that "gender" is a useful translation of the Greek word "*genos*" here, which is "type, kind." Unlike the words "type" or "kind," the word "gender," I think, better represents the characteristic that Aristophanes' persona is trying to isolate within the larger category of "humanity." Although current debates have (correctly) made a distinction between sex and gender (sex as a biological dimorphism, and gender as a cultural construct), I would argue that this text makes no such distinction, and that there is evidence that it conflates both physiological sex and culturally inscribed gender when it talks of its early humans (e.g., the claim that the word "androgyne" is now used as an insult). Indeed, in Plato's day a standard terminology did exist for differentiating between male and female members of the human species. One of the most regular ways to describe men and women was to use the word phule—"tribe"; hence there was the "tribe" of men and the "tribe" of women. It is perhaps noteworthy that this text does not use the noun "tribe" when it talks of its new human categories. It is conceivable, then, that Aristophanes' persona is struggling for a new vocabulary when he talks of his primordial humans; perhaps the word "gender" is a more accurate translation for the word genos than might previously have been supposed.

4. The claim that this third gender was both male and female in form and in name is literally the case: the word "*androgyne*" in ancient Greek is a compound word meaning "man-woman." Hence, the compound word "androgyne" accurately reflects the physical state of the gender it describes.

5. This rather circular logic (pardon the pun) is derived from the Greek belief that the sun (*Helios*) was "male" and that the earth (*Ge*) was "female." The moon (*Selene*) was de-

picted as either female or androgynous, depending upon which mythological tradition was being used.

6. Ephialtes and Otus were two giants who tried to conquer the Olympian gods by piling Mounts Ossa and Pelion on the gods' home, Mount Olympus. Here, the description of the mortal/spherical assault on Olympus uses the verb "*epithesomenon*," which literally means "to place something on top of something else for the subject's benefit." It is possible that the text's description of the sphere's attack is also making a joking reference to the giants' failed attempt to top Olympus with Ossa and Pelion.

7. Zeus is referring to a drinking game that required each contestant to leap onto a greased wineskin, and to try to maintain his or her balance. This sport's difficulty may have been increased by having the contestant try the jump on only one leg.

8. Young cicadas hibernate in the ground for years before they emerge from the dirt en masse, a life cycle that led many ancients to believe that adult cicadas "copulated" with the earth, and that their offspring were born from the ground.

9. Hence, sexual intercourse is a temporary, partial return to our former state of wholeness—a point I emphasize here to make the text's later argument a little easier to follow.

10. In ancient Greece, if a coin, called a "*sumbolon*," or "symbol, token" in English, was broken in half, and one half was handed to person A, and the other was handed to person B, then the two coin halves could serve as a form of contractual recognition, be it for business, personal affairs, or politics (cf. Kenneth Dover's *Symposium* commentary [Cambridge: 1980], 118nd4).

11. The flatfish, or flounder, is a large, flat fish that lives almost exclusively on the sea bottom, lying on its side and burrowing itself into the sand. It also possesses a bizarre optical organization: both eyes are located on one side of its face, which enables the fish to observe more of its surroundings without moving. Between this fish's very flat shape and the strange placement of its eyes, it can give an observer the impression that it is "one half" of a larger whole, which must have had two eyes on the other side as well.

12. In Athens, all women, no matter what their age or rank, were considered to be legal minors, and they were perpetual wards of the adult male head of their households. Since it was assumed that women were sexually insatiable, unreliable children, they were kept indoors a great deal of the time, and contact between women and outside men was minimized to avoid illegitimate offspring. Sexual contact with an Athenian female which was not first cleared with her legal guardian, then, was considered to be "adultery." This, combined with the fact that all men in ancient Athens, be they married or single, could legally consort with "hetairai," or "female companions," meant that, in the mind of an Athenian at least, any man who would commit adultery must be sexually excessive. As for Athenian women, they were not supposed to participate in any sort of sexual activity outside of marriage. The above-mentioned "hetairai" were not Athenian citizens, and as a result their sexual behavior was of less concern to the male Athenian citizenry; even so, any woman who showed sexual initiative was considered to be sexually rapacious.

13. This passage is our only extant evidence from classical Attic literature of female-to-female eroticism. After much internal debate, I have refrained from using the word "lesbian" as a translation of the Greek term "*hetairistriai*," which literally translates as "companionesses," because the modern sense of the word "lesbian" is anachronistic. In ancient Greek, the term "lesbian" meant "a woman of sexual inventiveness," *not* a woman whose sexual and relationship interests focus solely upon other women. I have also rejected the literal translation "companionesses," because in English this word lacks the erotic connotation important to the context. Further translational difficulty derives from our uncertainty of whether the ancient Greeks conceived of sexuality in the same way as we do, that is, were there women in ancient Greece who adhered to a lifestyle that, as a rule, rejected men and embraced women alone? Or, for that matter, were there men who, as a rule, rejected women and preferred the

company of men alone? Although Aristophanes' speech appears to answer these questions, there are those who believe there is a great deal of room for debate; yet, what is certain is that, at this point in the text, Aristophanes' persona is describing women who prefer erotic contact with women, rather than with men. To a twentieth-century English-speaking audience, women such as these are lesbians; in my effort to maintain the work's ancient Greek nuance whenever possible, however, I have chosen to avoid the potential for anachronistic confusion. For more information on the translation of the word "*hetairistriai*," see Kenneth J. Dover, *Greek Homosexuality* (Cambridge: Harvard University Press, 1989), 172. For the record, the modern term "lesbian" is derived from the name of the island Lesbos, home to Sappho, a seventh-century B.C.E. poet and teacher famous for her expressive love poems to some of her female students. Sappho's feelings for her students do not appear to have been condemned; indeed, her attentions could be compared to the practice in many Greek cities of an older male beginning a relationship with a younger male, usually an adolescent, as a form of initiation into and preparation for adult life.

14. At last, the text explicitly articulates the nature (*phusis*)/custom (*nomos*) dichotomy so important to much of Greek literature and philosophy, which often examines this duality's potential as a source of friction or cohesion in human society.

15. This speech does imply that such a wondrous reconnection can happen to either a woman or a man; however, the text's immediate and cultural context allows Aristophanes' persona to use the masculine pronoun as his default pronoun.

16. Oracles were (and, perhaps, still are) notorious for their indecipherable vagueness, and they were only understandable after the fact. One famous example is reported in Herodotus's *Histories*, 1.53. Croesus, the king of Lydia, was contemplating war with neighboring Persia, and so he sought advice from the Delphic Oracle in Greece. Croesus's envoys asked the question: "Should Croesus send an army against the Persians," and the Oracle responded: "Should you go to war with Persia, a great empire will fall." Croesus mistakenly believed this oracle was a promise of success. Hence, in 456 B.C.E., Croesus invaded Persia and lost horribly, only realizing in hindsight that the "great empire" to fall would be his own.

17. Hephaestus was the god of craftsmanship, which explains his role here as a "mender" of sundered souls.

18. Hades was the god of the underworld and the dead, and deceased mortals were said to dwell in his house. In time, Hades' name became synonymous with the realm he ruled.

19. Hence, Eros in this text has a stronger sense than mere "love." This Eros is the yearning for and the pursuit of an individual—a very active form of desire.

20. Xenophon's *Hellenika*, 5.2.5–7; around 385 B.C.E. a city in Arcadia called Mantinea was conquered and dispersed by the Spartans (Lacedaemonians) because of its pro-Athenian leanings.

21. Dice, or "tallies," were often cut in half and shared by friends as a sign of their friendship.

22. The Greek for "lover" here is "*paidika*," which specifically means "boy lover," that is, the younger half of a male-to-male pederastic relationship. I believe, however, that the sentence's opening emphasis upon *inclusion* (men, women, and the entire human race) gives this particular deployment of *paidika* a broader "object" sense, more consonant with the modern, generic term "lover," or perhaps even, "love-object."

Chapter 15: Boswell, "Revolutions, Universals, and Sexual Categories"

1. For particularly articulate examples of "nominalist" history, see Robert A. Padgug, "Sexual Matters: On Conceptualizing Sexuality in History," *Radical History Review* 20 (1979): 3–33; and Jeffrey Weeks, *Coming Out: Homosexual Politics in Britain from the Nineteenth Century to*

the Present (London, 1977). Most older studies of homosexuality in the past are essentially realist; see bibliography in John Boswell, *Christianity, Social Tolerance, and Homosexuality* (Chicago, 1980), 4n3.

2. It is of substantial import to several moral traditions, for example, whether or not homosexuality is a "condition"—an essentially "realist" position—or a "lifestyle"—basically a "nominalist" point of view. For a summary of shifting attitudes on these points within the Christian tradition, see Peter Coleman, *Christian Attitudes to Homosexuality* (London, 1980); or Edward Batchelor, *Homosexuality and Ethics* (New York, 1980).

3. Note that at this level, the debate is to some extent concerned with the degree of convention that can be sustained without loss of accuracy. It is conventional, for instance, to include in a history of the United States treatment of the period before the inauguration of the system of government that bears that title, and even to speak of the "colonial United States," although while they were colonies, they were not the United States. A history of Greece would likewise, by convention, concern itself with all the states that would someday constitute what is today called "Greece," although those states may have recognized no connection with each other (or even have been at war) at various points in the past. It is difficult to see why such conventions should not be allowed in the case of minority histories, so long as sufficient indication is provided as to the actual relationship of earlier forms to later ones.

4. Padgug, "Sexual Matters," 59.

5. For the variety of etiological explanations to date, see the brief bibliography in Boswell, *Christianity*, 9n9. To this list should now be added (in addition to many articles) three studies: Alan Bell and Martin S. Weinberg, *Homosexualities: A Study of Diversity among Men and Women* (New York, 1978); Bell and Weinberg, *Sexual Preference: Its Development in Men and Women* (Bloomington, Indiana, 1981); and James Weinrich, *Sexual Landscapes* (New York, 1987). An ingenious and highly revealing approach to the development of modern medical literature on the subject of homosexuality is proposed by George Chauncey Jr., "From Sexual Inversion to Homosexuality: Medicine and the Changing Conceptualization of Female Deviance," *Salmagundi* 58–59 (Fall 1982–Winter 1983): 114–146.

6. Moralia 767: *Amatorius*, trans. W. C. Helmhold (Cambridge, MA: 1961), 415.

7. Boswell, *Christianity*, pt. 1 passim, esp. 50–59.

8. See Boswell, *Christianity*, 125–27.

9. *Greek Anthology*, trans. W. R. Paton (Cambridge, MA: 1918), 1.65.

10. Daphnis and Chloe, 4.11. The term *"paiderastēs"* here cannot be understood as a reference to what is now called "pedophilia," since Daphnis—the object of Gnatho's intrerest—is full grown and on the point of marriage. It is obviously a conventional term for "homosexual."

11. For Plato and Pollianus, see Boswell, *Christianity*, 30n56; Athenaeus uses *"philomeirax"* of Sophocles and *"philogynēs"* of Euripides, apparently intending to indicate that the former was predominantly (if not exclusively) interested in males and the latter in females. Cf. R. Foerster, ed., *Scriptores physiognomici* (Leipzig, 1893), 1:29.36, where the word *"philogynaioi,"* "woman lover," occurs.

12. Casina, V.4.957.

13. Epigrams, 2.47.

14. Capitolinus, 11.7.

15. Boswell, *Christianity*, 127.

16. 2.4: Hostis si quis erit nobis, amet ille puellas: gaudeat in puero si quis amicus erit.

17. Saadia Gaon, *Kitāb al-'Amanat wa'l-I* ᶜ tikhadāt, ed. S. Landauer (Leyden, 1880),

10.7.294–297 (English translation by S. Rosenblatt in *Yale Judaica Series,* vol. 1: *The Book of Beliefs and Opinions*).

18. Ibid., 295.

19. Ibid.

20. *Kitāb mufākharāt al-jawārī wa'l-ghilmān,* ed. Charles Pellat (Beirut, 1957).

21. See discussion in Boswell, *Christianity,* 257–258.

22. "Le Livre des caractères de Qostâ ibn Loûqâ," ed. and trans. Paul Sbath, *Bulletin de l'Institut d'Egypte* 23 (1940–1941): 103–139. Sbath's translation is loose and misleading and must be read with caution.

23. Ibid., 112.

24. ". . . waminhim man yamīlu īlā ghairihinna mini 'lghilmāni" (ibid.). A treatment of the fascinating term *"ghulām"* (pl. *ghilmān*), whose meanings range from "son" to "sexual partner," is beyond the scope of this essay.

25. Qustā discusses this at some length (133–136). Cf. F. Rosenthal, "ar-Râzî on the Hidden Illness," *Bulletin of the History of Medicine* 52, no. 1 (1978): 45–60, and the authorities cited there. Treating "passive sexual behavior" (i.e., the reception of semen in anal intercourse) in men as a hereditary condition generally implies a conflation of Types A and C taxonomies in which the role of the "insertee" is regarded as bizarre or even pathological. Attitudes toward *ubnah* should be taken as a special aspect of Muslim sexual taxonomy rather than as indicative of attitudes toward "homosexuality." A comparable case is that of Caelius Aurelianus: see Boswell, *Christianity,* 53; cf. remarks on Roman sexual taboos, below.

26. Weeks, *Coming Out,* 12.

27. See Boswell, *Christianity,* 159–161.

28. *Aelfric's Lives of Saints,* ed. and trans. W. W. Skeat (London, 1881), 33.

29. Discussed in Boswell, *Christianity,* 316ff.

30. *"Sodomia"* and *"sodomita"* are used so often and in so many competing senses in the High Middle Ages that a separate study would be required to present even a summary of this material. Note that in the modern West, the term still has overlapping senses, even in law: in some American states "sodomy" applies to any inherently nonprocreative sex act (fellatio between husband and wife, e.g.), in others to all homosexual behavior, and in still others only to anal intercourse. Several sodomy statutes have in fact been overturned on grounds of unconstitutional vagueness. See, in addition to the material cited in Boswell, *Christianity,* 52, 183–184; Giraldus Cambrensis, *Descriptio Cambriae,* 2.7; J. J. Tierney, "The Celtic Ethnography of Posidonius," *Proceedings of the Royal Irish Academy* 60 (1960): 252; and *Carmina Burana: Die Lieder der Benediktbeurer Handschrift. Zweisprachige Ausgabe* (Munich, 1979), 95.4.334 ("Pura semper ab hac infamia/nostra fuit minor Britannia"; the ms. has "*Bricciavia*").

31. Walter Map, *De nugis curialium* 1.23, trans. John Mundy, *Europe in the High Middle Ages, 1150–1309* (New York, 1973), 302. Cf. discussion of this theme in Boswell, *Christianity,* chap. 8.

32. Prologue, 669ss. Of several works on this issue now in print, see especially Monica McAlpine, "The Pardoner's Homosexuality and How It Matters," *PMLA* (January 1980): 8–22; and Edward Schweitzer, "Chaucer's Pardoner and the Hare," *English Language Notes* 4, no. 4 (1967): 247–250 (not cited by McAlpine).

33. See Boswell, *Christianity,* 233.

34. 8565ss; cf. *Roman de la Rose* 2169–2174, and Gerald Herman, "The 'Sin against Nature' and Its Echoes in Medieval French Literature," *Annuale Mediaevale* 17 (1976): 70–87.

35. Rolf Lenzen, ed., "Altercatio Ganimedis et Helene: Kritische Edition mit Kom-

mentar," *Mittellateinisches Jahrbuch* 7 (1972): 161–186; English translation in Boswell, *Christianity,* 381–389.

36. Boswell, *Christianity,* 392–398.

37. *The Anglo-Latin Satirical Poets and Epigrammatists,* ed. Thomas Wright (London, 1872), 2:463.

38. Since the publication of my remarks on this issue in *Christianity,* 28–30, several detailed studies of Greek homosexuality have appeared, most notably those of Félix Buffière, *Eros adolescent: La Pédérastie dans la Grèce antique* (Paris, 1980); and K. J. Dover, *Greek Homosexuality* (Cambridge, MA: 1978). Neither work has persuaded me to revise my estimate of the degree to which Greek fascination with "youth" was more than a romantic convention. A detailed assessment of both works and their relation to my own findings will appear in my forthcoming study on the phenomenology of homosexual behavior in ancient and medieval Europe.

39. Artemidorus Daldianus, *Onirocriticon libri quinque,* ed. R. Park (Leipzig, 1963), 1.78.88–89. (An English translation of this work is available: *The Interpretation of Dreams,* trans. R. J. White [Park Ridge, NJ: 1975].)

40. "non est pedico maritus:/ quae faciat duo sunt: irrumat aut futuit" Martial 2:47 (cf. note 14, above: *"pedico"* is apparently Martial's own coinage).

41. *Ceveo* is to *futuo* or *pedico* what *fello* is to *irrumo:* it describes the activity of the party being entered. The vulgar English "put out" may be the closest equivalent, but nothing in English captures the actual meaning of the Latin.

42. *Futuo/pedico* and *ceveo* are likewise both active.

43. Hunayn ibn Ishāq, trans., *Kitāb Taʿbīr ar-Ruʾyā,* ed. Toufic Fahd (Damascus, 1964), 175–176.

44. [This section was added by Boswell in March 1988, five years after the original article was composed.—ED.]

45. For an overview of this literature since the material cited in note 1, see most recently Steven Epstein, "Gay Politics, Ethnic Identity: The Limits of Social Constructionism," *Socialist Review* 93/94 (1987): 9–54; also John D'Emilio, *Sexual Politics, Sexual Communities: The Making of a Homosexual Minority in the United States, 1940–1970* (Chicago, 1983); and the essays in Kenneth Plummer, ed., *The Making of the Modern Homosexual* (London, 1981). See also note 46.

46. Three recent writers on the controversy (Steven Murray, "Homosexual Categorization in Cross-Cultural Perspective," in Murray, *Social Theory, Homosexual Realities,* Gai Saber Monograph No. 3 [New York, 1984]; Epstein, "Gay Politics"; and David Halperin, "Sex before Sexuality" [in this collection]) identify among them a dozen or more "constructionist" historians, but Murray and Halperin adduce only a single historian (me) as an example of modern "essentialist" historiography; Epstein, the most sophisticated of the three, can add to this only Adrienne Rich, not usually thought of as a historian. As to whether my views are actually "essentialist" or not, see further.

47. See, for example, Halperin, "Sex before Sexuality." Much of the controversy is conducted through scholarly papers: at a conference on "Homosexuality in History and Culture" held at Brown University in February 1987, of six presentations four were explicitly constructionist; two of these were by classicists. On the other hand, the standard volume on Attic homosexuality, K. J. Dover, *Greek Homosexuality* (New York, 1985), defies easy classification but falls closer to an "essentialist" point of view than a "constructionist" one, and Keith DeVries's *Homosexuality and Athenian Society* is a nonconstructionist survey of great subtlety and sophistication. See also David Cohen, "Law, Society, and Homosexuality in Classical Athens," *Past and Present* 117 (1987): 3–21. For the (relatively few) recent studies of periods between Athens and the late nineteenth century, see Saara Lilja, *Homosexuality in Republican and Augustan Rome*

(Helsinki, 1983) (Societas Scientiarum Fennica, Commentationes Humanarum Litterarum, 74); Alan Bray, *Homosexuality in Renaissance England* (London, 1982); James Saslow, *Ganymede in the Renaissance: Homosexuality in Art and Society* (New Haven, 1986); Guido Ruggiero, *The Boundaries of Eros: Sex, Crime, and Sexuality in Renaissance Venice* (New York, 1985); Claude Courouve, *Vocabulaire de l'homosexualité masculine* (Paris, 1985).

48. An expression I use to include both women and men.

49. Of course, if a constructionist position holds that "gay person" refers only to one particular modern identity, it is then, tautologically, not applicable to the past.

Chapter 16: Halperin, "Sex Before Sexuality"

More extensive notes for this essay are available in its longer version, "One Hundred Years of Homosexuality," in David M. Halperin, *One Hundred Years of Homosexuality and Other Essays on Greek Love* (New York: Routledge, 1990).

1. Wrongly, no doubt: the same entry in the *OED* records the use of the word by J. A. Symonds in a letter of the same year, and so it is most unlikely that Chaddock alone is responsible for its English coinage. See R. W. Burchfield, ed., *A Supplement to the Oxford English Dictionary* (Oxford, 1976), 2:136, s.v. homosexuality.

2. The terms "homosexual" and "homosexuality" appeared in print for the first time in 1869 in two anonymous pamphlets published in Leipzig and composed, apparently, by Karl Maria Kertbeny. Kertbeny (né Benkert) was an Austro-Hungarian translator and *littérateur* of Bavarian extraction, not a physician (as Magnus Hirschfeld and Havelock Ellis—misled by false clues planted in those pamphlets by Kertbeny himself—maintained); he wrote in German under his acquired Hungarian surname and claimed (rather unconvincingly) in the second of the two tracts under discussion not to share the sexual tastes denominated by his own ingenious neologism.

3. George Chauncey, "From Sexual Inversion to Homosexuality: Medicine and the Changing Conceptualization of Female Deviance," in *Homosexuality: Sacrilege, Vision, Politics,* ed. Robert Boyers and George Steiner = *Salmagundi* 58–59 (1982–83): 114–146 (quotation at 116). Cf. Michel Foucault, *The History of Sexuality, Volume I: An Introduction,* trans. Robert Hurley (New York, 1978), 37–38; Claude Féray, "Une histoire critique du mot sexualité," *Arcadie* 28, nos. 325–328 (1981), esp. 16–17, 246–256; Jeffrey Weeks, "Discourse, Desire and Sexual Deviance: Some Problems in a History of Homosexuality," Kenneth Plummer, ed., *The Making of the Modern Homosexual* (London: Hutchinson, 1981), 76–111, esp. 82ff.; John Marshall, "Pansies, Perverts, and Macho Men: Changing Conceptions of Male Homosexuality," in Plummer, ed., *The Making of the Modern Homosexual,* 133–154; Arnold I. Davidson, "Closing Up the Corpses: Diseases of Sexuality and the Emergence of the Psychiatric Style of Reasoning," in *Reason, Language and Method: Essays in Honour of Hilary Putnam,* 295–325; George Boolos, ed. (Cambridge: Cambridge University Press, 1990). To be sure, the formal introduction of "inversion" as a clinical term (by Arrigo Tamassia, "Sull' inversione dell' istinto sessuale," *Rivista spermentale di freniatria e di medicina legale* 4 [1878]: 97–117: the earliest published use of "inversion" that Havelock Ellis, *Sexual Inversion = Studies in the Psychology of Sex,* vol. 2, 3rd ed. [Philadelphia, 1922]: 3, was able to discover) occurred a decade *after* Kertbeny's coinage of "homosexuality," but Ellis suspected the word of being considerably older: it seems to have been well established by the 1870s, at any rate, and it was certainly a common designation throughout the 1880s. "Homosexuality," by contrast, did not begin to achieve currency in Europe until the Eulenburg affair of 1907–1908 and even thereafter it was slow in gaining ascendancy. The main point, in any case, is that "inversion," defined as it is by reference to gender deviance, represents an age-old outlook, whereas "homosexuality" marks a sharp break with traditional ways of thinking.

4. Chauncey, "From Sexual Inversion to Homosexuality," esp. 117–122, citing W. C.

Rivers, "A New Male Homosexual Trait (?)," *Alienist and Neurologist* 41 (1920): 22–27; the persistence of this outlook in the United States, along with some of its practical (military, legal, and ecclesiastical) applications, has now been documented by Chauncey, "Christian Brotherhood or Sexual Perversion? Homosexual Identities and the Construction of Sexual Boundaries in the World War I Era" (chapter 18 in this volume), in a study of the role-specific morality that once governed sexual attitudes and practices among members of the U.S. Navy.

5. See Chauncey, "From Sexual Inversion to Homosexuality," 122–125; Marshall, "Pansies, Perverts, and Macho Men," 137–153; Arnold I. Davidson, "How to Do the History of Psychoanalysis: A Reading of Freud's *Three Essays on the Theory of Sexuality*," in Françoise Meltzer, ed., *The Trial(s) of Psychoanalysis, Critical Inquiry* 13 (1986–1987): 252–277, esp. 258–271; Jerome Neu, "Freud and Perversion," in Earl E. Shelp, *Sexuality and Medicine* (Dordrecht, Netherlands: Reidel, 1987), vol. 1, 153–184, esp. 153ff.

6. The new scientific conceptualization of homosexuality reflects, to be sure, a much older habit of mind, distinctive to northern and northwestern Europe since the Renaissance, whereby sexual acts are categorized not according to the modality of sexual or social roles assumed by the sexual partners, but rather according to the anatomical sex of the persons engaged in them. This habit of mind seems to have been shaped, in its turn, by the same aggregate of cultural factors responsible for the much older division, accentuated during the Renaissance, between European and Mediterranean marriage patterns; northern and northwestern Europe typically exhibits a pattern of marriage between mature coevals, a bilateral kinship system, neolocal marriage, and a mobile labor force, whereas Mediterranean societies are characterized by late male and early female marriage, patrilineal kinship organization, patrivirilocal marriage, and inhibited circulation of labor.

7. See Foucault, *The Archaeology of Knowledge and the Discourse on Language*, trans. A. M. Sheridan Smith (New York, 1972), 190, for the introduction of this concept; for its application to the history of sexual categories, see Arnold I. Davidson, "Sex and the Emergence of Sexuality," *Critical Inquiry* 14 (1987–1988): 16–48, esp. 48.

8. *A Problem in Modern Ethics*, quoted by Jeffrey Weeks, *Coming Out: Homosexual Politics in Britain, from the Nineteenth Century to the Present* (London, 1977), 1.

9. While condemning "homosexuality" as "a bastard term compounded of Greek and Latin elements" (2), Ellis acknowledged that its classical etymology facilitated its diffusion throughout the European languages; moreover, by consenting to employ it himself, Ellis helped further to popularize it. On the philological advantages and disadvantages of "homosexuality," see Féray, "Une histoire," 174–176.

10. This passage, along with others in a similar vein, has been well discussed by Marshall.

11. Marshall, "Pansies, Perverts, and Macho Men," 148, who goes on to quote the following passage from the preface to a recent survey by D. J. West, *Homosexuality Reassessed* (London, 1977), vii: "A generation ago the word homosexuality was best avoided in polite conversation, or referred to in muted terms appropriate to a dreaded and scarcely mentionable disease. Even some well-educated people were hazy about exactly what it meant." Note, however, that Edward Westermarck, writing for a scholarly audience in *The Origin and Development of the Moral Ideas*, could allude to "what is nowadays commonly called homosexual love" (2:456) as early as 1908. Westermarck's testimony has escaped the *OED* supplement, which simply records that in 1914 George Bernard Shaw felt free to use the word "homosexual" adjectivally in the *New Statesman* without further explanations and that the adjective reappears in *Blackwood's Magazine* in 1921 as well as in Robert Graves's *Good-bye to All That* in 1929. The French version of "homosexuality," by contrast, showed up in the *Larousse mensuel illustré* as early as December 1907 (according to Féray, "Une histoire," 172).

12. The earliest literary occurrence of the German loanword "homosexualist," of which the *OED* is similarly ignorant, took place only in 1925, to the best of my knowledge, and it illustrates the novelty that evidently still attached to the term: in Aldous Huxley's *Those Barren*

Leaves, we find the following exchange between a thoroughly modern aunt and her up-to-date niece, who are discussing a mutual acquaintance.

> "I sometimes doubt," [Aunt Lilian] said, "whether he takes any interest in women at all. Fundamentally, unconsciously, I believe he's a homosexualist."
>
> "Perhaps," said Irene gravely. She knew her Havelock Ellis. (Part 3, chap. 11)

(The earliest occurrence of "homosexualist" cited in the *OED* supplement dates from 1931.)

13. According, once again, to the dubious testimony of the *OED*'s 1976 supplement, 2:85, s.v. heterosexuality. (Note that Kertbeny, the coiner of the term "homosexual," opposed it not to "heterosexual," but to *normalsexual:* Féray "Une histoire," 171.) On the dependence of "heterosexuality" on "homosexuality," see ibid., 171–172; Harold Beaver, "Homosexual Signs (*In Memory of Roland Barthes*)," *Critical Inquiry* 8 (1981–1982): 99–119, esp. 115–116.

14. John Boswell, "Revolutions, Universals and Sexual Categories," chap. 15 in this volume. Boswell himself, however, argues for the contrary position, which has been most baldly stated by Vern L. Bullough, *Homosexuality: A History* (New York, 1979), 2, 62: "Homosexuality has always been with us; it has been a constant in history, and its presence is clear."

15. See Foucault, *The History of Sexuality,* 43:

> As defined by the ancient civil or canonical codes, sodomy was a category of forbidden acts; their perpetrator was nothing more than the juridical subject of them. The nineteenth-century homosexual became a personage, a past, a case history, and a childhood, in addition to being a type of life, a life form, and a morphology, with an indiscreet anatomy and possibly a mysterious physiology. Nothing that went into his total composition was unaffected by his sexuality. It was everywhere present in him: at the root of all his actions because it was their insidious and indefinitely active principle; written immodestly on his face and body because it was a secret that always gave itself away. It was consubstantial with him, less as a habitual sin than as a singular nature.

Cf. Randolph Trumbach, "London's Sodomites: Homosexual Behavior and Western Culture in the 18th Century," *Journal of Social History* 11 (1977): 9; Weeks, *Coming Out,* 12; Richard Sennett, *The Fall of Public Man* (New York, 1977), 6–8; Padgug, "Sexual Matters: On Conceptualizing Sexuality in History," *Radical History Review* 20 (1979): 59–60; Féray, "Une histoire," 246–247; Alain Schnapp, "Une autre image de l'homosexualité en Grèce ancienne," *Le Débat* 10 (March 1981): 107–117, esp. 116 (speaking of Attic vase paintings): "One does not paint acts that characterize persons so much as behaviors that distinguish groups"; Pierre J. Payer, *Sex and the Penitentials: The Development of a Sexual Code, 550–1150* (Toronto, 1984), 40–44, esp. 40–41: "There is no word in general usage in the penitentials for homosexuality as a category. . . . Furthermore, the distinction between homosexual acts and people who might be called homosexuals does not seem to be operative in these manuals. . . ."

16. Foucault, *The Use of Pleasure,* 10, 51–52, remarks that it would be interesting to determine exactly when in the evolving course of Western cultural history sex became more morally problematic than eating; he seems to think that sex won out only at the turn of the eighteenth century, after a long period of relative equilibrium during the Middle Ages.

17. Boswell, "Revolutions, Universals, and Sexual Categories," 194 in this volume. Bullough, *Homosexuality,* 3, similarly appeals to Aristophanes' myth as "one of the earliest explanations" of homosexuality.

18. Boswell, "Revolutions, Universals, and Sexual Categories," 194 in this volume; cf. Auguste Valensin, "Platon et la théorie de l'amour," *Études* 281 (1954): 32–45, esp. 37.

19. To be sure, a certain symmetry does obtain between the groups composed, respectively, of those making a homosexual and those making a heterosexual object choice: each of them is constituted by Aristophanes in such a way as to contain both males and females in their dual capacities as subjects and objects of erotic desire. Aristophanes does nothing to

highlight this symmetry, however, and it may be doubted whether it should figure in our interpretation of the passage.

20. The term "boy" (*pais* in Greek) refers by convention to the junior partner in a pederastic relationship, or to one who plays that role, regardless of his actual age; youths are customarily supposed to be desirable between the onset of puberty and the arrival of the beard.

21. For an explication of what is meant by "a certain (nonsexual) pleasure in physical contact with men," see note 25 below.

22. See Kenneth J. Dover, *Greek Homosexuality,* (Cambridge: Harvard University Press, 1989), esp. 73–109; a general survey of this issue together with the scholarship on it can be found in my essay, "Plato and Erotic Reciprocity," *Classical Antiquity* 5 (1986): 60–80.

23. Nor does Aristophanes make any allowance in his myth for what was perhaps the most widely shared sexual taste among his fellow Athenian citizens—namely, an undifferentiated liking for good-looking women and boys (that is, a sexual preference not defined by an exclusively gender-specific sexual object choice). Such a lacuna should warn us not to treat Aristophanes' myth as a simple description or reflection of contemporary experience.

24. Public lecture delivered at Brown University, February 21, 1987.

25. In "Plato and Erotic Reciprocity," I have argued that—in this one respect, at least—the picture drawn by Plato's Aristophanes, *if* taken to represent *the moral conventions* governing sexual behavior in classical Athens rather than the reality of sexual behavior itself, is historically accurate. To be sure, the pederastic ethos of classical Athens did not prohibit a willing boy from responding enthusiastically to his lover's physical attentions: Aristophanes himself maintains that a philerast both "enjoys" and "welcomes" (*khairein, aspazesthai:* 191e–192b) his lover's embraces. But that ethos did stipulate that whatever enthusiasm a boy exhibited for sexual contact with his lover sprang from sources other than *sexual* desire. The distinction between "welcoming" and "desiring" a lover's caresses, as it applies to the motives for a boy's willingness, spelled the difference between decency and degeneracy; that distinction is worth emphasizing here because the failure of modern interpreters to observe it has led to considerable misunderstanding (as when historians of sexuality, for example, misreading the frequent depictions on Attic black-figure pottery of a boy leaping into his lover's arms, take those paintings to be evidence for the strength of the junior partner's sexual desire). A very few Greek documents seem truly ambiguous on this point, and I have reviewed their testimony in some detail in the notes to "Plato and Erotic Reciprocity": see, esp. 64nn10–11; 66n14.

26. The notable exceptions are Bullough, *Homosexuality,* 3–5, who cites it as evidence for the supposed universality of homosexuality in human history, and John Boswell, *Christianity, Social Tolerance, and Homosexuality: Gay People in Western Europe from the Beginning of the Christian Era to the Fourteenth Century* (Chicago, 1980), 53n, 75n.

27. See P. H. Schrijvers, *Eine medizinische Erklärung der männlichen Homosexualität aus der Antike (Caelius Aurelianus "De Morbis Chronicis IV 9")* (Amsterdam: B. R. Brüner, 1985), 11.

28. I have borrowed this entire argument from Schrijvers, 7–8; the same point had been made earlier by Boswell, *Christianity,* 53n33.

29. Translation, with emphasis added, by I. E. Drabkin, ed. and trans., *Caelius Aurelianus: "On Acute Diseases" and "On Chronic Diseases"* (Chicago, 1950), 413.

30. As the chapter title, "De mollibus *sive subactis,*" implies.

31. Compare Aeschines, *Against Timarchus,* 185: Timarchus is "a man who is male in body but has committed a woman's transgressions" and has thereby "outraged himself contrary to nature" (discussed by Dover, *Greek Homosexuality,* 60–80). On the ancient figure of the *kinaidos,* or *cinaedus,* the man who actively desires to submit himself passively to the sexual uses of other men, see the essays by Winkler and by Maud W. Gleason in David Halperin, John J. Winkler, and Froma I. Zeitlin, eds., *Before Sexuality: The Construction of Erotic Experience in the Ancient Greek World* (Princeton, 1990). Davidson, "Sex and the Emergence of Sexuality," 22,

is therefore quite wrong to claim that "[b]efore the second half of the nineteenth century persons of a determinate anatomical sex could not be thought to be really, that is, psychologically, of the opposite sex."

32. The Latin phrase "*quod utranque Venerem exerceant*" is so interpreted by Drabkin, *Caelius Aurelianus,* 901n, and by Schrijvers, *Eine medizinische Erklärung,* 32–33, who secures this reading by citing Ovid, *Metamorphoses,* 3.323, where Teiresias, who had been both a man and a woman, is described as being learned in the field of *Venus utraque.* Compare Petronius, *Satyricon* 43.8: *omnis minervae homo.*

33. I follow, once again, the insightful commentary by Schrijvers, 15.

34. I quote from the translation by Drabkin, 905, which is based on his plausible, but nonetheless speculative, reconstruction (accepted by Schrijvers, 50) of a desperately corrupt text.

35. Anon., *De physiognomonia,* 85 (vol. 2, 114.5–14 Förster); Vettius Valens, 2.16 (76.3–8 Kroll); Clement of Alexandria, *Paedagogus,* 3.21.3; Firmicus Maternus, *Mathesis,* 6.30.15–16 and 7.25.3–23 (esp. 7.25.5).

36. Thus, Boswell, "Revolutions, Universals, and Sexual Categories," argues that the term "pederast," at least as it is applied to Gnathon by Longus in *Daphnis and Chloe,* 4.11, is "obviously a conventional term for 'homosexual' " (note 10), and he would presumably place a similar construction on *paiderastês* and *philerastês* in the myth of Plato's Aristophanes, dismissing my interpretation as a terminological quibble or as a misguided attempt to reify lexical entities into categories of experience.

37. Artemidorus, *Oneirocritica,* 1.2 (8.21–9.4 Pack).

38. John J. Winkler, "Unnatural Acts: Erotic Protocols in Artemidorus' Dream Analysis," in *The Constraints of Desire: The Anthropology of Sex and Gender in Ancient Greece* (New York, 1989).

39. I say "phallus" rather than "penis" because (1) what qualifies as a phallus in this discursive system does not always turn out to be a penis (see note 46), and (2) even when phallus and penis have the same extension, or reference, they still do not have the same intension, or meaning: "phallus" betokens not a specific item of the male anatomy *simpliciter,* but that same item *taken under the description* of a cultural signifier; (3) hence, the meaning of "phallus" is ultimately determined by its function in the larger sociosexual discourse: it is that which penetrates, that which enables its possessor to play an "active" sexual role, and so forth: see Gayle Rubin "The Traffic in Women: Notes on the 'Political Economy' of Sex," in Rayna R. Reiter, ed., *Toward an Anthropology of Women* (New York, 1975), 157–210, esp. 190–192.

40. Foucault, *The Use of Pleasure,* 215.

41. In order to avoid misunderstanding, I should emphasize that by calling all persons belonging to these four groups "statutory minors," I do not wish either to suggest that they enjoyed the *same* status as one another or to obscure the many differences in status that could obtain between members of a single group—for instance, between a wife and a courtesan—differences that may not have been perfectly isomorphic with the legitimate modes of their sexual use. Nonetheless, what is striking about Athenian social usage is the tendency to collapse such distinctions as did indeed obtain between different categories of social subordinates and to create a single opposition between them all en masse, and the class of adult male citizens. On this point, see Mark Golden, "*Pais,* 'Child,' and 'Slave,' " *L'Antiquité classique* 54 (1985): 91–104, esp. 101 and 102n38.

42. Paul Veyne, "La famille et l'amour sous le Haut-Empire romain," *Annales (E.S.C.)* 33 (1978), 55; and "Homosexuality in Ancient Rome," in Philippe Ariès and André Béjin, eds. *Western Sexuality: Practice and Precept in Past and Present Times,* trans. Anthony Forster (Oxford, 1985), 26–35.

43. I have borrowed this analogy from Arno Schmitt, who uses it to convey what the

modern sexual categories would look like from a traditional Islamic perspective: see Gianni DeMartino and Arno Schmitt, *Kleine Schriften zu zwischenmännlicher Sexualität und Erotik in der muslimischen Gesellschaft* (Berlin, 1985), 19.

44. Maurice Godelier, "The Origins of Male Domination," *New Left Review* 127 (May–June 1981): 3–17 (quotation on 17); see also, Godelier, "Le sexe comme fondement ultime de l'ordre social et cosmique chez les Baruya de Nouvelle-Guinée: Mythe et réalité," in Armando Verdiglione, ed., *Sexualité et pouvoir* (Paris, 1976), 268–306, esp. 295–96.

45. "Une bisexualité de sabrage": Veyne, "La famille et l'amour," 50–55; cf. the critique by Ramsay MacMullen, "Roman Attitudes to Greek Love," *Historia* 32 (1983): 484–502.

46. By "phallus" I mean a culturally constructed signifier of social power: for the terminology, see note 39. I call Greek sexuality phallic because (1) sexual contacts are polarized around phallic action—that is, they are defined by who has the phallus and by what is done with it; (2) sexual pleasures other than phallic pleasures do not count in categorizing sexual contacts; (3) in order for a contact to qualify as sexual, one—and no more than one—of the two partners is required to have a phallus (boys are treated in pederastic contexts as essentially unphallused [see Martial, 11.22; but cf. *Palatine Anthology*, XII: 3, 7, 197, 207, 216, 222, 242] and tend to be assimilated to women; in the case of sex between women, one partner—the "tribad"—is assumed to possess a phallus equivalent [an overdeveloped clitoris] and to penetrate the other.

47. Foucault, *The Care of the Self*, 3–36, esp. 26–34; S. R. F. Price, "The Future of Dreams: From Freud to Artemidorus," *Past and Present* 113 (November 1986): 3–37, abridged in *Before Sexuality*.

48. "Translations" (1972), lines 32–33, in Adrienne Rich, *Diving into the Wreck: Poems, 1971–1972* (New York, 1973), 40–41 (quotation on 41).

Chapter 17: Kennedy and Davis, "The Reproduction of Butch-Fem Roles"

The original version of this paper was written for the International Scientific Conference on Gay and Lesbian Studies, "Homosexuality, Which Homosexuality?" at the Free University of Amsterdam. We want to thank the conference organizing committee for granting permission to publish the paper in this volume, especially since the conference is publishing its own proceedings. We thank Christina Simmons and Kathy Peiss for their careful reading of this chapter, and helpful suggestions for revisions. We also thank Lisa Duggan, Joan Nestle, Bobbi Prebis, and David Schneider for their general support of our work and the reading of a draft of this essay.

1. See, for instance, Del Martin and Phyllis Lyon, *Lesbian/Woman* (New York: 1972); Audre Lorde, "Tar Beach," *Conditions* 5 (1979): 34–47; Joan Nestle, "Butch-Fem Relationships, Sexual Courage in the 1950s," *Heresies* 12 (1981): 21–24; John D'Emilio, *Sexual Politics, Sexual Communities: The Making of a Homosexual Minority in the United States, 1940–1970* (Chicago: 1983) Esther Newton, "The Mythic Mannish Lesbian: Radclyffe Hall and the New Woman," *Signs* 9 (Summer 1984): 557–575. Butch-fem roles are also apparent in twentieth-century novels and pulp fiction. For an example of the former, see, for instance, Gale Wilhelm, *We Too Are Drifting* (New York: 1935); and of the latter, Ann Bannon, *Beebo Brinker* (Greenwich, CT: 1962).

2. Our research is part of the work of the Buffalo Women's Oral History Project, founded in 1978 with three goals: (1) to produce a comprehensive, written history of the lesbian community in Buffalo, New York, using as its major source oral histories of lesbians who came out before 1970; (2) to create and index an archive of oral history tapes, written interviews, and supplementary materials; and (3) to give this history back to the community from which it derives. Madeline Davis and Elizabeth Lapovsky Kennedy are the directors of the project. Avra Michelson was an active member from 1978 to 1981. Wanda Edwards has

been an intermittent member of the project since 1981, particularly in regard to research on the black lesbian community and on racism in the white lesbian community.

3. For a helpful overview of essentialist positions, see Diane Richardson, "The Dilemma of Essentiality in Homosexual Theory," *Journal of Homosexuality* 9 (Winter 1983): 79–90.

4. For a helpful discussion of this nineteenth- and early twentieth-century literature, see George Chauncey Jr., "From Sexual Inversion to Homosexuality: The Changing Medical Conceptualization of Female 'Deviance' " in *Salmagundi* 58/59 (Fall 1982/Winter 1983): 114–46; and Newton, "The Mythic Mannish Lesbian," 565–568.

5. It is with hesitation that we call these psychological theories "essentialist." Can there be an essentialist approach other than one that attributes homosexuality to genetic factors? Freudian theory certainly has the potential to explain the construction of homosexual identity in the context of social and cultural forces. But until recently, it has only rarely been used in this way. Rather, most psychiatrists have worked with a model that dichotomized heterosexual and homosexual behavior and considered the former as normal and the latter as pathological. Carroll Smith-Rosenberg makes this point in her article, "The Female World of Love and Ritual: Relations between Women in Nineteenth-Century America," *Signs* 1 (Autumn 1973): 2–28. For an article that delineates some of the complex factors distinguishing an essentialist approach from a social constructionist approach and suggests some confusion in our current thinking about these distinctions, see Steven Epstein, "Gay Politics, Ethnic Identity: The Limits of Social Constructionism," *Socialist Review* 93–94 (May–August 1987): 9–56.

6. Radclyffe Hall, *The Well of Lonliness* (1928; rpt. London: 1974). For useful discussions of the novel's contribution to homosexual resistance, see Jonathan Katz, *Gay American History: Lesbians and Gay Men in the U.S.A.* (New York: 1976), 397–405; and Jeffrey Weeks, *Coming Out: Homosexual Politics in Britain, From the Nineteenth Century to the Present* (London: 1977), 107–111.

7. The dominant ideas about homosexuality are not monolithic; contradictory ideas exist alongside one another. The idea that homosexuality is a sickness or a moral flaw and can spread among people is also prevalent. The different ideas about homosexuality can be more or less homophobic depending on the context—the time period or the social group.

8. Katz, *Gay American History*, 6–7.

9. For a discussion of the conditions that might have given rise to lesbian communities at this time, see Ann Ferguson, "Patriarchy, Sexual Identity, and the Sexual Revolution," *Signs* 7 (Autumn 1981): 158–172. The earliest references to lesbian bar communities appear in French fiction, Emile Zola's *Nana* (1880) and Guy du Maupassant's "Paul's Mistress" (1881). For a discussion of these sources, albeit a negative one, see Lillian Faderman, *Surpassing the Love of Men: Romantic Friendship and Love between Women from the Renaissance to the Present* (New York: 1981), 282–284. For commentary on early-twentieth-century lesbian communities, see Gayle Rubin's introduction to *A Woman Appeared to Me,* by Renée Vivien (Nevada: 1976), iii–xxvii; Vern Bullough and Bonnie Bullough, "Lesbianism in the 1920s and 1930s: A Newfound Study," *Signs* 2 (Summer 1977): 895–904; and Eric Garber, "Tain't Nobody's Business: Homosexuality in Harlem in the 1920s," *The Advocate* 342 (May 1982): 39–43.

10. One of our narrators gave us an upper-class woman's obituary she had saved, which said that this woman was survived by a lifelong companion. From this lead we found other obituaries and learned of a group of women who had been active in business and the arts in the 1920s and 1930s. A copy of these articles is on file at the Lesbian Herstory Archives, P.O. Box 1258, New York, NY 10016.

11. This hypothesis was shaped by our personal contact with Buffalo lesbians who came out in the 1940s and 1950s and by discussion with grassroots gay and lesbian history projects around the country, in particular, the San Francisco Lesbian and Gay History Project, the Boston Area Gay and Lesbian History Project, and the Lesbian Herstory Archives. In addition, we were influenced by the early social constructionist work in lesbian and gay history. See, in

particular, Katz, *Gay American History;* Rubin, "Introduction" to *A Woman Appeared to Me;* and Weeks, *Coming Out.* We want to thank all these people, who have been inspirational to our work.

12. All quotations are taken from the oral histories collected for this project between 1978 and 1986.

13. For further discussion of Buffalo bar life and the development of the lesbian community, see Madeline Davis, Elizabeth Lapovsky Kennedy, and Avra Michelson, "Buffalo Lesbian Bars in the Fifties," paper presented at the National Women's Studies Association, Bloomington, IN, May 1980, and "Buffalo Lesbian Bars: 1930–1960," paper presented at the Fifth Berkshire Conference on the History of Women, Vassar College, Poughkeepsie, NY, June 1981. Both papers are on file at the Lesbian Herstory Archives and have been rewritten for our monograph *Boots of Leather, Slippers of Gold: The History of a Lesbian Community.*

14. For a detailed discussion of our research on butch-fem roles, see Madeline Davis and Elizabeth Lapovsky Kennedy, "Butch/Fem Roles in the Buffalo Lesbian Community: 1940–1960,"paper presented at the Gay Academic Union Conference, Chicago, October 1982. This paper is on file at the Lesbian Herstory Archives.

15. For additional information on butch-fem roles and sexuality in the Buffalo lesbian community, see Madeline Davis and Elizabeth Lapovsky Kennedy, "Oral History and the Study of Sexuality in the Lesbian Community: Buffalo, New York, 1940–1960," *Feminist Studies* 12 (Spring 1986): 7–26.

16. Katz, *Gay American History,* 209–211.

17. Weeks, *Coming Out,* 89, and *Sex, Politics and Society: The Regulation of Sexuality since 1800* (London: 1981), 115–117.

18. Newton, "The Mythic Mannish lesbian."

19. We do not mean to relegate butch-fem roles to history. They are unquestionably meaningful for a number of lesbians today. This analytical framework explains why they continue today, as well as alerts us to expect that their current meaning is somewhat different than it was in the 1960s.

20. The concept of prepolitical comes from Eric Hobsbawm, *Primitive Rebels: Studies in Archaic Forms of Social Movement in the Nineteenth and Twentieth Centuries* (New York: 1959), 2.

21. The DA—the letters stand for duck's ass—was a popular hairdo for working-class men and butches during the 1950s. All side hair was combed back and joined the back hair in a manner resembling the layered feathers of a duck's tail, hence the name. Pomade was used to hold the hair in place and give a sleek appearance.

22. Alfred Kinsey, Wardell B. Pomeroy, Clyde E. Martin, Paul H. Gebhard, *Sexual Behavior in the Human Female* (1953; rpt. New York: 1965), 468–476.

23. She could have been exposed to these ideas through Hall's *The Well of Loneliness,* which she had read.

Chapter 18: Chauncey, "Christian Brotherhood or Sexual Perversion?"

1. This is a revised version of a paper originally presented at the conference "Among Men, Among Women: Sociological and Historical Recognition of Homosocial Arrangements," held at the University of Amsterdam, June 22–26, 1983. I am grateful to Allan Bérubé, John Boswell, Nancy Cott, Steven Dubin, James Schultz, Anthony Stellato, James Taylor, and my colleagues at the Amsterdam conference for their comments on earlier versions.

2. The Newport investigation was brought to the attention of historians by Frank Freidel, *Franklin D. Roosevelt: The Ordeal* (Boston, 1954), 41, 46–47, 96–97, and by Jonathan Katz, *Gay American History: A Documentary* (New York, 1976), 579n. Katz reprinted the Senate report

in *Government versus Homosexuals* (New York, 1975), a volume in the Arno Press series on homosexuality he edited. A useful narrative account of the naval investigation is provided by Lawrence R. Murphy, "Cleaning Up Newport: The U.S. Navy's Prosecution of Homosexuals after World War I," *Journal of American Culture* 7 (Fall 1984): 57–64.

3. Murphy J. Foster presided over the first court of inquiry, which began its work in Newport on March 13, 1919, and heard 406 pages of testimony in the course of 23 days (its records are hereafter cited as *Foster Testimony*). The second court of inquiry, convened in 1920 "to inquire into the methods employed . . . in the investigation of moral and other conditions existing in the Naval Service; [and] to ascertain and inquire into the scope of an authority for said investigation," was presided over by Rear Admiral Herbert O. Dunn and heard 2,500 pages of testimony in the course of 86 days (hereinafter cited as *Dunn Testimony*). The second trial of Reverend Kent, *U.S. v. Samuel Neal Kent,* heard in Rhode Island District Court in Providence beginning January 20, 1920, heard 532 pages of evidence (hereinafter cited as *Kent Trial*). The records are held at the National Archives, Modern Military Field Branch, Suitland, Maryland, R.G. 125.

4. I have used "gay" in this essay to refer to men who identified themselves as sexually different from other men—and who labeled themselves and were labeled by others as "queer"—because of their assumption of "feminine" sexual and other social roles. As I explain below, not all men who were homosexually active labeled themselves in this manner, including men known as "husbands," who were involved in long-term homosexual relationships but nonetheless maintained a masculine identity.

5. *Foster Testimony:* Ervin Arnold, 5, F. F. Brittain, 12, Thomas Brunnel, 21; *Dunn Testimony:* Albert Viehl, 307, Dudley Marriott, 1737.

6. Frederick Hoage, using a somewhat different construction than most, referred to them as "the inverted gang" (*Foster Testimony,* 255).

7. *Foster Testimony:* Arnold, 5; *Dunn Testimony:* Clyde Rudy, 1783. For a few of the many other comments by "straight" sailors on the presence of gay men at the YMCA, see *Dunn Testimony:* Claude McQuillin, 1759, and Preston Paul, 1836.

8. A man named Temple, for instance, had a room at the Y where he frequently took pickups (*Foster Testimony:* Brunelle, 207–208); on the role of the elevator operators, see William McCoy, 20, and Samuel Rogers, 61.

9. *Foster Testimony:* Arnold, 27; Frederick Hoage, 271; Harrison Rideout, 292.

10. Ibid.: Hoage, 267; Rogers, 50; Brunelle, 185.

11. Ibid.: Gregory A. Cunningham, 30, Arnold, 6; *Dunn Testimony:* John S. Tobin, 720–721.

12. For an elaboration of the conceptual distinction between "inversion" and "homosexuality" in the contemporary medical literature, see my article, "From Sexual Inversion to Homosexuality: Medicine and the Changing Conceptualization of Female Deviance," *Salmagundi* 58–59 (Fall 1982–Winter 1983): 114–146.

13. *Foster Testimony:* Rogers, 50–51.

14. For example, an article that included the following caption beneath a photograph of Hughes dressed in women's clothes: "This is Billy Hughes, Yeo. 2c. It's a shame to break the news like that, but enough of the men who saw 'Pinafore' fell in love with Bill, without adding to their number. 'Little Highesy," as he is affectionately known, dances like a Ziegfeld chorus girl" (" 'We Sail the Ocean Blue': 'H.M.S. Pinafore' as Produced by the Navy," *Newport Recruit* 6 [August 1918]: 9). See also, for example, "Mayor Will Greet Navy Show Troupe: Official Welcome Arranged for 'Jack and Beanstalk' Boys," which quoted an admiral saying, "It is a corker. I have never in my life seen a prettier 'girl' [a man] than 'Princess Mary.' She is the daintiest little thing I ever laid eyes on" (*Providence Journal,* May 26, 1919, 9). I am grateful to Lawrence Murphy for supplying me with copies of these articles.

15. *Dunn Testimony:* John S. Tobin, 716; *Foster Testimony:* Charles Zipf, 377, confirmed by Hoage, 289, and Arnold (*Dunn Testimony,* 1405). The man who received the women's clothes was the Billy Hughes mentioned in the newspaper article cited in the previous note. I am grateful to Allan Bérubé for informing me of the regularity with which female impersonators appeared in navy shows during and immediately following World War I.

16. Ibid., Hoage called it a "faggot party" and "a general congregation of inverts" (267); Brunelle, who claimed to have attended the party for only fifteen minutes, noted the presence of the sailors and fighters; he also said only one person was in drag, but mentioned at least two (194, 206); John E. McCormick observed the lovers (332).

17. For the straight sailors' nicknames, see *Foster Testimony:* William Nelson Gorham, 349. On the ubiquity of nicknames and the origins of some of them, see Hoage, 253, 271, and Whitney Delmore Rosenszweig, 397.

18. *Dunn Testimony:* Hudson, 1663.

19. *Foster Testimony:* Rideout, 76–77.

20. Ibid.: Cunningham, 29. For other examples, see Wade Stuart Harvey, 366; and *Dunn Testimony:* Tobin, 715.

21. *Foster Testimony:* George Richard, 143; Hoage, 298.

22. Ibid.: Rideout, 69; see also Rogers, 63; Viehl, 175; Arnold, 3; and passim.

23. An investigator told the navy that one gay man had declined to make a date with him because "he did not like to 'play with fire' . . . [and] was afraid Chief Brugs would beat him up" (*Foster Testimony:* Arnold, 36); the same gay man told the court he had traveled to Providence with Brugs two weekends in a row and gone to shows with him (Rogers, 53–54). Speaking of another couple, Hoage admitted he had heard "that Hughes has travelled with Brunelle separately for two months or so" and that "they were lovers." He added that "of course that does not indicate anything but friendship," but that "naturally I would suspect that something else was taking place" (Hoage, 268).

24. Ibid.: Hoage, 313.

25. Ibid.: Arnold, 5.

26. Ibid.: Viehl, 175; Brunelle, 235; Rideout, 93. Hoage, when cross-examined by Rosenszweig, denied another witness's charge that he, Hoage, had *boasted* of browning Rosenszweig, but he did not deny the act itself—nor did Rosenszweig ask him to do so (396).

27. Ibid.: Hoage, 271; Rogers, 131–136.

28. Ibid.: Rogers, 39–40; other evidence tends to confirm Rogers's contention that he had not known openly gay men or women before joining the navy. For other examples of the role of the war in introducing men to gays, see Brunelle, 211; and in the *Dunn Testimony,* Rudy, 1764. For extended discussions of the similar impact of military mobilization on many people's lives during World War II, see Allan Bérubé, "Marching to a Different Drummer: Lesbian and Gay GIs in World War II,"; and John D'Emilio, *Sexual Politics, Sexual Communities: The Making of a Homosexual Minority in the United States, 1940–1970* (Chicago: University of Chicago Press, 1983), 23–39.

29. *Foster Testimony:* Rideout, 78.

30. *Dunn Testimony:* E. M. Hudson questioning Bishop James De Wolf Perry, 609 (my emphasis).

31. Ibid.: Jeremiah Mahoney, 698.

32. Ibid.: Tobin, 717.

33. Witnesses who encountered gay men at the hospital or commented on the presence of homosexuals there included *Foster Testimony:* Gregory Cunningham, 29, Brunelle, 210, John

McCormick; *Dunn Testimony:* 1780, and Paul, 1841. Paul also described some of the open homosexual joking engaged in by patients (*Foster Testimony,* 393–394).

34. *Foster Testimony:* Hervy, 366; Johnson, 153, 155, 165, 167; Smith, 221.

35. Ibid.: Johnson, 153; Smith, 169.

36. Ibid.: Smith, 171.

37. Ibid.: Hoage, 272. Hoage added that "[t]rade is a word that is only used among people temperamental [i.e., gay]," although this does not appear to have been entirely the case.

38. Ibid.: Hoage, 269, 314; Rudy, 14. The decoy further noted that, despite the fairy's pleas, "I insisted that he do his work below my chest."

39. Frederick Hoage provided an example of this pattern when he described how a gay civilian had taken him to a show and dinner, let him stay in his room, and then "attempted to do what they call 'browning.' " But he devoted much of his testimony to *denying* that *his* "tak[ing] boys to dinner and to a show," offering to share his bed with sailors who had nowhere else to say, and giving them small gifts and loans had the sexual implications that the court obviously suspected (*Foster Testimony:* Hoage, 261, 256, 252, 281–282). For other examples of solicitation patterns, see Maurice Kreisberg, 12, Arnold, 26; *Dunn Testimony:* Paul, 1843. Edward Stevenson described the "trade" involved in military prostitution in *The Intersexes: A History of Semisexualism* (Privately Printed, 1908), 214. For an early sociological description of "trade," see Albert Reiss Jr., "The Social Integration of Queers and Peers," *Social Problems* 9 (1961): 102–120.

40. *Foster Testimony:* Rudy, 13.

41. *Dunn Testimony:* Paul, 1836; see also, for example, Mayor Mahoney's comments, 703.

42. *Foster Testimony:* James Daniel Chase, 119 (my emphasis); Zipf, 375.

43. Ibid.: Walter F. Smith, 169.

44. See, for example, the accounts of Hoage, 271–272, and Rideout, 87 (*Foster Testimony*).

45. *Foster Testimony:* Smith, 169.

46. Alfred Kinsey, Wardell Pomeroy, and Clyde Martin, *Sexual Behavior in the Human Male* (Philadelphia, 1948), 650–651.

47. *Foster Testimony:* Arnold, 6; *Dunn Testimony:* Arnold, 1495.

48. *Kent Trial,* 21.

49. Ibid., defense attorney's interrogation of Charles McKinney, 66–67. See also, for example, the examination of Zipf, esp. 27–28.

50. Ibid., Zipf, 2113, 2131 (the court repeatedly turned to the subject). The "manly" decoy was Clyde Rudy, 1793.

51. The ministers' efforts are reviewed and their charges affirmed in the Senate report, 67th Congress, 1st session, Committee on Naval Affairs, *Alleged Immoral Conditions of Newport (R.I.) Naval Training Station* (Washington, DC: 1921), and in the testimony of Bishop Perry and Reverend Hughes before the Dunn Inquiry.

52. *Dunn Testimony:* Rev. Deming, 30; Rev. Forster, 303.

53. Hudson quoted in the Senate report, *Alleged Immoral Conditions,* 8; seel also *Dunn Testimony:* Tobin, 723, cf. Arnold, 1712. For the ministers' criticism, see, for example, Bishop Perry, 529, 607.

54. *Foster Testimony:* Hoage, 319.

55. Ibid.: Brunelle, 216. He says the same of Kent on 217.

56. *Kent Trial,* cross-examination of Howard Rider, 296.

57. Ibid.: Malcolm C. Crawford, 220–223; Dostalik, 57–71.

58. *Foster Testimony:* interrogation of Hoage, 315, 318.

59. *Dunn Testimony:* Deming, 43.

60. *Kent Trial:* Kent, 396, 419, 403.

61. Ibid.: Herbert Walker, 318–320; Bishop Philip Rhinelander, 261–262; Judge Darius Baker, 277; see also Rev. Henry Motett, 145–149, 151.

62. Ibid.: interrogation of C. B. Zipf, 37–38.

63. *Dunn Testimony:* Rev. Deming, 42; Bishop Perry, 507.

64. Ibid.: Perry, 678.

65. Jonathan Katz argues that such a perspective was central to Puritan concepts of homosexuality. "The Age of Sodomitical Sin, 1607–1740," in his *Gay/Lesbian Almanac: A New Documentary* (New York, 1983), 23–65. But see also John Boswell, "Revolutions, Universals, and Sexual Categories," chap. 15 in this volume.

66. This argument was first introduced by Mary McIntosh, "The Homosexual Role," *Social Problems* 16 (1968): 182–192, and has been developed and modified by Jeffrey Weeks, *Coming Out: Homosexual Politics in Britain from the Nineteenth Century to the Present* (London, 1977); Michel Foucault, *The History of Sexuality: An Introduction,* trans. Robert Hurley (New York, 1978); Lillian Faderman, *Surpassing the Love of Men: Romantic Friendships and Love between Women from the Renaissance to the Present* (New York, 1981); Kenneth Plummer, ed., *The Making of the Modern Homosexual* (London, 1981); and Katz, *Gay/Lesbian Almanac.* Although these historians and sociologists subscribe to the same general model, they disagree over the timing and details of the emergence of a homosexual role, and McIntosh's original essay did not attribute a key role in that process to medical discourse.

67. D'Emilio has provided the most sophisticated analysis of this process in *Sexual Politics, Sexual Communities.* See also Toby Moratta, *The Politics of Homosexuality* (Boston, 1981), and the pioneering studies by Jeffrey Weeks and Lillian Faderman cited in note 66.

68. One would also hesitate to assert that a single definition of "homosexuality" obtains in our own culture. Katz has made a similar argument about the need to specify the meaning of homosexual behavior and identity in his *Gay/Lesbian Almanac,* although our analyses differ in a number of respects (see my review in *The Body Politic* 97 (1983): 33–34).

69. Lillian Faderman, in "The Mordification of Love between Women by Nineteenth-Century Sexologists," *Journal of Homosexuality* 4 (1978): 73–90, and *Surpassing the Love of Men,* is the major proponent of the argument that the medical discourse stigmatized romantic friendships. Alternative analyses of the role of the medical literature and of the timing and nature of the process of stigmatization having been proposed by Martha Vicinus, "Distance and Desire: English Boarding-School Friendships," *Signs: Journal of Women in Culture and Society* 9 (1984): 600–622; Carroll Smith-Rosenberg, "The New Woman as Androgyne: Social Disorder and Gender Crisis, 1870–1936," in *Disorderly Conduct: Visions of Gender in Victorian America* (New York, 1985), 245–296; and Chauncey, "From Sexual Inversion to Homosexuality." On the apparent ubiquity of the early-twentieth-century public image of the lesbian as a "mannish woman," see Esther Newton, "The Mythic Mannish Lesbian: Radclyffe Hall and the New Woman," *Signs* 9 (1984): 557–575. Nineteenth-century medical articles and newspaper accounts of lesbian couples stigmatized only the partner who played "the man's part" by dressing like a man and seeking male employment but found the "womanly" partner unremarkable, as if it did not matter that her "husband" was another female so long as she played the conventionally wifely role (see Chauncey, 125ff.). The medical reconceptualization of female deviance as homosexual-object choice rather than gender-role inversion was under way by the 1920s, but it is difficult to date any such transition in popular images, in part because they remained so inconsistent.

Chapter 21: Siegel, "Dry-Cleaning the Troops"

A fuller explication of the ideas expressed in this essay can be found in the author's earlier piece, "Second Hand Prejudice, Racial Analogies and Shared Showers: Why 'Don't Ask, Don't Tell' Won't Sell," *Notre Dame Journal of Law, Ethics and Public Policy* 9 (1995): 185–213.

1. *Palmore v. Sidoti,* 466 U.S. 429, 433 (1984).

2. *City of Cleburne v. Cleburne Living Center, Inc.*, 473 U.S. 432, 450 (1985).

3. *Gregory v. City of Chicago,* 394 U.S. 111 (1969).

4. *Texas v. Johnson,* 491 U.S. 397 (1989).

5. *Fricke v. Lynch,* 491 F. Supp. 381 (R.I. 1980).

6. *"Lifting the Ban on Gays in the Military,"* Senate Armed Services Committee Hearings, Statement of David A. Schlueter, Professor of Law, St. Mary's University, Federal News Service, March 23, 1993.

7. Simone de Beauvoir, *The Second Sex* (New York: Knopf, 1951).

8. Joshua Meyrowitz, *No Sense of Place: The Impact of Electronic Media on Social Behavior* (New York: Oxford University Press, 1985), 204–205.

9. *Harris v. Forklift Systems,* 510 U.S. 17 (1993).

10. Anna Quindlen, "To Feed or Not to Feed," *New York Times,* May 25, 1994, A21.

11. Kathleen Lant, "The Big Strip Tease: Female Bodies and Male Power in the Poetry of Sylvia Plath," *Contemporary Literature,* 34: 620–669.

12. "Ban on Male Nurses Tending Pregnant Women Upheld," *Los Angeles Times,* September 13, 1994, A24.

13. Richard Cohen, "Closing the Door on Crime," *Washington Post Magazine,* September 7, 1986, W13.

14. Ellis Cose, *The Rage of a Privileged Class* (New York: Harper Collins, 1993), 55–56.

15. Ibid., 61–62.

16. *Thomasson v. Perry,* 895 F. Supp. 820 (E. D. VA 1995), aff'd., 80 F.3d 915 (Cir. 4 1996), cert. den., 117 S. Ct. 358 (1996); *Richenberg v. Perry,* 97 F. 3d 256 (Cir. 8 1996), pet. for cert. filed, 65 U.S.L.W. 3728 (April 16, 1997); *Philips v. Perry,* 106 F. 3d 1420 (Cir. 9 1997); cf. *Able v. U.S.*, 1997 U.S. Dist. LEXIS 9331 (E. D. NY 1997).

Chapter 23: Stramel, "Outing, Ethics, and Politics"

1. Richard Mohr, "The Outing Controversy: Privacy and Dignity in Gay Ethics," in *Gay Ideas: Outing and Other Controversies* (Boston: Beacon Press, 1992): 11–48. See also Mohr's "The Case for Outing" chapter 22 in this volume. Other articles on outing can be found in Timothy Murphy, ed., *Gay Ethics: Controversies in Outing, Civil Rights, and Sexual Science* (New York: Harrington Park Press, 1994).

2. For a fuller discussion of the right to privacy and a thorough defense of my claim that outing ordinarily violates privacy, see my dissertation, "Gay Virtue: The Ethics of Disclosure," University of Southern California, 1996.

Chapter 24: Knight, "How Domestic Partnerships Threaten the Family

1. For example, Seattle-based Exodus International, a Christian ministry with more than 125 chapters around the United States, regularly publishes testimonies of how former homosexuals became healed from homosexuality and sexual addiction, and the National Associa-

tion of Research and Therapy of Homosexuality, based in Encino, California, reports many successful treatments.

2. "D.C. Officials Seek to Revive Domestic Partners Initiative," *Washington Post,* March 1, 1993, D5.

3. "Report of the 14.06 Task Force," University of Michigan, March 29, 1994, 3–5.

4. Human Rights Campaign List, "Employers with Domestic Partner Policies," September 23, 1996; David J. Jefferson, "Gay Employees Win Benefits for Partners at More Corporations," *Wall Street Journal,* March 18, 1994, A1. Also, Ken McDonnell of the Employee Benefit Research Institute in Washington, D.C., estimates that about fifty companies have adopted partner benefits; cited in Robert Bellinger, " 'Domestic-Partner Benefits' Emerge," *Electronic Engineering Times,* November 8, 1993, 75.

5. Bellinger, "'Domestic-Partner Benefits'," 75.

6. Human Rights Campaign List, "Employers"; Jefferson, "Gay Employees"; and Thomas A. Stewart, "Gay in Corporate America," *Fortune,* December 16, 1991, 50, also Ann Merrill, "Domestic Partners: Many Companies Talking about Issue, but Few Have Done Anything about It," *Minneapolis Star-Tribune,* January 26, 1994, 1D.

7. January 1997 telephone survey of federal agencies by FRC cultural studies intern Maggie Cole.

8. Michelangelo Signorile, "Bridal Wave," *Out* (December/January 1994): 161.

9. Franklin E. Kameny, "Deconstructing the Traditional Family," *The World & I* (October 1993): 383–395.

10. Thomas Stoddard, "Why Gay People Should Seek the Right to Marry," in William B. Rubenstein, ed., *Lesbians, Gay Men and the Law* (New York: Free Press, 1993) 398, 400.

11. Paula Ettelbrick, "Since When Is Marriage a Path to Liberation?" in Rubenstein, ed., *Lesbians, Gay Men,* 401–405.

12. *Maynard v. Hill,* 125 U.S. 190, 205 (1888).

13. "Legal Definition of the Family," *Harvard Law Review* 104 (1991): 640.

14. Roberta Achtenberg et al., "Approaching 2000: Meeting the Challenges to San Francisco's Families," *The Final Report of the Mayor's Task Force on Family Policy* (San Francisco: City and County of San Francisco, June 13, 1990), 1.

15. "Health Care Benefits Expansion Act of 1992" (Washington, D.C.: District of Columbia City Council, 1992) sec. 2 and 3.

16. Ibid., sec. 4 and 5.

17. *Marvin v. Marvin,* 18 Cal. 3d 660, 557 P.2d 106, 134 Cal. Rptr. 815 (1976).

18. The case is now on appeal as *Sharon Lynne Bottoms v. Pamela Kay Bottoms,* No. 1930–93–2, Court of Appeals of Virginia at Richmond, Nov. 15, 1993.

19. *Georgia P. v. Kerry B.,* cited in "Lesbian Co-Parenting," *National Center for Lesbian Rights Newsletter* (Spring 1994): 4.

20. *Wanda J. v. Steven Wayne J.,* "Lesbian Custody, "*National Center for Lesbian Rights Newsletter* (Spring 1994): 4.

21. "Senator Attends Marriage Rights Meeting," *Island Lifestyle* (April 1994): 15.

22. *Baker v. Nelson* (1971), as cited in Stoddard,"Why Gay People Should Seek," 400.

23. Ibid.

24. "Texas Platform Agreement for Next Year's March," *Washington Blade,* May 22, 1992.

25. See, for instance, Leon McKusick et al., "AIDS and Sexual Behavior Reported by Gay Men in San Francisco," *American Journal of Public Health,* 75, no. 5 (May 1985): 493–496; Alan

P. Bell and Martin S. Weinberg, *Homosexualities: A Study of Diversity Among Men and Women* (New York: Simon and Schuster, 1978), 308–309. Also, M. Pollak, "Male Homosexuality," in P. Aries and A. Bejin, eds., *Western Sexuality: Practice and Precept in Past and Present Times* (New York: Blackwell, 1985) 40–61.

26. A. P. M. Coxon et al., "Sex Role Separation in Diaries of Homosexual Men," *AIDS* (July 1993): 877–882.

27. G. J. Hart et al., "Risk Behaviour, Anti-HIV and Anti-Hepatitis B Core Prevalence in Clinic and Non-clinic Samples of Gay Men in England, 1991–1992," *AIDS* (July 1993): 863–869, as cited in "Homosexual Marriage: The Next Demand," position analysis paper by Colorado for Family Values, Colorado Springs, May 1994.

28. Doug Sadownick, "Open Door Policy," *Genre* (April 1994): 34.

29. Ibid., 35, 36.

30. William Aaron, *Straight* (New York: Bantam Books, 1972): 208; cited in Joseph Nicolosi, *Reparative Therapy of Male Homosexuality* (Northvale, NJ: Jason Aronson, 1991), 125.

31. Pitirim Sorokin, *The American Sex Revolution* (Boston: Porter Sargent, 1956), 77–105.

32. Nancy E. Roman, "Unmarried Couple Lose Rental Case," *Washington Times*, June 3, 1994, A1.

33. Ibid., A8.

34. Ibid.

35. The laws were enacted in 1989. Nan D. Hunter et al., *The Rights of Lesbians and Gay Men: An American Civil Liberties Union Handbook* (Carbondale: Southern Illinois University Press, 1992), 106.

Chapter 26: Card, "Against Marriage"

1. Betty Berzon claims that her book *Permanent Partnerships: Building Lesbian and Gay Relationships That Last* (New York: Penguin, 1988) is about "reinventing our gay and lesbian relationships" and "learning to imbue them with all the *solemnity* of marriage wihout necessarily imitating the heterosexual model" (7), and yet by the end of the book, it is difficult to think of anything in legal ideals of the heterosexual nuclear family that she has not urged us to imitate.

2. Mary Daly, *Gyn/Ecology: The Metaethics of Radical Feminism* (Boston: Beacon Press, 1978), 113–152.

3. Virgina Held, *Feminist Morality: Transforming Culture, Society, and Politics* (Chicago: University of Chicago Press, 1993).

4. See, for example, Kath Weston, *Families We Choose* (New York: Columbia University Press, 1991); Phyllis Burke, *Family Values: Two Moms and Their Son* (New York: Random House, 1993); and Suzanne Slater, *The Lesbian Family Life Cycle* (New York: Free Press, 1995). In constrast, Berzon (*Permanent Partnerships*) uses the language of partnership, reserving "family" for social structures based on heterosexual unions, as in chapter 12, subtitled "Integrating Your Families into Your Life as a Couple."

5. Warren J. Blemenfeld, "Same-Sex Marriage: Introducing the Discussion," *Journal of Gay, Lesbian, and Bisexual Identity* 1, no. 1 (1996): 77; Evan Wolfson, "Why We Should Fight for the Freedom to Marry: The Challenges and Opportunities That Will Follow a Win in Hawaii," *Journal of Gay, Lesbian, and Bisexual Identity* 1, no. 1 (1996): 79–89; Victoria A. Brownworth, "Tying the Knot or the Hangman's Noose? The Case against Marriage," *Journal of Gay, Lesbian, and Bisexual Identity* 1, no. 1 (1996): 91–98.

6. Richard D. Mohr, *A More Perfect Union: Why Straight America Must Stand Up for Gay Rights* (Boston: Beacon Press, 1994), 31–53.

7. Wolfson, "Why We Should Fight,"

8. Mohr, *A More Perfect Union,* 31–53.

9. John Boswell, *Same-Sex Unions in Premodern Europe from Late Antiquity to the Renaissance* (New York: Pantheon, 1994).

10. Mohr, *A More Perfect Union,* 49–50.

11. Berzon, *Permanent Partnerships,* 266; Christine Pierce, "Gay Marriage," *Journal of Social Philosophy* 28, no. 2 (1995): 5.

12. See Clair M. Renzetti, *Violent Betrayal: Partner Abuse in Lesbian Relationships* (Newbury Park, CA: Sage, 1992); Kerry Lobel, ed., *Naming the Violence: Speaking Out about Lesbain Battering* (Seattle, WA: Seal Press, 1986); David Island and Parick Letellier, *Men Who Beat the Men Who Love Them: Battered Gay Men and Domestic Violence* (New York: Harrington Park Press, 1991).

13. Emma Goldman, "Marriage and Love," in *Anarchism and Other Essays* (New York: Dover, 1969).

14. Boswell, *Same-Sex Marriage.*

15. Radclyffe Hall, *The Well of Loneliness* (New York: Pocket Books, 1950); there have been many editions of this work—it was originally published in 1928.

16. Pierce, "Gay Marriage," 13.

17. Ibid.

18. Claudia Card, *Lesbian Choices* (New York: Columbia University Press, 1995).

19. Berzon, *Permanent Partnerships,* 163–182.

20. Betty Mahmoody, with Wiliam Hoffer, *Not without My Daughter* (New York: St. Martin's, 1987).

21. Claudia Card, "Gratitude and Obligation," *American Philosophical Quarterly* 25, no. 2 (1988): 115–127; and "Gender and Moral Luck," in Owen Flanagan and Amelie Oksenberg Rorty, eds., *Identity, Character, and Morality: Essays in Moral Psychology* (Cambridge, MA: MIT Press, 1990).

22. See, for example, Sandra Faulkner, with Judy Nelson, *Love Match: Nelson vs. Navratilova* (New York: Birch Lane Press, 1993).

Chapter 27: Mohr, "A Gay and Straight Agenda"

1. *New York Times,* April 1, 1996, A1.

2. *The Advocate,* March 7, 1995, 24.

Index

About the Contributors

· · · · ·

Daryl J. Bem is professor of psychology at Cornell University, where he has been on the faculty since 1978. Prior to that, he was on the faculties of Stanford University and Carnegie-Mellon University, and he taught at Harvard as a visiting professor. In addition to his work on sexual orientation, his specialty areas include belief and attitude change, psi (ESP) phenomena, self-perception, and personality theory. He is a fellow of both the American Psychological Association and the American Psychological Society.

· · · · ·

John Boswell was the A. Whitney Griswold Professor of History at Yale at the time of his death in 1994. He is best known as the author of the seminal and controversial work *Christianity, Social Tolerance, and Homosexuality* (1980). His other books include *The Kindness of Strangers: The Abandonment of Children in Western Europe from Late Antiquity to the Renaissance* (1988) and *Same-Sex Unions in Premodern Europe* (1994).

· · · · ·

David Bradshaw is assistant professor of philosophy at the University of

Kentucky. His articles on ancient philosophy and the philosophy of religion have appeared in *Apeiron, Ancient Philosophy,* and *The Thomist.*

.....

William Byne is director of the Neuroanatomy Laboratory in the Department of Psychiatry at the Mount Sinai Medical Center in New York City; a psychiatrist with the Columbia Center for Lesbian, Gay, and Bisexual Mental Health; and a lecturer at Columbia University. His research examines correlations between brain structure and function. He is a member of the International Academy for Sex Research and on the editorial boards of *Gender and Psychoanalysis, The Journal of Homosexuality,* and *The Journal of Lesbian, Gay, and Bisexual Psychotherapy.*

.....

Claudia Card is professor of philosophy at the University of Wisconsin, with teaching affiliations in women's studies and environmental studies. She is the author of *Lesbian Choices* (1995) and *The Unnatural Lottery: Character and Moral Luck* (1996) and editor of *Feminist Ethics* (1991) and *Adventures in Lesbian Philosophy* (1994).

.....

George Chauncey is professor of history at the University of Chicago and has also taught at Rutgers and New York University. His book *Gay New York: Gender, Urban Culture, and the Making of the Gay Male World, 1890–1940* (1994) won the Los Angeles Times Book Prize for History, the Frederick Jackson Turner Award, and the Merle Curti Social History Award from the Organization of American Historians. He is also the coeditor of *Hidden from History: Reclaiming the Gay and Lesbian Past* (1989) and is currently at work on *The Strange Career of the Closet: Gay Culture, Consciousness, and Politics from the Second World War to the Stonewall Era.*

.....

John Corvino is lecturer in the philosophy department at Wayne State University in Detroit, Michigan. His articles on homosexuality have appeared in *The Harvard Gay and Lesbian Review* and in the anthologies *Do We Need*

Minority Rights? (1996) and *The Philosophy of Sex* (1997). A popular teacher, he has lectured widely on the morality of homosexuality.

.....

Madeline Davis is a librarian and curator for the Temple Beth Zion Library and Judaica Museum, a singer/songwriter, poet, historian, actress and gay/lesbian activist in Buffalo, New York. She is coauthor of *Boots of Leather, Slippers of Gold: The History of a Lesbian Community* (1993) and winner of a Lambda Literary Award in lesbian studies in 1994. She is a contributor to numerous anthologies, including the forthcoming collection *Fem(me): Histories, Generations, Futures,* ed. Elizabeth Crocker and Laura Harris (1997). She is currently coediting a collection titled *Lusty Autumn: Lesbians and Sex after Midlife.*

.....

John Finnis is professor of law and legal philosophy at the University of Oxford, Biolchini Professor of Law at the University of Notre Dame, and a fellow of the British Academy. He has taught law and philosophy at Oxford since 1966, apart from two years as head of the Department of Law in the University of Malawi in the late 1970s. His best-known books are *Natural Law and Natural Rights* (1980), *Fundamentals of Ethics* (1983), *Nuclear Deterrence, Morality and Realism* (1987), and *Moral Absolutes* (1991).

.....

Carla Golden is associate professor of psychology at Ithaca College and a fellow of the American Psychological Association. She has taught courses in developmental psychology, the psychology of women, and women's studies at Smith College (1977–1983), Ithaca College (1983–present), and the University of Pittsburgh's Semester at Sea Program. Dr. Golden has lectured widely and written on feminist psychoanalytic theories of gender, as well as on the development of women's sexuality. She is coeditor of *Lectures on the Psychology of Women* (1996).

.....

David M. Halperin teaches queer theory at the University of New South Wales in Sydney, Australia. Among his contributions to gay studies are *One Hundred Years of Homosexuality and Other Essays on Greek Love* (1990) and

Saint Foucault: Towards a Gay Hagiography (1995). He is also an editor of *Before Sexuality: The Construction of Erotic Experience in the Ancient Greek World* (1990), *The Lesbian and Gay Studies Reader* (1993), and *GLQ: A Journal of Lesbian and Gay Studies.*

. . . . .

Daniel A. Helminiak is a psychotherapist at Pittsburgh Pastoral Institute and author of *What the Bible Really Says about Homosexuality* (1994). He holds Ph.D.'s in theology and psychology and is a fellow of the American Association of Pastoral Counselors. As a Roman Catholic priest, he ministered widely among lesbians and gays. His other books are *The Same Jesus: A Contemporary Christology, Spiritual Development: An Interdisciplinary Study, The Human Core of Spirituality: Mind as Psyche and Spirit,* and *Religion and the Human Sciences: An Approach Via Spirituality.*

. . . . .

Leah Himmelhoch received her B.A. in classics from Yale University and her M.A. and Ph.D. in Greek language and literature from the University of Texas at Austin. Her doctoral dissertation explored the image of the charioteer as a symbolic expression of male social and political power in Greek poetry. Her other classical interests include ancient conceptions of gender, Greek poetry (especially Attic tragedy), ancient warfare, and the response of Roman literature to Greek precedents.

. . . . .

Elizabeth Lapovsky Kennedy was a founding member of the Women's Studies Department at the State University of New York at Buffalo and a professor in the Department of American Studies/Women's Studies for twenty-seven years. She is currently in the process of moving to the University of Arizona, Tucson, to head the Women's Studies Department. She is coauthor of *Feminist Scholarship: Kindling in the Groves of Academe* (1985) and of *Boots of Leather, Slippers of Gold: The History of a Lesbian Community* (1993), which won the Jesse Bernard Award and a Lambda Literary Award in 1994. She is also the author of numerous articles on lesbian communities and histories.

. . . . .

Robert H. Knight is director of cultural studies at the Family Research Council (FRC). A former news editor and writer for the *Los Angeles Times*, Knight was a 1989–1990 media fellow at Stanford's Hoover Institution and a senior fellow for cultural policy studies at the Heritage Foundation. He has written extensively on homosexuality and homosexual activism, and he wrote and directed a video documentary on Alfred C. Kinsey, *The Children of Table 34*. FRC Research Assistant Dan Garcia and *Lambda Report* Editor Peter L. LaBarbera contributed to his article.

.....

Andrew Koppelman is assistant professor of law at Northwestern University; he has also taught at the University of Texas at Austin and at Princeton University. He holds a J.D. and Ph.D. from Yale University and is the author of *Antidiscrimination Law and Social Equality* (1996) as well as numerous articles.

.....

Mitchell Lasco earned his master's degree in counseling psychology from the University of Cincinnati, where he specialized in matters of gender and violence. He is currently a doctoral candidate in developmental psychology at New York University and conducts research in the Neuroanatomy Laboratory in the Department of Psychiatry at Mount Sinai Medical Center. His current research interests include correlating variations in brain structure with variations in gender identity, gender role and sexual orientation.

.....

John Luddy is a former Marine infantry officer who has written extensively on social issues in the U.S. military. At the time he wrote his contribution to this volume, he was a defense policy analyst at the Heritage Foundation, a prominent Washington think tank. He currently serves as defense and foreign policy aide to Senator James M. Inhofe of Oklahoma, a member of the Senate Armed Services and Select Intelligence Committees.

.....

Richard D. Mohr, professor of philosophy at the University of Illinois at Urbana, is the author of four books: *The Platonic Cosmology* (1985); *Gays/Justice: A Study of Ethics, Society, and Law* (1988); *Gay Ideas: Outing and Other*

Controversies (1992); and *A More Perfect Union: Why Straight America Must Stand Up for Gay Rights* (1994). Mohr has also written for magazines and newspapers, including the *Chronicle of Higher Education, The Advocate, Christopher Street, The Nation, Reason* magazine, the *Chicago Tribune,* and the *Boston Globe.*

. . . . .

Carol Queen is a cultural sexologist, writer, and bisexual activist who lives and works in San Francisco. Her essays have been widely published in queer and sex community anthologies, including *Bi Any Other Name, Bisexual Politics: Theories, Queries and Visions,* and *Bisexuality: Psychology and Politics of an Invisible Minority*; she also writes extensively on censorship, sex work, and alternative eroticism, and is a member of the Feminists for Free Expression speaker's bureau. Queen is also internationally known for her erotic writing.

. . . . .

Plato is a Greek philosopher who lived from 427 to 347 B.C.E.

. . . . .

The Ramsey Colloquium is a group of Jewish and Christian theologians, ethicists, philosophers, and other scholars who meet periodically to consider questions of morality, religion, and public life. It is sponsored by the Institute on Religion and Public Life in New York City. The colloquium is named after Paul Ramsey (1913–1988), the distinguished Methodist ethicist.

. . . . .

Jonathan Rauch, a contributing editor of *National Journal* magazine in Washington, is the author of three books—most recently, *Demosclerosis: The Silent Killer of American Government*—and many articles. A native of Phoenix, Arizona, he now lives in Washington, D.C. and has been a frequent contributor to *The New Republic,* where the article in this collection appeared previously.

. . . . .

Thomas E. Schmidt, who holds a Ph.D. from Cambridge University, is a

New Testament scholar whose research focuses on ethics in the biblical world. He is the author of *Straight and Narrow? Compassion and Clarity in the Homosexuality Debate* (1995).

.....

Paul Siegel is professor of communication arts at Gallaudet University and adjunct professor of journalism law and ethics at George Mason University and American University. His most recent book, *Outsiders Looking In: A Communication Perspective on the Hill/Thomas Hearings,* is available from Hampton Press (1996).

.....

Edward Stein teaches philosophy and lesbian and gay studies at Yale University. He specializes in philosophy of science, philosophy of psychology, epistemology, and ethics. His books include *Forms of Desire: Sexual Orientation and the Social Constructionist Controversy* (1992), *Without Good Reason: The Rationality Debate in Philosophy and Cognitive Science* (1996), and *Sexual Desires: Science, Theory and Ethics* (1998).

.....

James S. Stramel is adjunct instructor of philosophy at Santa Monica College, where he teaches ethics and sexual ethics. He received his M.A. and Ph.D. in philosophy from the University of Southern California. His dissertation, *Gay Virtue: The Ethics of Disclosure,* examines several ethical approaches to questions regarding disclosures of homosexuality by self or others; in it he develops and defends a neo-Aristotelian virtue ethics of gay identity disclosure.

.....

Frederick Suppe is professor of philosophy and chairperson of the History and Philosophy of Science program at the University of Maryland, College Park. He is well known for his contributions to philosophy of science including *The Structure of Scientific Theories* and *The Semantic Conception of Theories and Scientific Realism,* and the forthcoming two-volume *Facts, Theories, and Scientific Observation.* He is also the author of roughly 100 articles, including many on scientific issues pertaining to homosexuality.

. . . . .

Thomas Williams is assistant professor of philosophy at the University of Iowa. A specialist in medieval philosophy, he has published translations of Augustine and Anselm, as well as articles on Duns Scotus.